Caribbean Series 11

Sidney W. Mintz, Editor

Previous Volumes in the Caribbean Series

Mexican Liberalism in the Age of Mora, 1821-1853

by Charles A. Hale

New Haven and London   Yale University Press   1968

Designed by Marvin Howard Simmons,
set in Baskerville type,
and printed in the United States of America by
Vail-Ballou Press, Inc., Binghamton, N.Y.
Distributed in Great Britain, Europe, Asia, and
Africa by Yale University Press Ltd., London; in
Canada by McGill University Press, Montreal; and
in Latin America by Centro Interamericano de Libros
Académicos, Mexico City.

for
Lenore Rice Hale

Preface

This book had its origin more than ten years ago as a doctoral dissertation on the conflict of political ideas in Mexico during the postindependence generation. As I studied further in Mexican and especially in European history, I came to appreciate the inadequacies of my interpretation. Lacking a conceptual framework of my own, I had unwittingly adopted a stereotyped view. In this view Mexican liberalism was an effort to deny the Spanish heritage and to forge a new government and society based on solutions drawn eclectically from France, England, and the United States. Conservatism was simply a defense of the Spanish past.

Gradually I recognized that Mexico had inherited the Hispanic reform tradition with its central orientation toward state authority. I discovered Alexis de Tocqueville's writings and through them saw the comparisons that could be made between the structure of institutions in France and Mexico. I found that on many issues the distance between liberals and conservatives in Mexico was less great than I had thought. With a new comparative perspective, I reread the major sources of my dissertation and added numerous others. The result is an entirely different study, having as its focus a definition of Mexican liberalism within a broader Western context.

In the course of my work, I have received aid from many quarters, first from two teachers. E. Dwight Salmon initially aroused my interest in Mexican history. Frank Tannenbaum taught me to look for continuities in the Hispanic tradition. I am greatly indebted to my many Mexican friends and colleagues. José Miguel Quintana allowed me free reign in his exceptional private library. Ernesto de la Torre Villar, Jan Bazant, and Daniel Olmedo, S.J., led me to important source materials. Moisés González Navarro took a keen interest in my project from the beginning and has been generous with his time and knowledge on numerous occasions since. From their various vantage points, Fredric L. Cheyette, Peter Czap, Jr., and Robert A. Potash provided intellectual stimulus during the early stages of writing. I took good advantage of Robert F. Florstedt's offer of an extended loan of his dissertation on José María Luis Mora.

Charles Gibson read the manuscript and raised several important questions. The manuscript was also read and ably criticized by Hugh M. Hamill, Jr., and Richard M. Morse, both of whom gave me needed intellectual and moral support at difficult moments. The study was underwritten by two grants (1962 and 1965–66) from the Joint Committee on Latin American Studies of the Social Science Research Council and the American Council of Learned Societies. The Graduate College of the University of Iowa paid for the typing. Craig Simpson and Alan E. Schorr assisted me in the chores of indexing and proofreading.

I am indebted to my parents for the extraordinary interest they have shown in my work over many years. Finally, my wife's critical sense, instinctive good judgment, and steady encouragement have made this a far better book than it would have been otherwise.

Contents

Introduction

Not long ago I was discussing my plan for this book with a learned and genial Mexican cleric. When I told him that I was having difficulty assessing judiciously the prevailing Mexican interpretations of liberalism, he responded with a knowing smile: *"Sí, todavía hay mucha pasión en eso."* His phrase stuck with me; for despite the lapse of a century, postindependence thought and policy is not a subject to be treated dispassionately.

The writing of history in Mexico has been inevitably affected by the country's experience of social upheaval, civil war, and foreign invasion—a heritage of conflict unique for its intensity in all of Latin America. The political process since 1810 has been subject to two contrasting interpretations, with only minor variations or departures. It has been seen as a succession of senseless efforts to destroy Hispanic traditions, to substitute alien ideals and values, and by so doing to condemn the country to perpetual anarchy, dictatorship, and moral corruption. Or this process has been interpreted as a continuing liberal and democratic struggle against the forces of political and clerical oppression, social injustice, and economic exploitation. The two lines of interpretation were first established by the arguments of the combatants themselves in the first generation after independence; and within the particular assumptions of each successive era, they have been continually reproduced by later historians. At the center of each has been the increasingly intense concern for forging a nation. Thus nationalism and ideological conflict have been the principal determinants in Mexican political historiography.

The first school of interpretation was initiated by Lucas Alamán, a figure who will loom large in this book. It identified the Mexican nation with the Hispanic heritage and revealed a nostalgia for the peace and apparent prosperity of New Spain, and particularly for the role played by the Catholic Church in colonial society. It has been as fiercely nationalist as the opposing school, especially in the twentieth century. Such historians as José Vasconcelos, Mariano Cuevas, and José Bravo Ugarte have seen materialism, anticlericalism, and the influence of the United States as subversive and alien forces against which the nation must continually defend itself. Though the lesser in importance of the two, the conservative school has maintained its vitality and may ultimately become merged with the varied oppositionist interpretations of the twentieth-century revolution.[1]

The second of the schools, the liberal, has very much predominated in Mexican historiography. With the defeat by Benito Juárez in 1867 of the allied forces of Maximilian, the French army, and the native conservative party, "the triumph of liberal ideas was to decisively orient the future of Mexico."[2] From that time on, national destiny came to be officially associated with liberalism, however differently successive generations envisioned the specific elements of that destiny.

Following 1867, the liberal view of nineteenth-century history was most concisely summarized in 1900 by Justo Sierra. In a book that has enjoyed wide popularity and continuing influence, he stated that "Mexico has had only two revolutions." The first was the Revolution for Independence; the second was the great Reform of 1854 to 1867. Both were for Mexico part of the same social process: "The first was emancipation from Spain; the second was emancipation from the colonial regime; two stages in the same work of creating an autonomous national individual."[3] In another place Sierra spoke, using liberal terminology, of the three great "disentailments" of Mexican history: that of Independence, "which gave life to our national personality"; that of the Reforma, "which gave life to our social personality"; and that of Peace,

1. For the latter see Robert A. Potash, "Historiography of Mexico Since 1821," *Hispanic American Historical Review* [hereafter *HAHR*], *40* (1960), 411 ff.

2. François Chevalier, "Conservateurs et libéraux au Mexique. Essai de sociologie et géographie politiques de l'indépendance a l'intervention française," *Cahiers d'histoire mondiale, 8* (1964), 474.

3. Justo Sierra, *Evolución política del pueblo mexicano* (Mexico, Fondo de Cultura Económica, 1950), p. 185.

"which [with the 'normal' influx of foreign capital] gave life to our international personality." [4]

Justo Sierra's interpretation was a product of the official philosophical positivism that underlay the thirty-year rule of Porfirio Díaz. Conflict over abstract ideals was seen to have ended in 1867. Under the firm and necessary guidance of Don Porfirio, the country had entered the "industrial" era of practical economic progress and social regeneration. From these assumptions positivist historians found one part of the liberal heritage—constitutionalism —archaic, while they continued to find inspiration in the liberal work of anticorporate and anticlerical reform. This ambivalent attitude toward liberalism was apparent in Sierra, but it found its best expression in Emilio Rabasa's *La Constitución y la dictadura* of 1912. Believing that a written constitution could not effectively be in advance of the stage of a people's social evolution, Rabasa criticized the constitution-makers of 1857 for limiting executive power, and thus making extraconstitutional dictatorship inevitable. Rabasa became in effect an apologist for authoritarian government and praised equally the dictatorships of Benito Juárez and of Porfirio Díaz. A strong executive in a country like Mexico was the "inevitable realization of sociological laws." [5] Within the liberal school of historiography, there has continued, despite changing intellectual premises, a subcurrent questioning early liberal faith in the magic that could be worked through constitutional forms.

The assumptions of Sierra and Rabasa, and the last of Sierra's stages in Mexican history, have, of course, been repudiated since 1910; for the revolution which began in that year was directed against the dictatorship and social exploitation of the Díaz regime. Yet Sierra's concept of Mexican history as evolution toward fulfillment of national and liberal ideals remains essentially unchanged. The liberal era of 1810–67 can now be interpreted as preparing the way for the "social constitutionalism" of 1917, the adherence to political liberties, and even the policies of economic transformation of the last two decades.

Jesús Reyes Heroles has in recent years argued forcefully the

4. Ibid., p. 295.

5. Emilio Rabasa, *La Constitución y la dictadura* (Mexico, Porrua, 1956), p. 67 and passim.

"continuity" of Mexican liberalism from the nineteenth to the twentieth century. "The revolutionary idea appears as the completion, the total integration of historical evolution, of history itself." Revolutionary Mexicans should not feel it necessary to free themselves from their past. "We have a historical capital [in liberalism] which we must preserve and increase." To overlook this is "to forget that our generation is not its own offspring." [6] Liberalism as a body of thought and policy becomes far more than a delimited historical phenomenon of the nineteenth century. It is for contemporary Mexico the basic point of ideological orientation.

It has been said that much of recent Mexican historical writing is a product of the "law of the centennials." The great symbolic dates of a century ago, 1854 (the Revolution of Ayutla), 1857 (the Constitution), 1858–61 (the Three Years War), 1862 (the May 5 defeat of the French at Puebla), have each in their turn evoked quantities of books and essays, occasionally probing but more often merely glorifying these heroic liberal and patriotic events. The hand of the government is very apparent in the majority of these efforts. For instance, 1967 marked the centennial of the victory of Juárez over Maximilian. To mark the occasion there was organized in 1965 a Patronato Nacional para la Celebración del Centenario de la Victoria de la República, including in its ranks Mexico's most distinguished historians and social scientists. On the occasion of its founding, the group's president, Raul Noriega, delivered a speech entitled "Mexican Liberalism," in which he referred to liberalism as an "irreducible and supreme force in the voice of our government." In concluding, he reaffirmed the view that Mexico is "a nation with a revolutionary and liberal sense of existence." [7] The centennial, which completes the heroic liberal cycle, will undoubtedly yield numerous works of history.

Recent preoccupation with *lo mexicano,* the attempt to find, with the aid of existentialist philosophy, peculiar elements of a Mexican ethos, has in a sense reinforced this identification of

6. Jesús Reyes Heroles, *El Liberalismo mexicano* (Mexico, Universidad Nacional Autónoma Mexicana [hereafter UNAM], 1957–61), *3,* xix. See also "Continuidad del liberalismo mexicano," in *Plan de Ayutla* (Mexico, UNAM, 1954), pp. 343–74.

7. Noriega, speech delivered July 16, 1965, in *Novedades* (July 25, 1965). Noriega referred to the initiative of the PRI, the official party.

liberalism and national ideals. One such interpreter, Francisco López Cámara, after beginning a search for the origins of a Mexican "political mentality," or "political consciousness," said that he was inevitably drawn to liberalism, the assumptions of which largely govern today's mental outlook and institutional orientation. "To write the history of Mexican liberalism is equivalent, therefore, to pursuing, in its most essential elements, the development of the Mexican's political consciousness." [8] López Cámara, unlike Reyes Heroles, conceives of Mexican liberalism as developing *sui generis* out of a growing popular reaction to pre-1821 social conditions. Only after a "liberal consciousness" was formed indigenously did foreign ideas have any acceptance. Liberalism for López Cámara becomes something thoroughly Mexican at its origin, a part of the national ethos at independence.

There is recent evidence of the beginnings of a critical interpretation of nineteenth-century experience, which may transcend the traditional dictates of ideology. It has appeared particularly in the multivolume *Historia moderna de México* under the direction of Daniel Cosío Villegas. Uninfluenced by the "law of centennials," Cosío Villegas and his collaborators set out to demonstrate that the years 1867–1910 constituted the formative period of modern Mexico. It was then that the bases of the modern administrative state were formulated, that the work of economic modernization began, and, lamentably, that a tradition for the abridgment of constitutional liberties became established. Though a vigorous defender of liberal constitutionalism, Cosío Villegas openly attacks the manipulation of historical evidence characteristic of current centennial historiography.[9] By eschewing the centennial idea and the overt effort to seek precedents for current policies in a protean liberalism of the nineteenth century, Cosío Villegas and his followers have opened the way to a critical and dispassionate understanding of the recent Mexican past.

I was once told by a distinguished Mexican anthropologist that

8. Francisco López Cámara, *La Génesis de la conciencia liberal en México* (Mexico, El Colegio de México, 1954), p. 9.

9. Daniel Cosío Villegas, *La Constitución de 1857 y sus críticos* (Mexico, Hermes, 1957), pp. 13–15. Most of the book is directed against Emilio Rabasa's 1912 apology for authoritarian executive power, the continuity of which Cosío laments in present-day Mexico.

being a foreigner (and especially, perhaps, a Protestant North American) I could not hope to comprehend Mexican history. His assertion has frequently troubled me, for it contains some truth. I have come to believe, however, that it may be the detached foreigner who is best able to bring fresh understanding to a sensitive historical topic like Mexican liberalism. The outsider can disengage liberalism from present-day ideology and examine it comparatively within its own historical context—the Atlantic world of the early nineteenth century. Liberal thought and policy in Mexico can be properly understood only if it is related to the broader Western experience of which it was a part. This is not to deny the uniqueness of Mexican history or to posit liberal thought as a mere "reflection" of European ideas. Rather we must examine Mexican peculiarities from the point of view of Europe. In studying liberalism in Mexico, we should keep in mind what Louis Hartz calls the "two necessary parts of all comparative analysis," in this case European continuities (or influences) and Mexican particularities.[10]

In order to define Mexican liberalism we must compare the institutional and social situation of the country with relevant areas of the Atlantic world, particularly Spain, France, England, and the United States. This is necessary to determine why, of the large body of thought available in the West, the ideas of certain European thinkers and the policies of certain nations appealed to the Mexicans and why others did not. We can thus identify and attempt to explain the particular points of orientation and emphasis in Mexican thought and policy. We are concerned with tracing the influences of European liberal thought in Mexico, but we should also go further and demonstrate how the comparative situation and the problems of Mexico set the terms of liberal argument. These questions are the explicit concern of Chapter 2 and in part of Chapter 5, but they will command our attention implicitly throughout the book.

In our discussion of Mexican liberalism there will lurk another larger question—to be raised again specifically in Chapter 9. How significant in the long run has liberalism been in Mexico? To

10. See Hartz, "Comment" (in the symposium on his *The Liberal Tradition in America*), *Comparative Studies in Society and History*, 5 (1962–63), 281.

what extent has the country departed from the psychological and cultural inheritance of traditional Spain? In other words, was Western liberalism "exotic" to the Mexican cultural tradition? These are the problems that provide our orientation for the study of liberalism in Mexico.

This book will treat substantively the period 1821 to 1853, which lies between two heroic landmarks of the Mexican liberal tradition—the Revolution for Independence and the Reforma. Liberalism in Mexico has most often been equated with the latter era, and indeed the study of the Reforma would form a logical sequel to this book. The earlier years were characterized by extreme political instability and have often been dismissed as the "Age of Santa Anna"—after the chieftain who most often occupied the presidential chair. Justo Sierra labeled the period "anarchy," though he saw it as punctuated by a few premature attempts at reform. It has been the least studied period of Mexican history, in contrast, for instance, to the same years in Argentina. In Argentina interest in these years has not been eclipsed by heroic epochs at either end. Moreover, the caudillo Juan Manuel de Rosas has found a school of ardent nationalist admirers in every generation, whereas Antonio López de Santa Anna has invited only scorn. Without ignoring the bewildering political turmoil in Mexico between 1821 and 1853, indeed in hopes of further explaining it, my intention is to examine the era through its ideas. In this formative period of Mexican liberalism can be found the points of orientation and conflict for the entire century.

The focus will be narrowed further, to the ideas of José María Luis Mora (1794–1850), the major liberal theorist of the pre-Reforma period. He was not a prolific writer; his published works constitute only five volumes. Yet much of Mora's thought emerges from the debates of the first constitutional congress of the State of Mexico, in which he was the principal figure, and from the assumptions that underlay the three journals he edited between 1821 and 1834. Mora's voluminous personal papers are also important, though they contain little unpublished material written by him. His formal writing ended in 1837, with the publication of his works in Paris.

In addition, we have brief but important evidence of his ideas in the reports he sent as minister to England during the critical years 1846 to 1850. The correspondence of this period to and from Mora affords strong testimony to the respected and influential place he had in the minds of midcentury liberal leaders. He was regarded as a kind of unofficial adviser to the Mexican government prior to his death in 1850. Mora is not presently in the first rank of Mexican liberal heroes. His views on social questions, on land, and on economic development are in general disrepute. However, if we are to understand the nineteenth century on its own terms, we must emphasize Mora. Not only was he the most significant liberal spokesman for his generation but his thought epitomizes the structure and the predominant orientation of Mexican liberalism.

This book is intended, however, to be more than an intellectual portrait of José María Luis Mora. Mora must be placed in a broader context of ideas and institutions, both within Mexico and within the Atlantic world. Although Mora's ideas form the principal substance of Chapters 3, 4, and 5, I have introduced in Chapters 6, 7, and 8 topics that were of less concern to him. These topics, and where Mora stood on them, are nevertheless crucial in identifying what liberalism was—and what it was not. In these latter chapters, and occasionally elsewhere, other figures emerge —Fray Servando Teresa de Mier, Lorenzo de Zavala, Mariano Otero, Estevan de Antuñano, and even Lucas Alamán—who may at times seem to challenge Mora in importance. My intention throughout is not primarily to study Mora, but to offer a definition of Mexican liberalism during the era in which he was ultimately the key figure.

I have found intriguing the evidence of coalescence between liberals and conservatives in a situation where ideological conflict has always been assumed the prevailing pattern. In numerous ways liberals and conservatives were not always so far apart. They shared many common assumptions, especially on social questions. Thus, the ranking political conservative, Lucas Alamán, figures significantly in this study of liberalism, partly to point up by contrast the arguments of the liberals, but also to suggest that there may be points of continuity in Mexican thought and policy that run deeper than political liberalism and conservatism.[11]

11. I have explored this problem further in "José María Luis Mora and the Structure of Mexican Liberalism," *HAHR, 45* (1965), 196–227.

Be this as it may, I would never contend that ideological conflict has been insignificant in Mexico since independence. It is perhaps the major point of differentiation between the Mexican experience and that of other principal countries of Latin America—Argentina, Brazil, and Chile. Our definition of liberalism for all of Latin America has been influenced (perhaps unduly) by the Mexican case. Since the terms of ideological struggle in Mexico were set in the years between 1821 and 1854, we need to establish its exact characteristics. Whatever points of coalescence can be discovered between conservatism and liberalism, the reality of Mexico's unique midcentury civil war cannot be overlooked. Before proceeding to analyze liberalism, we must commence at the end of our story and describe the conflict of ideas that emerged in Mexico after 1846.

1

War, National Crisis, and the
Ideological Conflict

Following a border skirmish at the Rio Grande on April 25, 1846, Mexico and the United States were at war. Within a few months Zachary Taylor's troops had overrun the North, reaching Monterrey and Saltillo. Simultaneously, an expedition under Winfield Scott landed at Veracruz and pushed inward along the ancient road of conquest, arriving at the gates of Mexico City by August 1847. There were scattered Mexican displays of heroic resistance, but disorganization and poor leadership played havoc with any concerted attempt at national defense. The capital fell and was occupied by the invaders. The Mexican government fled to Querétaro. By February 1848, an ignominious peace treaty had been accepted by the hapless Mexicans, though not without serious opposition from the radical-liberal (*puro*) group, which favored a last-ditch stand. With the rapid subjection of the country and the loss of half its territory, the once proud nation of 1821 was left stunned.

The shock of military disaster, coming after a dismal decade of mediocre leadership and internal anarchy, evoked among articulate Mexicans the fear that national existence itself was in jeopardy. Such an easy victory by its powerful neighbor meant that Mexico might at any time be absorbed by the United States, especially since there was a movement for that purpose already afoot north of the Rio Grande.[1] Moreover, the years 1847–49 witnessed the outbreak of the Caste Wars, those violent uprisings of heretofore peaceful Indians in Yucatán and the Huasteca. Ethnic conflict threatened to engulf the entire country. The mood of the day was

1. See John D. P. Fuller, *The Movement for the Acquisition of All Mexico, 1846–1848* (Baltimore, Johns Hopkins University Press, 1936).

one of crisis, provoking a disposition toward self-examination and
a renewed search for remedies to Mexico's ills.

A dramatic increase in the volume and intensity of intelligent
political expression marked the years after 1846. There emerged
several daily newspapers, containing acute editorials on varied
national questions. Between 1846 and 1848 at least four such
major dailies in Mexico City engaged in vigorous debate unknown
in the previous decade. The oldest of the newspapers was the
moderate-liberal (*moderado*) *El Siglo XIX*. Except for a year during the war, it ran for several decades after its first issue in 1841. *El
Monitor republicano* appeared in 1846 to combat the short-lived
conservative *El Tiempo;* it ran continuously until 1853. Perhaps
most forceful of all was *El Universal,* organ of the militant conservatives between 1848 and 1855.[2] Political leaders and thinkers of
the day, men such as Lucas Alamán, Mariano Otero, Manuel Díez
de Bonilla, Francisco Zarco, and Manuel Piña y Cuevas, used the
editorial pages to express their views (though articles were un-
signed and authorship difficult to identify). This was also the
period of Alamán's great *Historia de Méjico,* the histories of
Cuevas and José María Tornel, and of numerous and important
pamphlets.

Curiously enough, this self-examination and ferment of ideas
took place in a period of relative political calm. Concurrent foreign invasion and internal contention for power had so exhausted
the country that by 1848 cries for peace and stability were heard
from all sides. The perennial rebel general, Mariano Paredes y
Arrillaga, was defeated by government forces in late 1848.[3] Thereafter, the regime of the restored "constitutional" president, José
Joaquín de Herrera, was marked by an absence of pronunciami-

2. *El Monitor republicano* (Feb. 14, 1846, to Apr. 30, 1853) was a continuation
of *El Monitor constitucional* (Dec. 21, 1844, to Feb. 13, 1846). *El Siglo XIX* (Oct.
8, 1841, to Dec. 31, 1845) was continued as *Memorial histórico* (Jan. 1 to Feb. 28,
1846) and then as *Republicano* (Mar. 1, 1846, to July 11, 1847). *El Siglo* resumed
publication on June 1, 1848. *El Tiempo* ran from Jan. 24 to June 7, 1846. *El
Universal* began publication on Nov. 16, 1848.

3. For details see Hubert H. Bancroft, *History of Mexico* (San Francisco, 1883–
88), 5, 548–50, and Thomas E. Cotner, *The Military and Political Career of José
Joaquín de Herrera, 1792–1854* (Austin, University of Texas Press, 1949), pp.
174–83.

entos. Herrera's successor, Mariano Arista, faced increasing factionalism, but there was no serious political crisis until late 1852. The peace was a shaky one, however, produced by the "indifference of the majority for public affairs, the fatigue of the parties, and the destruction of the army." [4]

The self-critical mood was reflected well in a remarkable essay written in December 1847, probably by Mariano Otero. It was published both as a pamphlet and as a serial in *El Monitor*.[5] The author tried to explain the military defeat and the absence of popular national resistance of the kind seen in Spain when Napoleon invaded in 1808. For him the answer lay in Mexico's basic social afflictions, which produced hopeless division in time of crisis. Otero divided society into the "people in general," the "productive" classes, and the "unproductive" classes. He then proceeded to demonstrate why none had shown patriotic concern. What interest can the Indians (the "people in general") take, he asked, in the defense and "preservation of a system of which they are the victim"? The plight of the Indians is pitiable. They are still exploited as they were during colonial times, and they have no real place in society. Among the "productive" groups, those engaged in commerce have been beset by high tariffs, internal taxes, and corrupt customs officials. Those engaged in agriculture have become mere dependents of the church, which has absorbed three-quarters of the landed property. If the "productive" classes have little patriotic incentive, he continued, the "unproductive" or privileged groups—principally clergy and army—have even less. The upper clergy, living in wealth and splendor apart from the nation, even incited open revolt against the forced loan decreed by the government for the war. The defeat of 1847, moreover, demonstrates the decay of the army. The Indians are potentially

4. Letter from Mariano Otero to José María Luis Mora (Feb. 12, 1849), in Génaro García, ed., *Documentos inéditos o muy raros para la historia de México*, "Papeles inéditos y obras selectas del Doctor Mora," 6 (Mexico, Bouret, 1906), 136.

5. [Mariano Otero], *Consideraciones sobre la situación política y social de la república mexicana en el año 1847* (Mexico, 1848). Several authorities have suggested Otero as the author, including Jesús Reyes Heroles who notes that the method of analysis employed is that of Otero's 1842 pamphlet (*Liberalismo*, 2, 379). The moderate approach to peace and reforms further suggests Otero. It ran in *El Monitor* on June 13–15, 17–21, 23–24, 1848.

good soldiers if led by intelligent officers, but unfortunately this latter group is completely degenerate.

This unprecedented self-indictment was followed by an even more startling conclusion: *"In Mexico that which is called national spirit cannot nor has been able to exist, for there is no nation."* [6] Such sentiment was not isolated. *El Siglo* in its first postwar issue (June 1, 1848) asked if Mexico was "really a society or [only] a simple collection of men without the bonds, the rights, or the duties which constitute one." Yet some could take solace in defeat. *El Monitor* asserted on July 7, 1848, that in one sense Mexico had gained from the war, for it was now "in a condition capable of receiving reforms that would never have taken hold previously." As President Herrera's minister of relations, Mariano Otero spoke of a "new era" of "life or death" for the republic and called for the patriotic services of all.[7]

In this time of national crisis, there emerged a new generation of Mexican liberals. These were men who had experienced the war and who went on to champion the cause of reform in the 1850s and 1860s. Ignacio Ramírez at twenty-seven was editing a satirical journal called *Don Simplicio*. On the eve of the war he commented that "we really don't want federalism, nor centralism, nor monarchy, but only revolutions." [8] His cynical tone soon gave way to an ardent defense of republican institutions, in order to meet the strictures of *El Tiempo*. He was assisted by his contemporary Guillermo Prieto, soon to become minister of finance under Arista in 1851.

The somewhat younger Francisco Zarco was at eighteen made *oficial mayor* under Luis de la Rosa in the 1847 government at Querétaro. By 1853 he was editor of *El Siglo,* a job he was to hold for the next decade. Benito Juárez and Melchor Ocampo were governors of their respective states of Oaxaca and Michoacán

6. Otero, *Consideraciones,* p. 42. Mora as minister to England was presenting to Europeans a similar view of the state of the country. See letter to Secretaría de Relaciones, Sept. 6, 1848, in Luis Chávez Orozco, ed., *La Gestión diplomática del Doctor Mora,* Archivo histórico diplomático mexicano, 35 (Mexico, Sec. de Rel. Ext., 1931) , p. 108.

7. Mariano Otero, *Ministerio de relaciones interiores y esteriores* (Mexico, 1848) , a four-page directive to the state governors, dated June 4.

8. *Don Simplicio. Periódico burlesco, crítico y filosófico por unos simples,* Jan. 14, 1846.

during the war years. The brilliant Mariano Otero would have joined the ranks of these future leaders of the Reforma, but he was struck down by cholera in 1850 at the age of thirty-three. *El Siglo* commented that "the liberal party has lost an athlete whose shoes no one can fill." [9]

Undoubtedly the most dramatic political development of these years was the appearance of a militant conservative opposition. Not only was it a political movement of real force, capturing power in 1853, but its spokesmen provided the most penetrating and forceful arguments in the great debate of the postwar period. To attribute conservatism and the burgeoning ideological conflict entirely to the war crisis would be wrong, for certainly elements can be traced back to 1833 if not to 1810. Lucas Alamán's position had been taking shape gradually since the 1820s. Gutiérrez de Estrada's famous monarchist appeal dates from 1840, and Alamán started publishing his histories in 1844. Nevertheless, it was the war that gave focus to a well-articulated and self-conscious "conservatism" (the term had not been used earlier). The war pointed up an ideological cleavage which was to characterize Mexican political life until 1867.[10]

Under the leadership of Lucas Alamán, the conservative party made its debut by winning the municipal elections for control of the Ayuntamiento of Mexico City on July 15, 1849. Its municipal ascendancy was short-lived, however, for the liberal government immediately began to maneuver for its overthrow, which was effected when Alamán resigned in December.[11] The conservatives entered the old insurgent, Nicolás Bravo, in the national elections

9. *El Siglo,* June 26, 1850. Otero's last year was spent apart from politics, "lamenting in a quiet corner of my house the sad state of public affairs." See letter to Mora (May 13, 1849) in García, *Documentos, 6,* 142.

10. The term "conservative" in its modern political usage is said to have originated with Chateaubriand and Lamennais, who jointly founded a journal called *Le Conservateur* in 1818 to combat the partisans of the French Revolution. See Roberto Michels, "Conservatism," in *Encyclopedia of the Social Sciences* (New York, Macmillan, 1931), *4,* 231b. In Mexico Lucas Alamán's *El Tiempo,* in its introductory issue, did state that "our principles are essentially conservative," but the term was not generalized until the appearance of *El Universal* in Nov. 1848. *El Tiempo's* concern had focused more on the specific issue of monarchy. See also the remarks of Chevalier, "Conservateurs et libéraux," pp. 457–58.

11. This interesting episode is treated in José C. Valadés, *Alamán, estadista e historiador* (Mexico, Robredo, 1938), pp. 449–71, and in Cotner, pp. 194–97.

of 1851, and when he failed, they turned to Santa Anna. The
period of conservative control of the Mexico City Ayuntamiento
saw numerous appeals to party organization, particularly in *El
Universal*.[12] The impact of the new conservatism should not be
underrated. Otero commented in 1849 on the welcome that *El
Universal* and Alamán's histories were receiving, in contrast to
Gutiérrez de Estrada's pamphlet in 1840 and *El Tiempo* in 1846.
Edmundo O'Gorman has recently asserted that, contrary to the
"official Jacobin view," popular support in 1854 was stronger for
conservative than for liberal ideas.[13]

It is evident from the tone and the content of the sharpening
debate that the conservative resurgence had put the liberals on the
defensive. As *El Universal* itself acknowledged, the conservatives
had been outside politics since independence. The regimes of
Agustín de Iturbide (1821-23) and Anastasio Bustamante (1830-
32) could be claimed by the postwar conservative party as only
quasi-conservative precursors. Thus the conservatives of 1848
could strike with impunity at what was most vulnerable in Mexico's troubled course since independence. Starting from the same
point as the liberals, namely concern over the survival of Mexico
as a nation, the conservatives were able to exploit the crisis to their
advantage.[14] Their basic argument—a simple one, but hard to
combat in the dark days of 1847—was that independent Mexico
had broken with its past, had taken on alien institutions and principles, and thus had condemned itself to internal anarchy and ex-
ternal weakness.

The chief conservative spokesman was Lucas Alamán, undoubtedly the major political and intellectual figure of independent
Mexico until his death in 1853. A man of indefatigable energy and
diverse talents, Alamán was not only a prolific writer, whose works
fill twelve stout volumes, but also the guiding force in several ad-

---

12. *El Universal,* July 7, Aug. 2 and 6, 1849.

13. Otero to Mora (May 13, 1849), in García, *Documentos, 6,* 140–41; O'Gorman,
"Precedentes y sentido de la revolución de Ayutla," *Plan de Ayutla,* pp. 174–75.

14. For examples see Lucas Alamán, *Historia de Méjico desde los primeros
movimientos que prepararon su independencia en el año de 1808, hasta la época
presente* (Mexico, 1849–52), *1,* xii [dated Aug. 27, 1849]; *El Universal,* Jan. 14 and
July 14, 1849; Luis G. Cuevas, *Porvenir de México,* ed. Francisco Cuevas Cancino
(Mexico, Jus, 1954), pp. 3–8.

ministrations and an active promoter of economic development.

One can follow a rough pattern in Lucas Alamán's life that runs from activist to writer, from statesman and entrepreneur to *pensador*. It is important to note that his conservatism hardened only in the 1840s, particularly after 1846. The great bulk of Alamán's writing was done in his later years. Besides his histories, he was generally acknowledged to be the editor of *El Tiempo* and of *El Universal*. History was Alamán's principal weapon and the cornerstone of what could be called conservative political philosophy in Mexico. *El Tiempo* announced its appearance in Burkean terms by explaining that its title signified a search in the past (*tiempo pasado*) for lessons to guide in the present (*tiempo presente*), which in turn contains the seeds of the future (*tiempo por venir*). Destructive natural phenomena, such as earthquakes and volcanic eruptions, it added, cannot be a model for human development. "We thus reject from our ideas of progress all violent and revolutionary means." [15]

On September 16, 1849, *El Universal* opened its attack on Mexico's accepted revolutionary tradition by asserting that Miguel Hidalgo's Grito de Dolores should no longer be considered Independence Day. Instead, there appeared on September 27 an article entitled "The Great Day of the Nation," commemorating Agustín de Iturbide's entry into Mexico City in 1821. The liberal newspapers *El Siglo* and *El Monitor* rose immediately to the defense of Hidalgo and of September 16, and a fierce debate ensued. It was symbolic of the broader conflict of ideas over the social and political bases of independent Mexico and the country's relation to its colonial and Hispanic past.

Alamán announced on several occasions that the purpose of his historical writing was to combat popular disrespect for Mexico's Spanish heritage and the idea that independence constituted a necessary break from it. He set out to demonstrate through history that Hernán Cortés was the founder of the Mexican nation, that three centuries of colonial rule had been on the whole beneficial and progressive, and that Mexico's only road to salvation in the present crisis was to reject liberal and disruptive doctrines and return to time-honored practices. By 1851 Alamán was claiming suc-

15. *El Tiempo*, Jan. 24, 1846.

cess for his efforts and pointed to recent patriotic orations as evidence.[16] Alamán's conservative appeal through history had begun on February 18, 1844, when he proposed to the Ateneo Mexicano, a group of scholars and men of letters, that he prepare ten "dissertations" covering "our national history from the epoch of the Conquest to our day." He completed this effort nine years and eight volumes later, a few months before his death in June 1853.[17]

Alamán's treatment of New Spain in his *Disertaciones* focused on Cortés and the Conquest. His approach was largely biographical, not unlike that of his contemporary, William H. Prescott. Alamán emphasized the constructive as well as the military and destructive achievements of Cortés and described in detail his organization of the government of Mexico City, his agricultural and mining enterprises, and his founding of charitable institutions.[18] It should be added that Alamán's historiographical mission to solidify Cortés' stature served a practical purpose as well. Alamán had served during two decades as agent for the Sicilian Duke of Terranova y Monteleone, the present heir to Cortés' huge sixteenth-century feudal patrimony. As early as 1828, Alamán defended Monteleone's holdings against liberal attacks on the grounds "that we are not the nation despoiled by the Spaniards, but one in which everything originated with the Conquest." [19]

Characteristic of Alamán's historical argument was the third volume of *Disertaciones* (1849), devoted entirely to a history of peninsular Spain between 1500 and 1810. It was as if he were deliberately baiting the liberal Hispanophobes of his day. Spain

16. See Alamán's letter to Monteleone (Dec. 3, 1851), *Documentos diversos* (Mexico, Jus, 1945–47), *4*, 604. Cf. Otero to Mora (May 13, 1849), García, *Documentos, 6*, 140–41.

17. Alamán, *Disertaciones sobre la historia de la república megicana, desde la época de la conquista que los españoles hicieron . . . hasta la independencia* (3 vols. Mexico, 1844–49). See notice in *El Siglo*, June 9, 1844.

18. Alamán, *Disertaciones, 2*, 1–126. Alamán acknowledged his debt to Prescott and annotated the Spanish translation of the latter's *Historia de la conquista de Méjico* (2 vols. Mexico, 1844).

19. Alamán, "Exposición que hace a la cámara de diputados del congreso general el apoderado del Duque de Terranova y Monteleone," *Documentos, 3*, 477. In a letter of Dec. 3, 1851, Alamán claimed that his historical writings had helped gain public acceptance of the duke's holdings (ibid., *4*, 604).

and Mexico were one historically, and Mexicans should recognize their tie to the great tradition of the Catholic Kings and the eighteenth-century Bourbons. Still, Alamán's treatment of the Colony in *Historia,* Vol. 1, was balanced, and it is cited and even translated today as a perceptive and useful synthesis. He accorded high praise to the civilizing efforts of the early missionaries, the Jesuits, and a handful of statesmanlike viceroys; yet he was not blind to the principal colonial grievances.

Being a Creole aristocrat himself, Alamán recognized the political and social inferiority imposed on the Creoles. He often spoke, too, of the industriousness of that group. He had no sympathy for Spanish restrictions on colonial industry and agriculture. Moreover, he condemned the Inquisition, though he regarded the church, spiritual and temporal, as the soul of Mexico's Hispanic heritage. For him, independence was both inevitable and beneficial, prepared for by three centuries of generally enlightened and progressive policies. It was not independence itself that Alamán questioned, but rather the use it had been put to by republican Mexico.[20]

Alamán made most effective use of history as a weapon in his interpretation of the Revolution for Independence. The force of his argument was not based on mere polemic but rather on the documentation and detail of his five large volumes. His *Historia de Méjico* remains the standard treatment of the 1810–21 period, and it has never been equaled by a "liberal" version. This fact may reflect the durability of Creole conservatism in the Mexican tradition. The interpretation embedded in Alamán's narrative is clear and unequivocal: there was not one revolution; there were two. The first was led by Miguel Hidalgo in 1810 and lasted ten years till it disintegrated in 1820; the second took place briefly in 1821 under Agustín de Iturbide. In no way, asserted Alamán, could the first revolution be considered a war of "nation against nation," nor was it "a heroic effort of a people struggling for their liberty," try-

20. See Alamán, *Historia, 1,* 83, 346; *5,* 109–10; also *El Tiempo,* Jan. 25, 1846. His disillusionment with Mexico's misuse of the gift of independence was baldly stated as early as 1835 in "Borrador de un artículo que salió como editorial de un periódico en 1835 con motivo del aniversario de la independencia," *Documentos, 3,* 349–50.

ing to "shake off the yoke of an oppressor power." Hidalgo's insurrection was rather a "rising of the proletarian class against property
and civilization," led by many "lost souls or ex-criminals noted for
their vices." This first revolution caused a "reaction of the respectable segment of society in defense of its property and its families,"
which "stifled [by 1820] the general desire for independence."
Moreover, "the triumph of the insurrection would have been the
greatest calamity that could have befallen the country." [21]

Lucas Alamán grew up in a wealthy and distinguished family in
the prosperous mining city of Guanajuato, which was the first
target of the Revolution of 1810. As a youth of seventeen he experienced siege by Hidalgo's Indian hordes and saw the death of
the enlightened Spanish intendant Riaño, a family friend. Alamán
escaped with his family to Mexico City, but, he wrote in 1849, the
"shout of death and destruction . . . still resounds in my ears
with a terrible echo." His memories of 1810 were revived by the
entry of the American army into Mexico City in September 1847.
Though his house escaped sacking, he noted that some of his
neighbors were not so fortunate.[22] Alamán concluded that Father
Hidalgo was merely a demagogue, appealing to mob anarchy and
the exaggerated democratic doctrines of the French Revolution.
His use of the Virgin of Guadalupe as an emblem was a blasphe-
mous linking of religion and violence. After disorder had been un-
leashed by Hidalgo, it was impossible for more disciplined leaders
like José María Morelos and Ramón López Rayón to control its
fury. Alamán found admirable qualities in several of the later insurgent leaders, but the movement as a whole could be termed a
disaster.

21. See Alamán, *Historia*, *4*, 722–24; also *5*, 352. Alamán was reiterating the
arguments of royalist propagandists in 1810. In fact, there is a striking parallel
between the "psychological warfare" conducted by the post-1847 conservatives and
by the 1810 royalists. Both appealed with great effectiveness to Creole social conservatism (see below, Chap. 7). See the interesting discussion by Hugh M. Hamill,
Jr., "Early Psychological Warfare in the Hidalgo Revolt," *HAHR*, *41* (1961),
206–35.

22. Alamán, *Historia*, *1*, 379; "Autobiografía," *Documentos*, *4*, 14; letter to
Monteleone, Sept. 28, 1847, in ibid., 450–51. Alamán remarked ironically that the
American occupation of Mexico City on Sept. 16 was perhaps a form of divine
retribution, commemorating Hidalgo's insurrection (*Historia*, *2*, 225).

The second revolution was the climax of Alamán's *Historia*. It was a frankly conservative movement directed against the anticlerical and democratic principles of the Spanish cortes (assembly) and the Constitution of 1812, both of which had been reactivated in 1820. Independence was achieved as a mere breaking of political ties with Spain. Iturbide was correct, maintained Alamán, in refusing to recognize a connection between the 1810 insurrection (against which he had fought as a royalist commander) and his harmonious movement. Independence was thus "brought about by the same people who until then had been opposing it." [23] Alamán was explicit in denying the "vulgar error" current in 1821 that independence was a resurgence of the pre-Conquest nation of Anahuac after three centuries of Spanish oppression. The nation that emerged in 1821 was for Alamán the product of sixteenth-century conquest, guided by Hispanic principles of authority, religion, and property. Alamán summed up his position in words his friend Manuel Terán had used in 1824: "I have never considered myself other than a rebellious Spaniard." [24]

This interpretation of the Revolution for Independence was tied closely to an Iturbide cult which flourished in the conservative writings of 1846 to 1853. Not only did he emerge as the hero of Alamán's *Historia* and as the subject of much praise in the conservative press, but he was the focus of Luis G. Cuevas' *Porvenir de México,* which was subtitled a "judgment on [Mexico's] political state in 1821 and 1851." The work was a long nostalgic essay, evoking the halcyon days of 1821 when Mexico was a great and extensive nation, strong from the unifying and conservative principles of Iturbide's Plan of Iguala. Though both Cuevas and Alamán were harsh in their judgment of Iturbide's self-styled empire, clearly it was not his actions in detail that mattered, but rather the principles he espoused and the social groups he represented. Mexico's present anarchy did not begin in 1821, but rather with the overthrow of Iturbide by men "who had embraced un-

23. Alamán, *Historia, 4,* 725; *5,* 108, 351–52; also "Noticias biográficas del Lic. D. Carlos Ma. Bustamante," *Documentos, 3,* 308.

24. See Alamán, *Historia, 1,* 190 n. Alamán found Bustamante, the chronicler of the wars of independence, particularly guilty of the Aztec myth. See "Noticias," *Documentos, 3,* 327.

thinkingly the system of changing everything" and had thus
negated "union which is the strength of nations." [25]

The political use of history by the postwar conservatives posed a
challenge to liberal and republican Mexico. The liberals were
asked to acknowledge the inner contradictions of the independence movement, to choose, as it were, between Hidalgo and
Iturbide. Should the nation find the principles of reconstruction
in the Indian upheaval of 1810 and the revolutionary idea of
popular sovereignty? Or, should the 1821 movement be the model,
acknowledging the social supremacy of Creole aristocrats, established church, and traditional views of authority? The dilemma
this conservative challenge posed for the liberals can be seen by a
brief consideration of their interpretations of the Revolution for
Independence before 1847. In general, the revolution had been
accepted as an integral movement, begun by Hidalgo and completed by Iturbide. Beginning with the multivolume chronicle of
Carlos María de Bustamante in the 1820s and continuing with the
Independence Day orations of subsequent years, the emphasis was
clearly on the heroic achievements of Hidalgo and Morelos. Yet,
the revolutionary years could be referred to as one movement,
embodying the forces of liberalism, progress, and popular sovereignty against three hundred years of Spanish tyranny.[26]

The major liberal narratives of the revolutionary era had been
written by Lorenzo de Zavala and José María Luis Mora in the
early 1830s. Although these critical accounts differed in important
ways, they both accepted the basic premise that the Revolution for
Independence was an integral movement. For Zavala and for
Mora—and this is where they differed sharply from Lucas Alamán—independence itself was the great event. They were less con-

25. See Cuevas, *Porvenir*, pp. 148, 198. Further examples of the effort to glorify
Iturbide can be seen in *El Tiempo*, Feb. 6 and 26, Mar. 30, 1846; *El Orden*, Sept.
27, 1853. Alamán found ridiculous the makeshift "coronation" and the tawdry
imperial trappings. See *Historia*, 5, 624–41.

26. Carlos María de Bustamante, *Cuadro histórico de la revolución de la
América mexicana* (6 vols. Mexico, 1823–32); Mariano Otero, "Discurso que en la
solemnidad del 16 de septiembre de 1841 pronunció en la ciudad de Guadalajara,"
El Siglo, Oct. 22–23, 1841, and "Oración cívica," ibid., Sept. 23, 1843; Andrés
Quintana Roo, *Discurso pronunciado . . . en el glorioso aniversario del 16 de
septiembre de 1845* (Mexico, 1845); Manuel Díaz Mirón, *Discurso que pronunció
el 16 de septiembre de 1845, aniversario del grito de Dolores"* (Veracruz, 1845), p. 6.

cerned with the date of independence and what that date symbolized than with the fact that Mexico had broken with Spain, had repudiated the Colony, and was on a new course. By 1849, Alamán, although accepting independence as a fait accompli, was dubious as to the benefits it had brought.

Zavala and Mora did differ from each other, however, as to how they viewed the struggle for independence. Lorenzo de Zavala's interpretation was presented against a summary dismissal of the colonial era. "Since the time prior to the events of 1808 is a period of silence, of sleep, and of monotony . . . the interesting history of Mexico begins only in that memorable year." [27] The conventional black legend of Spanish cruelty, oppression, and religious fanaticism introduced the reader to the events of the revolutionary era. Mexico, Zavala maintained, was not prepared for independence in 1808 or in 1810. It was a sentiment that matured over a decade, nurtured by the heroic actions of Hidalgo and Morelos, the liberal constitutionalism of the Spanish cortes, and the growth abroad of the idea that Mexico was a nation. Thus by 1819 the people were convinced that independence was necessary, and the stage was set for the bold and politically astute leadership of Iturbide.

José María Luis Mora approached the central theme of independence as a Creole whose distaste for Spanish domination was more than matched by his hatred of revolutionary violence. Whereas Lorenzo de Zavala, also from a prominent Creole background, had grown up in Yucatán away from the social violence of the revolutionary years, Mora, like Alamán, was deeply affected by early memories of Hidalgo's Indian upheaval in Guanajuato. Zavala was exposed to the *philosophes,* including Rousseau, through his teacher, the priest Pablo Moreno; and in 1813 at twenty-five he joined the Sanjuanistas, a reformist group under clerical leadership which had emerged with the Spanish Constitution of 1812. As a young radical intellectual and editor of journals, Zavala was imprisoned in 1814 at San Juan Ulúa in the wave of royalist reaction following the restoration in Spain of Ferdinand VII. He returned to Mérida after three years, and 1821 found him

27. Lorenzo de Zavala, *Ensayo histórico de las revoluciones de Mégico, desde 1808 hasta 1830* (Paris and New York, 1831–32) , *1*, 9.

in Madrid as a Mexican delegate to the reconvened Spanish cortes. Thus Zavala's experience was that of a radical, constantly in opposition to Spanish authority.

Mora, on the contrary, had spent the war years studying in royalist Mexico City, whence he fled after his father's fortune had been confiscated by Hidalgo's troops.[28] Mora, therefore, was more sympathetic to the Colony than was Zavala, though less so than Alamán. Mora pursued the theme of independence to its sixteenth-century origins, beginning with the plot of Don Martín Cortés in 1563. He made it clear, however, that he was not at all interested in the efforts of Indians to shake off Spanish rule, since "they did not constitute the Colony that we are concerned with." [29]

The key to Mora's interpretation of the Revolution for Independence was his careful discussion of the events of 1808–10. His ideal of the perfect revolution would have been a well-planned coup d'etat by a few enlightened Creole leaders. He admired the three colonial officials, Bishop Abad y Queipo of Michoacán, and the intendants Manuel Flon and Juan Antonio Riaño. These men were critics of the colonial regime until 1810 and, Mora maintained, "were aware of the inevitable necessity of independence." [30] Mora sympathized with the 1809 Creole independence plot in Valladolid and implicitly contrasted it with the upheaval of the following year. The tone of Mora's condemnation of Hidalgo's demogogic leadership and of his failure to control violence, plunder, and despoilment of property, approached that of Alamán, with one crucial difference. Mora concluded that Hidalgo's revolt "was as necessary for the attainment of independence as it was

28. Mora related his 1810 experience in *Obras sueltas* (2d ed. Mexico, Porrua, 1963) , p. 169. For Zavala's early career see the thorough study by Raymond Estep, *Lorenzo de Zavala, profeta del liberalismo mexicano* (Mexico, Porrua, 1952) , pp. 21–45.

29. Mora, *Méjico y sus revoluciones* (Paris, 1836) , *3*, 196–97 [hereafter *Revoluciones*]. His essay "Méjico en diversas tentativas para establecer su independencia" was first published under a different title in *El Indicador de la federación mejicana, 3*, 117–273 (Mar. 5 to Apr. 2, 1834) .

30. Mora, *Revoluciones, 3*, 359–61; *4*, 45–46. Of Riaño Mora said: "If independence had sprung from the constituted authorities, if it had been carried out as it had been planned during the viceroyalty of Iturrigaray [1808], . . . Riaño would not have rejected it." See ibid., *4*, 40. Mora held this view despite the fact that Riaño, like Abad y Queipo, was a Spaniard.

harmful and destructive to the country." Recognizing the strength
and the benighted resistance of the Spanish regime in 1809, he
went as far as to say that it was necessary to oppose power with
strength of numbers (meaning the Indian masses). Mora's interpretation emerged ambivalent. He pointed up much more sympathetically than did Zavala the Creole reaction (of "true patriots") against Hidalgo. Yet he concluded that 1810 was a necessary
evil.[31]

Mora's interpretations of Mexican history and his positions on
the great issues of reform were consistently more complex than
those of Zavala. Zavala, a Yucatecan who ended up a Texan, was
always an outsider. He had experienced the ideological but not the
social conflicts of the revolutionary era. Mora, on the other hand,
carried with him always the conflicting sentiments of his early
years. Like many Creoles from central Mexico (though unlike
Alamán), he had to weigh his resistance to Spanish domination
and to much of the Hispanic tradition against his fear of social
upheaval, epitomized by the Hidalgo revolt. He was among the
Creoles who reacted against Hidalgo, and yet he could not be a
wholehearted royalist. We know, for instance, that he lost a
brother, Manuel, who in 1812 had passed from the royalist to the
insurgent cause, served valiantly, and died as an officer under
Ramón López Rayón.[32] Mora's engagement in the issues of the
Revolution for Independence helps to explain his significance
within nineteenth-century Mexican liberalism.

Mora's history of the revolutionary years was left unfinished,
the narrative ending in 1812; so we have little evidence on his
interpretation of subsequent events. We do know, however, that
Mora welcomed Agustín de Iturbide's triumph in the *Semanario
político y literario,* which he was editing in 1821. Moreover, in a

31. Mora's ambivalence can be seen in ibid., *4,* 1–2, 8, 23, and 43; also *3,* 376.
Mora and Zavala specifically disagreed on whether or not the Creoles in Mexico
City would have welcomed Hidalgo had he won the nearby battle of Las Cruces.
Cf. ibid., *4,* 82, with Zavala, *Ensayo, 1,* 56. Hamill argues that Hidalgo could well
have led a successful Creole coup against Spanish rule, but chose instead a broad
appeal to include the Indians and Castes, thus antagonizing most of the
Creoles. See *The Hidalgo Revolt: Prelude to Mexican Independence* (Gainesville,
University of Florida Press, 1966).
32. Mora, *Revoluciones, 4,* 419.

passage on the execution of Hidalgo, Mora concluded that the
evils of the 1810 revolution could ultimately be overlooked, since
"it opened the way to the other [revolution] which was orderly,
glorious, and beneficent." [33] Lorenzo de Zavala, an even stronger
partisan of Iturbide in 1821 than was Mora, treated the career of
the liberator and emperor in considerable detail. The Plan of
Iguala was a "political masterpiece," he asserted.

> [It] was not the tumultuous cry of Dolores of 1810—there
> were no Indians armed with hoes, stones, and slings, those
> who shouted in confusion and disorder: Death to the Span-
> iards, long live Our Lady of Guadalupe. This time there was
> a leader reputed for valor, who, supported by national senti-
> ment, with disciplined troops, spoke in the name of the peo-
> ple and demanded rights now already too well known.[34]

Zavala went on to relate Iturbide's growing ambition, his rejection
of the idea of constitutional monarchy, and his misguided eleva-
tion to the throne. Though Zavala was one of those who turned
against the empire in 1822 in favor of republicanism, he clearly
incorporated Iturbide into his pantheon of founders of the Mexican nation.

Liberal historiography had tried to weave into one fabric the
discordant elements of the years 1808–21. Despite hostility to Iturbide in 1823 and despite his subsequent overthrow, exile, and execution, little effort was made by liberal spokesmen to penetrate the
significance of his brand of "revolution." His remains were
brought to Mexico City in 1838 and interred amid official pomp
and circumstance without significant opposition.[35] By and large,
the myth of the integral Revolution for Independence persisted.
In 1846 the liberal orator, Luis de la Rosa, used the lesson of
Iturbide to combat the monarchist pretentions of El Tiempo.

33. Ibid., pp. 156–57. See also his reference to "the illustrious Iturbide," ibid.,
p. 383.

34. Zavala, Ensayo, 1, 117–18.

35. Except for the chronicler Bustamante, who felt the action to be imprudent.
The occasion appeared to have benefited primarily the poor léperos who infested
Mexico City. They turned out in droves to jeer and to snatch purses. See
Vicente Riva Palacio, ed., México á través de los siglos (Mexico, 1888–89), 4, 416–
17.

Still, Iturbide himself emerged as "glorious liberator" who was used by the "privileged classes." Rosa saw the revolution itself as a struggle of the people against aristocracy, the former winning out by 1823. Following the challenge by *El Universal* in 1849, *El Siglo* entered the debate and accused the conservative party of retarding the independence of Mexico ten years.[36] The polemic raged the rest of the fall and sporadically in the coming years, yet one must conclude that the postwar liberals ultimately refused to make the hard choice between Hidalgo and Iturbide. Mora's dilemma continued to plague them, a dilemma that was reflected in the social aspect of their reform program.

The conservatives did not limit their ideological offensive to using history to rebut liberal and republican Mexico. At the heart of their attack was a political program to save the country from disaster. On August 25, 1840, José María Gutiérrez de Estrada addressed a ninety-six-page "letter" to President Anastasio Bustamante, expressing his disillusionment with Mexico's fruitless republican experiments and calling for a convention to establish a constitutional monarchy. The tone of his argument was moderate, well fortified with European analogies, and self-consciously presented as "liberal"; yet the pamphlet evoked a furious reaction. It was so ill received that Gutiérrez was forced into hiding, then into exile; the publisher, Ignacio Cumplido, was jailed. Mme. Calderon de la Barca remarked that the pamphlet "seems likely to cause a greater sensation in Mexico than the discovery of the gunpowder plot in England."[37] *El Mosquito mexicano* referred to it as the *only* question of the day.

Gutiérrez de Estrada, like Lucas Alamán, had been a loyal servant of the republic, who became increasingly disillusioned with its record of political anarchy. Gutiérrez, who came from a wealthy and aristocratic family in the outlying province of Campeche, served as a diplomat in the late 1820s, married in Spain, and then lived out the stormy years 1830 to 1834 in Mexico City.

36. Rosa, *Discurso pronunciado en la alameda de esta capital* (Mexico, 1846); *El Siglo*, Sept. 25, 1849.

37. Calderon de la Barca, *Life in Mexico: The Letters of Fanny Calderon de la Barca*, ed. by H. T. and M. H. Fisher (Garden City, Doubleday, 1966), p. 341. See also Cumplido, *Manifestación al público del impresor . . . con motivo de su prisión* (Mexico, 1840). Cumplido insisted that he was a publisher, not a censor.

He was attacked by the reformers in 1833, barely escaped proscription by the notorious *ley del caso,* and then served briefly as foreign minister in 1835. He was an intimate friend of Mora, who portrayed Gutiérrez in 1837 as a liberal. Gutiérrez ultimately resigned his ministry post out of disgust for the machinations of Santa Anna and his cronies, and left for Europe.[38]

Gutiérrez made his proposal for constitutional monarchy after what he termed a "prolonged and painful . . . struggle between my reason and my pure and sincerely republican heart." [39] But experience has shown us, he wrote, the impossibility of imposing republican institutions, whether federalist or centralist in form, upon our society. The United States cannot be our model, though we have tried to make it so. "Everything in Mexico is monarchical," he asserted, and a constitutional monarchy in the "person of a foreign prince" would guarantee more liberty and certainly more peace than would a republic. Gutiérrez presented his "letter" in a period of particular political turbulence, so vividly described by Mme. Calderon. He had just returned to be greeted by a federalist revolt, led by General José Urrea and Valentín Gómez Farías, which laid seige to the capital, captured the president, and heightened the general sense of impending chaos.[40]

Gutiérrez de Estrada fortified his argument by frequent reference to European experience, especially that of France and Spain. He cited the recent Constitution of 1837 in Spain, a compromise between the radical Constitution of 1812 and the conservative Estatuto Real of 1834. He quoted from Odillon Barrot, leader of the "dynastic opposition" to the July Monarchy in France, and from Casimir Perrier, an opponent of Charles X and later a minister under Louis Philippe. The Revolution of 1830 made a great impression on Gutiérrez. Eschewing republicanism in favor of a liberal constitutional monarchy, the French demonstrated the course Mexico should follow. As Chateaubriand had said in 1830:

38. See José C. Valadés, "José María Gutiérrez de Estrada (1800–1867)," *Enciclopedia yucatanense* (Mexico, Ed. Oficial de Yucatán, 1944–47), 7, 141–204; Mora, *Obras,* p. 162.

39. Gutiérrez de Estrada, *Carta dirigida al escmo. sr. presidente de la república sobre la necesidad de buscar en una convención el posible remedio de los males que aquejan a la república* (Mexico, 1840), p. 84.

40. For details of these events see Bancroft, 5, 220–25.

"A representative republic perhaps will be the state of the future in the world, but its time has not yet arrived." [41] If France, the leader of the civilized world, is not ready for a republic, asked Gutiérrez de Estrada, how can we expect to be?

Gutiérrez was a more outspoken Francophile than any other writer of his generation. His arguments were reasonable, his position moderate. Yet, like Zavala, he was on the periphery of the national experience. Whereas Zavala, as we shall see in Chapter 6, sought his political utopia in the United States, Gutiérrez turned to France. Bernardo Couto wrote to Mora that since the appearance of Gutiérrez de Estrada's *Carta,* "everyone is speaking in public the language of the most exalted republicanism." [42] The idea of bringing a foreign monarch to a New World republic which had supposedly freed itself in 1821 from the decadence of Europe, struck a dissonant chord in Mexican opinion, to which Gutiérrez was insensitive. Gutiérrez was not alone in his use of European example; in fact, Mexican thought in the pre-Reforma period was saturated with it. Still, Gutiérrez de Estrada epitomized the Europeanized aristocratic intellectual, and his proposals were regarded as seditious.

Despite its repudiation in 1840, by 1846 monarchism was again being proclaimed, this time by Lucas Alamán's newspaper *El Tiempo.* The arguments of Gutiérrez were given new force, less now by reference to European example and more by reference to national history and conditions. Gutiérrez had emphasized the necessity of fitting institutions to the conditions of Mexican society; *El Tiempo* was more specific. Beginning with the three guarantees of Iturbide's Plan of Iguala, its program advocated respect for the "military hierarchy," an aristocracy of merit and of wealth, and "support for the Catholic religion of our ancestors" (and the property necessary to uphold it decently). This was all to be preserved by a "representative monarchy." [43]

41. Quoted in Gutiérrez, *Carta,* p. 43.

42. Letter of Oct. 25, 1840, Mora Correspondence, 1794–1844 (University of Texas). Earlier Gutiérrez had written: "You know that I am cosmopolitan in my principles, that I love civilization . . . and that I have always singled out France." See ibid. (Feb. 28, 1839).

43. The outright support of monarchy in *El Tiempo* was withheld until the dramatic "profession of faith" of Feb. 12, 1846.

In the midst of internal anarchy and foreign war, *El Tiempo* placed its hopes on Mariano Paredes y Arrillaga, who had risen to the presidency by military rebellion in December 1845. When Paredes rejected the idea of calling a foreign prince, *El Tiempo* ceased publication in protest (June 7, 1846). National defeat in 1847 made the conservatives believe monarchy all the more necessary. Gutiérrez de Estrada was now in Europe where he worked continuously for the monarchist cause until it succeeded in 1863.[44] In Mexico, the conservatives spoke more guardedly, but monarchist proposals were close to the surface in *El Universal*. Otero remarked to Mora at the founding of *El Universal* that it "is ultra-absolutist in tone. It indicates that the former monarchist and antirepublican party wants to maintain its sacred fire." [45] During the subsequent years, *El Universal,* joined in 1852 by *El Omnibus* and *El Orden,* continued to attack the republic by pointing up the contrast between colonial peace and republican anarchy and suggesting by innuendo that monarchy would prove Mexico's solution. Alamán avoided advocating outright monarchism in his *Historia,* but his intention was unmistakable.[46]

Just as José María Gutiérrez de Estrada had found encouragement for his monarchist proposals in the French Revolution of 1830, so the postwar conservatives were drawn toward French events in 1848. *El Universal* expressed shock on November 16, 1848, to see "that civilizing part of the world . . . given over to the horrors of complete anarchy," and it compared the June Days to the barbarian invasions. Actually, news of social upheaval in France was unsettling to Mexicans of both parties. Mariano Otero

44. Gutiérrez wrote two pamphlets at this time: *México en 1840 y en 1847* (Mexico, 1848), elaborated the themes of 1840; and the other, *Le Mexique et l'Europe ou exposé de la situation actuelle du Mexique et des dangers qui peuvent en résulter pour l'Europe si elle ne prend des mesures efficaces pour y remédier* (Paris, 1847), emphasized the North American menace to European interests.

45. Letter of Feb. 12, 1849, García, *Documentos,* 6, 136–37. Otero also identified Manuel Piña y Cuevas and Manuel Díez de Bonilla as editors.

46. See Alamán, *Historia,* 5, 110, 905. Jorge Gurria Lacroix, *Las Ideas monárquicas de don Lucas Alamán* (Mexico, Inst. de Historia, 1951), insists Alamán was a monarchist his entire life, but his claims cannot be documented. See Moisés González Navarro, *El Pensamiento político de Lucas Alamán* (Mexico, El Colegio de México, 1952), pp. 122–26. For his part, Alamán explicitly denied such an assertion (*Historia,* 5, 807 n.). See also Arturo Arnáiz y Freg, "Prologo," *Lucas Alamán, semblanzas e ideario* (Mexico, UNAM, 1939).

wrote to Mora in October that though the February revolution
had probably scuttled temporarily the plans of the Mexican
monarchists, there was now no telling where the reaction would
end, either in France or in Mexico.[47]

By 1849 *El Universal* was finding solace in this reaction. On
October 19 it announced that, in light of recent events, democracy
was clearly discredited in favor of the "other principle, which is
called conservative because it incorporates the elements of life and
well-being of societies." France exemplified the struggle between
order and disorder, between "the majesty of the old systems and
the ridiculous aspirations of the new revolutionary spirit." The
Mexican liberals, always moderate in their social views, were
ambivalent toward the Revolution of 1848. Mora wrote approv-
ingly of French efforts to "repress the communist tendencies" in
the June upheaval. If there was a "democratic" and "socialist"
current in Mexico that was stimulated by the events of France, it
did not take shape until the mid-1850s.[48]

The continuing fear of North America, carefully nurtured by
the conservative press, was accompanied in 1852 and 1853 by
much discussion of a Hispanic-American alliance. José Vasconcelos attributed the idea to Lucas Alamán, and credited him with
perpetuating the Bolivarian dream of forging a league of Hispanic
nations to resist the Yankee menace.[49] The conservative press
pointed to Chile as a model of conservative progress, "the only
former Spanish colony which . . . has been spared the disasters
which all the others have experienced." [50] Hispanic America, said
El Universal, must awaken to the foolishness of ultrademocratic
ideas; the war with the United States has proved that. The North
Americans are the "Islamites" of the nineteenth century, who can
be stopped only by "an alliance of all peoples of Hispanic origin."

47. Letter of Oct. 14, 1848, García, *Documentos*, 6, 121. Otero, as minister of
relations, commissioned Mora to keep him informed of monarchist activities in
Europe.

48. Mora to Relaciones, July 28, 1848, Chávez Orozco, *Gestión*, p. 85; also *El Siglo*,
Sept. 14, 1849, and Francisco Fagoaga to Mora, Oct. 12, 1848, García, *Documentos*,
6, 115–16.

49. See González Navarro, *Pensamiento*, p. 99.

50. Algunos Mexicanos, *Manifiesto a la nación* (n.p., n.d., 1851?) , p. 18. See also
El Universal, June 18, 1852, and July 23, 1853. *El Universal* showed particular interest in South American events during 1853.

Throughout 1853 *El Universal* continued to advocate the alliance, but the idea lost ground in the face of new concerns.

The political expedients of the conservatives (short of their final effort to bring Maximilian in 1864) were always less impressive than their arguments. In 1853 they were trapped by their own logic. Insisting historically on the choice between Hidalgo and Iturbide, they found themselves turning for leadership to that reincarnation of Iturbide, General Antonio López de Santa Anna. The plan for importing a foreign monarch had yet to mature; so the conservatives, encouraged by clerical and military rebellions in Jalisco and Michoacán, brought the perennial caudillo back from his South American exile. Alamán and his colleagues hoped Santa Anna would provide a convenient facade for a regime built on genuine conservatism.

Alamán wrote to the general, instructing him on the course he should follow. The letter was a summary of conservative principles, most important of which was "to conserve the Catholic religion . . . as the only link which binds all Mexicans when all the others have been broken." [51] Santa Anna returned, took power on April 20, and chose Alamán as his minister of relations. But Alamán died on June 2 and with him passed any hope of controlling Santa Anna. In the manner of Iturbide, the general became the master and instituted his own brand of "conservative principles." He made himself "Most Serene Highness" amid much pageantry. The conservative dream of Lucas Alamán was made ridiculous, and his colleagues turned even more decidedly to foreign monarchy.

As we have seen, the initiative in the growing ideological conflict, first in 1846 and then in 1848 and after, was taken by the conservatives. Faced with an attack on their basic political principles, the liberals were forced to defend what they had previously taken for granted, namely, the validity of republican institutions and the benefits of independence over colonial rule. This liberal response, however, was slow to take form, partly because of divisions within what could be called the "liberal party." There were

51. The text (Mar. 23, 1853) can be found in Riva Palacio, *México, 4,* 807–09. For a conservative view of relations with Santa Anna, see *El Partido conservador en México* (Mexico, 1855).

distinctly two liberal wings, and they had been in sharp conflict during the war. In January 1847 the moderados had balked at the attempt of the radical anticlerical government of Valentín Gómez Farías to raise fifteen million pesos by mortgaging or selling at public auction clerical property held in mortmain. The puros did not favor the peace negotiations and afterward referred to the Peace of Guadalupe Hidalgo as a "creature of the moderados." [52] The postwar governments of Herrera and Arista were controlled by the moderados and thus were reluctant to initiate critical reforms.

The war had an equal impact on both groups, as seen in the immediate postwar analysis of national problems. If anything, the moderate position, as represented by Mariano Otero and *El Siglo,* dominated. *El Monitor,* which came later to be the militant spokesman for reform of the church, was moderate in 1847 and 1848. In fact, one is struck in studying the liberal press of the immediate postwar years by how timid the specific reform suggestions were.[53] It was not until 1851 that the liberals enunciated a reform program as bold as the one of 1833.

Symptomatic of divisions in the ranks were the frequent calls for liberal unity. Melchor Ocampo saw the difficulties: the liberals could not unite following some traditional principle of authority, but must draw together freely their individual opinions and interests. The liberal party is "essentially anarchical," but with "full faith in infinite progress," it is sure to triumph. The human race cannot be kept in a "perpetual yesterday." [54] The most obvious unifying issue was the defense of the republican and revolutionary heritage against conservative attacks. On June 18, 1851, *El Monitor* ran an article entitled, "Necessity of a True Union of Moderados and Puros," and concluded that there were now only two

52. See Wilfred H. Callcott, *Church and State in Mexico, 1822–1857* (Durham, Duke University Press, 1926), pp. 181–91. The moderados did not fare well in subsequent liberal historiography, primarily because of their hesitancy on anticlericalism. See Riva Palacio, *México, 4,* 699, 718; Justo Sierra, *Juárez, su obra y su tiempo* (Mexico, UNAM, 1956), p. 30, and *Evolución,* p. 193.

53. See *El Siglo* in the early issues following its resumption on June 1, 1848; also *El Monitor,* July 1848; also Otero, *Consideraciones.*

54. Ocampo to D. A. García (Mar. 8, 1853), *Obras completas* (Mexico, Vásquez, 1900–01), 2, 291.

parties in the country: the conservative and the republican. The liberals saw that they must now prove that Mexico was better off as an independent republic than as a Spanish colony. The conservatives were really trying to "destroy liberty and annul independence, so that the nation could again become a flock of sheep." [55] A series of articles in *El Monitor* during January 1852 pursued the same theme, condemning monarchist-conservative ideas "as a museum curiosity." The polemic continued in 1852–53, as *El Omnibus* and *El Orden* assailed republican *El Siglo* by drawing an idealized picture of the Colony. [56]

Hence, the liberal reform program that did emerge, in spite of a continuing division in the ranks, was based on a defense of the federal republic. The year 1847 saw a return to federalism after a decade under the centralist Constitution of 1836. In full reaction against the monarchist designs of the conservatives, the liberal revolt of August 1846 had made the restoration of the federal system its primary objective. A constitutional congress met, and, as the Americans were approaching Mexico City in May, the Acta de Reformas was adopted. Inspired by Mariano Otero, it reinstated with modifications the Constitution of 1824. [57] Although the adoption of the Acta came amid much praise of federalism, in the subsequent years there was little specific response by the liberals to conservative attack on the federal system. In defending the "federal republic," they spoke only in general terms of the benefits of republicanism. It was apparent that in the face of conservative opposition, federalism as a system was now taken for granted. The important implications for liberalism of federalist limitation of central power were no longer of concern as they had been in the 1820s.

With military defeat the liberals recognized that Mexican society was out of joint. This was the principal theme of Mariano Otero's pamphlet, written in December 1847, and it was a recur-

55. *El Siglo,* Apr. 3, 1850.

56. See *El Omnibus,* Oct. 9, Nov. 20, 1852; *El Orden,* Aug. 7, 1853.

57. For the text of the Acta and the various congressional proposals preceding it, see Felipe Tena Ramírez, ed., *Leyes fundamentales de México* (Mexico, Porrua, 1964), pp. 442–77. The most significant innovation of the Acta (art. 25) was the *juicio de amparo,* which instituted a type of judicial review of constitutionality. See below, Chap. 6.

rent concern in the subsequent years.[58] The principal liberal remedy was a program of European colonization which would strengthen the middle-class property holders. They were the basis of the liberal party, asserted *El Monitor* (June 24, 1849). Mora, Otero, and Guillermo Prieto questioned indiscriminate colonization (see below, Chap. 6), fearing that the northern provinces might go the way of Texas; but they were in the minority. *El Monitor* on August 31, 1848, called urgently for an increase in population, "opening wide the doors of our land to all foreigners, whatever be their origin and their faith." The great obstacle to an indiscriminate colonization program had always been the opposition to religious tolerance for non-Catholics. Once again in 1849, a colonization law was scuttled on the toleration issue, after a long and heated debate in the congress.[59] European colonization remained a will-o'-the-wisp for the liberals throughout the nineteenth century.

It was the church that came increasingly to absorb the attention of the militant liberals. Anticlericalism again became the focus of reform, just as it had been earlier in 1833. In time of crisis the presence of this vast property-holding institution, which absorbed a large percentage of the liquid capital of the country and which lived as a separate juridical entity, was particularly intolerable. Moreover, the church had shown no patriotic loyalty in the face of foreign invasion.

Yet, it was anticlericalism which above all caused the division in liberal ranks between moderados and puros. *El Siglo,* the organ of the moderados, was far milder in its advocacy of church reform than was *El Monitor.* The governments of Herrera and Arista were only moderately anticlerical, as we have seen. Herrera was particularly cautious. He announced to congress on January 1, 1851, that "throughout my administration the clergy of the republic have suffered no attacks upon their property." As a devout Catholic Herrera took a special interest in the welfare of Pius IX who had been forced to flee from Rome in the Revolution of 1848. Herrera went so far as to invite him to reside in Mexico, a measure

---

58. See *El Monitor,* June 18, 21, 1851, and *El Siglo,* Mar. 8, 1851.
59. Cotner, p. 312. See also the observations of Otero to Mora (Feb. 12, 1849), García, *Documentos, 6,* 137.

that won approval in congress along with a grant of 25,000 pesos to aid the Pope in crisis. Cordial relations with the papacy did allow Herrera, however, to win papal assent to a new Patronato agreement, in which the government would exercise the right of presenting candidates for vacancies in the ecclesiastical hierarchy.[60]

Therefore, when Melchor Ocampo, as Governor of Michoacán, became involved (1851) in an acrimonious debate with a local priest, he spoke for a radical minority of liberals. The debate began when "a priest from Maravatío" (D. Agustín Dueñas) published a condemnation of Governor Ocampo's proposal before the Michoacán legislature to reform the parish fees. These fees for baptisms, marriages, and funerals, which provided a livelihood for priests, were governed in Michoacán by a law unchanged since 1731. Payment was scaled according to one's class and caste, a provision now theoretically obsolete in an egalitarian republic. Actually the maximum charge (for "Spaniards") was the one most often levied, leading Ocampo to remark: "By virtue of our emancipation from Spain, we are all Spaniards."

Ocampo was demanding reform of a system that was squeezing the poor parishoner and encouraging illegitimacy. Ocampo was careful to state, however, that many priests were men of exemplary conduct, who would starve themselves rather than levy unjust fees. He had high praise for Juan Cayetano Portugal. As Bishop of Michoacán until his death the previous year, Portugal was an enlightened leader who had done much to improve the conduct of his priests.[61]

The crux of the polemic, which grew into five separate essays that El Monitor reprinted, was the question of "sovereignty." Dueñas was disputing Ocampo's assertion that since these were essentially taxes paid for civil functions, the government should control their collection and reform as it had in the eighteenth

60. On Herrera and the church, see Cotner, pp. 280–89.

61. Ocampo, "Respuesta primera" (Mar. 8, 1851), in La Religión, la iglesia y el clero (Mexico, Empresas Editoriales, 1948), p. 32. The "priest from Maravatío" may well have had encouragement from Michoacán's new bishop, Clemente José Munguía, a man of philosophic depth, who came to be one of the church's most forceful and prolific apologists. Munguía deserves a study. See Chevalier, "Conservateurs et libéraux," pp. 460–61.

century.[62] Bishops, insisted Ocampo, were no more "sovereign" now than they had been under the Bourbon kings. Ocampo, as we shall see in Chapter 4, was treating a question that was at the heart of nineteenth-century liberalism. *El Monitor* carried the attack to the other well-known anticlerical issues—mortmain property, privileged jurisdiction, control of education, and registry of vital statistics.

Almost daily from August through November 1851, *El Monitor* concentrated on the issue of mortmain and called openly for nationalization of church property, against the violent opposition of *El Universal* and of another clerical newspaper, *Voz de la religión*. *El Monitor* deplored the fact that

> private fortunes decline and vanish while the clergy, without suffering any of these misfortunes [imposed on the individual by outside circumstances], doubles its capital every twenty years and continues to absorb the free wealth of the individual property owner.[63]

Corporate entailed wealth was deemed an obstacle to progress. The aim of reform must be to free property holders from the clutches of the church and to transfer their allegiance instead to the nation. "Each new proprietor will be a new defender of institutions and of stability," and "peace, order, and liberty will have gained." Melchor Ocampo and the editors of *El Monitor* reaffirmed the 1833 liberal vision of a modern and progressive secular society based on free individual initiative (see Chapter 5 below).

The years from 1846 to 1853 were critical in the life of the Mexican nation, now shaken to its foundations by political anarchy, foreign invasion, military collapse, and social upheaval. Thinking Mexicans could with reason doubt if theirs was really a nation and if it would continue to exist. Out of crisis came a fresh analysis of the great national problems and new proposals for their solution. In no way, however, did the crisis of 1847 bring unity to Mexico. On the contrary, it gave rise to a profound schism which was to control the country's destiny for two decades. Although struggle

---

62. Ocampo, "Respuesta quinta" (Oct. 20, 1851), in *La Religión,* pp. 122–24.
63. *El Monitor,* Sept. 19, 1851.

remained in the realm of ideas during the immediate postwar years, it was a genuine conflict nonetheless. The ensuing civil war of 1854 to 1867 was at bottom ideological, and the political strife of that era cannot be understood without knowing precisely what ideas men were fighting over.

The ideas in contention did not emerge spontaneously in 1847. The new element was the definition of a clearly expressed and self-conscious conservative argument, which, as a kind of psychological warfare, managed to exploit the crisis of republican Mexico for its own ends. By the vigorous use of history as a weapon of political debate, the conservatives, under the leadership of Lucas Alamán, succeeded in pointing up conflicts in the Mexican past that were previously either unperceived or ignored.

The inner contradictions of the Revolution for Independence were Alamán's particular target, and the result was his magisterial *Historia de Méjico*. By asking the liberals to choose between Hidalgo and Iturbide, Alamán hit at the liberals' most vulnerable point, the social basis of their liberalism. When the liberals were faced with a stirring of the Indian masses, either in 1810 or in the contemporary Caste Wars, they recoiled from egalitarianism. In this they were no different from contemporary liberals throughout the Atlantic world when confronted with the "social question." Mexican liberals could talk of the need for a society of free property holders or of an "aristocracy of talent" without facing the real condition of two-thirds of the population. Their's was a social question, though, which presented unique problems, because this two-thirds majority was an ethnically distinct group.

Despite these social fallacies and the political division in liberal ranks, the conservative challenge, coming as it did in the wake of the disastrous war, did much to revive and give focus to a vigorous liberal program which had been formulated earlier in the 1820s and 1830s. Let us now turn to an analysis of that liberalism.

2

The Structure of Political Liberalism

The liberal program, as it was reformulated in Mexico following the war with the United States, contained two conflicting objectives. On the one hand, there was the drive to free the individual from the shackles that bound him under the Spanish system. The liberties of the individual must be guaranteed against irresponsible power; thus freedom of the press, speech, and, ideally, freedom of religion were of great significance. The representative institutions of a federalist republic, and even a measure of municipal autonomy, must be strengthened. Moreover, protecting property rights and advancing economic liberty through laissez-faire were also directed toward the objective of individual freedom. Authoritarian state power must be limited.

On the other hand, the liberals wanted to free Mexico from the regime of corporate privilege. A modern, progressive nation must be juridically uniform under a fiscally strong secular state. Its citizens' allegiance to the civil state must not be shared with the church, with the army, or with any other corporation, such as the university or the Indian community. This objective embraced educational reform, the attack upon the *fueros,* secularization, colonization, and even land reform.[1]

On the surface, these objectives, which were present in liberal programs throughout the Atlantic world, might not seem to conflict. In certain national contexts—for instance, England and the United States—the contention was less pronounced than in others. To understand Mexican liberalism, however, it is important that we demonstrate the nature of the conflict, even in its ideal form.

1. Cf. Felipe Tena Ramírez' contribution to *El Constituyente de 1856 y el pensamiento liberal mexicano* (Mexico, Porrua, 1960) .

Therefore, let us move obliquely and seek the affinities of structure that emerge between Mexico and Western Europe. This chapter will focus on Europe.

In France, to understand the development of a liberal and revolutionary ideology, one must consider the nature of the old regime. The same would be true for Mexico. Any such study from the point of view of liberalism first encounters the phenomenon of feudal institutions. The term "feudalism" has frequently been used to describe the colony of New Spain and even the more recent Mexico. Viewed comparatively, the case of New Spain presents two interrelated problems. First, New Spain was part of the Western world, and, unlike other areas to which "feudalism" has been applied, did not evolve independently of Europe. Second, in speaking of feudalism in New Spain, essentially we are comparing society and institutions of the sixteenth and seventeenth centuries with a Europe of several centuries earlier.

There are generally two ways of defining feudalism that are of value to this discussion. Considered narrowly, feudalism may be seen as a set of legal institutions and relationships based on the obedience and service (primarily military) of a free vassal toward a lord in exchange for protection and maintenance. Thus feudalism embraced a number of key terms, particularly "lord," "vassal," "homage" or "fealty," and the "fief." The last was a grant, usually of land, by the lord to maintain the vassal. This system in essence became a mode of political organization and saw its classic development between the Loire and the Rhine from the tenth to the thirteenth centuries. Political power became a private possession, and the rights to land (or to the fief) became equivalent to rights of government.[2]

Feudalism may also be defined in broader terms as a form of society. Marc Bloch has stated that the fundamental features of European feudalism included the following: a subject peasantry economically tied to the land; the existence of the "service tenemeant" (that is, the fief), through which the holder exercised authority; a class of warriors which held a supreme place in society; and, finally, ties of dependence between man and man which

2. See F. L. Ganshof, *Feudalism* (London, Longmans, 1952).

permeated all levels of society, on one level between lord and vassal, on another between lord of the manor and serf.[3]

In view of these definitions of European feudalism, New Spain can best be characterized as having a variant of feudal society without the corresponding feudal political institutions. François Chevalier has described vividly the formation of this feudal society in the early seventeenth century. It resulted from a period of economic decline, a shrinking of the Indian population, and from a consequent falling back on the land by the Creole population. The hacienda, acquiring its "Magna Carta" by the Crown's general settlement of land titles, became the base for a landowning aristocracy. In the manner of post-Carolingian Europe, the large landowner created a style of lordly largesse, assumed de facto authority over his dependents, and dominated a subject Indian peasantry which was tied to the land through peonage.[4] This society persisted with little change until 1910.

At the heart of the feudal system, by any definition, were the institutions of vassalage and the fief. To what extent did these develop in New Spain? The precedents in medieval Spain were meager. Owing largely to the Reconquest, there was an absence of systematic lord-vassal relationships. The fief, which depended on more stable agrarian conditions than the struggle against the Moslems could provide, did not take root as in France. Moreover, the authority of the king never completely disappeared in Spain, because of his continually revived role as war leader against the infidel.

Despite these limited precedents, the conquest and colonization of America produced the *encomienda,* an institution with feudal potentialities. The Crown and the *encomendero* were initially parties to a feudal contract. The encomienda, though not a grant of land, was a fief or benefice by which the encomendero received rent in the form of a portion of the tribute owed to the Crown by the Indians under his control. This was payable at first in services

3. Marc Bloch, *Feudal Society* (Chicago, University of Chicago Press, 1961), p. 446.

4. Chevalier, *La Formation des grands domaines au Mexique* (Paris, Inst. d'Ethnologie, 1952).

and later in money or goods. The encomendero swore fealty to the Crown and was often obligated in the early days to supply horses or retainers to fight the Crown's enemies, particularly in the frontier areas. In the early 1550s, when Viceroy Velasco sought royal aid for the campaign against hostile Indians, the reply was that responsibility lay with the encomenderos, since "the encomiendas are rents which His Majesty gives to the encomenderos because they defend the land." [5]

Yet we know that the encomienda as a feudal military institution declined after 1550, partly because of a general reluctance on the part of the restless encomenderos to engage in organized campaigns, but more decisively because of the hostility of the Crown. One of the remarkable facts in the history of New Spain was the rapid decline of this incipient feudal warrior class, who "became pensioners of the Crown, a tamed nobility without any real vitality." [6]

The nature of the Castilian state is the crux of any consideration of feudal institutions in New Spain. The sixteenth-century Spanish monarchy, though the strongest in Europe, was in many aspects still medieval. Its administrative apparatus was developing rapidly, and a vast royal bureaucracy could be laid down in New Spain after 1535; but it was not yet "a unitary and rationalized whole." [7] Thus the conquest and colonization of New Spain was carried through by individuals, the recipients of royal concessions or contracts. The Crown was the source of privileges freely given, as in the case of the early encomienda and the later grant of latifundia (large landholdings).

The church became the most privileged entity. It was both a historic estate from Spanish and medieval traditions and a functional corporation in its role of Christianizing the Indian popula-

5. Quoted in Lyle N. McAlister, "Social Structure and Social Change in New Spain," *HAHR, 43* (1963), 360.

6. Ibid., p. 361. The Crown did grant a vast feudal patrimony to Hernán Cortés in 1529, but immediately began to undermine the rights of jurisdiction originally extended to the conquistador and to his descendants (Chevalier, *Formation,* pp. 167–76).

7. Quoted from Mario Góngora, *El Estado en el derecho indiano, época de fundación, 1492–1570* (Santiago de Chile, Editorial Universitaria, 1951), p. 301, by Richard M. Morse, "The Heritage of Latin America" in Louis Hartz, *The Founding of New Societies* (New York, Harcourt, 1964), p. 139.

tion.[8] Even the Indian communities, refashioned under royal direction toward 1600, were granted privileges and thus juridical protection against the encroachment of latifundia. Still largely a medieval monarch, the king was first of all a judge, exercising through his agents jurisdiction among the competing privileged entities. Thus the *audiencia,* or supreme tribunal, became the key institution of royal administration in New Spain. As Chevalier remarks repeatedly, "it was the jurists who governed the country." [9]

In summarizing the comparison between New Spain and the feudal society of medieval Europe, we find that the affinity rests mainly on the hacienda (manor) system and a subject peasantry. Moreover, the general medieval tone of Mexican society, provided by the omnipresence of the church and by the great variety of privileges and jurisdictions, is readily apparent. The peculiarity of Mexico's "feudal" heritage from the sixteenth century is more easily understood by considering one of Marc Bloch's observations. The manor, originating in the Roman villa, predated the establishment of feudal institutions proper and in turn outlasted them. The essentially separate evolution of the two is confused because in Europe they reached their peak concurrently.[10] In New Spain "manorialism" arose after the decline of incipient feudal institutions and concurrently with royal bureaucracy, ideally the antithesis of feudalism.

Marc Bloch concluded his famous work with the statement that "the originality of . . . [European feudalism] consisted in the emphasis it placed on the idea of an agreement capable of binding the rulers." [11] This contractual agreement provided the basis for the medieval system of representative bodies, a system that never

8. McAlister, "Social Structure," p. 353.

9. See Chevalier, *Formation,* pp. 194, 269, 405; also J. H. Parry, *The Audiencia of New Galicia in the Sixteenth Century* (Cambridge, Cambridge University Press, 1948) , p. 3.

10. Bloch, *Feudal Society,* p. 442. A comparison of European manors and Spanish American latifundia cannot, of course, be carried very far. Unlike the medieval serf, Indian "serfs" were ethnically and culturally distinct from their masters. See Margali Sarfatti, *Spanish Bureaucratic-Patrimonialism in America* (Berkeley, University of California, Inst. of International Studies, 1966) , pp. 46 ff. The significance of this difference for Mexican liberalism will be explored more fully in Chap. 7.

11. Bloch, *Feudal Society,* p. 452.

took root in New Spain. The *cabildo* or *ayuntamiento* (municipal corporation) did flourish as a local representative institution in the early days of colonization, but its autonomy was undermined after 1550. The closest approach to a cortes came in 1542 when there were widespread petitions and even some meetings of colonists to protest the abolition of the encomienda system in the New Laws for the Indies. Charles V would hardly have let develop in America an institution that had so recently challenged his authority in Spain. In short, "the medieval imprint which the [colonial] system as a whole bore was not that of parliamentary representation, but that of pluralistic, compartmented privilege and of administrative paternalism." [12]

Between the sixteenth and the eighteenth centuries the structural differences between Mexico, Spain, and France became less pronounced. As absolute monarchy progressed in Europe, it did so at the expense of the political prerogatives of the nobility and of traditional representative institutions. This process came earlier and was more advanced in Spain than in France, but it was similar in both countries. The old nobility of the two countries were drawn into the court, made more dependent on the Crown for privileges, and replaced or circumvented in the governing councils. After experiencing rebellious nobles in the Fronde, Louis XIV curtailed the *parlement,* the only effective institution in France to serve as a check on royal edicts. Though reviving considerably in the eighteenth century, the parlements became controlled by a small group of families which inherited their seats.

In short, by the mid-eighteenth century the society of Western Europe had become more aristocratic. Broader and yet more exclusive than the old nobility, aristocracy was based on the institution of family, which had a tendency "to diffuse itself through the

12. Morse, "Heritage," p. 144. Morse uses Max Weber's term "patrimonialism" to describe the socioadministrative structure of colonial Spanish America, as opposed to Weber's other type of traditional domination—"feudalism." This definition has recently been developed systematically by Sarfatti. "Patrimonialism" is the most precise term for what I have described in New Spain. However, since I am primarily concerned with defining Mexican liberalism, I have preferred to speak more loosely in terms of "feudal institutions" (or the lack of them) , "corporate privilege," and so forth. These were the terms that had meaning to nineteenth-century liberals.

institutions of government, not to mention those of religion." [13]
Municipal government in the eighteenth century had degenerated
into a petty oligarchy. The same thing could be said of the cabil-
dos of New Spain, at least prior to the introduction of the intendant system. Lucas Alamán noted that many of the principal
Creole families prior to independence were mineowners who purchased Jesuit property and became large landowners as well.[14]
Mora and others spoke of the sharp economic and social division
between upper and lower clergy, a pattern similar to that in
France and Spain before 1789. Economic and bureaucratic growth
lent new opportunities to the aristocratic elite and served to
sharpen the sense of juridical and economic privilege.

The European aristocracy thought in terms of "orders" or
"estates." Society was seen to be divided into a myriad of corporate
entities, groups of people tied by similar occupation, function, or
interest, who were represented through "constituted bodies."
These might be the parlements, provincial assemblies, or estates
general in France, the cortes in Spain, or parliament in England.
The only entity approaching a constituted body in New Spain was
the cabildo. The term "constituted body," as Palmer uses it, has a
political meaning. It is the outgrowth of the medieval idea of representation or feudal limitation on royal authority. But there was
a broader sense of corporate privilege which went beyond any tie
to political function or initiative. When the eighteenth-century
aristocracy came to talk of "liberties" or "rights" they were as
often as not speaking of fiscal or juridical privilege in nonpolitical
terms.

This dichotomy between privilege and liberty was sharpest in
Spain and Mexico, where historic political representation was
weak or nonexistent. In Spain the defense of aristocratic or clerical
privilege could be tied, if only vaguely, to the memory of representation by estates in a now defunct cortes. In Mexico not even
the memory of representation existed, except through the cabildo.
Privilege and liberty became more easily confused in France than

13. Robert R. Palmer, *The Age of the Democratic Revolution: A Political History of Europe and America, 1760–1800* (Princeton, Princeton University Press,
1959–64), *1*, 29.
14. Alamán, *Historia, 1*, 101.

in Spain, for instance by the aristocratic caste which controlled the parlements and challenged the king in the eighteenth century. The dichotomy was scarcely present in England. Among eighteenth-century constituted bodies, the English parliament was the model, for through it a privileged aristocracy exercised political initiative and constituted, unlike the French *parlementaires,* a true governing class. Blackstone referred to parliament as the "great corporation or body politic of the kingdom." It was both, in a way that was unique to the eighteenth-century world.

In concluding this cursory institutional survey, we come back to the special character of New Spain. Mariano Otero was aware of it when he tried to explain the apparent social and political anarchy of Mexico in 1842. We have erred, he wrote, "in not recognizing that our society had its own features, and that it was in no way similar to the European societies with which we are always comparing ourselves." [15] The crucial difference, according to Otero, was that the Mexican aristocracy, despite primogeniture and an array of noble titles, did not "exercise civil jurisdiction, nor did it have any political influence." It was a privileged group and lived lavishly in the cities, leaving estates to administrators. Colonial government was a "true despotism, without intermediate classes, and this power was essentially foreign." Society, by the end of the colonial period, was incoherent, each group or class defending its own "abuses and privileges" and incapable of concerted political action.[16] In reducing the political prerogatives of the aristocracy, the continental enlightened despots were attempting to move toward a situation which was essentially that of Otero's Mexico.

Political liberalism in Europe grew up within the theoretical as well as the institutional conflicts of the old regime. Feudal government was in effect upheld by medieval theory, which posed limitations on political authority in the name of Natural Law or God's just ordering of the universe. This Law, while it decreed a fixed

15. Otero, *Ensayo sobre el verdadero estado de la cuestión social y política que se agita en la república mexicana* (Mexico, 1842), p. 36.

16. Otero used this analysis to argue optimistically the republican and democratic destiny of the country. Despotism, being foreign by tradition, was impossible. Without a political nobility, there could be no constitutional monarchy. For him the only cohesive force was a growing middle class and the only appropriate form of government a republic (ibid., p. 54).

hierarchical order to society and a natural obedience to rulers, always distinguished between "tyrants" and the "just prince." The tyrant was irresponsible, in harmony neither with God's law nor with the community of the governed. The tyrant, according to the extreme position of a John of Salisbury, could be overthrown, even killed. Political theory based on Natural Law regained vitality during the Reformation and was used by Protestants and Catholics alike, by the author of *Vindiciae contra tyrannos* and by Mariana and Suárez, to justify popular resistance to the ungodly prince.[17] Ultimately, this line of theory culminated in John Locke, who gave it a secular orientation and a radically new social premise. Thus, constitutionalism, as it was expressed for example in France following the reign of Louis XIV, was supported both by the heritage of medieval theory and by insitutional practice.

As we have seen, however, political events were moving in the opposite direction, especially on the continent. Absolutism was built upon the twelfth-century revival of Roman Law, but more particularly upon modern theory which separated the religious from the secular sphere—Machiavelli, Luther, Bodin, and Hobbes. The new concept was sovereignty, that supreme power, according to Jean Bodin, that distinguished the state from other groupings in society. Whereas Bodin clung to the idea of a society made up of multiple corporations, Thomas Hobbes reduced it to sovereign and subjects. According to him, warring individuals in the state of nature gave over their authority by contract to a sovereign who then ruled them absolutely for their own welfare. Though absolute monarchy in practice conformed more to the pattern of Bodin than to that of Hobbes, the opposition of the monarchy to corporate privilege became increasingly apparent.

Modern liberalism partook of both these traditions, but it did so amid changing conceptions of man and society, conceptions that are most conveniently seen in the ideas of John Locke. Attacking absolutist theory, Locke found government to be derived from a contract between the people and their governors. The natural state of man is one of liberty and equality, and it is governed by a "law of nature," or reason. This law "teaches all mankind who

17. See John N. Figgis, *Political Thought from Gerson to Grotius: 1414–1625* (New York, Harper, 1960).

will but consult it, that being all equal and independent, no one ought to harm another in his life, health, liberty, or possessions." [18] To avoid the inconveniences of enforcing this law in the state of nature, men entered into a community, and in turn delegated authority to a governing majority.

At the same time, according to Locke, man has a natural right to property. Every man "has a 'property' in his own 'person.' The 'labor' of his body and the 'work' of his hands . . . are properly his." [19] The fruits of Nature, given by God to men in common, are made individual when man mixes his labor with what is common. It is for "the mutual preservation of their lives, liberties and estates, which I call by the general name—property," that men join in society and put themselves under a government. It follows then, in Locke's view, that if a government becomes tyrannical and goes against these inalienable rights of man, it can be dissolved by the people.

Locke's theory denied any notion of unified or unlimited sovereignty. It also put political authority on a new basis—individual rights, which included the inalienable right of property. That there were ambiguities in Locke's theory is evident from the different way his ideas were interpreted in England and on the continent. Locke wrote his treatise to justify the Revolution of 1688; and it was used in the eighteenth century to sanctify the historic rights and property of Englishmen, as expressed through their aristocratic representatives in parliament. In France, Locke was interpreted more abstractly, largely because of the weakness of traditional political institutions below the monarchy.[20] Out of this divergence grew a conflict between liberties and liberty, between historically acquired rights (privileges) and abstract natural rights, between constitutionalism and sovereignty. Thus Guido de Ruggiero has seen a grand dialectic in "the two typical forms of Liberalism, the French and the English," which, by the time Edmund Burke faced the French Revolution in 1790, "seem

18. Locke, *Two Treatises of Civil Government* (London, Dent, 1924), Chap. 2.
19. Ibid., Chap. 5.
20. George H. Sabine, *A History of Political Theory* (New York, Holt, 1937), p. 547.

irreconciliable in their mutual contradiction." [21] Ruggiero's scheme admittedly oversimplifies the problem, but used with caution, it can aid us in understanding Mexican liberalism.

Despite what came to be the dominant tendency toward rationalism and abstraction in French political thought, there was a sustained though unsuccessful effort to revive the ancient French constitution, particularly by Montesquieu and by the later parlementary spokesmen of the French aristocracy. Charles Louis de Secondat, Baron de la Brède et de Montesquieu, grew up a provincial aristocrat in the last days of Louis XIV's reign and inherited a seat in the Parlement of Bordeaux. This background, in addition to his visit to England in 1729–31 and his extensive study of the English constitution, made him the consistent and outspoken enemy of "despotism." He was both empirical and a rationalist in his approach. From observation of the English constitution he developed a legalistic scheme in which the legislative, executive, and judicial powers were delicately balanced, forming an ideal check on arbitrary power. As an aristocrat he naturally enough ignored the inner and more organic aspect of English politics, namely its control by a privileged oligarchy.

Yet Montesquieu's emphasis upon a constitution as the guarantor of civil and political liberty made him the classic spokesman for constitutionalism in countries where the institutional limitations on sovereign power were weak or nonexistent. His *Spirit of the Laws* was the best known French book in North America. He was equally esteemed for a very different reason by later continental liberals and by Mora in Mexico in the 1820s; for "Montesquieu could be invoked wherever individual liberty was threatened by irresponsible power." [22]

The French parlements, in their effort after 1760 to reconstitute France as a limited monarchy, drew heavily from Montesquieu who had argued that France like England had the institutions necessary to establish political liberty. He had seen in France a

21. Ruggiero, *The History of European Liberalism* (Boston, Beacon, 1959), p. 347. Ruggiero, influenced by Hegel, sees a synthesis resulting from the conflict of the two forms in the nineteenth century.

22. Kingsley Martin, *The Rise of French Liberal Thought* (New York, New York University Press, 1954), p. 166.

great number of "intermediate bodies," from the nobility and the parlements down to towns, guilds, and professional groups, each as a corporate entity with its own legal status. Each of these balanced one another and provided a moderating influence on the monarch.[23] In the years from 1760 to 1789 the French king and his ministers were at war with the parlements, beginning with the reaction to the tax decrees of 1763, enacted by the king to meet the expenses of war and of a growing bureaucracy. The decrees included the continuation of the *vingtième,* a modern tax levied primarily on income from land, and another tax on property in office. The parlements began to speak of themselves as making up one true national representative body. Louis XV in 1766 refused to recognize the magistrates of the parlements as other than "my officers, charged with the truly royal duty of rendering justice to my subjects." There were for him only the traditional estates of the kingdom (which had not met since 1614).[24]

The parlements were abolished in 1770 by Louis XV's vigorous minister Maupéou, only to be restored in 1774 by the more conciliatory Louis XVI. But the new king also appointed a series of reformist ministers, Turgot, Necker, Brienne, and Calonne, who pursued the same radical program of fiscal and administrative modernization. The parlements decried what they termed the effort to promote an "equality of duties" and thus "to overturn civil society, whose harmony rests only on that gradation of powers, authorities, preeminences and distinctions which holds each man in his place and guarantees all status against confusion." [25] This was the theoretical basis of the "aristocratic resurgence" which culminated in the calling of the estates general in May 1789. The Bourbon monarchs were attempting to attack the basic problem of corporate privilege in society, but until 1789 their effort had little success. The parlements won wide support when they labeled Bourbon policy "despotism."

The most serious threat to privilege and constitutionalism, however, came from another quarter, from the ideas of Jean Jacques Rousseau. Translated into political terms, the constituted

23. Palmer, *1,* 56–57.
24. Ibid., pp. 94–96.
25. Quoted in ibid., p. 451.

bodies faced a war on two fronts, against the king on one side and the people on the other. Monarchy and what came to be democracy were akin in their common opposition to aristocratic privilege. But Rousseau was attacking more than privilege in the *Social Contract*. Unlike the physiocrats and Voltaire, he was critical of the entire old regime as he saw it, including the monarchy. His radical equality and sense of community left no room for hierarchy, no room for subjection of man to man. "Each man, in giving himself to all, gives himself to nobody."

He began as Locke did with man in the state of nature, but then said that man became truly free only by joining with his fellows. Rousseau distinguished between "natural liberty" and "civil liberty," between man acting instinctively and man acting justly. Legitimacy, morality, justice, were thus derived from the social compact. Unlike Locke, Rousseau saw no legitimate rights, such as property, which preceded the social contract. Of basic importance for Rousseau was not "the individual personality of each contracting party" but rather "the moral and collective body" created by "this act of association." This body is the sovereign: "those who are associated in it take collectively the name of *people,* and severally are called *citizens.*" [26]

Rousseau's model was based, apart from his own city-state of Geneva, on the republics of Antiquity; thus he had no place for representative government, which he regarded as feudal and barbarous. The English for him were not a free people. He saw liberty only as a positive thing, achieved when the people collectively, democratically, appropriated the state. He had no sense of liberty as the negative limitation of authority in the interest of sacred individual rights. The growth of liberal representative government, therefore, owed more to eighteenth-century aristocratic constitutionalism than to Rousseau's popular sovereignty. Still, a government could not be termed liberal in the modern sense until representation was based on individuals, rather than on estates, communities, or corporate groups.[27]

Liberalism and democracy appeared contradictory when Rousseau's ideas were later used to support Robespierre's revolutionary

26. Rousseau, *The Social Contract* (New York, Dutton, 1950), Bk. I, Chap. 6.
27. See Palmer, *I*, 125, 166–67.

government. And yet democracy grew out of the "ideal premises of modern liberalism," out of both its negative and positive aspects. "They may be summarized in two formulae: the extention of individual rights to all members of the community, and the right of the people as an organic whole to govern itself." [28]

The two aspects of liberalism were contained in the Declaration of the Rights of Man and Citizen of August 1789. Palmer calls the declaration the most important single document of the eighteenth-century revolution in the West because it laid down the principles of the modern democratic state. But since democracy is only one part of political liberalism, the contradictions within the document are for us the point of interest. The declaration asserted the "natural and imprescriptible rights of man, liberty, property, security, and resistance of oppression" (article ii), at the same time stating that "law is an expression of the will of the community" or the general will (vi). "Every community in which a separation of powers and a security of rights is not provided for lacks a constitution" (xvi), yet "the nation is the source of all sovereignty" (iii). While guaranteeing individual freedom against authority, the declaration set up a new sovereignty rooted in the people, or the community. Ruggiero has said that the declaration left Montesquieu and Rousseau face to face. It attempted to bring together as the "natural rights of man" two conflicting tendencies which at their extremes represented aristocratic constitutionalism and democratic despotism.[29]

This question must be seen in the context of the events of the French Revolution to appreciate its relevance to Mexico. The basic constitutional problem of the French Revolution was how to maintain individual liberty while establishing effective legal equality in the face of entrenched corporate privilege. On the dramatic night of August 4, 1789, the national assembly "abolished feudalism."

"Feudalism" meant primarily the vestiges of peasant obligations

28. Ruggiero, p. 370. Isaiah Berlin, in *Two Concepts of Liberty* (Oxford, Oxford University Press, 1958), pp. 29–33, asserts that the core of rationalism is the positive conception of liberty, the "nation of self-direction or self-control." Rousseau is his example, in whose view "liberty, so far from being incompatible with authority, becomes virtually identical with it."

29. See Ruggiero, pp. 66–73; also Martin, pp. 192–95.

under the manorial regime. It also meant the differences between nobles and commoners in taxation, property in office, the guild system, provincial liberties, and in general, juridical distinctions by orders and by persons. The greatest of corporations was the church, and its power was undermined by the abolition of tithes and annates. The August 4 decrees were followed by the nationalization of church property in November 1789, and by the Civil Constitution of the Clergy in 1790. To enforce this broad enactment of legal equality and secularism, the power of the civil state had to be greatly expanded. The elimination of the provinces in favor of uniform and centrally controlled departments completed the pattern.

The problem can be further seen in the debates over the Constitution of 1791. The two major arguments in the constituent assembly were presented by Abbé Sieyès and J. J. Mounier. Mounier wanted a balanced government, Sieyès wanted the "people as a constituent power," essentially Rousseau's idea of popular sovereignty in its active or creative form.[30] Sieyès had been the champion of the third estate in 1789; he now wanted a single-chamber legislature with the king subjected to its authority. Mounier, though speaking militantly against an aristocratically ordered society, held out for two chambers and the royal veto. Instead of the assembly having the full constituent power, Mounier believed that the king must be recognized as coauthor of the constitution. In arguing for two chambers, Mounier used the example of the American Senate. The problem was that an upper house in France would consist of aristocrats and clergy, a thought that was intolerable in France after 1789.

Moreover, the hostility to the king had grown since May 1789. He no longer was the antagonist of the aristocrats but was seen to identify increasingly with them. In the face of a democratic revolution, the king showed his true aristocratic colors. The result was a victory for the unicameral legislature and for a mild suspensive veto. "To explain why Sieyès prevailed in every case is to explain a good deal of the Revolution."[31]

The French Revolution in its early phases may have been a

30. See Palmer, *1*, 489 ff.
31. Ibid., p. 491.

battleground for contending conceptions of government, but from the outside it came to be associated with one dominant set of ideas, essentially those of the Abbé Sieyès. This association is due in good part to Edmund Burke. Burke's characterization of France was really more applicable to the Jacobins of 1793 than to the moderate revolutionaries of 1790, but from his English aristocratic vantage point, the Revolution was a single entity. It was Edmund Burke who sanctified the English constitutional system in the face of what he saw as the French conception of liberty "in all the nakedness and solitude of metaphysical abstraction." Against the destructive work of 1789, he threw up the example of the English Revolution of 1688, "made to preserve our *ancient* constitution of government which is our only security for law and liberty." In France he saw, like Tocqueville after him, the "old fanatics of single arbitrary [monarchical] power" reborn as "our new fanatics of popular arbitrary power." [32]

Palmer maintains that Burke's philosophy did not emerge primarily as a critique of the French Revolution or even as a reaction against the rationalism of the Enlightenment. Rather it was forged in the political battles of the 1780s in England to preserve parliament against monarchical and popular reformers. It was then that Burke made famous the doctrine of "prescription"— rights derived from long-accustomed practice—as the basis for the constitution. It was then that he opposed electoral reform put forward as the "supposed rights of man." [33] Yet it was the French Revolution, epitomizing all those tendencies he deplored in England, that crystallized his ideas and gave them wide currency. Burke defended English liberties in strongly aristocratic and even feudal terms as "an *entailed inheritance* derived to us from our forefathers . . . locked fast as in a sort of family settlement; grasped in a kind of mortmain forever." [34] Thus the established order in England (or elsewhere) could be defended in the name of ancient customs or historic liberties against democratic leveling, regicide, and an abstract conception of liberty. Burke inspired the

---

32. Burke, *Reflections on the Revolution in France* (London, Dent, 1910), p. 24.
33. See Palmer, *1*, 66, 286, 308–14.
34. Burke, p. 31.

conservatives, those who rejected the changes brought by the French Revolution, but he also introduced continental liberals to the spirit of English liberalism, as we will see with Benjamin Constant.

For comparative purposes a word should be added about North America, though it will be treated in more detail in Chapter 6. Palmer notes that the Abbé Sieyès was expressing the same democratic idea of the "people as a constituent power" that had been formulated in the American Revolution. And yet Sieyès was untouched by the American experience. The American Revolution had a great impact in France, but perhaps Sieyès represents one way in which it was not relevant to the French reformers.

The rights of man in America did not have to be instituted as in France by first tearing down the regime of aristocratic, clerical, and corporate privilege. A Sieyès, who had to establish in reality the idea that the third estate was the nation, could draw few analogies from America, where there had always been but one estate. Sieyès probably shared Turgot's earlier disappointment that the American constitutions established, in the English manner, too many different bodies, "instead of bringing all the authorities into one, that of the nation." In France, as Turgot recognized, a dispersal of power meant in social terms the continued entrenchment of aristocratic privileges as obstacles to change. In America historic liberties and a separation of powers could be championed as a rational formula—the natural or universal rights of man. Nature and History were not in conflict in America, as they necessarily had to be in France. Ruggiero's two liberalisms, the French and the English, could be joined harmoniously in the new society of North America.[35]

The next chapter is concerned with Mexican constitutional liberalism of the 1820s, especially as expressed by José María Luis Mora. No one figure was of greater significance in that movement than Benjamin Constant, the leader of the French school of doctrinaire or constitutional liberals from 1810 to 1830. To establish Constant's importance for Mexico we must do more than identify the traces of his influence, quotations from his works, and refer-

35. See Palmer, *1*, 181, 234–35, 268.

ences to him; these are all available in abundance. We must ask
why he was so relevant to Mora and to his fellow constitutionalists
of the 1820s. Let us consider, with an eye to comparison, the historical context in which Constant wrote.

Benjamin Constant is best known for his psychological and
romantic novel *Adolphe*. He had a turbulent personal life, notorious particularly for his decade of intimacy with Mme. de Staël. His
political life was equally turbulent. He was active in widely differing regimes, yet his political ideas were remarkably consistent.[36]
Constant presented the classic modern defense of individual liberty against the invasions of arbitrary power. He reasserted, in
postrevolutionary terms, the basic liberal themes of Montesquieu,
and he was important in Mexico for the same reason as was his
predecessor. Constant was searching for ways to guarantee civil
liberty in a country where secondary or intermediate institutions
were weak.

Constant's ideas were formulated in reaction to the French
Revolution and Napoleon. Still, he remained a liberal, in the
sense that he accepted the changes of the revolutionary era and did
not want to return to 1789. He shared Tocqueville's later dictum
that "in the French Revolution there were two impulses in opposite directions, which must never be confounded; the one was
favorable to liberty, the other to despotism." [37] Unlike the English or unlike Tocqueville's Americans, Constant saw that the
French had to *become* a free people, "like slaves that broke their
chains." The problem now was to consolidate the liberty that had
been gained, a problem made more acute "when twenty-five years
of storm have destroyed the ancient institutions of a people." Far
from an absence of government, he saw in the Revolution the
"continuous and universal presence of an atrocious government,"

36. Constant himself made a point of this fact in "Principes de politique ap-
plicables a tous les gouvernements représentatifs et particulièrement a la constitution actuelle de la France" (1815), *Cours de politique constitutionnelle ou collection des ouvrages publiés sur le gouvernement représentatif,* ed. E. Laboulaye (2d
ed. Paris, 1872), *1,* iv. As the title indicates, the *Cours* is a collection of pamphlets
and tracts, each of which was first published separately.

37. Tocqueville, *Democracy in America* (New York, Knopf, 1954), *1,* 100. On the
definition of "liberal," as used in France, see Stanley Mellon, *The Political Uses of
History; a Study of Historians in the French Restoration* (Stanford, Stanford University Press, 1958).

not anarchy but a new concentration of central power.[38] This ambivalence toward the Revolution is the key to Constant's constitutional liberalism.

Constant did not deny popular sovereignty, the principal political doctrine of the Revolution. He could not have remained a liberal in France and have done so. Yet his "Principes de politique" opened with a critique of popular sovereignty. The "body of citizens as a whole (*universalité des citoyens*) is the sovereign," but it does not follow that "they can dispose absolutely (*souvereinement*) of the existence of individuals. There is a part of individual existence that necessasily remains individual and independent."[39] Constant distinguished between the legitimate general will and illegitimate force. First of all, popular sovereignty must be defined precisely and its limits established. According to Constant, this is what Rousseau failed to do, with the result that his *Social Contract*, "so often invoked in favor of liberty," became "the most awful auxiliary of all types of despotism."

The critique of Rousseau was a persistent theme in Constant's writings. Constant, like Rousseau, maintained an admiration for the republics of Antiquity, but Constant always distinguished between antique and modern liberty. He recognized that the citizens of Greece and Rome were a small oligarchy, but, more important, that antique liberty was seen entirely as "active participation of the collective power." Civil liberty was unknown. It was this antique emphasis upon collective participation, as opposed to individual security, that was revived in Rousseau and that became an instrument of tyranny under revolutionary governments.[40]

38. See Constant, "De l'Esprit de conquête et de l'usurpation, dans leurs rapports avec la civilisation européene," *Cours*, *2*, 239; "Observations sur le discours pronouncé par S. E. le ministre de l'intérieur en faveur du projet de loi sur la liberté de la presse," *Cours*, *1*, 504; also "Principes de politique," *Cours*, *1*, 75.

39. Constant, "Principes de politique," *Cours*, *1*, 9. Isaiah Berlin's conclusion in *Two Concepts of Liberty* (pp. 48 ff.) is clearly inspired by Constant's philosophy of "negative liberty."

40. See Constant, "De l'Esprit de conquête," *Cours*, *2*, 205–06, 225. Ruggiero discusses the distinction between civil and political liberty, pp. 51–52. Constant wrote a later treatise entitled *De la Liberté des anciens comparée a celle des modernes* (1819). I use the adjective "antique" as opposed to "ancient," which during this period referred usually to the Middle Ages and not to Antiquity; for example, in Mme. de Staël's famous "In France liberty is ancient; despotism is modern."

Constant did his most significant political writing between 1814 and 1820 as a partisan of constitutional monarchy. Born in Lausanne in 1767, he did not come to France permanently until Robespierre's fall in 1794, when he joined the moderate republican circle of Mme. de Stäel. He was eliminated from his post in the Tribunate by Napoleon in 1802, and he remained a bitter opponent of the emperor until 1814. The following year Constant was persuaded by his new-found love, Mme. Récamier, to accept a position in the Council of State during the Hundred Days. He wrote his "Principes de politique" during this period. Thus the form of government per se was never his concern, for he believed that his basic liberal and constitutional principles could be applied universally. Nevertheless, monarchy was the context in which Constant was most at home, and following in the spirit of Montesquieu, England was his model. "The continent [under Napoleon]," he wrote in December 1813, "was nothing but a vast dungeon, deprived of all communication with that noble England, generous asylum of thought, illustrious refuge of the dignity of the human race." [41] It was the continuity of English institutions, the preserving of liberty over such a long period, that particularly drew Constant to that country's experience.

All the French constitutions have proclaimed liberty, he said, and yet it has been constantly violated. "We must have positive safeguards," not mere pronouncements. With England in mind, he kept returning to the need for "intermediate bodies," which would stand between the individual and the state. There was much in Constant that was faintly aristocratic, as there was with all nineteenth-century liberals of his persuasion; and yet he repudiated the French nobility as it was in 1789. In arguing for a hereditary assembly on the model of England, he objected to comparison with the French old regime. The French nobility had no function, he said. "It was in no way an intermediary body that kept the people in order and that watched over liberty. It was a corporation without a base and without a fixed place in the social body." [42] Thus he distinguished between privileged corporations

41. Constant, preface to the first edition of "De l'Esprit de conquête," in *Cours*, 2, 130.

42. Constant, "Principes de politique," *Cours*, 1, 36.

and intermediate bodies, which, as we will see, could only be done by rooting the latter in the one privilege not destroyed by the Revolution—individual property.

Constant's system of liberty was founded first of all upon "the existence of a numerous and independent representation," the parliamentary heritage from the early years of the Revolution. Beyond that, the inviolability and neutrality of royal power, combined with the responsibility of ministers and of lower officials, was a point of particular importance. The hostility to ministers, as potential agents of tyranny, went back at least to Richelieu. In Constant's view, they could only be controlled by allowing deputies the right of accusation and by setting up as in England the upper chamber as judge in cases of ministerial encroachment upon individual rights.

At the same time, the judicial power must be secured and judges must be made irremovable. During the whole Revolution, Constant asserted, "neither tribunals, judges, nor trials were free." Constitutional liberals from Montesquieu to Tocqueville and Laboulaye always saw in strengthened judicial institutions a counterweight to administration.[43] Constant was an advocate of the jury system, "that much slandered institution." A jury made up of citizens and proprietors has a stake in preventing attacks on individual security. This has been proved in England. Moreover, the jury system would help guarantee the vital liberty of press and opinion. Freedom of the press is what ties the "great bodies of the state" to the people as a whole, provided it is controlled as liberty, not license. Again, citizen juries will have an interest in making this distinction. For instance, the king (or the emperor in 1815) must in his neutral status be above attack, on pain of severe punishment.

Finally, freedom of religion must be guaranteed. Constant shared with the romantic movement of his day a sympathy for the "religious sentiment," however unorthodox.[44] This sentiment, he

43. See ibid., pp. 154–55; Tocqueville, *Old Regime and the French Revolution* (Garden City, Doubleday, 1955), p. 175; Laboulaye, introd. to the first edition (1861) of Constant, *Cours, 1,* xliv.

44. See, for example, in Constant, "Principes de politiques," *Cours, 1,* 133. Constant later wrote a five-volume work entitled *De la Religion considerée dans sa source, ses formes et ses développments* (Paris, 1824–31).

said, can only develop with freedom of worship. As under Louis
XIV, suppression can only lead to skepticism. But the effort of the
revolutionaries to enforce irreligion was just as odious to him as
enforced orthodoxy. Open anticlericalism was not a part of Constant's scheme of liberty, though he stoutly maintained a separation of religious and civil authority.

One chapter of Constant's "Principes de politique" was entitled
"On Municipal Power, Local Authorities, and a New Type of
Federalism." Constant was oppressed by *uniformity,* "the great
word today"; and in the name of liberty he sought a remedy. The
Revolution had destroyed the municipalities in favor of "equality" and more efficient administration. The vitality of local authority must be restored. He wanted local checks on central
authority, not a loose association of governments or powers.[45]
Constant in the French tradition assumed the strength (and even
the necessity) of central power. The problem was to find limits to
it. Like Tocqueville later, he developed a nostalgia for communal
traditions, true local patriotism, and even for rural values.

> The magistrates of the smallest communes delight in beauti-
> fying them, and they maintain ancient monuments with care.
> There is in almost every village a learned man who loves to
> relate its rural annals, which are listened to with respect.
> . . . The attachment to local customs is tied to all the sen-
> timents that are disinterested, noble, and pious. . . . Variety
> is life; uniformity is death.[46]

Free municipalities, independent of the executive power, were for
Constant a bulwark of individual liberty.

The anchor of Constant's entire system was the institution of
property. The experience of the Revolution confirmed its importance. Without property as a balance, men of all professions took
up "chimerical theories" and "inapplicable exaggerations." Property must be an essential condition for those exercising rights as
candidates and as electors. Indigence condemns men to the posi-

---

45. "We must introduce into our administration much federalism, but a federalism different from that which has been known until now" ("Principes de politique,"
Cours, 1, 101).

46. Constant, "De l'Esprit de conquête," *Cours, 2,* 173–74.

tion of children in public affairs. Constant claimed sympathy for the "laboring class"; they have shown courage and patriotism, he said. Yet they are not able to know their country's interests. This knowledge can only be acquired by leisure "which is indispensable for acquiring knowledge and rectitude of judgment. Only property assures this leisure; only property makes men capable of exercising political rights." [47] Moreover, landed property is preferable to industrial property. Constant never maintained that industrial capitalists should be excluded from exercising political rights, but he did hold them in suspicion. He spoke of the "moral preeminence" of landed property, the tie to family tradition, to memory. Constant was looking for liberty but also for a bulwark against the awesome changes of the revolutionary era. "I confess that I have much reverence for the past, and each day . . . that reverence increases." The aristocratic roots of constitutional liberalism were always apparent in Constant, as was nostalgia for the local and the rural in the face of modernization.

Any attempt to uncover the structure of political liberalism in the Atlantic world must center on France. Obviously, John Locke, Edmund Burke, and Jeremy Bentham were not Frenchmen. English thought and English institutions were crucial to liberals everywhere. Yet France provided the classic situation in which liberalism as a body of theory was directed toward political and ultimately social change. By definition, liberal theory was elaborated with reference to an ancien régime; the model was France. In identifying Mexican liberalism we begin with France. Nevertheless, it is Spain that provides the historical context of most immediate relevance to Mexico.

We have seen some of the points of institutional affinity between France and Spain. Similarly, liberalism in Spain can be termed a variant of the French pattern, with certain distinct differences. Immediately apparent in eighteenth-century Spain, by comparison with France before 1789, is the absence of political conflict. This can be explained partly by the weakness of a Spanish commercial and professional middle class which in France came to pose a challenge to aristocratic pretentions in politics. More significant for our purposes, however, was the strength of attachment

47. Constant, "Principes de politique," *Cours, 1,* 54.

to the monarchy. Spain was a "true" enlightened despotism under Charles III, without political challenge from "constituted bodies." The cortes was dormant and the audiencias were adjuncts of the Crown, not defenders of an ancient constitution as were the parlements in France.

Recent students of eighteenth-century Spain emphasize the strength of regalism. Jean Sarrailh particularly notes the depth of patriotism that permeated the small enlightened elite in their search for reform. Influences from France were naturally strong, but even the leaders of enlightenment were sharply critical of the tendency to imitate things French. Economic reform was predicated on knowing the resources of the country, its mines, industries, and agricultural resources. The only real threat to royal power was the church; but under Charles III, the Crown prevailed in curtailing the Inquisition, in directing university reform, and in expelling the Jesuits. The attachment to Crown and to country was complemented by a strong religious orthodoxy which, unlike France, remained generally unquestioned among enlightened Spaniards. In fact "devotion to the Catholic religion . . . was probably the strongest force in Spanish society at the end of the eighteenth century." [48]

The corollary to this attachment to king, country, and religion was the dearth of constitutionalist political thought amid the outpouring of economic and social literature in late eighteenth-century Spain.[49] Gaspar Melchor de Jovellanos provided the exception, but even his concern for studying the Spanish constitution awakened little response before 1789. Two traditional prerogatives of the cortes, the right of consent to new taxes and the right of consultation in grave circumstances, were dropped by Charles IV in the 1805 codification of the laws, without noticeable protest.[50] The American Revolution, which caused so much stir in France, went virtually unnoticed in Spain. This remarkable

48. Richard Herr, *The Eighteenth-Century Revolution in Spain* (Princeton, Princeton University Press, 1958), p. 33; also p. 85.

49. Pedro Rodríguez de Campomanes, for example, never questioned traditional absolutist assumptions. See Ricardo Krebs Wilckens, *El Pensamiento histórico, político y económico del conde de Campomanes* (Santiago de Chile, Editorial Universitaria, 1960), pp. 67 ff.

50. Jean Sarrailh, *L'Espagne éclairée de la seconde moitié du xviiie siècle* (Paris, Impr. Nationale, 1954), p. 579.

unity under Charles III was expressed well by Jovellanos himself in his eulogy on the monarch upon his death in 1788. The discourse was a virtual catalogue of concerns of the leaders of enlightenment, specific programs achieved or at least initiated by the Crown. Charles III, said Jovellanos, tried to make of his reign a true period of "regeneration." [51]

It was the French Revolution which drove a wedge into this apparent Spanish unity and which initiated the "two Spains" of more recent times. The French Revolution raised the fear that the now vibrant spirit of inquiry would extend to the sacrosanct realms of politics and religion. The result was a wholesale reaction by Floridablanca, chief royal minister, against all reformist thought that was judged to be "French." This reaction against "modern ideas," after such a concerted royal effort to foster reform, caused division, particularly considering the weakness of the new monarch, Charles IV. In England, patriotic response to the French Revolution could center in a defense of historic English institutions and liberties, as expressed by Edmund Burke. In Spain, where historic liberties were dormant, patriotism had to turn on increased absolutism in church and state, to the dissatisfaction of "enlightened" Spaniards.

Because of the extremes of the French Revolution, any program of reform, even along the lines of enlightened despotism, became easily suspect. Anticlericalism, abetted by the royal need to disentail church property to meet the expenses of war, was discredited because of its association with the extremist Civil Constitution of the Clergy. In 1798 Jovellanos was eliminated as minister of grace and justice amid a general reaction within the church against any kind of reform.[52] These divisive forces could be controlled only by the loyalty that the monarch as a symbol of unity commanded. Thus in 1808, when Napoleon persuaded both Charles IV and Ferdinand VII to abdicate, Spain was plunged into an extreme constitutional crisis.

The crisis can best be examined through the thought of Gaspar

---

51. Jovellanos, "Elogio de Carlos III, leído en la real sociedad económica de Madrid el día 8 de noviembre de 1788," in *Biblioteca de autores españoles* [hereafter *BAE*], *46* (Madrid, Atlas, 1951), 314b. On Jovellanos see also Luis Sánchez Agesta, *El Pensamiento político del despotismo ilustrado* (Madrid, Inst. de Estudios Políticos, 1953).

52. See Herr, pp. 414–21.

Melchor de Jovellanos, the major Spanish intellectual figure from
1780 to 1810. Not only was he important in his own right, but his
ideas generally were a major influence in Mexican liberalism.
Moreover, his political thought demonstrates the problem of constitutional liberalism in Hispanic nations. We have seen Jovellanos already as the apologist for enlightened despotism in 1788.
Born into a family of the lesser nobility in the Asturias, Jovellanos
was educated in theology and later in law. He obtained a royal
appointment as magistrate in the criminal court of Seville and
later in Madrid in 1778. He always remained close to the Crown
until he was caught up in the conflicting crosscurrents of clericalism and anticlericalism under Charles IV. After his banishment in
1798, Jovellanos remained out of public life until the crisis of
1808, when he became the leading figure in the Junta Central of
Seville.

In 1780, on being elected to the Royal Academy of History,
Jovellanos made an appeal for "the necessity of bringing together
the study of legislation with that of our history and antiquities."
This famous discourse initiated an interest in Spanish constitutional history, which remained, however, a distinct undercurrent
until 1808. There was always a lingering conflict between Jovellanos' enthusiastic regalism and his concern for the "ancient Spanish constitution." From both points of view, the high point of
Spanish history was the reign of Ferdinand and Isabella, which was
followed by a period of political absolutism and economic decline
under what he termed the "Austrian" Hapsburgs. Yet in 1788,
when he was surveying the advance of enlightenment and economic progress, Jovellanos depreciated the Middle Ages, the great
period of constitutional development.[53]

Jovellanos' constitutionalism remained academic and speculative until 1808; only thus could he have continued an unquestioned supporter of Bourbon enlightened despotism. With the
Napoleonic invasion, however, the constitutional issue took on an
immediate practical importance. When the two monarchs abdi-
cated their respective claims to the throne on May 3, 1808, in

53. See "Elogio," *BAE, 46,* 312–13. Jovellanos' "Discurso . . . sobre la necesidad
de unir al estudio de la legislación él de la historia y antigüedades" was later
reprinted by Mora. See below, p. 122.

Bayonne, they were defying a basic law of the kingdom, the inalienability of the Crown. The monarchy was not a private possession but rather belonged "to the entire lineage, failing that, to the people." [54] The assumption of power by a series of regional juntas during the summer of 1808 could be justified by Spanish law. The major opposition to these juntas came from the Council of Castile which claimed authority in the crisis. No province, it said, can "judge this Supreme Tribunal except the monarch or the entire nation united in the cortes which represents it."

Out of the regional juntas came the Junta Central, created at Aranjuez on September 25, 1808, and then forced to flee to Seville in November before Napoleon's advancing armies. It claimed supremacy in the name of the Spanish people and denied any adherence to "the old authorities" (especially the Council of Castile). In the unwieldy thirty-five-man junta, Jovellanos was clearly the leader. He headed the committee on calling a cortes, and was the prime mover on the committees of finance, legislation, and education. His writings pertaining to these areas constitute "the testament of the Enlightenment," and they "project before the eyes of their readers the task of organizing a new Spain." [55]

Jovellanos' major political tract was an impassioned defense of the Junta Central, written in 1810 in the heat of dramatic events. He upheld the work of the centralized junta and its claim to authority, refuting regional critics and more particularly the strictures of the Council of Castile. He also enunciated a program of constitutional liberalism. Like Benjamin Constant, Jovellanos rejected Rousseau's popular sovereignty. Both men looked to the example of England and sought in intermediate institutions the bulwark of liberty against excessive authority. Jovellanos was the more conservative, partly because of his aristocratic origins but also because the popular revolutionary process in Spain was less radical than in France. Both men were partisans of monarchy; but as a postrevolutionary French liberal, monarchy was no longer an article of faith for Constant, as it very much was for Jovellanos. It is significant that a republic was never declared in Spain.

54. See Miguel Artola, *Los Orígenes de la España contemporanea* (Madrid, Inst. de Estudios Políticos, 1959), *1*, 104 ff.

55. Ibid., p. 266.

"According to Spanish public law, the fullness of sovereignty resides in the monarch"; thus it would be heresy to assert that "a nation whose constitution is completely monarchical is sovereign." [56] This was a basic assumption of Jovellanos. And yet he was speaking as a member of a revolutionary junta which claimed the right, derived from the people, to create a government. The Junta Central is a legitimate organ in harmony with the constitution. When any people is attacked from outside, deprived of the "king which it adored" and enslaved by false authorities, "it naturally enters into the necessity of defending itself, and consequently acquires an extraordinary and legitimate right of insurrection." This is very different, he maintained, from the "ordinary right of insurrection," which the "French, in the frenzy of their political principles, gave to the people in a constitution that was put together in a few days." [57]

Jovellanos' attitude toward unified sovereignty was necessarily ambivalent, an ambivalence he shared with political liberals in other Hispanic nations. The monarch was sovereign; his authority was sanctioned by the historic constitution, as well as by the practice of the Bourbons. Now, a form of de facto popular sovereignty had emerged with the removal of the king and the subsequent popular insurrection. The problem was that sovereignty, whether lodged in king or people, conflicted with the concept of a historic constitution.

Jovellanos rejected the idea that the constitution was defunct and that the "people as a constituent power" must create a new one. Reasserting his earlier views of 1780, Jovellanos maintained that the custom of calling a cortes "is the true source of the Spanish constitution," a practice that in effect limited the monarch in favor of the rights of the nation.[58] He believed that the main purpose of the Junta Central was to prepare for a cortes, to which end he devoted much of the "Memoria." In this effort to seek out the

56. Jovellanos, "Memoria en que se rebaten las calumnias divulgadas contra los indivíduos de la junta central del reino," *BAE, 46,* 597b. The "Memoria" proper is followed by lengthy notes and a series of appendixes which include committee reports and other documents. Many of Jovellanos' most significant ideas are found in the notes and appendixes.

57. Ibid., p. 584b.

58. Ibid., p. 598b.

basis of a historic constitution, it was once again England that provided the model. Jovellanos sensed the historic and circumstantial pressures for arbitrary authority and advocated a balance of powers. He disregarded those who accused him of wanting to "make us Englishmen," by emphasizing "the great analogies that exist between [the English constitution] and the ancient Spanish constitution." [59] He was referring particularly to the historic similarity between cortes and parliament.

The basic problem in calling a cortes was the French problem of 1789: Should it meet by estates or as one body? Jovellanos held out for two chambers, one of privileged orders and one representing the towns. Two chambers were essential to a monarchy

> because no [monarchy] can be sustained without an intermediate hierarchical body, which, on the one hand will contain the irruptions of supreme power against the liberty of the people, and, on the other, those of popular license against the legitimate rights of the Sovereign.[60]

The concept of nobility had not been destroyed in Spain as in France, and Jovellanos clung to the idea that the privileged order could play an important constitutional role. He dismissed the concern of those who said that nobles in a cortes would be creatures of the Crown. "Deprived of their ancient representation, it was very natural for them to draw near to the Crown, the only source of honors and privileges." If the cortes were closed to nobles employed at court, and if the constitutional functions of the nobility were restored, this group would no longer be oppressive to the people.

Unfortunately, the concept of a vigorous nobility was a contradiction in terms in the Spain of 1809, just as it was in the France of 1789. Jovellanos, though, was no conservative upholder of a privi-

---

59. Ibid., p. 573b. John H. R. Polt demonstrates the critical influence of English thought on Jovellanos in *Jovellanos and His English Sources*, Transactions of the American Philosophical Society, new ser., 54, pt. 7 (Philadelphia, 1964).

60. Quotation from the majority (3-2) decision of the cortes committee of the Junta Central, of which Jovellanos was the chairman, dated June 22, 1809 ("Memoria," *BAE*, 46, 596b). Jovellanos elsewhere defined "popular license" as "the excessive pretentions of the democratic spirit" (p. 602b) and "the democratic fury" (p. 550a).

leged corporate society. His "Informe de ley agraria" of 1795 was a forthright attack on entailed property and upon the privileges of a degenerate aristocracy and church establishment. He maintained that the virtue he believed to be characteristic of nobility had turned into mere inherited privilege, and he sought vainly for a rebirth of the glorious medieval traditions of noble leadership through a representative cortes.[61]

The struggle for constitutional liberalism in Spain was more difficult than it was in France, both because the traditional institutional checks on monarchical authority were weaker, and because the regime of corporate privilege was still intact. Benjamin Constant had firmer ground on which to build. Jovellanos' tenuous bicameral position was soon overwhelmed by the dissenting opinion of 1809, as expressed by Rodrigo Riquelme:

> in order that the sacred and imprescriptible rights of the Spanish people be shielded in the future from all usurpation and violence, I believe that said cortes should constitute a true national representation.[62]

Historical constitutionalism lost out to the Cortes of Cádiz, a unicameral assembly on the French pattern, which declared in the Constitution of 1812 that "sovereignty resides essentially in the nation." Jovellanos died in 1811, politically isolated. He had tried, he said, to find a middle way between destroying everything and starting afresh, and slavishly keeping old forms. He was left between the Cortes of Cádiz and the old regime in a dilemma that had unique Hispanic features. An aristocrat who supported enlightened despotism, Jovellanos became a de facto advocate of revolutionary popular sovereignty while trying to cling to its antithesis, the ancient constitution of the Spanish kingdom.

There were, as in France, strong points of continuity between the Bourbons and the revolutionary assembly. An intense national consciousness was present in the revolution of 1808–12, the heri-

61. For Jovellanos' views on the nobility see Polt, pp. 57–59, and Sarrailh, pp. 518–24.

62. Minority opinion in report of the cortes committee (Jovellanos, "Memoria," *BAE, 46,* 596b) .

tage of Bourbon enlightenment and political unification.[63] The Cádiz regime, short as it was, continued the Bourbon efforts to bring legal and administrative unity to the country. It attacked seigneurial privileges, the guilds, and local and special jurisdictions. The new goal, one only dimly perceived by the Bourbons, was a nation based on legal equality and proportional taxation. Legal codification was proposed, a measure supported by Jovellanos in 1809. Most dramatic was the anticlerical program which included disentailment of church property to meet the growing financial crisis. We will examine these reformist efforts by the Cortes of Cádiz in the coming chapters as they relate specifically to Mexican liberalism. Suffice it to say now that the work was short-lived, brought to an end by the return of Ferdinand VII and his suppression of the constitution in May 1814.

We have seen the parallels between constitutional liberalism in France and in Spain, the points of similarity between Constant and Jovellanos. Constant, however, was a postrevolutionary figure and had to begin by accepting the changes of the revolutionary era; particularly, he had to accept the triumph of popular sovereignty. Though he was clearly nostalgic for the past and though he betrayed aristocratic longings, the idea of securing liberty by a *historic* constitution was no more than a memory. New guarantees must be erected. Similarly, after 1812 in Spain purely historic liberties could hardly provide much inspiration. It was for this reason that in 1820, when the Constitution of 1812 was restored by revolution, Benjamin Constant's works were immediately translated and offered enthusiastically to the Spanish nation. "Since the happy moment that our beloved monarch declared himself constitutional, we have spoken in Spain of nothing but *constitution*." [64]

63. Artola, *1,* 171. Much of Artola's argument is based on an analysis of the responses to the *consulta al país,* a general solicitation of opinion on the state of the country initiated by the Junta Central in 1809. The consulta was similar to the request for *cahiers de doléances* in France in 1789.

64. Constant, *Curso de política constitucional,* trans. and ed. Marcial Antonio López (Madrid, 1820) , *1,* i–ii. This three-volume edition was reprinted in Bordeaux in 1823. López justified his effort partly by the fact that the French editions of Constant were three times as expensive as his, an added factor that may have encouraged Mexicans to read Constant in Spanish. In any case, the López edition was the only one in Spanish available to Mexicans from 1823 to 1825.

And since there was no better place to seek sure definitions of this
term than in Constant, presenting his ideas in Spanish seemed a
particularly worthy project to Marcial Antonio López, his translator.

The edition was a free selection and arrangement of chapters
from Constant's works, abridged for particular relevance to Spain.
Of special interest to us are the "observations" by translator López
at the end of each chapter. He presented Constant's ideas to a
hopefully liberal Spain in fervent tones. In discussing "extraordinary tribunals, and the suspension and abbreviation of formulas
of justice," López spoke of the "terrible events occurring in a
space of six years," of "martyrs of liberty," and of actions of unjust
and tyrannical ministers.[65] Constant had appeal in Spain (and in
Mexico) mainly because a López (or a Mora) could identify with
the context and the spirit in which Constant wrote. They faced
revolutionary upheaval and arbitrary authority just as Constant
had in 1815. Therefore, they shared Constant's sense of urgency in
establishing safeguards for individual freedom, an urgency that
was not felt in the Anglo-Saxon environment.

Within the broader framework of political ideas and institutions of the Atlantic world, we can identify the structural elements
of Mexican political liberalism. In part, the tension within the
Mexican liberal program alluded to at the beginning of this
chapter was a variation of the contending positions of "English"
and "French" liberalism. Inner conflict between the elements of
these two ideal types can be discerned in all Western nations. Yet
in Mexico, as in Spain, there were institutional and cultural peculiarities that gave liberalism a special orientation. The institutions
upon which English liberalism was built were weaker in Spain
than in France; in Mexico these institutions were almost nonexistent. On the other hand, the regime of corporate (particularly
clerical) privilege, which was destroyed in France with the Revolution, was largely intact in Mexico, as it was in Spain. This fact,
added to the historic supremacy of the central power in Hispanic
countries, made the establishment of a constitutional regime particularly difficult.

These special institutional configurations help explain the in-

65. López, "Observaciones," in Constant, Curso, 1, 258–59.

fluence, or the relevance to the Mexicans, of the ideas of certain political thinkers, for example Benjamin Constant and Gaspar Melchor de Jovellanos, from among the general reservoir of European political thought. They were facing similar problems. On the basis of these assumptions, let us examine Mexican political liberalism of the 1820s and 1830s, principally through the ideas of José María Luis Mora, the most significant liberal spokesman of his generation.

3

Mora and Mexican Constitutionalism

In 1821, D. Joseph María Servin de la Mora Díaz Madrid began his career as a liberal political journalist.[1] Three years later at the age of thirty he became the leader of a small group of delegates which drew up the first constitution for Mexico's most populous and important state. By 1832, he was the acknowledged theorist of the national reform party, a champion of anticlericalism and of a utilitarian vision of social progress.

Mora's early life gave little indication of his future liberalism. His parents were prosperous Creoles, proud to be "Old Christians . . . with no mixture of mulattos or other bad ancestry which might stain or in any way obscure our refined lineage."[2] The loss of the family fortune to Hidalgo's men did not interfere with Mora's education. At the age of twelve he had been brought to the capital to begin his studies in the Colegio de San Ildefonso, the most prominent of the old Jesuit schools. Mora was a brilliant student, and after the traditional public disputations, he received a licentiate in sacred theology in 1819. Soon thereafter he began to teach at San Ildefonso. Concurrently, he took Holy Orders and held the position of deacon in the Archbishopric of Mexico. Mora showed prowess as a preacher and on Ascension Day, 1820, proclaimed in the Cathedral of Mexico that the truth of Jesus Christ would triumph "over the tyranny of the Caesars and over philosophical pride."[3] As of 1820 it appeared that Mora had settled

1. Mora's complete name appeared on his Bachelor's diploma of 1812 (Mora Documents, 1806–38, University of Texas). The "Luis" began to appear in his name, inexplicably, in 1827.

2. Quoted by Robert F. Florstedt in "The Liberal Role of José María Luis Mora in the Early History of Independent Mexico" (Ph.D. dissertation, University of Texas, 1950), p. 3. On Mora see also Arturo Arnáiz y Freg, "Prologo," *José María Luis Mora, ensayos, ideas y retratos* (Mexico, UNAM, 1941).

3. Sermon, Mora Documents, 1806–38.

into the traditional religious and academic life of the colonial capital.

The origins of Mora's liberalism are obscure, and one can only hazard explanations from scraps of evidence. Like many Creole liberals of his generation, he emerged from a priestly education. Clearly, there was an infusion of rationalist philosophy into the traditional scholastic curriculum of San Ildefonso. Mora had a peculiarly inquiring mind. By 1817 he was already an avid book collector, and he held the post of librarian at his school. A few years later an English traveler remarked that Mora had the best library in Mexico. His early career, however, was not all success. His academic appointment at San Ildefonso came only after he had failed in two previous attempts to secure a *catedra* at the Royal and Pontifical University. He also failed to receive a canonship at the Cathedral, for which he aspired in late 1820. His political opponents later claimed that his anticlericalism stemmed from these personal experiences, an allegation he vigorously denied.[4] Though he was insulated from the turmoil of the revolutionary years, Mora was caught up in the "constitutional euphoria" of 1820, which must have struck him personally at a critical time. In any event, with the restoration of the Spanish Constitution of 1812, Mora entered politics on December 3, 1820, as an intermediate elector (*compromisario*) from the parish of El Sagrario in Mexico City. By the following November a liberal Mora was extolling the glories of independence as editor of the *Semanario político y literario*.

Despite his priestly and conservative background, it is apparent that Mora was intellectually prepared to embrace the cause of constitutionalism in 1821. Mora's first articles contained a secular and liberal theory of politics which in two principal characteristics remained unchanged for a decade. The first of these characteristics was an admiration for the Spanish Constitution of 1812. The other was an identification with French constitutional liberalism, particularly the thought of Benjamin Constant.

It is significant that Mora in 1821 showed high regard for the Constitution of 1812. Mexican independence, he believed, was justified because the Spanish cortes did not treat Mexico in accor-

4. Florstedt, "Liberal Role," p. 39.

dance with the liberal provisions of the constitution. The problem lay in "the insistence of its authors to diminish American representation and to block the influence which the natives of these countries could and must have in the government of the peninsula." There was nothing in the constitution itself, however, "contrary to the interests of America." Mexico was deceived by the mother country and thus "the social compact was dissolved." [5]

The break with Spain took place amid the constitutional optimism that swept Mexico with the reenactment of the 1812 document. We have seen this excitement already in the Spain of 1820. In Mexico, under the aegis of a free press, scores of pamphlets appeared expressing a "constitutional determinism," the theme of which was that under a benign constitution Mexico's problems would disappear.[6] Iturbide's swift and bloodless coup in 1821 intensified this atmosphere of political optimism. It was the heyday of the Western Hemisphere idea, the notion that the newly freed nations of America shared a unique destiny apart from the Old World. Yet despite the natural antipeninsular overtones of the break with Spain, the Mexican liberals had little quarrel with the principles of the Spanish constitution, no more than they had had in 1812.

An unusual and exasperating product of these halcyon years was the writing of Francisco Severo Maldonado. This priest and scholar from Guadalajara had embraced Hidalgo's cause in 1810 and had published the first revolutionary journal, *El Despertador americano*. The following year, however, he abandoned the revolution and began to write for the royalists. In 1820 we find him an enthusiastic supporter of the Constitution of 1812, and in 1821 a partisan of Iturbide. During the next two years he published three editions of a work he called variously *Nuevo Pacto social* and *Contrato de asociación*, in effect proposals for an ideal constitution of political and social organization. Elected as a delegate to the Spanish cortes, Maldonado asserted in 1821 that

the code is applicable to a certain extent to all nations, and capable likewise of giving the Spanish Revolution the charac-

5. Mora, *Obras*, pp. 467–68.
6. See Reyes Heroles, *Liberalismo, 1,* 37–118.

ter of grandeur and importance that it merits, making it the first step toward the reduction of the whole human race into one large family of brothers.[7]

His schemes revealed strong traces of Jean Jacques Rousseau, but on the whole they remained an odd blend of liberal individualism, utopian socialism, and traditional corporate theory. He spoke constantly of equalizing classes, particularly by land reform, and yet he called for politically "active" and "passive" citizens based on property ownership. Property holders were "the real pillars of the association." [8] He envisioned a corporate society in which each functional group was separated from the others by prescribed salary, rank, and dress. Maldonado called for universal free education, and yet he wanted the church to have control over the "moral and spiritual regeneration of the nation." A union of church and state was at the center of his plan.

His views on land reform and his corporatist theories have attracted interest among twentieth-century observers who see them as presaging certain provisions of the Constitution of 1917.[9] He may also have exerted influence on his younger compatriot from Guadalajara, Mariano Otero. A testimonial in the *Águila mexicana* (July 13, 1824) gave evidence that his utopian schemes impressed some people, at least in Guadalajara. In the main, however, Maldonado is a marginal figure in any consideration of nineteenth-century liberalism. His ideas provide an extreme example of the

7. Maldonado, *Nuevo Pacto social propuesto a la nación española, para su discusión en las próximas cortes de 1822 y 1823* (Guadalajara, 1821), also reprinted in *El Fanal del imperio mexicano, 2,* (Mexico, 1822). The quotation is taken from the latter edition, p. 26; *Contrato de asociación para la república de los estados unidos de Anahuac*, 1st ed. in *Fanal, 2;* 2d ed. (Guadalajara, 1823). The *Fanal* was a publication in which Maldonado intended to reprint important works in law and political economy, partly because European books were so expensive. He did reprint from De Pradt, Condado, Volney, and the Mexican Mier in addition to his own works, but the *Fanal* ceased after two volumes.

8. Maldonado, "Nuevo Pacto social," *Fanal, 2,* 216–17.

9. See Paulino Machorro Narváez, *Don Francisco Severo Maldonado* (Mexico, Polis, 1938), p. 99, and Reyes Heroles, *Liberalismo, 3,* 550–53. The best biography of Maldonado (1775–1831) is by Juan B. Iguíniz, in *Disquisiciones bibliográficas* (Mexico, El Colegio de México, 1943). On Rousseau's influence see Jefferson R. Spell, *Rousseau in the Spanish World Before 1833* (Austin, University of Texas Press, 1938), pp. 250–51.

constitutionalist excitement that engulfed Mexico's first independent years.

In identifying the context in which Mexican constitutional liberalism developed, the association with French experience was of equal importance to the Spanish. Mora's second political essay of March 13, 1822, carried the characteristic title "The Supreme Civil Authority Is Not Unlimited." Parts of the essay could well have been written by Benjamin Constant. Mora outlined a contract theory of government based both upon natural rights and upon utilitarian considerations. He then proceeded to describe the unique opportunities for free American nations to constitute themselves following legislative examples from Europe and North America. This was merely introductory, however, to his principal theme, namely "to assign the general limits within which the authority of all government must be contained, without subjecting ourselves blindly to the doctrines of European publicists." The "publicist" he had chiefly in mind was Rousseau, for Mora's essay constituted a critique of popular sovereignty, which was similar to the first chapter of Constant's "Principes de politique." The "authority of society is not absolutely unlimited, as Rousseau judged it to be"; as such it is "essentially and inevitably tyrannical." This has been proved by experience; for

> as the celebrated Constant observes, the horrible outrages against individual liberty and civil rights committed in the French Revolution arose in large part from the vogue of this [Rousseau's] doctrine, which is not only illiberal, but the fundamental principle of despotism.[10]

Mora went on to say, as did Constant, that the form of government was not important. The people could be despotic as in France during the Revolution, while monarchs could be liberal as in England and Spain [!]. "Despotism, then, is nothing else but the absolute and unlimited use of power," and it can come in many forms.

These lines were written following a decade of upheaval which

10. Mora, *Obras*, p. 473. José Miranda refers to Mora as the "Mexican Constant" in his brief essay "El Liberalismo mexicano y el liberalismo europeo," *Historia mexicana, 8* (1959), 518. Constant's impact in Argentina was also great; see Mario C. Belgrano, "Benjamin Constant y el constitucionalismo argentino," *Boletín del instituto de historia argentina "Doctor Emilio Ravignani," 6*, 2d ser. (1961), 1–57.

for Mora was not unlike the recent revolutionary experience of the French and Spanish people. He still regarded Agustín de Iturbide as a constitutional ruler, an assumption that was short-lived. The reality of Iturbide the despot, however, only strength-ened Mora's constitutionalist convictions. Iturbide became for Mora what Napoleon had been for Constant; in fact Mora fre-quently compared the two emperors. Examples from recent French history permeated Mora's political thought of the twenties. Whenever he turned to the question of civil rights, to the problem of maintaining individual liberty against invasions of arbitrary power, to the criticism of exaggerated notions of political equality or of misinterpreted popular sovereignty, he was likely to include a reference to the French Revolution, to the Reign of Terror, or to Napoleon. These discussions were often graced by quotations from Constant, Montesquieu, or from lesser constitutionalists such as Droz or Daunou.[11]

Although Constant was of more immediate significance to Mora, it was Montesquieu whom he quoted more frequently. Mora re-garded Montesquieu as the classic liberal thinker, "the pathfinder for liberal institutions," even though he lived before the era of "political revolutions" and thus could not "know the spirit of contemporary republics or monarchies."[12] Mora's constitutional-ist orientation was shared by Lorenzo de Zavala during the early twenties, despite the fact that they later came to be political oppo-nents in the State of Mexico. Zavala claimed to have translated Daunou's *Essai sur les garanties individuelles* (1818), a popular tract of the constitutional liberal school. Moreover, Zavala sharply criticized Rousseau's *Social Contract,* which he said had been

11. French authors, French history and law, and the French language seem very much to predominate in Mora's library (for example, he apparently read Blackstone in French). The library was sold to the State of Guanajuato after Mora's death and is now housed in the Biblioteca de la Universidad de Guanajuato. Unfortunately, his books are merged with the unclassified general collection and are identifiable only by a French bookseller's penciled notation, *"vendu a M. Mora,"* which appears in some of the volumes. I was unable to find an inventory of the supposedly seven to eleven thousand volumes. I am grateful to Ernesto Scheffler for many courtesies while in Guanajuato. On the sale of Mora's library, see Florstedt, "Liberal Role," pp. 547–48.

12. *Actas del congreso constituyente del estado libre de México* (Mexico and Toluca, 1824–31), *6,* 892 (Feb. 24, 1826).

badly applied in France, leading to Robespierre and the Reign of Terror. Thus French experience best exemplified a favorite maxim of constitutional liberalism, namely that "the first step taken [by public authority] against the security of the individual is the sure precursor of the ruin of nation and government." [13]

As the decade wore on, José María Luis Mora was increasingly plagued by the difficulties of Mexico's transition from colony to independent republic. Benjamin Constant had pondered the problem of preserving the safeguards to individual liberty in the wake of a destructive revolution. Mora viewed Mexico's problem in much the same way. How can a nation "which has adopted the republican system just after emerging from a despotic regime, [a nation] which has conquered its liberty by force of arms," prevent the reign of demagogues? When the old regime has been overthrown, how can a "well-constituted society" be achieved? How, "in a new people that has never known liberty because of its inexperience," can factionalism be avoided and individual security be guaranteed? Like Constant, Mora accepted revolutionary change, though often with reluctance. The problem was to preserve liberty and avoid the extremes of anarchy and despotism. As the case of France demonstrated, a country that has lived under an oppressive regime does not achieve freedom by the mere act of breaking chains. Free political institutions must be created. This was the principal task of Mora and his fellow liberals.[14]

The focus of Mexican political liberalism during the first independent decade was the formation of a constitutional system. The labor of framing a basic legal structure consumed the efforts of the nation's small group of intellectuals and provided a heady atmo-

13. On Daunou see Zavala, *Ensayo, I,* 184. The Mexican edition (1823) of Daunou's *Ensayo sobre las garantías individuales que reclama el estado actual de la sociedad* does not identify the translator. Pierre Claude François Daunou (1761–1840), legist, historian, and statesman, was a Girondist who later prepared the Constitutions of the Years III and VIII. He eventually turned away from Napoleon and became a liberal during the Restoration. On Rousseau see Zavala, *Proyecto de reforma del congreso* (Mexico, 1822), pp. 3–4. The quotation is from Mora, *Obras,* p. 511.

14. The sentiments of this paragraph were best expressed in two of Mora's essays in *El Observador* during 1827: "Discurso sobre los medios de que se vale la ambición para destruir la libertad" and "Discurso sobre la libertad civil del ciudadano," reprinted in *Obras,* pp. 498–512.

sphere of political optimism. Disillusionment set in after 1827, but until then a faith in the magic of constitutions held sway. This optimism was part of a strong tendency on the part of the liberals to identify themselves with the utopian destiny of the United States, where the adoption of a liberal constitution seemed to have assured unlimited progress. In 1824 Mexico took on the federal form of organization, as opposed to the prevailing centralist systems of Spain and France. If Mexican liberalism was cut from the continental pattern, how do we explain federalism, a form that persists to this day? First, let us turn to the institutional side of the question.

Fortunately, the problem of federalist origins has now been thoroughly studied. Nettie Lee Benson has demonstrated that the state governments of the federal system grew naturally out of the institution of the provincial deputation, provided for in the Spanish Constitution of 1812. Miguel Ramos Arizpe, delegate to the cortes from the northern Mexican province of Coahuila, was the prime mover in the creation of the provincial deputation. He later became the leader of the federalist party in the Constituent Congress of 1823–24 and is generally acknowledged to be the "father" of Mexican federalism. In a report to the Spanish cortes in 1811 on the conditions of Mexico's northern provinces, Ramos Arizpe called for an elective "executive council (*junta gubernativa*) or provincial deputation" to be established in each province.[15]

There was a conflict in the cortes between the American and the Spanish delegates over the powers to be granted to provincial institutions. The Spaniards accepted *diputación,* a neutral term, as opposed to *junta,* which, especially in view of recent events in Spain, connoted to them a body with legislative powers. The resulting articles 324 to 337 stated that provincial government would consist of a diputación made up of seven elected members presided over by a *jefe superior,* to be appointed by the king. The deputation also included an intendant, likewise a royal appointee, who was to preside in the absence of the jefe superior (sometimes

15. See Benson, *La Diputación provincial y el federalismo mexicano* (Mexico, El Colegio de México, 1955), p. 21 and passim; also her translation of Ramos Arizpe's 1811 *Report that . . . Presents to the August Congress* (Austin, University of Texas Press, 1950), p. 37.

called *jefe político*) . The American deputies were unsuccessful in their attempt to have the powers of these royal appointees limited.[16] Constitutionally then, the provincial deputation was a locally elected administrative body, decisively controlled by two centrally appointed officials.

What was from the Spanish point of view a centralist form of provincial organization became de facto more decentralized within Mexico. There was no viceroy provided for in the Constitution of 1812. Thus each jefe político was made responsible to king and cortes in Spain, while constitutionally independent of other provinces and of the central government in Mexico City. This was the legal precedent upon which the resurgent regionalism and subsequent federalism of the years 1822 to 1824 could be based. In fact, the deputations were barely organized before Ferdinand VII suppressed the constitution on May 4, 1814, and reinstalled the traditional colonial administration. The deputations were restored along with the constitution in 1820. The number was increased in April 1821, upon urging from American delegates to the cortes, from the original six to a total of fourteen. Each of the former intendancies of the Bourbon system was to have a deputation.[17]

The juridical relation of the central government in Mexico to the provincial deputation was not settled with independence. The Treaty of Córdoba left the Constitution of 1812 intact, except

16. Benson, *Diputación*, p. 15. The first article (324) of this chapter of the constitution stated that "the government of the provinces will reside in the jefe superior, named by the king in each of them." It was the second article (325) which said: "In each province there will be a deputation termed provincial, for the purpose of promoting its prosperity, presided over by the jefe superior." These provisions were spelled out in greater detail in a decree for provincial government issued by the cortes on June 23, 1813. See Manuel Dublán and José María Lozano, eds., *Legislación mexicana* (Mexico, 1876–1904) , *1*, 413–24.

17. See map in Benson, *Diputación*, p. 66. Tlaxcala was added soon thereafter. The intendancies formed the units for the deputations in 1821 and later for the states of the federal system. The powers of the Bourbon intendant were not unlike those of the 1812 jefe superior. The former was also a royal appointee and only vaguely responsible to the viceroy. And yet the intendant fostered a spirit of provincial and municipal autonomy, at least in Argentina. See John Lynch, *Spanish Colonial Administration, 1782–1810: the Intendant System in the Viceroyalty of the Rio de la Plata* (London, University of London Press, 1958) . Intendants in Mexico, particularly such figures as Riaño and Flon, deserve study. It might even be discovered that the intendancies formed the ultimate antecedent for Mexican federalism.

where it specifically conflicted with the Plan of Iguala. And yet a central government was created under Iturbide. When the rebellion against Iturbide came in late 1822, the resulting provincial Plan of Casa Mata implied that complete control over provincial administrative matters would fall to the deputations. Apparently, now that neither a Spanish nor a Mexican central government existed for the provinces, the jefe político became de facto a provincially elected figure.[18] In the absence of a central government, the provinces set about to create one. The result was the federalist Constitution of 1824. In the strict sense, it was a federalism that "did not disunite the united, but rather one which joined together what had been disunited." [19] With the removal of the central authority, first of Madrid (1821) and then of Mexico City (1823), the action of the Mexican provinces was similar to that of the peninsular provinces from 1808 to 1812. In both cases it was the provinces that re-created a central government. But once re-created (whether according to centralist or federalist formulas), the central authority began to assume again its traditional supremacy over the provinces.

Since the provincial deputations provided the institutional antecedents for the states of a federal republic, and since the Spanish constitution—except where it specifically conflicted with new enactments—was still in effect in Mexico, it would logically follow that the Constitution of 1824 should show strong traces of the 1812 document. This was indeed the case, as examination of the text will show. The Spanish inspiration for the Constitution of 1824 was somewhat disguised by the obvious major departures, these being a republic as opposed to a monarchy, the federalist as opposed to the centralist form, and the necessary two chambers instead of one. It can generally be stated, however, that apart from articles pertaining to these features, "the nerves, the real spirit of the constitution" were derived from Spanish sources.[20] This can be seen first of all in the similarity of phrase, beginning with the

18. After the election of deputies to the constituent congress in Sept. 1823, the first-named deputy assumed the functions of jefe político. See Benson, *Diputación*, pp. 82–84; also her "The Plan of Casa Mata," *HAHR*, 25 (1945), 45–56.

19. Reyes Heroles, *Liberalismo*, *1*, 358.

20. See J. Lloyd Mecham, "The Origins of Federalism in Mexico," *HAHR*, *18* (1938), 179.

introductory clauses, in the general plan of dividing topics, in the consecutive numbering of articles, and even in the order of topics themselves. In the spirit of traditional Spanish legislation, the powers of authorities in both documents were often specifically defined. General precepts were mixed with regulatory details.

The Spanish constitution was one-third longer than the Mexican, owing to special articles pertaining to the king, an elaborate election law written into the constitution, and articles concerning provincial and municipal government. Because of its Spanish spirit, the Mexican constitution was still at least twice as long as the vaguely worded United States Constitution of 1787. One can point, moreover, to special 1812 creations which appear in the 1824 document: the Government Council (articles 113–16) to operate during recesses of the legislature; the proclamation of the exclusive Catholic faith (3) ; and the perpetuation of ecclesiastical and military *fueros* (154) . The judicial system, except where changes were made necessary by the federal form, was drawn from the Constitution of 1812.[21] Since the Constitution of 1824 omitted detail on matters that are left to state control in a federal system, we must turn to provincial constitution-making to test further the claim of Spanish influence. To do this, it is instructive to examine the case of the State of Mexico, where José María Luis Mora became the leader of the constitutional convention in 1824.

We have only fragmentary evidence concerning Mora's political activities during the critical years 1822 to 1824. In March 1822, he was sworn in as a member of the provincial deputation of Mexico. In the deputation Mora was closely associated with the faction of José María Fagoaga. This group, soon to be strongly anti-Iturbide, had called for a Bourbon prince for Mexico according to the Treaty of Córdoba, as well as favoring the liberal and anticlerical provisions of the Constitution of 1812.[22] Mora's work in the pro-

21. James Q. Dealey, "The Spanish Source of the Mexican Constitution of 1824," *Texas State Historical Quarterly, 3* (1900) , 167.

22. See Florstedt, "Liberal Role," pp. 55–56, who cites Lucas Alamán's sympathetic treatment of this group. Mora's close friend, Bernardo Couto, wrote of him after his death that Mora "was strongly inclined toward moderate monarchy [as a form of government], a fact that would be hard to believe from an examination of his writings after 1833." Couto's statement is the sole evidence for this possibility, but it is a perfectly plausible one. See Couto, "Dr. D. José María Luis Mora," in Manuel Orozco y Berra, ed., *Apéndice al diccionario universal de historia y de geografía* (Mexico, 1855-56) , 2, 888.

vincial deputation involved educational reform and a study of the perpetual problem of Mexico City drainage.[23] Mora was apparently a leader of the six-man deputation, just as he came to be later of the state congress. He openly criticized Iturbide, was arrested, but managed to escape actual imprisonment.

Though Mora's career at this stage gives concrete evidence of the institutional continuity from provincial deputation to state government, Mora himself was not an ardent federalist. He did sign a manifesto of the Mexico deputation in March 1823 supporting the Plan of Casa Mata. Yet by July he had clearly disassociated himself from extreme provincial sentiment which was demanding a new national constituent congress. He now deplored the ascendancy of "provincial egoism," ungrateful for the efforts of the national representatives "to clear the ground of so many poisonous weeds which had taken root and grown in the shade of despotism." The deputations have exceeded their powers, he continued, and "they are breaking the social bond that unites them with the other provinces." Mora's call was for union against disintegrating provincialism, for which he has understandably been called a "centralist." [24] The case of Mora's "centralism" is an example of the fluidity of federalist-centralist categories in the 1820s. In part, Mora's argument was an expression of the interests of Mexico's central and most powerful province against the pretentions of an outlying region like Guadalajara.[25] Yet Mora's position was similar to that of Fray Servando Teresa de Mier, the respected national deputy from Monterrey, a vigorous antagonist of both Iturbide and the centrifugal forces of provincialism.

Because of his "prophetic" opposition to extreme federalism in 1824, Mier was appropriated as a hero by later conservatives and long called a "centralist." A recent analysis has reestablished him as a "federalist." Mier served in both the reconvened first congress (March to October 1823) and the later constituent congress

23. On the latter Mora prepared (or supervised the preparation of) a *Memoria que para informar sobre el origen y estado actual de las obras emprendidas para el desagüe de las lagunas del valle de México* (Mexico, 1823).

24. Mora, "La Diputación provincial de Méjico a todos los pueblos de la nación" (July 1823), MS. in Mora Documents, 1806–38. Mora is called a "centralist" by Florstedt in "Liberal Role," p. 73.

25. See Charles W. Macune, Jr., "A Test of Federalism: Relations Between the Province and State of Mexico and the Mexican Nation, 1823–1824," *Paisano, 4* (1965), 45–46.

(November 1823 to October 1824), and held to a consistent position in each. All want a republic, he wrote in April 1823.

> We only differ in that some want it confederated, and I with the majority want it central, at least for ten to twelve years, because there do not exist in the provinces the necessary elements for each state to be sovereign; and all would become disputes and divisions.[26]

Like Mier, Mora clearly opposed the drive for extreme provincial autonomy that motivated men like Miguel Ramos Arizpe, Lorenzo de Zavala, and Valentín Gómez Farías, all in the majority in the 1824 national congress. Yet Mora, as a member of the provincial deputation and later as a state legislator, became by necessity a defender of state prerogatives. Moreover, he was proud of the efforts of the provincial deputations and in 1826 said that "they worked positively in many matters and made the federation." [27]

Recent Mexican interpreters have attributed more importance to federalism as a political than as a juridical doctrine. Only by adopting federalism, writes Jesús Reyes Heroles, could liberalism evolve and democratic institutions be consolidated. "The equation liberalism-federalism, so peculiar to our political evolution, obeyed an authentic necessity." [28] That there were differences of juridical viewpoint in 1824 between a Mora, a Mier (or even an

26. Mier to Ayuntamiento of Monterrey (April 2, 1823) in *Diez Cartas, hasta hoy inéditos* (Monterrey, Impresos Modernos, 1940), p. 5. On Mier's federalism see Benson, "Servando Teresa de Mier, Federalist," *HAHR, 28* (1948), 514–25. The reconvened first congress, prior to convoking the later constituent congress, produced a "Constitutional Plan" on May 16, 1823. It called for a federal republic and limited autonomy for the provinces. See Tena Ramírez, *Leyes*, pp. 147–52; Mecham, "Origins," p. 169. Mier's ideas and career will be dealt with at greater length in Chap. 6.

27. *Actas, 8,* 680 (Oct. 12, 1826). A closer study of the "federalism" of the majority leaders of 1824 should be made. For instance, Zavala, who presented the Constitution of 1824, had also signed his name to the more centralist "Plan" of May 16, 1823.

28. Reyes Heroles, *Liberalismo, 3,* 395; also 338. Cf. Felipe Tena Ramírez, *Derecho constitucional mexicano* (Mexico, Porrua, 1963), esp. pp. 103–04: "But if in the domain of comparative law Mexican federalism does not count, for us it represents the only reality worthy of our attention and study." Since Tena Ramírez admits the de facto centralization of Mexico, is he not in effect arguing the "reality" of a *mythical* federalism?

Alamán) on the one hand, and a Ramos Arizpe, a Zavala, or a Gómez Farías on the other, is unquestionable. However, by 1833 these differences had given way to a liberal coalescence in which agreement on federalism was assumed. Other issues took the ascendancy. We are led to suggest, then, that federalism as a juridical form was not a distinguishing feature of Mexican political liberalism.

On March 3, 1824, the constituent congress of the State of Mexico began its sessions in the impressive eighteenth-century Palace of the Inquisition in Mexico City. There it remained until the city was made a federal district. On February 27, 1827, after almost daily meetings, the congress adjourned in the "uninhabitable quarters" of the dilapidated convent of San Juan de Dios in the town of Texcoco. The task of the congress was staggering. Mexico was one of the largest and by far the most populous state, embracing in addition to its territory of today, the present state of Morelos, part of Hidalgo, and most of Guerrero. Besides its work of drawing up a constitution, a treasury and tax system, an election law, the bases of an elaborate judicial system with detailed regulations for civil and criminal procedure, and a law of municipalities, the congress was the target for myriad petty requests and local petitions. The Villa de Guadalupe would request permission to levy a tax on pulque carried through its confines. A porter would demand back pay. A town council would seek congressional support in its dispute with a local priest. In the administrative confusion brought by independence, the congress served as viceroy, audiencia, and intendant in the eyes of citizens and local communities.

The congress was reasonably harmonious; the majority of the deputies were members of the former Fagoaga group that had made up the provincial deputation. In fact, the State of Mexico became embroiled in a bitter factional struggle beginning in late 1826 between the congressional group and the followers of Lorenzo de Zavala. The conflict was given focus by the political activity of the Masonic lodges, the congress belonging to the *escoces* [Scottish Rite] group and Zavala to the *yorkino* [York Rite] group. There is no direct evidence that Mora was an escoces, but Zavala and others asserted that he became a *novenario,* an offshoot of the escoceses, in 1827.[29] As far as the ideas of the deputies were concerned, it is clear from the debates that Mora was the intellectual leader, and that in most cases his views prevailed. He was chairman of the two key committees of legislation and constitution.

The first order of business was to draw up a preliminary law (Ley Orgánica Provisional) to govern the state until the constitution could be written.[30] In the opening debates on the law, Mora presented some of his most characteristic constitutional views. He found that the law as presented did not place proper limits upon the legislative power. This failing "is what has caused all the evils suffered during the last fifty years by the peoples [of Europe] who have adopted the representative system." In a familiar vein, he said that "the evil is not in the depositary of power; it is in power itself."[31] He then proceeded to cite examples from Rome, and from the French and Spanish revolutions. In France, "despite the pompous declarations of rights," the Convention through its laws of exception rivaled the pre-1789 despotism. In Spain, similar laws "accelerated, if they did not cause, the ruin of the constitution." The "power of society" must be circumscribed; the judicial power must be made inviolable; and the bases of criminal and civil justice laid down. "Man," he said, "does not come into society to seek rights; these are given him by Nature. He comes rather to gain for himself security in exercising them." Mora was in part replying to José Ignacio de Nájera who often took a more egalitarian and

29. See Zavala, *Ensayo*, 2, 36; also José María Tornel, *Breve Reseña histórica* (Mexico, 1852), p. 133. At least three of the nineteen deputies, Francisco Guerra, Manuel Cortázar, and Agustín Valdovinos, had been delegates or alternates to the Spanish cortes. See N. L. Benson, ed., *Mexico and the Spanish Cortes, 1810–1822* (Austin, University of Texas Press, 1966), passim.

30. The text of the Ley Orgánica, dated Aug. 6, 1824, can be found in *Decretos del congreso constituyente del estado de México* (Tlalpam, 1830), *1*, 23–36. This was the only volume to appear.

31. Speech of May 13, 1824, in *El Sol*, May 31, 1824. A few of the early speeches of the congress were printed textually in *Águila* and *El Sol*. Generally the *Actas* carried only the minutes and not verbatim speeches. Thus, unless otherwise indicated, a quotation from the *Actas* will be the secretary's version. *Águila* ran the minutes for several months and only sporadically thereafter; *El Sol* carried them until the end of 1825. Thus, the *Actas* are a more complete source for the work of the congress than the newspapers.

popular position.[32] Always an advocate of the separation of powers and an opponent of popular sovereignty, Mora said a few days later (May 17) that "national sovereignty is the sum of individual sovereignties . . . [it] cannot be communicated in itself."

Apart from Mora's general views in the congress, which merely reinforce his better known statements of constitutional liberalism elsewhere, we should examine three areas of special congressional concern. These were: the organization of municipal government; the establishment of the judicial system, especially the introduction of trial by jury; and the framing of an election law. Mora played a key role in each.

Perhaps the most interesting problem to emerge from the debates of the congress pertained to local and municipal organization. None of the Mexican federal constitutions of the nineteenth century devoted a single article to municipalities, since in a federal system this was a matter to be left to the states.[33] Yet when we turn to the sessions of the congress of the State of Mexico, the municipalities become a dominant issue and one that provides a special insight into an important aspect of liberalism.

Although the deputies did not agree on the proper way to organize the municipalities, they were of one mind on their present plight. The *ayuntamientos* were degenerate. All the deputies referred to the deplorable condition of the municipalities, but perhaps most eloquent was Manuel de Villaverde, himself from Corte de la Sierra (Zacualtipan), a town of 400 families in the Huasteca. He claimed intimate knowledge of the countryside and asserted that except for a few towns of "the first rank," the municipal corporations

> are formed of persons who are absolutely inept, without political ideas and even without education, who never take interest in public concerns, and who view our political events with indifference as if they were taking place in Italy.[34]

32. See the debate of May 12, 1824, *Actas, 1,* 265–66. Mora reasserted many of the same arguments when the draft constitution was being discussed. See *Actas, 7,* 425–26 (June 5, 1826).

33. Tena Ramírez, *Derecho,* p. 139. His chapter on the municipality makes no reference to nineteenth-century state laws on the subject.

34. *Actas, 1,* 280–81 (May 13, 1824).

Mora said the councils were often made up of servants and day laborers. Villaverde presented a chronicle of local tyranny, in which the people had always been "victims immolated at the whim of their mandarins." A woman was routed from her house at bayonet point by town officials in the middle of the night for refusing to return to her husband. An eighteen-year-old boy was thrown into a filthy prison and bound with an enormous chain because he refused to marry a fallen woman.

Villaverde said the situation had changed little with the intendant system; the only solution now was to abolish ayuntamientos in all but the largest towns and replace them with a single elected magistrate (*alcalde de paz*). According to Mora the present condition of the ayuntamientos stemmed from the time of the provincial deputations, when in the absence of central authority, "the spirit of disorder" reigned supreme.[35]

The deputies disagreed on the extent to which liberty should be accorded to the ayuntamientos. Should they be allowed to administer their own affairs or should a superior official be charged with full responsibility over the municipalities in his district? The provisional constitution provided for a system of prefects and subprefects, both officials having elaborate specific powers of intervention in municipal affairs. Mora took sharp exception to this plan in his general speech of May 13, 1824. He made a frank plea for more local freedom and responsibility, and held to this position consistently thereafter.

> If these [prefects and subprefects] are to intervene in everything; if they are to determine everything; if nothing can be done without their consent; the creation of municipal bodies along with the prefects is completely useless. It is not only ridiculous but also contrary to the system we have adopted for superior authorities to stoop to minutiae which degrade them and distract them from their serious endeavors.

Moreover, Mora believed that the best way to upgrade the municipalities was to give them more responsibility over their own

35. For Mora's views see *Actas*, *1*, 461, 2d ser., June 23, 1824 (blocks of pages were occasionally repeated in the *Actas*); *3*, 26, 33–35 (Nov. 8, 9, 1824); also the previously cited MS. of July 1823.

affairs. He optimistically argued that with time "they will be the prime movers of the public prosperity." Mora even intimated in one heated discussion that the opponents of municipal freedom were really those who saw their old position of seigneurial lordship being undermined by an independent town council.[36]

The leaders of the move toward further control of municipal activities were the previously mentioned Villaverde and José María de Jáuregui, a consistent leader in the congress. These men felt that strict control by the appointed prefects and subprefects was the only way to curb the local oligarchs. When the matter of municipal codes was raised, Jáuregui remarked that the laws of the Spanish cortes on this subject were too general. If the French constituent assembly prescribed municipal codes, he added, we as a mere state government should certainly do it for our municipalities. Jáuregui and Mora agreed on many issues but were opponents on local administration. Following Mora's remarks on municipal liberty, Jáuregui replied:

> I am well informed on this lovely theory of Benjamin Constant upon which to a certain degree is built the edifice of the federal system. But I think that the country where it could be reduced to perfect practice would be at the peak of civilization.[37]

Civilization is needed for municipal liberty, he concluded. He was agreeing with the position of Marcial Antonio López, the 1820 translator of Constant, who had said that the Spanish municipalities were not as developed as the French, and that the best way to stimulate them was by government action.[38]

More than a pragmatic problem, therefore, the government of the municipalities became a question of liberal principles. Mora had said that keeping the municipalities "under degrading tutelage" would "pull down and demolish the bases of the federal

---

36. See *Actas*, 7, 460 (June 9, 1826). For Mora's views on upgrading the municipalities see ibid., 7, 34 (Mar. 8, 1826), 459–60 (June 9, 1826); 2, 31–32 (July 6, 1824); 5, 433–34 (Oct. 11, 1825). The problem of the hacienda in municipal affairs was generally overlooked by the liberals because of their reluctance to attack private property rights. See Chaps. 5 and 7, below.

37. *Actas*, 1, 274 (May 13, 1824).

38. López, "Observaciones," in Constant, *Curso*, 2, 21.

system." He was inspired by Constant's "new type of federalism," by which Constant meant not the loose confederation of Switzerland or the United States, but one that entailed decentralization within a system where the presence of a central power was assumed (see above, page 60). This was perhaps the true nature of Mora's "centralism" in 1823 and of his assertion in 1827 that "our federalism has been created in the opposite manner from that of the United States . . . from the center to the circumference." [39] Mora's view of local liberty bears more analysis, however, for his position can be easily misunderstood. In his May 13, 1824, speech he emphasized that he thought of the ayuntamientos as administrative and not as legislative bodies. The question can be raised, then, was Mora really interested in municipal liberty?

We have seen his concern over the degeneracy of the ayuntamientos. His remedy was that more administrative responsibility should be given to them. He did not oppose the prefect system, however. He always assumed its necessity in order to maintain unity, especially after the provincial disorder of the 1822–23 period. At that time, the ayuntamientos paid no attention to the provincial deputations. The disorder resulted from the fact that "there was no authority watching over the conduct of the municipal bodies, in order to make them take up their duties." [40] He went on to explain that the Spanish Constitution of 1812 had been little concerned with specific American problems; thus for the small area of Spain the jefe político was sufficient. Prefects and subprefects were not created, though in a subsequent law provision for a *jefe político subalterno* appeared.[41]

The use of the term "prefect" itself, obviously taken from the Napoleonic provincial official of 1800, revealed strong assumptions of administrative centralization on the part of the delegates. What Mora appeared to want was a balance between extreme centralization on the French pattern, where superior officials intervened in

39. Mora, *Obras,* p. 632. This assertion was often made by critics of federalism who wanted to show the unnatural quality of the Mexican federal system. Mora, however, was by 1827 an unquestioning supporter of political federalism, which became thereafter part of the liberal creed.

40. *Actas,* 2, 40–41 (July 8, 1824).

41. Law of June 23, 1813, Chap. III, arts. iii and xxxiii, in Dublán and Lozano, *1,* 420, 423.

minute local decisions, and de facto autonomy which, under Mexican conditions, could lead only to municipal degeneracy.[42] The decree of the Spanish cortes (June 23, 1813), elaborating the provisions of the constitution on provincial administration, served as his model in drawing up the state law of ayuntamientos (approved on February 9, 1825). In this law, Mora managed to win acceptance for his concept of municipal "liberty," defeating the earlier provision for undue authority in the hands of prefects and subprefects.[43]

The deputies were caught on the horns of a characteristic dilemma of continental liberalism. Constant had said that "uniformity is death"; he had sought local autonomy and variety. Yet, having lived through the revolutionary era, he recognized the need for a strong centralized administration. Mora in Mexico wanted local initiative developed; he saw it as the true basis of the federal system and one aspect of his scheme for limiting absolute authority in the interests of individual liberty. Yet given local ignorance and the reign of petty oligarchs, centralized administrative control was necessary to combat privilege and foster progress. The result was his compromise system of prefects *and* administrative ayuntamientos. It was a conception of local government that drew its inspiration from continental structures and not from the example of the Anglo-Saxon self-governing community. Mora shared the more general conflict within political liberalism between the desire to guarantee individual liberties and the necessity to adhere to patterns of rationalized administration.[44] The colo-

42. See *Actas*, 7, 458 (June 9, 1826). The first use of the term "prefect" in Mexico was in the "Constitutional Plan" of May 16, 1823 (see n. 26 above) in which each province was to be governed by a prefect and a provincial congress. On the French prefect, see Jacques Godechot, *Les Institutions de la France sous la révolution et l'empire* (Paris, Presses Universitaires, 1951), pp. 509 ff. The prefect, a key figure in turning "the inconsistent, irrational, frustrated and inhibited centralism of the [French] old regime into a juggernaut of modern bureaucracy," was unchallenged during the Restoration, either by the ultraroyalists or by the liberals. See Alan B. Spitzer, "The Bureaucrat as Proconsul: the Restrauration Prefect and the *Police Générale*," *Comparative Studies in Society and History*, 7 (1965), 392 and passim.

43. Cf. the 1825 decree (*Decretos*, pp. 54–66) and the pertinent articles of the state constitution (*Decretos*, pp. 154–57) with the earlier Ley Orgánica provisions (*Decretos*, pp. 29–35). The latter had only one article devoted to the ayuntamientos.

44. Mora introduced the law to rationalize the "monstrous" territorial limits of

nial term *"subdelegado"* also came into the discussions of the prefect system. The question was to what extent the new prefects and subprefects really embodied the functions of the old territorial judges of the Bourbon intendant system. Mora was quick to point out that the prefects had no judicial powers, but implied that as administrative agents they were indeed replacing the Bourbon officials.[45]

The municipal policy of the congress raises again the issue of federalism. Within the formal framework of a federalist constitution, Mora and his colleagues, despite differences among themselves, were following centralist patterns of administration. Mora spoke of "federalism" when referring to local institutions, but what he meant was some measure of administrative decentralization at the lowest level, under the surveillance of appointed officials. The prefect system was incorporated into the national centralist Constitution of 1836 (Law VI, article 16), along with the reorganization of the provinces by "departments" and detailed regulations for the ayuntamientos. The system was instituted again on a national scale under Porfirio Díaz.[46]

Since the members of the Mexico state congress revealed centralist sympathies, perhaps what we have is the anomoly of a centralist state constitution within a federalist system. In any event, the issue of centralism versus federalism was not vital to Mora's liberalism. Perhaps this is true as well for more ardent juridical federalists such as Gómez Farías and Zavala. We can conclude, then, that within Mexican political liberalism, continental and late colonial administrative assumptions ran deeper than formulas of juridical federalism and local autonomy.[47]

One of the principal activities of the state congress was the establishment of a judicial system. The rational administration of

---

partidos within the state. See *Actas, 4,* 82 (Mar. 22, 1825). A decree of Apr. 8, 1825 (*Decretos,* pp. 68–70) detailed the new organization of partidos, each of which was to have a *cabecera* (head town) where the subprefect resided. The redrawing of territorial limits was the cause of numerous disputes and petitions to the congress.

45. *Actas, 2,* 35–40 (July 7–8, 1824).

46. See Tena Ramírez, *Derecho,* p. 140.

47. To test this point further, the work of the Jalisco congress in local organization might be compared with that of Mexico. Jalisco was the center of extreme federalist sentiment in 1824.

justice, governed by the doctrine of the separation of powers, was a cardinal tenet of constitutional liberalism, one to which José María Luis Mora was deeply committed.

> In a wisely constituted nation which has adopted for its government the representative system, the effective independence of the judicial power is the complement to the fundamental laws and the guarantee of public liberties.[48]

The difficulty of establishing an effective separation of powers at the various governmental levels constantly plagued the legislators. The three powers had been thoroughly confused in the colonial system. The problem of separating judicial from administrative matters in the myriad of local questions that were presented to the congress consumed much time. Not only did the liberals have to combat colonial practices, but also the heritage of the revolutionary years.

One of the persistent themes of Mora's essays in *El Observador de la república mexicana* was hostility to arbitrary judicial proceedings, either in criminal or political matters. Evoking the revolutionary tribunals of the French Revolution, he pointed out what might happen if rigid adherence to judicial independence broke down. Mora particularly attacked the revival in 1827 of military tribunals to dispatch criminal justice, based on decrees of 1811 and 1823. In 1826 he had argued vigorously for the inclusion of two articles in the state constitution, one (173) forbidding any authority to reopen closed cases (*juicios fenecidos*), the other forbidding judgment by commissions.[49] The latter was found to duplicate a provision in the federal constitution (148) and thus was dropped.

The administration of justice loomed large in Mora's thoughts during the years of the congress, for he was concurrently studying law. In fact, he petitioned the congress to be excused from certain preliminary courses and be admitted to the bar by special examination. His colleagues concluded "that he has unusual knowledge of natural and customary law, of political economy and other

48. Mora, *Obras,* p. 549.
49. Mora, "Discurso sobre los tribunales militares," in *Obras,* pp. 552–55; *Actas,* 6, 404–05 (Jan. 7, 1826).

sciences . . . and that he would be wasting his time in the university." To gain admittance to the bar, Mora presented before the state supreme court a dissertation outlining the advantages of the new system of justice, of which he had been the chief architect.[50]

From this and other statements of his juridical views, Mora appears to have been steeped in the writings of contemporary French jurists. He particularly mentioned Alphonse Bérenger de la Drôme's *De la Justice criminelle* (1818), François-Charles Louis Comte's translation of a work on jury trial by Richard Philipps (1819), and treatises by André-Marie-Jean Jacques Dupin. All three of these men were liberals. Comte was persecuted by Napoleon and by the Bourbons, but he managed to edit intermittently an opposition journal called *Censeur* during the Restoration. Dupin (*aîné*), though condemned as a political chameleon over his long life, was the chief legal advocate of the liberal opposition in the years from 1815 to 1830. Although most of the specific articles pertaining to administration of justice in the state constitution were taken from the Spanish Constitution of 1812, the only Spanish juridical writer referred to was Francisco Martínez Marina. He, like Jovellanos, was a student of Spanish legislation and history before 1808 and wrote a popular *Teoría de las cortes* in 1813. The general influence of Jeremy Bentham, as we will see in Chapter 5, permeated the juridical discussions of the congress, but it was the experience of the Spanish cortes and of the French liberals with which Mora identified himself most directly.

The state congress adopted a three-stage court system modeled after the Spanish, which Mora said provided surer justice for the poor than did colonial practices. Mora admitted that the English system of ambulatory judges was the best (his colleague Jáuregui strongly advocated its adoption) but said it was unfeasible in Mexico's underdeveloped provinces.[51] Instead, the constitution provided for a single judge in each *partido* and *distrito*, plus a supreme court. Mora's pet project was the introduction of trial by

50. Reprinted in Mora, *Obras*, pp. 525–30 (dated Mar. 1, 1827). On his petition, see *Actas*, *4*, 147 (Apr. 18, 1825).

51. Mora, *Obras*, p. 526. Jáuregui's arguments are in *Actas*, *5*, 487–92 (Oct. 19, 1825).

jury in criminal cases. This system of English origin evoked great enthusiasm among continental liberals and was widely adopted in Europe in the early nineteenth century. Benjamin Constant argued vigorously for juries in France. The Constitution of 1812 did not specifically provide for trial by jury. The Spanish legislators, according to Constant's translator, were most enthusiastic about this English institution but concluded that introducing it would be too brusque a change. They did leave the door open for future action, however, in article 307. Jáuregui's comment was that "in Spain it was not put into practice . . . because of deep-rooted absolutism (servilismo)." [52]

Enthusiasm for jury trial was based on a faith in the common sense of local people closest to the case being tried, free from traditional judicial corruption. Mora was inconsistent on how jurors should be named: on one occasion he argued for election by ayuntamientos; at a later time he said they should be appointed. He always maintained, however, that juries should be made up of property holders. "Only this class of citizens is truly independent and can inspire the confidence of both the legislator and the rest of the nation." [53] After Mora mentioned that trial by jury had already been adopted by Jalisco, Puebla, and Zacatecas, measures providing for the system were overwhelmingly passed on January 20, 1826.

At the heart of Mora's constitutional liberalism, like that of Constant, was the idea that individual liberty could be best guaranteed if the political process were entrusted to property holders. It was in his discussions of political rights and citizenship that Mora revealed most clearly his hostility to egalitarian theories of political democracy. His ideas on this subject were clearly expressed in the debates of the state congress on the electoral law and

52. Lopez, "Observaciones," in Constant, Curso, 1, 243–45; Jáuregui in Actas, 2, 109 (July 20, 1824). López waxed enthusiastic over jury trial in England, as did Mora in Obras, p. 527. Jáuregui quoted Constant in its support (Actas, 9, 24, Nov. 7, 1826). Interestingly enough, Mora also referred to an assertion by Martínez Marina that "before absolutism was well consolidated [in Spain], the principle was accepted that men should be judged by their equals" (Actas, 7, 374, Apr. 24, 1826).

53. Mora, Obras, p. 529. He argued for election, and against the French precedent of selection of jurors by the prefect, in the debate of May 19, 1826 (Actas, 7, 353–54). He reversed himself the following year (Obras, p. 527). Perhaps this inconsistency is another indication of Mora's ambivalence regarding local liberty.

also in his later essays. In fact, the political convulsions of the years 1827 and 1829 sharpened his conviction that only property owners could form a bulwark against anarchy and a safeguard for constitutional rights. In 1830 he wrote: "We are convinced that this exaggerated equality, understood literally, has been among us a seedbed of errors and an abundant source of misfortunes." [54]

Mora was presumably referring to the political crisis of 1828 which had elevated the Indian warrior of the independence movement, Vicente Guerrero, to the presidency. Mora's ideas on property undoubtedly reflected "Creole" or "aristocratic" opposition to resurgent political democracy, as suggested by Zavala and more recently by Reyes Heroles. The 1830 essays in *El Observador* discussed the term "aristocracy" at length, obviously sensitive to contemporary charges. In fact, in advocating property qualifications they defended the notion of "true" or "natural" aristocracy, "that government in which authority resides in the hands of the men, most outstanding for their virtue, talent, learning, and valor." [55] Constant in France could not have used the word "aristocracy" openly, but his sentiments were similar. In fact, Constant is quoted frequently in these Mexican discussions. Interestingly enough, Lorenzo de Zavala, the political democrat of 1828, was by 1831 also advocating that in order to avoid political intrigue and demagoguery, elections should be in the hands "of a respectable class of society, the property holders." [56]

Mora espoused on a national scale in 1830 what the state congress of Mexico had already put into effect in 1827. Electoral procedure in Mexico (both nation and state) was governed by the elaborate provisions of the Constitution of 1812. It was an indirect three-stage system, consisting of selecting municipal (*parroquial*) electors, who in turn chose district (*de partido*) electors. The latter then met to select the deputies to the cortes. This procedure was imitated in the June 17, 1823, election law to select deputies to the national constituent assembly in Mexico. It was again

54. Mora, "Discurso sobre la necesidad de fijar el derecho de ciudadanía en la república, y hacerlo esencialmente afecto a la propiedad," *Obras*, p. 630.

55. See "Aristocracia," *El Observador*, 2d ser., *3*, 241–42 (Sept. 22, 1830); also "Elecciones," *El Observador*, 2d ser., *1*, 164 ff.

56. See Zavala, *Ensayo*, *1*, 309; also *2*, 133, 374–75. The implications of this problem are discussed further in Chaps. 4 and 7, below.

adopted by the State of Mexico and written into its Constitution of 1827. The three laws, however, differed as to qualifications for political rights. The 1823 law was the most democratic, requiring no property qualifications to participate in any stage of elections, or to be a deputy. Moreover, all male residents over eighteen years of age could participate in municipal elections. The Spanish constitution imposed an undesignated "annual income from real property" on deputies (article 69), but none at the lower levels. The state constitution was the most conservative of the three. At the lowest level "citizenship" was defined as being a *vecino,* a one-year resident of the state, who had "an industrial art or profession" and who was the owner of real property within the state worth at least 6,000 pesos (article 19).[57]

Mora insisted that his idea of citizenship and political rights was modern and liberal, despite his attachment to property qualifications. He disagreed sharply with his colleague José Domingo Lazo de la Vega, who maintained that historically Spaniards had had political rights because vecinos had been named delegates to the cortes.

> Although the Spaniards had their cortes [Mora replied], they were only a vain resemblance of the representative system. There was no equality of representation nor did residence (*vecindad*) entail the rights which it does today. These are a modern discovery.[58]

Mora clearly gave preference to landed property. In the debates he succeeded in defeating a measure that "an industry or profession" would suffice; this could mean that the citizen was not really rooted in the place. By 1830 he acknowledged that a business income of 1,000 pesos could substitute for a landed property worth 6,000 pesos. Yet Mora's constitutional system, like that of Constant, was based on a rural civilization, where enlightened indi-

---

57. For the 1823 law, see Dublán and Lozano, *1,* 651–57. For the state law, see *Decretos,* pp. 135–36 and 166–67. The Constitution of 1824 omitted property qualifications for deputies.

58. *Actas, 8,* 154 (July 24, 1826). The argument arose from Mora's specific recommendation that *vecindad* entail a one-year residence, which "is necessary to demonstrate interest in the prosperity of the place." Duration of residence apparently was not a factor in the old Spanish concept of vecindad.

vidual property holders formed a responsible governing class.[59]

It is already evident from our discussion of Mexican constitutionalism that the wave of optimism that engulfed the early twenties became dissipated after 1826. The debates of the state congress after August of that year suddenly became dominated by the Toluca election controversy. Enlightened discussions gave way to heated partisan speeches. The Masonic lodges had emerged "as a permanent conspiracy against the tranquility of the state," to use Lucas Alamán's phrase. Politics had become bitter factionalism, disturbing the benign regime of Mexico's first president, the former insurgent Guadalupe Victoria. He entered office "amid the most prosperous circumstances," mused Alamán in 1852; "the parties had been repressed and the hope of a happy future coaxed the spirits of all." Victoria's government was one of coalition, short-lived since incompatibles such as Alamán and Ramos Arizpe were given cabinet posts. The president was well-meaning, but as Mier said, not born to govern. He believed naïvely that Mexico was destined to unlimited progress and that under the rule of law all factions would disappear. In short, it was as José María Tornel was later to remark, "the golden age of the republic." [60]

That the golden age had passed by mid-1827 was clear to Mora who had begun to edit El Observador. His "introduction" (June 6, 1827) drew a dismal picture of conspiracy, factional scheming, and personalist politics. A later article looked nostalgically back to the peace and harmony of 1825. The journal, then, became the organ of a determined constitutionalism: "The salvation of the republic must not depend on personal accidents, but on the undisturbed supremacy of the laws."

Mora and his colleagues demonstrated further their adherence to constitutionalism by applying its doctrines to a major socio-

59. Marcial Antonio López was critical of the failure of the Spanish constitution to fix citizenship to property rights, as Constant had advocated. See "Observaciones" in Constant, Curso, 1, 190; 2, 69–71. By 1830 Mora was advocating abandonment of the indirect system of elections, and the institution, instead, of direct elections on a national scale by property holders. See "Discurso sobre las elecciones directas," Obras, pp. 672–79.

60. See Alamán, Historia, 5, 812; Tornel, Breve Reseña, p. 30. There is a lengthy study on Victoria by Elmer W. Flaccus, "Guadalupe Victoria: Mexican Patriot and First President, 1786–1843" (Ph.D. dissertation, University of Texas, 1951).

political issue of the twenties—the expulsion of the Spaniards. This question, which completely absorbed the attention of the press in 1827, was one more decisive sign that the 1824–26 era of good feelings had ended. The explanation of this episode remains obscure. Some contemporaries saw it as a product of political factionalism, seized upon by demagogues in the yorkino group to discredit the pro-Spanish escoceses. Others viewed it as a legacy from the bitterness of the revolutionary wars, a popular resurgence of Hispanophobe sentiment, combined with a Creole desire to dislodge Spaniards from their ascendant position in economic life. Modern Mexican interpreters have judged it an inevitable reaction to Spain's intransigent attitude toward her former colony; or they have seen in it a growing popular and egalitarian movement against oligarchical control.[61]

It is undeniable that anti-Spanish feeling was uniquely strong in Mexico, a country that had seen the Indian upheaval led by Hidalgo and Morelos. This was demonstrated by the attempt of a mob of Independence Day enthusiasts in 1823 to desecrate the tomb of Hernán Cortés, the great symbol of Spanish oppression. Only by the adroit work of minister Lucas Alamán and a few friends, who moved Cortés' remains from one part of the Hospital de Jesús Nazareno to another, were the vandals foiled.[62] It might be expected that a movement to expel Spaniards would develop in a country that has always refused to erect a monument to its great conquistador. The episode that touched off the anti-Spanish reaction was the naïve conspiracy of Padre Joaquín Arenas, apparently an agent for the Spanish government, which was planning an invasion. He was apprehended in January 1827, and a popular wave of anti-Spanish sentiment swept the state legislatures.

For Mora, now editing El Observador, the issue was a clear case

61. Factionalism as a cause was stressed by Mora, by El Sol, and by El Observador. Zavala, more sympathetic to the movement, looked for deeper causes (Ensayo, 1, 272, 330; 2, 19, 41–42). Zavala's discussion revealed him at his best as a historian. For examples of modern views see Chávez Orozco, Historia de México, 1808–1836 (Mexico, Patria, 1947), p. 250; Reyes Heroles, Liberalismo, 2, 64. Fortunately, a thorough study of this episode, by H. D. Sims of the University of Pittsburgh, is under way.

62. Francisco De la Maza, "Los Restos de Hernán Cortés," Cuadernos americanos, 32 (1947), 153–74.

of civil liberty against irresponsible power. His basic principles of constitutional liberalism were at stake, and he argued an unpopular position with a vigor that demonstrated his deep convictions. The first few months of *El Observador* were devoted almost entirely to defending the rights of Spaniards. It must have been particularly galling to Mora that the question of expulsion first arose in the congress of the State of Mexico, now controlled by the yorkinos. Governor Lorenzo de Zavala allowed discussion of the matter on August 28, under what he termed later was heavy pressure, though he himself opposed expulsion.[63] Mora's argument was that the Spaniards, by virtue of the Treaty of Córdoba and the Plan of Iguala, were Mexican citizens with full natural rights: "the security against being molested in their persons, rights, and properties, and equality before the law to be treated like the rest of the natives of the republic." [64]

The issue of expulsion provided a focus for the characteristic tenets of Mora's liberalism. The parliamentary chamber, under the pressure of popular passions, had become like the French Convention. It was no longer an active instrument governed by "the will of the representatives," but a "passive body" subject to "the will of a small number of factious charlatans and adventurers." Calm and rational deliberation had given way to passion, and once again individual rights had been abridged in the name of the general will. When Generals Pedro Celestino Negrete and José Antonio Echávarri, Spanish-born patriots who had supported Iturbide in 1821, were arrested arbitrarily by the minister of war, a series of articles condemning the action appeared in *El Observador*. The author, Francisco Molinos del Campo, quoted long passages from Constant, that "respected genius of liberty" who had cited the danger of public authority encroaching upon the judicial power.[65]

Though civil rights formed the basis of Mora's defense of the

63. See Zavala, *Ensayo*, 2, 25 and passim. Zavala made the statement in 1832. For contemporary evidence of his views, see his manifesto to the congress in *El Sol*, Oct. 8, 1827. Tornel, a supporter of expulsion in 1827, assigned Zavala indirect responsibility (*Breve Reseña*, pp. 166–67).

64. Mora, *Obras*, pp. 540–41.

65. Mora, *Obras*, pp. 513–14, 575–78; *El Observador*, 1st ser., *1*, 153–206 (July 18, 1827).

Spaniards, he used other arguments as well. As an economist, he saw the blow to the small supply of capital in circulation, much of it in the hands of Spanish merchants. We don't even have the justification used by the Catholic Kings for expelling the Moors; whereas they differed in language and religion, "we have everything in common with the Spaniards." Mora also feared the opinion foreigners would have of Mexico. The French suffered greatly by their acts of proscription; how much less can Mexico, which needs so desperately a moderate internal regime and good relations abroad, afford to commit such actions. Mora kept returning, however, to the precepts of constitutional liberalism. It has been alleged, he wrote, that though individual guarantees would suffer, at least the *patria* would be saved. How is it possible "to distinguish public interest from individual interest and to suppose that social guarantees can be in opposition to public security and well-being?" [66]

In the Mexico of 1826 and 1827, political ideas were inseparable from partisan politics. The articles in *El Observador,* for all their lofty principles and doctrinaire adherence to constitutional ideals, were also the product of an embattled political faction. By 1827 the escoces party with which Mora was affiliated had lost control of both the State of Mexico and the national congress. The first blow had come in late September 1826, when ninety-seven state electors met as a junta in Toluca to choose deputies to the new state congress and to the national congress. Lorenzo de Zavala and his yorkino supporters staged a stunning coup and captured the delegation. This victory touched off a bitter controversy in which the constituent congress (still in Mexico City) charged fraud and illegal procedures.[67]

Mora led the bitter protests which the congress made to the national legislature, asking support for their decree annulling the elections. In one of his many speeches on the subject, Mora in-

66. Mora, *Obras,* pp. 539, 546–48, 584. *El Sol* (June 3, 1828) said ten million pesos would be taken out of circulation as a result of the expulsion. The first national law (Dec. 20, 1827) made numerous exceptions to those expelled. A second law (Mar. 20, 1829) eliminated the exceptions. See Dublán and Lozano, 2, 47–49, 98.

67. There is a detailed treatment of this episode in Florstedt, "Liberal Role," pp. 128–50. For Zavala's role see Estep, *Lorenzo de Zavala,* pp. 127–31. A central issue was Zavala's residency in the state, based on a flimsy title to property in Tlalpam.

sisted that the congress must have control over electoral juntas, recalling the "disasters of the French nation" when juntas reigned
supreme, and when the "first heroes of France were made to perish
by the blade of the guillotine." [68] He called for quick and firm
action against the opponents. Mora's reaction to the election controversy revealed signs of a proud and petulant intellectual, quick
to become embroiled in partisan politics. A contemporary British
traveler said that he was "perhaps too much of an enthusiast in
politics," a characteristic somewhat obscurred by the philosophic
tone of much of his writing.[69] Mora's efforts to dislodge the
yorkinos failed; in fact the yorkino-dominated national legislature
declared unconstitutional the state decree annulling the Toluca
elections.

On January 29, 1827, the beleaguered state congress packed up
and left Mexico City for Texcoco. Mora had insisted on moving
despite lethargy and opposition. The congress "must not remain
any longer in a city where a dominating faction is attempting to
ridicule its authority." [70] Mora and Jáuregui would have nothing
of the bureaucratic objections to the move raised by José María
Puchet, of the governor's council. Said Jáuregui: "The congress
. . . is prepared if necessary to have its sessions there in a cabin or
under a tree . . . like the Congress of Apatzingán." [71] For Mora,
the problem of the state capital was not governed entirely by
politics, however. It had been a concern of his over several years.
He had led the heated protests of the congress against the inevitable capitalization of Mexico City in late 1824. Opposition was
natural enough, since the act removed the economic, political, and

68. *Actas, 9,* 93–94 (Nov. 16, 1826).

69. See R. W. H. Hardy, *Travels in the Interior of Mexico in 1825, 1826, 1827,
and 1828* (London, 1829), p. 511. Mora's good friend Bernardo Couto noted the
polemical tone of much of his work ("Mora," p. 888). Young Melchor Ocampo was
antagonized by Mora when they met in Paris in 1840: "[Mora is] so exclusive a
partisan that he must be hard to get along with, except for those who in all their
conversations submit to holding no opinion" (*Obras, 3,* 41–42). Quoted by Florstedt,
"Liberal Role," p. 474.

70. *Actas, 9,* 311 (Dec. 29, 1826).

71. Ibid., p. 429 (Jan. 23, 1827). The temporary capital was moved to Tlalpam
in late Apr. 1827, where it remained until 1830, when Toluca became the permanent
site. The constitution was presented on Feb. 14, 1827, in a manifesto, *A los Habitantes del estado de México su congreso constituyente* (Mexico, 1827), signed by
Mora, Jáuregui, and José Nicolás Oláez.

cultural heart from the state—just as the capitalization of Buenos Aires was to do in Argentina.

The federal district question contributed to Mora's ambivalence on federalism. He was now put in the position of defending states rights as opposed to his seemingly centralist utterances of 1823.[72] Thereafter in the debates Mora consistently took the position that Mexico City was a deadening influence on local liberty and development. He defended the district court system by saying that it would force lawyers out into the countryside and aid in the dispersing of enlightenment and wealth to the state.[73] Also, district courts would meet "the appeals of the people who should be justly freed from the burden of coming to a corrupt [central] court, where favor, patronage, and money tip the balance of justice toward the party that can manipulate it." On another occasion Mora proposed unsuccessfully that the state capital be chosen by the ayuntamientos, and that in so doing they be informed of "the vigorous resistance which the congress has put up to the dismemberment of its territory." [74] Undoubtedly, Mora's strictures against the evil influence of Mexico City were sharpened by losing it as a state capital. Though born in the provinces, Mora was not basically a provincial spirit. His task was to square centralist assumptions with a liberal concern for decentralization and local development, in the light of pressing political considerations.

By 1830, Mora's constitutional liberalism was threatened. His zeal for establishing legal and constitutional guarantees for individual liberty against arbitrary authority had been undermined by factional politics. Enlightened and moderate rule by property holders had been challenged by demagogues, successfully manipulating popular passions. The political anarchy that so disillusioned Mora in 1827 did not abate in the succeeding years. The

72. For Mora's position on the federal district question, see *Actas, 4,* 240–44, 255–58 (May 17–19, 1825). On the issue generally, see Macune, "Test," pp. 53–57.

73. *Actas, 6,* 425 (Jan. 7, 1826). The specific question was whether the court should admit written reports of lawyers. They could thus avoid leaving Mexico City instead of actually consulting with poor clients in the country. Mora earlier refuted opponents of the district court system who asserted that lawyers could never be persuaded to leave Mexico City (*Actas, 5,* 247, 2d ser., Sept. 3, 1825). In 1830 Mora acknowledged that there were no lawyers at all in many of the *cabeceras de partido* (*Actas, 10,* 109, May 21, 1830).

74. *Actas, 5,* 261, 2d ser. (Sept. 6, 1825); *7,* 173 (Apr. 14, 1826).

escoces party and its offspring the novenarios were dislodged from power by 1828, after the failure of the Plan of Montaño, a rebellion led by Nicolás Bravo, the national vice-president. The victorious party split, however, over the elections of September 1828, since both candidates for president were yorkinos. Though Manuel Gómez Pedraza won the election, Vicente Guerrero's partisans rebelled, and after winning the Mexico City garrison in the Revolution of the Acordada, they declared Guerrero president. Guerrero assumed office in April 1829; but amid increasing anarchy, he in turn was overthrown by his own vice-president, Anastasio Bustamante, in December.

Mora was faced with the problem of how a constitutional system could be maintained in such chaotic circumstances. Mora's political writings of the year 1830 bear close examination, for they reveal a decided change of emphasis. This change is often elusive, often inconsistent; but in comparison with his ideas of a few years earlier, a new orientation is discernible.

Mora was never one to shun politics; he became an enthusiastic supporter of Anastasio Bustamante in 1830. *El Observador,* discontinued in early 1828, now resumed publication and welcomed the army that called itself "protector of the constitution and the laws." Mora was in a mood to accept the constitutionalist pronouncements of Bustamante's Plan of Jalapa at their face value. "Spreading with the speed of lightning to all the corners of the republic, [the Plan] was adopted in a very few days with astounding unanimity." [75] Mora was convinced that this was not just another political coup, but rather a true restoration of the laws.

Victory brought a general political housecleaning, including a decree that the constituent congress of the State of Mexico be reconvened. Mora was again the leader, this time of only eleven delegates whose job it was to prepare for a new regular congress. The state government was now clearly subordinate to the president. On April 26, 1830, Melchor Múzquiz sent a communication to the congress saying that "he had been given permission [by Bustamante] to take charge of this state." [76] The assembly met

75. Introd. to *El Observador,* 2d ser., *1* (Mar. 3, 1830), in *Obras,* p. 619. The general enthusiasm that greeted Bustamante was reminiscent of 1821.

76. *Actas, 10,* 48. For the events of 1830 involving Mora, see Florstedt, "Mora y la génesis del liberalismo burgues," *Historia mexicana, 11* (1961), 207–23.

from March 8 to August 14, 1830, convoked a new congress, and tried vainly to deal with the state's desperate financial plight.

Thus, we can find in Mora's writing of 1830 a continuing emphasis on constitutionalism. The following year he published *Catecismo político de la federación mexicana,* a simplified presentation in question and answer form of Mexico's constitutional system. "Sovereignty of the people" and the doctrine of the "general will" came under particular attack. A "competent authority," as established by the constitution, is quite distinct from the general will, he asserted.[77] Numerous quotations and maxims from Constant continued to fill the pages of *El Observador.* There were articles on freedom of the press and on the independent judiciary. This search for constitutional order led to Mora's effort, as we have seen, to institute nationwide property qualifications for citizenship. *El Observador* argued for rule by a "true aristocracy."

Mora also began to recognize, however, a dichotomy between this constitutional order and the state of society. In his "Philosophical Essay on Our Constitutional Revolution" he lamented the fact that none of the new republics of America "has been able to establish a solid government." What is the origin of this instability?

> The reply is too easy: these [new republics] have not adopted of the representative system anything but its forms and its exterior apparatus. They have tried to unite intimately the despotic and miserable laws and customs of the old absolutism with the principles of a system in which all must be liberty and openness.[78]

Mora now openly criticized the national legislators of 1824 for following the Constitution of 1812 too closely. This disenchantment with the Spanish code reflected Mora's conservatism of 1830, in turn closely related to the social assumptions of constitutional liberalism. He went on, however, to question all efforts to achieve public felicity by imposing theoretical political forms, "one of the follies of our time." [79] His faith in the miraculous effects of good

77. [Mora], *Catecismo político de la federación mexicana* (Mexico, 1831), p. 16. See also Mora, *Obras,* pp. 701–04; *El Observador,* 2d ser., *3, 313.*

78. Mora, *Obras,* p. 623.

79. Ibid., pp. 694, 724, 734–35 ("De la Eficacia que se atribuye a las formas de gobierno").

laws had vanished. He was disturbed by the deluge of petty concerns which slowed the legislative process. The work of the reconvened state congress involved a particularly heavy dose of trivia in the midst of a financial crisis.[80] Mora was even beginning to question the efficacy of deliberate lawmaking.

Cognizant of the divergence between society and liberal political forms, Mora turned to another theme—revolution. We have said that he was no revolutionary, that he had seen revolution as the abridgment of individual liberty in the name of a perverted popular sovereignty. Early in 1830 Mora attempted to classify different types of revolution and to penetrate the psychology of revolutionary change. His context was the bewildering popular agitation of 1827–29 and the coming of Guerrero to the presidency. Mora distinguished between revolutions like 1688 and 1776, which were directed toward fixed and limited objectives and had felicitous results, and others that involved a vast social restlessness. In the latter, "everyone wants to change his situation." [81] These are "the critical epochs of the human spirit," of which the French Revolution is the best example. Mora was still hostile toward the product of these revolutions—"this class of men, jealous of and inflamed against all distinctions of superiority . . . filled with Rousseau whom they understand poorly." Yet these 1830 passages indicated a new social awareness on Mora's part, the realization that there were contending forces in the society of his day.

A few months later Mora's new interest in revolution had turned to more open sympathy. Condemning as he so often had the extravagancies of the French revolutionaries and of their imitators in Spain, Mora admitted "that those follies were in part provoked or caused by the obstinacy and by the stratagems, which preserved insufferable abuses and which rejected reforms deemed necessary at the time." [82] He was now speaking of the "revolu-

80. See quote in Florstedt, "Mora y la génesis," p. 219. There was discussion on one proposal that, because he was incapacitated, the governor should be allowed to use a half signature on documents, except for communications to the state and national congresses (*Actas, 10,* 104–06, May 21, 1830).

81. Mora, *Obras,* p. 647. Zavala had similar concerns; see *Ensayo,* 2, 23.

82. Mora, *Obras,* "Sobre Cambios de constitución" (June 2, 1830), p. 738. See also *El Observador,* 2d ser., *3,* 385 (Oct. 20, 1830).

tions of the time" which must be valued in order to avoid the
"revolutions of men." What was needed was enlightened and firm
leaders, enlightened to appreciate the need for change, firm to
prevent rule by political factions. No longer could Mexicans rely
on political forms to assure social felicity. Society itself was out of
joint. Mora's emphasis had shifted to the "insufferable abuses" and
the "miserable laws and customs of the old absolutism." Were they
not the true source of Mexico's problems?

Mora had looked to Anastasio Bustamante as a political leader
who might restore the constitutional system and return society to
even keel. By the end of 1830, however, his enthusiasm for the
president had cooled. El Observador closed down on October 27,
1830, though Mora disclaimed any government coercion.[83]
Within a few months the Bustamante regime had displayed its
true principles, ones quite different from Mora's. For him the
failure of Bustamante was the final blow to his already shaky constitutional liberalism. Plagued by the same ambivalence toward
revolution that Constant had experienced in France, disillusioned
by years of political anarchy, Mora was coming to the conclusion
that liberal progress in Mexico must be achieved by other means.
Mora's crisis was his country's also, for the year 1830 marked a
turning point in Mexican political liberalism.

83. The still obscure question of Mora's break with Bustamante is discussed by
Florstedt in "Mora contra Bustamante," *Historia mexicana, 12* (1962), 26–52.

4

Mora and the Attack on Corporate Privilege

On April 9, 1824, José María Luis Mora and several of his fellow deputies introduced a proposal in the Mexico state congress, recently convened in the former Palace of the Inquisition:

> Being unable to comprehend the words of the deputies because of the din from the bells of Santo Domingo, we petition that the governor be instructed to reach an agreement with the prelate to suspend chimes during the hours of session.

The proposal was duly sent to committee whence it emerged for discussion on July 3. The result, which carried an insertion that the agreement be made "confidentially," was judged by deputy Nájera to be "very moderate and not commanding in tone, so that the prior of Santo Domingo will have no reason to be resentful." By July 12, the governor had succeeded in his negotiations, for the prelate agreed to silence the bells of the monastery from ten to one on the days of session. Feeling it wise to assure remaining on good terms with its close neighbor, the deputies resolved a few days later that their request did not include prayer bells at twelve nor their use in the coming festival of the patron saint.[1] The congress might well have felt the need for caution in framing its request, intruding as a fragile secular entity into the ancient corporate compound of the Dominican Order. The moderation of 1824 was soon to change, however, as Mora and his colleagues came to realize what the episode of the bells signified.

The change in Mora's thought that set in after 1830 was closely tied to political events. By the end of that year the Bustamante

---

1. After much discussion, the latter resolution omitted the words "moderate and necessary" preceding "use." For this episode see *Actas, 1,* 143; *2,* 17–18, 59, 155. In the reform law of Dec. 4, 1860 (art. 18), the use of church bells was finally made subject to civil ordinance.

regime had already stirred up opposition in the provinces because of its relentless campaign against Vicente Guerrero and Juan Álvarez in the South and because of the arbitrary changes it imposed on the state governments. Guerrero's capture and summary execution in February 1831 came as a shock, even to many who had opposed him as president in 1829. Evidence of Mora's political activities at this time is slim, though he later admitted to association with José Antonio Facio, Bustamante's war minister. He even said in 1832 that he was offered a cabinet post by Bustamante but that "nothing in the world would persuade me to accept it." [2] January 1832 saw the beginning of a series of provincial pronunciamientos against the central government, and by midyear the provinces were in full-scale rebellion.

Mora recalled that during late 1831 and 1832 he met frequently with José María Cabrera, an old collaborator on *El Observador,* and with Miguel Santa María, a diplomat, to discuss the political drift of the country. These three men as moderates tried vainly to persuade Bustamante to discard his unpopular ministers, particularly the proclerical Lucas Alamán and José Ignacio Espinosa Vidaurre. Mora then joined the growing provincial opposition and actively promoted the candidacy of Manuel Mier y Terán, one of Bustamante's military commanders and a man of learning and intelligence. Mora carried on a considerable correspondence with Terán during 1832. Perhaps he hoped to become the guiding force in a Terán regime, as Alamán had been under Bustamante. His hopes were dashed when Terán committed suicide on August 3, 1832, making Antonio López de Santa Anna de facto leader of the opposition.

Prior to this turn of events, Mora had also become associated with the regime of Francisco García in Zacatecas, which included Valentín Gómez Farías, senator from the state. In the face of increasing clericalism in Mexico City, Gómez Farías persuaded the Zacatecas congress to offer a prize for the best essay to be written on church and state in relation to property. He then urged Mora

2. Letter to Manuel Mier y Terán, June 29, 1832 in Mora, *Obras,* pp. 41–42 n. According to Mora, Facio opposed the proclericalism of the regime. The American minister, Anthony Butler, referred to Mora as "the Talleyrand of Mexico" because of his changing political affiliations during this period (Florstedt, "Liberal Role," p. 380).

to submit an essay, which the latter did in December 1831.[3] This important writing will engage our attention shortly.

Defeated militarily in the provinces, Bustamante resigned in September 1832, leaving a caretaker government under Melchor Múzquiz. Múzquiz in turn gave way to Manuel Gómez Pedraza. The latter was designated by the victorious provincial and military alliance to fill out his "constitutional" term, which supposedly had been interrupted when his 1828 opponent, Vicente Guerrero, usurped power. On April 1, 1833, a fragile coalition of civilian reformers under Vice-President Valentín Gómez Farías and military dissidents under President Santa Anna took office. Mora turned to journalism, and his new effort, *El Indicador de la federación mejicana,* welcomed Santa Anna as "regenerator and liberator": "Fame proclaims you father of your country . . . beside the illustrious Washington, the valiant model of virtue and patriotism." [4] Mora was appointed to the General Board of Public Instruction which served as an inner council for Vice-President Gómez Farías, the virtual chief executive during the next year. Santa Anna at first supported the reform legislation of the Gómez Farías regime, but by 1834 he turned to the military and clerical dissidents. The civil-military coalition fell apart, and the reformers were thrown out of power in May 1834.

Two years later in Paris, Mora reflected upon these events and concluded that Valentín Gómez Farías, whom he so much admired in other ways, had missed a chance to execute the reform program. At a critical moment he could easily have mustered the force necessary to arrest Santa Anna and decimate the opposition; but "he lacked the will, and in this he committed the greatest of all errors." When a "social change" has been undertaken, Mora continued, it must be carried through despite opposition. Gómez Farías was governed by "an excessive respect for constitutional forms," and thus refused to act forcefully in the time of crisis. Mora claimed that he had strongly urged those in command to use

3. C. Alan Hutchinson, "Valentín Gómez Farías: a Biographical Study" (Ph.D. dissertation, University of Texas, 1948), p. 127. For the events of the period, see Bancroft, *History of Mexico, 5,* 88–124; Florstedt, "Mora contra Bustamante"; Mora, *Obras,* pp. 30–46.

4. From a poem in *El Indicador, 1,* 124–26 (Oct. 30, 1833). See also ibid., pp. 183–84 (Nov. 13, 1833); p. 234 (Nov. 20, 1833).

the only means left open to them when faced by rebellion in 1834, "a dictatorial act of the legislature, of the president, or of both powers at once." A coup d'etat was needed. What had happened to the Mora of the 1820s, the doctrinaire adherent of constitutionalism? In the face of new political realities, he had apparently abandoned his constitutional liberalism. Mora now even began to reconsider a formerly taboo question: "Is it possible and rational to recognize an unlimited power in society?"[5]

How can we explain Mora's dramatic shift of orientation? It is apparent that Mora now saw the achievement of liberal goals in new terms. The problem was no longer to guarantee individual liberty by constitutional limitation upon arbitrary power, but rather to reform Mexican society so that individualism could have some meaning. Mora had begun to perceive the new problem in *El Observador* in 1830; by 1833 he saw it clearly:

> The position [of the 1833 regime] was difficult and had to culminate necessarily in one of two things: the ruin of the federation by the privileged classes; or the destruction of the privileged classes by the triumphant forces of the federation. In either case the constitution had to fall.[6]

Mora distinguished, however, between "unlimited power and power that departs from normal rules." He had no sympathy for the notorious *ley del caso* of June 23, 1833, by which some fifty supporters of the Bustamante regime were exiled from the country along with any others, according to the law, "found to be in the same category *(en el mismo caso)* ." This was for Mora a mere act of political vengeance, put through by the military wing of the 1833 coalition. Moreover, it included a number of Spaniards to whom Mora had been partial, and several friends such as Miguel Santa María, Joaquín Villa, Francisco Molinos del Campo, and José María Gutiérrez de Estrada. In fact, political allegiances were so fluid between 1829 and 1833 that Mora himself might well

5. Mora reprinted his "Reflecciones sobre facultades extraordinarias" (*El Indicador, 1,* 171–81, Nov. 13, 1833) in his later "Revista política" (pp. 133–48) of his 1837 *Obras.* For Mora's critique of Gómez Farías see *Obras,* pp. 52–53, 73, 153–54. Felipe Tena Ramírez discusses this question in *Derecho,* p. 203, comparing Alamán and Mora in their advocacy of extraordinary power.

6. Mora, *Obras,* p. 72.

have been included as a former supporter of the Bustamante regime.[7] Beyond mere political vengeance, Mora was advocating force against entrenched power in society, which he identified as the "privileged classes."

Until 1830, José María Luis Mora centered his efforts on the forging of a constitutional system and thus on the importance of a formal written constitution in guaranteeing individual liberty and social progress. We have seen that by 1833 his constitutionalist assumptions had been largely put aside. He continued to be interested in the constitution, but his approach to it was changing. In 1830 Mora started writing a survey of Mexico, frankly modeled on Alexander von Humboldt's *Political Essay on the Kingdom of New Spain* (1811), but updated for contemporary European readers.[8] In it he discussed at length the Constitution of 1824, including in addition to a legalistic description of its elements, an assessment of its strengths and weaknesses. "We must not delude ourselves," he wrote; "the Mexican constitution is full of imperfections." The essay was transitional. While maintaining a faith in the constitutional system reminiscent of his earlier writings, a new spirit of realistic analysis had entered.[9]

Most of the defects Mora noted in the Constitution of 1824 reflected his continuing constitutionalist concerns. For instance, he had argued for jury trial by property holders in *El Observador;* that proposal for reform was now repeated. Similarly, Mora again urged a property qualification for citizenship. He even advocated checks on the unlimited authority of the legislature. At the head of the list, however, were two new concerns. One was the reform of article 3, which provided for intolerance and for official protection of the Roman Catholic Church. The other was the suppression of article 154, which perpetuated clerical and military juridical privileges. Mora was ambivalent on the question of intolerance, a mat-

---

7. See ibid., pp. 146–47. The text of the law can be found in Riva Palacio, *México, 4,* 328. Many of those proscribed managed to remain in the country, including Gutiérrez de Estrada.

8. Mora, "Estado actual de Méjico," first published in *El Indicador, 1,* 73–123 (Oct. 23, 30, 1833); 2, 3–88 (Dec. 4, 1833). Mora noted at one point that it was "written in 1830," but the essay was obviously revised to include data through 1833–34. It was reprinted in *Revoluciones,* Vol. 1.

9. Ibid., 314–16.

ter that warrants special treatment later. The objection to article 154 was the heart of his new approach to the constitution. Moreover, it is interesting that by 1837, when he summed up the reform program of the Gómez Farías government, only two of the eight "principles" were of constitutionalist orientation—increased freedom of the press and the abolition of capital punishment for political crimes.[10] The presence of article 154 symbolized for Mora the gulf between Mexican social reality and a liberal and republican juridical order. It was now *society* that increasingly drew Mora's attention.

The realization among liberals that Mexican society was at variance with the new constitutional forms did not appear suddenly in 1830. It had been a subordinate theme throughout the 1820s. Not infrequently would a writer in *El Sol* or the *Águila,* or a speaker in one of the congresses, denounce specific vestiges of the colonial regime such as the tobacco monopoly, a blazon of the Inquisition still visible in the Church of Santo Domingo, the use of the term "audiencia" for the new supreme court, or the continuing colonial sales tax *(alcabala)*. What changed in 1830 was the assumption about how liberal progress could be achieved. It was the society exemplified by these vestiges of the past that must now be reformed. Our customs and habits are at variance with our liberal theories of government, wrote Lorenzo de Zavala in 1831. In this new mood, José María Luis Mora noted that although the term "republic" had replaced "empire" in 1823 as the official designation, "as long as the same institutions were maintained, both terms were inadequate to connote a society that was really nothing but the Viceroyalty of New Spain with some vague desires of becoming something else." [11] "Institution" now clearly had a new, social meaning for Mora that it had not had in the twenties.

Mora's new analysis found its classic expression in his identification of the "corporate spirit" *(espíritu de cuerpo)*. It was the corporate spirit that characterized the "ancient constitution of the

10. See Mora, *Obras,* pp. 53–54. Detailed discussion to follow. The 1830–33 enumeration of constitutional defects can be found in his *Revoluciones, 1,* 318 ff.

11. Zavala, *Ensayo, 1,* 23; Mora, *Obras,* p. 5. *Reformador* (Toluca), Nov. 20, 1833, welcomed the new realistic "spirit of analysis and discussion," as opposed to the "glitter of a false glory" of 1824.

country" and that the 1833 reformers found impossible to accommodate. They had to choose, Mora said, between the "federal representative system established by the constitution and the old regime based on the espíritu de cuerpo." Within the old regime there could be no "national spirit" because men identified with smaller corporate units rather than with the nation. If independence had come forty years earlier, a native would not have understood the term "Mexican." Far more vital would have been his designation within his corporate group. Speaking to him of "national interests would have been speaking to him in Hebrew." In a representative system he would have claimed to represent his cuerpo, not the nation. How much of this has really changed today? reflected Mora.[12]

He admitted that of the multitude of privileged bodies that existed in colonial Mexico, the only ones still maintaining juridical privileges were the church and the army. The Bourbons had begun to limit special privilege; the Constitution of 1812 carried the process further, affecting the Inquisition, the mint, the guilds, the Indian communities, and the university. Besides the two powerful privileged orders, however, there still remain the remnants of these other bodies. They exercise a kind of tyranny over their members, which inhibits personal independence and the development of a community of citizens enjoying equal rights and responsibilities. The espíritu de cuerpo imposed not only juridical and administrative barriers to unity and progress but grave economic obstacles as well. Mora was aware of the problem of corporate power during the 1820s. But as a state legislator he advised the assembly to "pass around these fueros and immunities as a necessary evil that is beyond [the assembly's] efforts to remedy." [13] Mora, like those who drew up the constitutions of 1812 and 1824, saw juridical privilege as a subsidiary liberal problem. By the early 1830s, however, he had concluded that most of the country's evils originated in the privileged orders which must be abolished.

12. See Mora, *Obras*, pp. 56–61.
13. See *Actas*, 5, 401, 412 (Oct. 6, 7, 1825). The matter under discussion pertained to judicial procedure for privileged persons (*aforadas*). See also *Actas*, 1, 66 (Mar. 18, 1824).

Mora's new orientation was accompanied by a fresh interpretation of the political process since independence. Inherent in events was a growing conflict between "progress" and "reaction" (*retroceso*). In his "Revista política" (1837), Mora defined the "political course of progress" as essentially the reform program of the Gómez Farías regime. The "course of reaction" was any attempt to deny these reforms. Anticlericalism formed the base of this reform program: the disentailment of church property; the abolition of the fueros (including those of the army) ; the curtailment of monasteries; and the advance of secular public education. Other elements of progress were the establishment of jury trial, freedom of opinion, and equal civil rights for foreigners.[14]

In Mora's view, conflict between the two parties had been muted by President Guadalupe Victoria's "irrational effort [after 1824] to amalgamate refractory elements." During the mid-twenties progress was represented by the state governments, reaction by the clergy and the military, with the central government a moderating neutral power. Moreover, political confusion was enhanced by the entry of the extraconstitutional Masonic factions, which were always more concerned, said Mora, with "persons than with things." After 1827 the escoceses supported the clergy and the yorkinos supported the army. Neither the men of progress nor the men of reaction yet had a fixed program. The cleavage developed in the critical year 1829: "The elements of the [Masonic] parties, which for two years had upset the country, ultimately dissolved to take on new forms . . . and to again introduce social questions under the guise of retrogression and progress." [15]

In Mora's new view of recent history, the Bustamante regime represented the ascendancy of the clergy and the military and the suppression of the states. The basic principle of this "Alamán administration" was to support the social status quo. Mora forgot that he never really had opposed the regime in the 1830 *El Observador* or in the state congress, as he was claiming in 1837 to have done as a consistent partisan of the "party of progress." History was bound to fall into a neater pattern now, in light of the

14. Mora, *Obras,* p. 4. Cf. n. 10, above.
15. "Examen crítico de la administración establecida en consecuencia del plan de Jalapa," *El Indicador, 1,* 3–4 (Oct. 9, 1833) ; Mora, *Obras,* p. 11.

conflicts of 1833–34. The men of progress came to power at last in April 1833, "the first time in the history of the republic that there had been a serious effort to tear out its evils by the roots . . . and to establish the bases of public prosperity in a solid and enduring manner." The principles of the Gómez Farías regime were the "general and irresistible tendencies of the civilized world." [16] Mexico for the first time was being brought abreast of the universal march of progress.

Mora's interpretation of the events of the previous decade was cast in the unmistakable terms of ideological conflict. He had identified what he saw as a deep and irreconcilable social struggle in Mexico between the privileged orders and liberal principles. In the 1820s, the antagonist had been an abstraction, arbitrary power, which was difficult to identify in terms of current politics. Now the enemy was the concrete old regime of corporate privilege, defended by the previous administration. In the 1830 *El Observador,* Mora had begun to reconsider "revolution," dismissed previously as only a source of arbitrary power. He now began to assert the need for revolution to root out the cuerpos. He even made reference to the contemporary French Revolution of 1830 and compared the Bustamante regime to that of Charles X.[17] Gómez Farías headed a revolutionary government, dedicated to reforming the corporate society in favor of individual liberty.

Yet because the party of progress failed in 1834, Mora was forced to conclude that the conflict between the two conceptions of society had reached an impasse. The old order persists, he wrote. The new order has not been established

> because the means have not yet been found either to combine the [liberal doctrines] with the existing remains of the old system, or to do away with those remains. In short, it is impossible to go backward or forward except with great difficulty.[18]

The change in Mora's thought from constitutionalism to a new ideology of institutional reform leads us to review a few points

---

16. Mora, *Obras,* p. 51; *El Indicador, 3,* 410 (Apr. 30, 1834).

17. See *El Indicador, 1,* 19 (Oct. 9, 1833).

18. Mora, *Revoluciones, 1,* 554 (the concluding passage of the volume). An analogous observation can be found in Zavala, *Ensayo, 2,* 136–37.

concerning the structure of political liberalism. Of special relevance was Mexico's peculiar institutional pattern, in which a variant of feudal society grew up within a patriarchal state. The strong medieval imprint in New Spain came not from feudal limitation on sovereign power through "representative" institutions, but rather from compartmented privilege and multiple jurisdictions under the paternal authority of the Crown. Mariano Otero referred to New Spain as a true "despotism," noting particularly the lack of political power in the Mexican aristocracy (see above, page 46). Lorenzo de Zavala also sensed this characteristic when he saw Mexico as "an image of feudal Europe without the spirit of independence and the energetic valor of that era." Mora, though he often betrayed aristocratic leanings in his writing, could find little to admire in the colonial nobility. It was a degenerate group, lacking a tradition of "heroic and brilliant actions," the base of true nobility. The Mexican nobles, he said, were primarily descendants of rich Spanish merchants who purchased titles from the Crown and established patrimonies. It was an "invertebrate society," thought of organically, but held together only by the power of the Crown.[19]

Mora believed that the 1833 liberals were faced with eliminating an oligarchy, "the inevitable regime of an ignorant people in which there neither is nor can be a monarch." Mora distinguished between an oligarchy of *families* and one of *classes*. The Revolution for Independence ruined the oligarchy of families, or nobility; on the other hand, it strengthened the oligarchy of classes, by which he meant the corporate groups of church and army. Since "the people" as such had never been strong under the Spanish regime, the new oligarchy triumphed. This was Mora's way of saying that the removal of the monarchy in a society without feudal political institutions, and one in which the nobility was completely dependent on royal favor, left the balance of power in favor of the corporate entities. This pattern of change is analogous to what Morse identifies in broader terms as the reemergence of

19. Zavala, *Ensayo, 1,* 18; Mora, *Revoluciones, 1,* 93; McAlister "Social Structure," p. 364. Mora's description of Mexican customs (*Revoluciones, 1,* 132–59) for European readers seemed designed to show that all the amenities of aristocratic society existed in the country.

"telluric creole social structures" which "again [after indepen-
dence] seized the stage." [20]

Mora asserted that the men of 1833 were fighting to maintain
the Constitution of 1824 against the corporate spirit fostered by
"the ancient constitution of the country." But Mora's *antigua
constitución* could never have become the bridge to modern constitutionalism, as it was for Jovellanos in Spain or even as it was in
France for Benjamin Constant. Mora intimated that the cuerpos
in Mexico thought of themselves historically as "representing" the
nation, but without a cortes representation was obviously a fic-
tion.[21] We are faced again with the dichotomy between "privilege" and "liberty," always sharper in Mexico than even in Spain
or in France (see above, page 45). Mora's cuerpos were hardly
the functional "constituted bodies" of the French old regime.
They were only the residual holders of juridical and economic
privilege in a patriarchal state which had lost its head. Thus constitutionalism, or the limitation of sovereign power in the name of
liberties, could not find strength in a historic national tradition.

The Mexican liberals never used the word "feudalism" when
referring to the regime of clerical and military privilege. Nor did
they, except in one instance, apply the term to the remnants of the
colonial nobility. The nobility was weak and never formed an
estate with representative functions. This of course was a Spanish
pattern merely accentuated in the New World. The strength that
the noble estate had in Spain was derived from the institution
of the *mayorazgo,* the right to entail property by primogeniture.
The mayorazgo served as compensation for a nobility which, in
an imperfectly feudalized state, had lost its juridiction in public
law.[22] Entailment by laymen spread to New Spain, but like the
nobility itself, it was weaker than in the mother country. The

20. Mora, *Obras,* p. 110 and Morse, "Heritage," p. 162.

21. Mora, *Obras,* pp. 56–57. Bishop Abad y Queipo (see below) defended clerical
immunities in 1799 as inherent in the *antigua constitución,* originating in the
fuero juzgo. Thus, immunities were granted to the clergy as a functional order in
exchange for services to society. Abad even cited Montesquieu for support against
what he saw as despotic attacks on the ancient constitution. Abad did not try,
however, to tie the immunities of the Mexican clergy to representation. See
"Representación sobre la inmunidad personal del clero," in Mora, *Obras,* pp.
178–80, 192–94, 204.

22. Artola, *Orígenes, 1,* 62.

mayorazgo was attacked vigorously by Jovellanos in his "Informe de ley agraria" of 1795. For him the institution was repugnant to the dictates of reason and nature. In 1820 the Spanish cortes suppressed all entails of property, including those of the church. The law was restated in Mexico on August 7, 1823, with the important exception of ecclesiastical entails. The fact that the mayorazgos were so easily suppressed in Mexico further attests to the weakness of the nobility.[23]

The liberals did use the term "feudal," however, to apply to the property of the Duke of Terranova y Monteleone, the Sicilian heir to Hernán Cortés. This vast patrimony with its secular jurisdiction over numerous people and communities was the result of a unique feudal grant (the Marquesado del Valle) to the conquistador in 1529. The Crown had thereafter eaten away at the jurisdictional rights, but a large domain with residual prerogatives still existed in 1821. This feudal remnant came under intermittent liberal attack from 1824 to 1833. Interestingly enough, the issue appeared very little before the Mexico state constituent congress, though most of the duke's domain lay within its jurisdiction. On at least one important occasion, however, Mora struck at the problem. In dicussing the law for town properties and revenues (*propios y arbitrios*), it became evident that Monteleone was disputing with the ayuntamientos of Cuernavaca and Toluca the right to collect fees from vendors using town plazas. Allowing such a perquisite, said Mora, is allowing feudalism, which is not recognized by "the system we have adopted." Monteleone might justly claim the right to hold individual properties, though even this is questionable because he is a foreigner. But seigneurial claims to rights over public property are intolerable.[24]

The issue was not pursued in the state congress, but it was raised by the social critic, José Joaquín Fernández de Lizardi, and again in the national congress in 1828. A Yucatecan delegate, José Matías Quintana, who introduced a proposal to nationalize Monteleone's property, asserted:

23. See law of Sept. 27, 1820, in Dublán and Lozano, *1*, 528–31; the Mexican law in ibid., pp. 662–64. *El Sol* carried the debates on the law beginning in the July 16, 1823, issue. Curiously, Father Mier was against the abolition of the mayorazgos.

24. *Actas, 3*, 185–89 (Dec. 9, 1824).

I understand that even now since independence there are cities, towns, and villages which still pay the feudal tribute to this conquistador. How can we reconcile the ideas of sovereign and feudal? If sovereignty rests in the nation, how can the nation pay tribute to a foreign lord? [25]

Lucas Alamán, as the duke's agent, defended the patrimony successfully for the moment (see above, page 18), but it became a prime target for the 1833 reformers. The result was expropriation of the Hospital de Jesús Nazareno and the other urban real estate belonging to Monteleone, to be used for public education.[26] The suppression of the mayorazgos, followed by the nationalization of Monteleone's property, was the closest Mexican approach to the French "abolition of feudalism" on August 4, 1789.

The shift of orientation in Mora's political thought was accompanied by a new assessment of Mexico's Spanish heritage. Mora was neither an apologist for the colonial regime nor an Hispanophobe. Though his attack on the corporate spirit was a condemnation of the Spanish colony, he freely admitted that "the base of Mexican character is completely Spanish." This sentiment was most manifest in his historical essay on the Conquest. In the style of Alamán and Prescott, his history was principally a biography of the conquistador, whom he portrayed as a political genius, a master of psychology, and a statesman of the first rank. While condemning the barbarous acts of the Conquest, such as the Cholula massacre, the lopping off of hands of fifty Tlascalan spies, or the torture of Cuauhtemoc, he refused to accept the popular "hatred against everything that is Spanish." Mora, like Alamán, saw the Conquest as the origin of the Mexican nation, and he concluded his essay by stating unequivocally: "The name of Mexico is so intimately tied to the memory of Cortés that the latter can never perish so long as the country exists." [27] It appears that Mora

25. In Alamán, "Esposición" (1828), *Documentos, 3,* 465–66. Also Fernández de Lizardi, *Baratas del pensador para los cuchareros y la nación* (Mexico, 1824), p. 4, and *Conversaciones del payo y el sacristán* (Mexico, 1824–25), *2,* Nos. 14–15.

26. Law of Oct. 26, 1833, in Dublán and Lozano, *2,* 574. For liberal attacks on Monteleone's property, see *El Telégrafo,* July 15, 1833; *El Fénix,* July 11, 1833 (reporting speeches in the congress); *Reformador,* Apr. 4, 1833; *El Indicador, 1,* 64 (Oct. 23, 1833).

27. Mora, *Revoluciones, 3,* 1–190. See also Victor Rico González, *Hacia un Concepto de la conquista de México* (Mexico, Inst. de Historia, 1953).

attributed most of the defects of the colonial regime to the Hapsburg period which he generally ignored in his historical writings.
After 1550, wrote Mora, Spain fell back on pride, ignorance, and
superstition; and under the aegis of the church, a "theocratic
dominion" was instituted.[28]

It was the reign of Charles III that marked for Mora the point
"when Spain and her colonies began to emerge from a state of
barbarism." After 1760 "the philosophic spirit" entered Spain,
and the Crown asserted the *regalía* (royal rights over the church)
and undertook commercial reforms.[29] Though Mora admitted the
significance of the educational work of the Jesuits, he believed the
expulsion of the order in 1767 to have been necessary. Charles III
merely acted against "the evils that are always brought to society
by a body which like the Company has taken over so much
power." It was under the "wise administration" of Charles III that
"Mexico embarked upon the high road to useful knowledge," and
that the "Mexican Enlightenment" began.[30]

After 1830 Mora found an affinity with the Spanish reform
spirit that commenced in the mid-eighteenth century. Though he
always emphasized the inevitability and necessity of Mexican independence from Spain (see above, Chapter 1), and though he
found the colonial heritage a burden to Mexican progress, he instinctively realized the permanence of the Hispanic bond. Just as
his constitutionalism was framed within the context of the Cortes
of Cádiz, so his drive to reform the corporate and "theocratic" society of Mexico found inspiration in the policies of the Bourbon
monarchs.

It would seem, therefore, entirely natural that José María Luis
Mora, as editor of *El Indicador,* should reprint six essays and dis-
courses of Gaspar Melchor de Jovellanos, written in Spain in the
1780s. Most of them dealt with the reform of education along scientific and utilitarian lines and relate best to the discussion in
Chapter 5. One of the essays, however, was the appeal by Jovel-

28. Mora, *Revoluciones, 3,* 231.

29. Ibid., *1,* 110–11, 222–23, 228–29.

30. Ibid., pp. 84–85. On the Jesuits see ibid., *3,* 259–71. Mora had great respect
for Charles III's minister Aranda, "that profound statesman," and reprinted the
text of his 1783 proposal to establish independent monarchies in America (ibid.,
pp. 275–83).

lanos (see page 64 above) to seek out Spain's historic constitution. Why Mora should reprint this particular writing at a time when he was defending the abridgment of constitutional forms to meet the threat of rebellion is at first puzzling. On further consideration, however, it reveals the particular relevance of Jovellanos to understanding Mora's liberalism.

Jovellanos, as we have seen, was caught between an attachment to Bourbon enlightened despotism and the search for liberty in a historic constitution. In this essay Jovellanos described the weakness of the cortes in Castile and its domination by the privileged orders, until Alfonso X was able in the Siete Partidas (1256–65) to "reduce legislation to a uniform system" and "form the idea of a general code." The cortes became thereafter the upholder of authority against feudal pretention and the bastion of popular liberty. Thus Spain entered her golden age, culminating in the reign of Ferdinand and Isabella, when royal authority reached "a degree of vigor which it never before had." [31] At that point the essay ended, leaving without comment the progress of royal absolutism in the seventeenth and eighteenth centuries and the consequent withering of the cortes.

Mora showed particular interest in "sovereignty," for an editor's note (presumably by him) referred the reader to Jovellanos' elaboration of the question in the 1811 "Memoria" in defense of the Junta Central. There Jovellanos had struggled with the inherent contradiction between sovereignty as being lodged historically in the monarch, and the limitations on sovereignty posed by a representative cortes. Moreover, Jovellanos was writing as a member of a revolutionary junta which had assumed de facto popular sovereignty (see above, page 65).[32] It can be inferred that Mora saw the 1809 predicament of Jovellanos as one not unlike his own in 1834; the pressures for unified sovereignty were overwhelming his constitutional liberalism. Mora, like Jovellanos, was no advocate of popular sovereignty. Both had explicitly attacked Rousseau's doctrine and its use by the revolutionaries in France.

31. Jovellanos, "Discurso," El Indicador, 3, 374–75 (Apr. 23, 1834).

32. The editor's reference is specifically to Appendix XII and n. 1 of Jovellanos' "Memoria," where the key passages are located: BAE, 46, 597–600, 619–21. Bernardo Couto ("Mora," p. 888) said Mora was "sole editor" of El Indicador.

Yet both men found themselves in situations where democratic doctrine was the logical corollary to their revolutionary stance.

The assault upon corporate privilege brought the question of democracy to the surface. *El Fénix de la libertad* emphasized the contradiction between fueros and "civil equality which is the inseparable companion of liberty." How can we have "absolute equality," the mark of a republic, along with "distinctions and privileges?" asked *La Oposición*. It is absurd to "sanction fueros and privileges in a popular government," wrote Lorenzo de Zavala. Because the revolutionary attack upon corporate privilege was necessarily carried out in the name of equality before the law, and because Mexico was no longer a monarchy, it was logical that assumptions about "democracy" should emerge. The question, of course, is how deep the assumptions went. Can we say, as does Jesús Reyes Heroles, that the struggle against the fueros brought together the "enlightened" and the "democratic" liberals, and that the "internal logic of the liberal movement had to carry it toward equality," assuring by the time of the Reforma the triumph of democratic liberalism?[33] It is a question that will concern us frequently in subsequent pages.

The case of Zavala, one of the "democratic liberals" by Reyes Heroles' categorization, is interesting. Unlike Mora, Zavala apparently saw no precedents for reform in the Hispanic past. He judged everything before 1808 darkness: "The entire colonial system was founded at the beginning on terror and ignorance." Far more than Mora, Zavala was the Jacobin revolutionary who condemned the old regime in its totality. Commenting on the abortive Spanish invasion of 1829, Zavala asserted that "a confused memory of the iniquities of the Spaniards, of their riches, of their monopolies, is all that will pass on to posterity."[34] The more outspoken "democratic" journals expressed a similar Hispanophobia.

Still, there is evidence that Zavala came to be disillusioned by democracy, in the sense of active participation by the mass of the

33. Reyes Heroles, *Liberalismo*, 2, xviii–xx, 194, 275, 279. For a sampling of democratic expression, see *El Fénix*, Mar. 31, 1832; *La Oposición*, Nov. 24, 1834, June 15, 1835; *Reformador*, Apr. 2, Oct. 27, 1833; Zavala, *Ensayo*, *1*, 24, 215; also *Juicio imparcial sobre los acontecimientos de México en 1828 y 1829* (Mexico, 1830), p. 30.

34. Zavala, *Ensayo*, *1*, 406; 2, 191.

people in the political process. We have seen that he urged property qualifications for voting, following his experience in the popular upheaval under Vicente Guerrero. As governor of the State of Mexico in 1833, he broached the question of democracy directly: "It is derived from natural law; it resides in the popular masses; and it is always present actively or passively in all revolutions." In Mexico the obstacles are such that "in reality there is not nor can there be democracy." How can there be, he asked, when of the 200,000 voting inhabitants of the state, two-thirds cannot read, one-half is naked, one-third knows no Spanish, and three-fifths are the instrument of the party in power? [35]

In other words, democracy meant the active participation of the rural Indian masses, which, for nineteenth-century liberal Creoles, was unthinkable. Significantly, one finds little trace of Jean Jacques Rousseau's influence, even among the most radical of the 1833 reformers. The sociological reality of Mexico made "equality" and "democracy" abstract terms, terms that could mean juridical equality in the face of corporate privilege, but not popular political participation.

Mora, like his more democratic colleagues in 1833, attacked the fueros in the name of "equality before the law" and "the people," but he conceived of an active political democracy even less than did Zavala. Thus he searched for inspiration in the Bourbon reform tradition. Charles III and his ministers such as Jovellanos and Campomanes pursued enlightenment and progress without encouraging the dangerous democracy of the French Revolution or even that of the Cortes of Cádiz. Yet Mora, like Jovellanos, was attuned to change, and his attitude toward revolutionary movements was always ambivalent. In framing a forceful reform program, his constitutional principles had to suffer. Jovellanos struggled with the concept of sovereignty in 1809, trying to reconcile it with Spain's historic constitution. Mora tried to do the same in 1833, though Mexico's constitution was only a decade old.

Despite differences of detail, Mora shared with Jovellanos the dilemma of Hispanic constitutionalism, the dilemma of trying to forge a constitutional system where historic precedents were weak

35. Zavala, *Memoria de la gestión de gobierno del estado de México durante el año de 1833* (Toluca, 1833), pp. 2–4.

or nonexistent, where monarchical attachments were strong, and where the regime of privilege was still intact. It was a dilemma that Benjamin Constant in France did not have to face. The Bourbon precedent was irrelevant to him, because corporate privilege had been decimated by the Revolution. He, as a political liberal, could be more consistent in seeking constitutional guarantees for individual liberty than was possible in Hispanic nations. Thus after 1830 Mora found Constant of less relevance to the problems of Mexico. French liberalism continued to be generally germane to Mora's thought, but in the form of the earlier anticorporate and especially the anticlerical policies of the Revolution. Because of institutional similarities within Hispanic countries which were now increasingly apparent, Mora turned particularly at this stage to the "native" reform tradition of the Bourbons and the Cortes of Cádiz.[36]

The principal target of the reform program of 1833 was the church, the single most powerful institution in society. The church refused to recognize that the new civil government commanded either the force or the respect of the Spanish monarchs. According to Zavala, Rome set the tone by never referring to Mexico as a republic, a government, or a state, but rather as "those regions called Mexican." [37] Mora often looked with nostalgia upon the commanding position the Crown had over the colonial church, in contrast to his day when a legislative assembly had to request, with discretion, that a Dominican prior control bell ringing so the deputies could conduct business. The main political problem the liberals faced was to recover state sovereignty, and their principal antagonist was the church.

The anticlerical attack, which drew so much of its inspiration from the Spanish reform tradition, was always conducted within the limits prescribed by Catholic religious orthodoxy. Mora emphasized that his assault upon "the abuses of superstition" and upon "the ambition and covetousness of the ministers of the altar"

36. Cf. Charles C. Griffin's discussion of Bourbon traces in Argentine, Chilean, and Colombian reform policies of the 1820s. See "The Enlightenment and Latin American Independence," in A. P. Whitaker, ed., Latin America and the Enlightenment (Ithaca, Cornell University Press, 1961), pp. 119–43.
37. Zavala, Ensayo, 2, 231.

did not constitute an attack upon religion. He explicitly disassociated himself from the struggle between the *impíos* and the
fanáticos during the French Revolution. Mexico had inherited
the religiosity of the mother country. Charles III asserted regalian
rights in Spain as a deeply pious prince who commanded the respect of the ecclesiastical hierarchy. This was a point often noted
by Mora. Despite the anticlerical atmosphere of the Cortes of
Cádiz, the Constitution of 1812 established Roman Catholicism as
the official religion, a feature copied in the Apatzingán Constitution of 1814, the Plan of Iguala, the Constitution of 1824, and
even (rather superfluously) in the Mexico State Constitution of
1827. Though religious tolerance came to be advocated, most
anticlericalism developed under the assumption that the state
would remain officially Catholic. As Mora saw it, the reform drive
was constantly plagued by the fact that the people could be easily
led to believe that religious beliefs and clerical pretentions were
one and the same.[38]

The problem of church and state in its most general form centered on the traditional question of patronage (Patronato) —the
right of the Spanish king to nominate or present candidates for
high ecclesiastical posts. It was a question that had caused legal
and political dispute between popes and princes throughout
Christendom since early medieval times. The understanding of
"patronage" was complicated by the fluctuations of actual regal
and papal power, so that there emerged a permanent conflict of
interpretation on exactly what the right consisted of. The "regalists" contended that royal patronage was laical, that its nature
was derived from its possessor, not its source, and that it was inherent in temporal sovereignty. The "canonists," on the other
hand, argued that the Pope, as absolute arbiter over Christendom,
had on occasion granted patronage, but that it was always a re-
vokable concession and not an inherent right of the holder. The
Real Patronato de las Indias was confirmed by three papal bulls
(1493, 1501, and 1508) which bestowed on the Spanish Crown

38. When the Bishop of Puebla became identified as the leader of the clerical
opposition in 1834, *El Indicador* went as far as to say that the present government
had tolerated him far longer than would have Philip II, "the most superstitious
of the Spanish monarchs" (*3*, 275, Apr. 2, 1834).

additional rights such as control over tithes, over the construction of churches, and over the territorial limits of dioceses—all of which went beyond royal patronage powers in the peninsula.[39] With the abdication of the Spanish king in 1808, followed by Mexican independence, the conflict between regalists and canonists emerged again. The Pope and the majority of the Mexican clergy claimed that patronage reverted to the Pope; the government assumed that it continued in the new sovereign authority.

Moreover, the problem of church and state after independence was complicated by the intrusion of the secular concept of sovereignty, in which temporal and spiritual spheres were separate and not united as under the Patronato. As Mariano Otero noted, these two concepts, patronage and separation, "were working at the same time and were directed substantially by the same spirit, and thus their action was often confused." [40] Both theories were advanced in the debates of the national Constituent Congress of 1823–24, but the problem was left tangled. The constitution gave congress powers to "issue instructions on celebrating concordats with the Holy See" and to "regulate the exercise of patronage within the entire federation." [41] The question of patronage, therefore, was not an issue in the Mexico state congress, but Mora led the effort to provide for a measure granting the right of *esclusiva* to the governor, that is—the power to reject any ecclesiastical appointee in the state.[42] The national government was under pressure to obtain an agreement with the papacy on the Patronato question, since after 1827 Mexico had no bishops. Its envoy to Rome, Francisco Vázquez, made little headway until the Bustamante administration abandoned claims to civil presentation, the heart of the Patronato. New bishops were installed, but

39. See J. Lloyd Mecham, *Church and State in Latin America* (Chapel Hill, University of North Carolina Press, 1934), pp. 1–13.

40. Otero, *Ensayo*, p. 58.

41. Reyes Heroles has an excellent account of these debates in *Liberalismo, 1*, 275–318. Besides Spanish regalism, the example of French Gallicanism was much cited in the congress, even the views of Henri Grégoire, the revolutionary bishop.

42. Art. 134, pt. 2 of the Constitution of 1827. Mora's views can be found in *Actas, 1*, 353 (May 26, 1824). Deputy Jáuregui had been a leading advocate of the national assumption of the Patronato in 1822; see his "Voto particular del . . . vocal de la soberana junta e individuo de la comisión eclesiástica, sobre patronato," *La Sabatina universal, 1*, 261–66 (Sept. 28, 1822).

the liberals viewed the action as a triumph for clericalism.[43]

The problem of the church was a subordinate concern for José María Luis Mora during the 1820s. His essays in *El Observador* seldom if ever touched upon church questions, and the problem of church and state only occasionally arose in the debates of the state congress. Nevertheless, the outlines of his later position can be discerned during this period, especially after the appearance of the papal encyclical of September 24, 1824. The Pope urged bishops in America to support the cause of Ferdinand VII, recently restored as absolute monarch in Spain.

The reaction in Mexico to this ill-advised papal move was widespread, partly because it coincided with the threat of Spanish reconquest supported by the Holy Alliance. On the national level Father Mier was particularly outspoken against this papal intrusion into Mexico's sovereignty, and he evoked the Gallican liberties of the French church under Louis XIV as an example to be followed.[44] In the Mexico state congress, Mora and Joaquín Villa proposed that a decree be issued, manifesting the government's intention to uphold religion in the state, while rejecting the idea that Mexico should return to Spanish tyranny. Moreover, the congress would offer a prize of 200 pesos for the best essay on the limits of papal power and its relation to national sovereignty. The winner was Bernardo Couto, Mora's former student, who emphasized that "the spiritual and the temporal are two entirely diverse orders." [45]

It was the Patronato problem and the furor over the papal encyclical that probably stimulated Mora to undertake the translation of a treatise on ecclesiastical law by Gaspard Real de Curban, a French scholar and royal councillor of the mid-eighteenth century. The translation, advertised by the publisher as helping to "fix the type of relations which should be established with the

43. Mecham, *Church and State*, pp. 406–07. On Bustamante see *El Indicador, 1*, 1–19 (Oct. 9, 1833).

44. Mier, "Comunicado," in *El Sol*, July 20, 1825; *Discurso . . . sobre la encíclica del Papa Leon XII* (Mexico, 1825). See also Mecham, *Church and State*, pp. 92–96.

45. See Norberto Pérez Cuyado, pseud., *Disertación sobre la naturaleza y límites de la autoridad eclesiástica* (Mexico, 1825), p. 52. The papal encyclical was discussed in the state congress on July 7, 23, 26, 1825: *Actas, 5*, 42, 131–33. The decree of July 27 is in *Decretos*, pp. 86–87. See also Florstedt, "Liberal Role," pp. 111–17.

Holy See," began with an elaborate discussion of the sources and history of canon law and the bases of church government. Volume two dealt with the relation between church and state, citing details from various European countries, especially France. The treatise as a whole was a vigorous defense of regalian rights, demonstrating that "ecclesiastical authority has no power, direct or indirect, over civil authority in temporal matters [including property]." Although Mora did not cite Real de Curban in his 1831 *Disertación,* the similarity of orientation and argument between the two is unquestionable.[46]

The problem of patronage emerged again in 1833 as part of the liberal reaction to the proclericalism of the Bustamante regime. According to Mora, there were two positions on the question among the reformers. One, held by Valentín Gómez Farías and Quintana Roo (minister of justice), was the government view calling for complete independence of the "civil coercive power" and the "spiritual [power] over conscience and conviction." The other, held by the legislature, called for the recovery by sovereign state authority of "all the prerogatives which had been enjoyed by the Spanish government before independence"—in other words, the exercise of the Patronato.[47] Mora favored the first position, separation, but it was separation within a state where Catholicism was constitutionally the official religion. Mora sympathized with, but never accepted, official religious tolerance, nor was it adopted as a principle by the reform government.

"Separation of church and state," under these circumstances, signified removal of church power from all temporal or civil areas, at the same time that the government protected the Catholic religion. "Protection" meant for Mora the obligation by the government to pay worship expenses and the salaries of church officials. Mora explicitly rejected the constitutional provisions on concor-

---

46. Real de Curban, *Derecho eclesiástico escrito en francés por M. de Real y traducido al castellano por J. M. M.* (2 vols. Mexico, 1826). To my knowledge, the only extant copy of the translation is in the Harvard Law Library. It comprises Vol. 7 of Real's *La Science du gouvernement* (Aix-la-Chapelle, 1751–64). A publisher's *Suscrición* for the volumes can be found in the Mora Documents, 1806–38, dated May 21, 1828. A first edition of Real's work can be found in Mora's library in Guanajuato.

47. Mora, *Obras,* p. 80.

dats and patronage, which had led to a "monstrous mixture" of civil and religious functions. Instead, "the naming of priests and bishops should be left to whoever wish to do it [i.e. within the church], coming to an understanding with Rome as it seems best to them." [48]

Mora's concept of government "protection" of religion can be easily misunderstood, for it was intimately tied to a radical attack on the civil prerogatives of the church, such as the privileged jurisdiction (fueros), the free accumulation of property, its sources of income, and its control over education and marriage. The capital presently in the hands of the church, he maintained, was more than sufficient to amortize the public debt and still pay the expenses of worship. Mora's plan for church-state relations approached that of the French Civil Constitution of the Clergy of 1790. As in the French plan, Mora would redraw the limits of dioceses, making them coextensive with the states (departments in France). Salaries for each ecclesiastical office as well as the number of clerics would be prescribed by the government. The French revolutionaries carried their program much further, however, by providing that bishops be chosen by civil electors in the departmental assemblies, and by establishing freedom of worship.[49] Mora's concept of "separation" lost out to a senate plan, called the *ley de curatos* (December 17, 1833), by which vacant parishes were to be filled according to the procedure of the colonial Patronato.[50]

One of the principal financial sources of clerical strength was the traditional tithe, the tax of one-tenth on the fruits of agricultural produce. The civil obligation to pay tithes, originating in

48. Mora, *Revoluciones, 1,* 341–42. On government assumption of worship expenses see *Obras,* p. 314, and "Cuestión importante para el crédito público," ibid., pp. 385–420, a detailed argument that the funds for such a policy were available. *Reformador* presented the same position on Dec. 19, 1833.

49. For the text of the Civil Constitution of the Clergy see John H. Stewart, ed., *A Documentary Survey of the French Revolution* (New York, Macmillan, 1951), pp. 169–81. Mora's position is discussed by Reyes Heroles, *Liberalismo, 1,* 317–18; *3,* 136.

50. See Mora, *Obras,* p. 81; Mecham, *Church and State,* p. 415. For the text of the law see Riva Palacio, *México, 4,* 336. The law was preceded by another, revoking the Bustamante plan for clerical election to benefices.

the vast papal grants to the Spanish Crown in 1501, was occasionally attacked as an abuse during the 1820s. In 1831 Mora discussed the tithe in detail, emphasizing that traditional civil control over the tithe incurred no obligation on the part of the state. In fact, the state was free to act as it pleased. Not only was the tithe an intolerable burden upon agriculture and upon the poor cultivator, but well over half the proceeds went to providing the upper clergy—bishops and canons of the cathedral chapters—a luxurious existence. A related ecclesiastical abuse was the imposition of parochial fees on poor parishioners to support the curates. These fees were also by tradition a civil obligation, which Mora said should be removed. He later claimed that the Gómez Farías government had been influenced by his argument in passing the law of October 27, 1833, which made the tithe a voluntary contribution only.[51] The attack upon the tithes, although technically an effort to "separate" church and state, was really aimed at giving the state more freedom of action to control the temporal church.

The 1833 reformers made less headway in eliminating what Mora had described as the symbol of corporate power—the ecclesiastical fuero. Earlier, the legislators of the State of Mexico, while having to accept the fuero as provided for in the Constitution of 1824, attempted to control its abuse. Mora showed particular concern for this problem, insisting that ecclesiastical courts which judged state citizens be located within the state. He feared that otherwise the ecclesiastical courts would evade government control by claiming to be outside the latter's jurisdiction.

Of greatest importance to Mora, however, was the provision that the state supreme court exercise the traditional *recurso de fuerza*, that is, the power of the audiencia to overrule an illegality in canon law or a trespass on secular jurisdiction committed by an ecclesiastical court. Insistence on the recurso de fuerza, said Mora, was part of "the protection the government must impart to its

51. Mora, *Obras*, p. 303 (including the text of the law). Mora greatly admired Bishop Juan Cayetano Portugal of Michoacán, who he said rectified the "vicious distribution" of the tithe soon after the law was passed (ibid., p. 301; also *Revoluciones*, *1*, 114, 213). The abolition of obligatory tithes was the only anticlerical measure of the Gómez Farías regime not to be abrogated in 1834–35. The 1833 regime never abolished parochial fees.

subjects." [52] The contest between a newly created state government and an ancient corporation was obviously lopsided, and the
natural liberal response was to call for the elimination of ecclesiastical jurisdiction on a national basis. On April 29, 1833, *El
Fénix* congratulated the congress for opening discussion on the
fueros which created "a state within the state itself." As Mora
noted later, however, the reformers passed no legislation and
settled for trying to undermine church power in other ways.[53]
The abolition of the fueros had to wait two decades.

Another effort to strengthen state authority, by disengaging it
from obligations to the church, centered on the monasteries. The
regular clergy had been under attack on utilitarian grounds since
the eighteenth century. Monasteries were said to serve no useful
function in society; in fact, they took valuable capital and human
resources out of circulation. Mora had urged the abolition of
monasteries since the days of the state congress. In 1833 the legislature repealed all laws that imposed civil coercion on monastic
vows, but it went no further. Juan José Espinosa de los Monteros
argued in congress that this law was merely an effort to carry out
article 30 of the constitution, which pledged the government to
protect the natural rights of citizens.[54] Espinosa later introduced a
proposal (which never passed) to limit the number of monasteries
and the number of monks in each, subjecting the monasteries
to frequent government inspection, and prohibiting monastic
vows from being taken until the age of twenty-five.[55]

In education, the reformers did go further, as we shall see in

52. See *Actas, 6,* 134 (Nov. 29, 1825). The *recurso de fuerza* was provided for in
art. 215, pt. 7 of the Constitution of 1827, copied from art. 261, pt. 8 of the Constitution of 1812. There was no provision for the recurso de fuerza in the Constitution of 1824, which meant that the legislators intended the matter be left to the
states. This fact only strengthened the position of the church and probably gave
added impetus to the drive on the fueros after 1830. For a good discussion of
colonial ecclesiastical jurisdiction and the recurso de fuerza, see Parry, *Audiencia,*
pp. 100–07.

53. In Mora, *Obras,* p. 73.

54. Ibid., p. 324. Mora reprinted the law of Nov. 8, 1833, in ibid., p. 321. Mora
had led the effort to insert an article in the Mexico state constitution, forbidding
any future establishment of monasteries without the permission of congress. It was
defeated, however, in a session at which Mora was absent. See *Actas, 7,* 436 (June 6,
1826) and *9,* 180 (Jan. 29, 1826).

55. In Mora, *Obras,* pp. 339–45.

Chapter 5, by abolishing the church-controlled university and re-placing it with a nationalized system of secular instruction. Also part of the reformers' program was the establishment of a civil register of vital statistics, civil matrimony, and municipal ceme-teries. "These were the intentions of the Administration of 1833," wrote Mora, "in order to begin controlling the civil status of individuals . . . laws [concerning which] now exist in the major-ity of the nations of Catholic Europe." [56]

José María Luis Mora's essay of 1831 on church property can be said to have provided the point of departure for nineteenth-century anticlericalism in Mexico. Mora, for the first time, ad-vanced a reasoned and learned argument for the legal right of the state to intervene in and to regulate the entailed property that gave material substance to the church's corporate power. Mora addressed himself to three questions: One, what is the nature and origin of ecclesiastical property? Two, who has the authority to regulate its acquisition, administration, and investment? And three, who has the authority to determine the expenses of worship and the means to cover them? Mora's answer to these questions was based on a premise inspired by Real de Curban, namely, that in Catholic countries the church can be considered both a mystical and a political body.[57] Mora was combating the clerical argument that once property passed into mortmain it became spiritualized and was thus beyond the reach of any secular authority.

Historically, Mora argued, the church passed through two stages, separated by the conversion of the Roman Emperor Con-stantine to Christianity in 312. Prior to that, the church was a mystical body, "the work of Jesus Christ, eternal and indefectable, forever independent of temporal power." The fathers of the early church expressly condemned any accumulation of property not used to maintain worship. Mora marshaled quotations from St.

56. Ibid., p. 77.
57. Cf. Real de Curban, *Derecho*, 2, Chap. 3, and Mora, "Disertación sobre la naturaleza y aplicación de las rentas y bienes eclesiásticos, y sobre la autoridad a que se hallan sujetos en cuanto a su creación, aumento, subsistencia o supresión," *Obras*, p. 281. The pamphlet was anonymously published (Mexico, 1833) and also included in *El Indicador*, 2, 257–339 (Jan. 22, 1834). For a typical clerical response see *Disertación que manifiesta la propiedad que los eclesiásticos tienen en sus bienes* (Mexico, 1834).

John Chrysostom, St. Ambrose, and St. Augustine to confirm his point. When Constantine became converted and decreed that Christianity was the official religion of the empire, the church emerged as a political body (*comunidad política*) with property, legal status, and a coercive power over its members.

Mora emphasized that the act of civil protection was never an obligation, since only individuals (and not governments) could be subjects of the church.[58] While as a mystical body the church could secure assistance from the faithful to cover the expenses of worship, as a political body it could receive this only at the sufferance of civil law. Mora, then, believed it was entirely justifiable for the church to hold property, but only as a comunidad política under due regulation by the secular power. Canon law, said Mora (following Real de Curban), was part ecclesiastical and part civil, and the "civil part consists of the faculties that temporal governments have expressly accorded to churches." In Catholic countries where the church is recognized as a political body, many papal and conciliar decrees on property are disregarded, for instance those of the Council of Trent in France and Spain.[59]

Having established the legal and historical grounds for secular regulation of church property, Mora went on to make a crucial distinction between community and individual property:

> The right of an individual to acquire property has never had limits. . . . With communities . . . [the laws] have consistently placed limits to its acquisition. . . . An individual's right of acquisition is natural, prior to society . . . by contrast, a community's right of acquisition is purely civil, subsequent to society, created by it and consequently subject to the limitations society wishes to put on it.[60]

This distinction concerning property was one Mora made at several points in the essay; and as we will see in Chapter 5, it is the key to understanding an important aspect of his thought. Furthermore, Mora separated communities or "moral bodies" from "the

58. Mora, *Obras*, p. 287. This was the argument on which the 1833 laws, removing civil coercion for monastic vows and tithe-paying, were based.

59. Ibid., pp. 291–92.

60. Ibid., p. 305. Mora concluded that undue accumulation of private property was lamentable but beyond legal control.

associations of individuals for commercial or industrial enterprises." The property of the first type is purely corporate, whereas
the holdings of commercial companies exist as "a common fund
whose component parts conserve the character of individual property." Mora concluded his liberal restatement of classic regalist
arguments by exhorting the Mexican clergy to return to Caesar
what was Caesar's and to follow the example of Jesus Christ, "who
protested repeatedly that his kingdom was not of this world but
purely spiritual."

There were at least three interrelated grounds on which the
liberal assault on church property was put forth. One, which we
will explore in the next chapter, was utilitarian and economic:
entailed capital should be given free circulation by individuals to
assure economic progress. Another, we have seen, was political and
legal: the corporate privilege and power of the church must be
eliminated in favor of a regime of equal rights and administrative
uniformity within the state. The third was fiscal: the perpetual
financial crisis of the new republic could be solved only by using
the disentailed property of the church to provide a base for public credit. The financial question was one that particularly concerned Mora, and he formulated several elaborate proposals on the
subject in 1833 and 1834. As a legislator in the reconvened constituent congress in 1830, Mora had observed the insolvency of the
State of Mexico. Resorting to church property in times of fiscal
crisis was a standard practice in continental nations. The French
revolutionaries had nationalized church property in November
1789. Charles IV in Spain had ordered disentailment of ecclesiastical holdings to cover royal bond issues in 1796 and 1804. The
Cortes of Cádiz was faced with bankruptcy and likewise attacked
the church in 1813.[61]

When José María Luis Mora began to probe the tangled question of Mexican church property, he turned for guidance to
Manuel Abad y Queipo, former Bishop of Michoacán. Mora's
attachment to Abad is intriguing. It seems odd that Mora should
have devoted considerable space in his *Obras sueltas* to reprinting
a series of memorials addressed by the bishop to the Spanish government between 1799 and 1810. Why, for instance, should Mora

61. See Artola, *1*, 509–18; cf. Mora, *Obras*, p. 331.

have included in his violently anticlerical volume Abad's forceful defense of clerical immunities? His principal reason for turning to Abad y Queipo is that he considered the bishop the leading expert on the statistics of church property, especially property belonging to chaplaincies and pious works. Mora admitted that he based his estimate of total mortmain holdings (80 million pesos) on Abad's figures. Prior to becoming bishop in 1810, Abad held the post of judge of wills, chaplaincies, and pious works in the diocese from 1784 to 1806.[62]

Mora's affinity for Abad y Queipo is based on more, however, than his respect for the bishop as a financial expert. We have seen Mora's reference to Abad as one of several enlightened Spaniards who, prior to 1810, would have welcomed independence under moderate Creole leadership. Abad was one of a group of late colonial reformers, an extention of the Bourbon "regeneration" in Spain, which found its leadership especially in Gaspar Melchor de Jovellanos.[63] Abad had advocated, as early as 1799, a series of reforms to alleviate the condition of the Indians and particularly to end their segregation from the whites. It was anomolous that Abad should suggest these changes in a petition, the main theme of which was the defense of clerical immunities against royal encroachment.[64]

Mora actually condoned Abad's defense of privilege. Given the abject condition of Indians and Castes and the rigid class divisions, "that type of theocratic government was the only kind that could have kept the ignorant and oppressed classes in submission." Thus it would have been "nonsense" to contemplate the abolition of clerical privileges in 1799. In 1833, however, the situation was different:

> The dignity of the government was disregarded by the rejection of its exercise of the former Patronato; landed property

62. See Lillian E. Fisher, *Champion of Reform: Manuel Abad y Queipo* (New York, Library Publishers, 1955), p. 12. For Mora's tribute to Abad see *Obras*, pp. 370–71.

63. See Victor A. Belaunde, *Bolívar and the Political Thought of the Spanish American Revolution* (Baltimore, Johns Hopkins University Press, 1938), p. 40. Abad had also condemned Hidalgo's revolt in 1810, a position Mora agreed with.

64. See Abad, "Inmunidad personal," Mora, *Obras*, pp. 207–09, and "Representación a la primera regencia" (May 30, 1810), in ibid., p. 258.

was bankrupt because of the encumbrances on capital from the pious funds; the public debt was nearly 128 million pesos. . . . [All of this] constitutes a social situation in which one cannot avoid the real necessity of proceeding promptly to the total abolition of the clergy as a civil class.

Whereas the traditionally strong royal government could tolerate, at least to a certain extent, the existence of the church as a corporate entity, its weak republican successor could not.[65]

Abad y Queipo's detailed discussion of church property was occasioned by the royal decree of December 26, 1804, in which landed property of chaplaincies and pious funds was to be disentailed and their capital was to provide a sinking fund for the amortization (*consolidación*) of royal *vales*. The vales were interest-bearing bonds, issued first in 1779 and circulated in Spain as legal tender, very much like the *assignats* in France. The issue had been increased several times, and beginning in 1796 the government resorted to church property to maintain their value.[66]

Abad protested that in Mexico, unlike Spain, property was mostly in specie and not in land. This specie was not in dead hands, he argued; rather it was actively providing two-thirds of the working capital for industry, commerce, and agriculture in the viceroyalty. Recalling this capital and liquidating landed property would cause economic disaster.[67] Mora agreed with Abad's analysis of the situation as of 1804, and criticized the decree as ruinous and impolitic. The pious funds, Mora said, had become "a kind of investment bank (*banco de avío*) to foment agriculture and the internal prosperity of the country." [68] At the same time, Mora

65. Mora, *Obras*, pp. 77–79. Mora's departure from his normal regalist position was clearly inconsistent. Perhaps he concluded that in 1799 the Indian menace was even more threatening than the power of the church. See Chap. 7, below.

66. On the *vales reales* see Herr, *Eighteenth-Century Revolution*, pp. 146, 384, 392.

67. Abad, "Representación a nombre de los labradores y comerciantes de Valladolid de Michoacán" (1805) , Mora, *Obras*, pp. 214–30, and "Escrito presentado a Don Manuel Sisto Espinosa" (1809) , ibid., p. 231. It is significant that Abad tried repeatedly to turn royal attention to private latifundia as the true obstacle to social and economic progress. See ibid., pp. 182–83, 224, 226.

68. Mora, *Revoluciones, 1*, 121–22. Mora added that the measure was a great source of hostility between Spaniards and Creoles prior to 1810 (ibid., *3*, 300) , a matter noted also by Alamán (*Historia, 1*, 172–75) . See also Henry G. Ward, *Mexico*

emphasized that the legality of the 1804 measure was never questioned, even by Abad, and that it could serve as a precedent for a
new and better-conceived secular occupation of church property.[69]

Mora's analysis stressed the "universal bankruptcy" of landed
property, which rendered it useless as a source of revenue. The
committee appointed by Gómez Farías in November 1833, to deal
with the financial question, concluded that land could not be
taxed "since the amount that encumbers it exceeds the value of
the property itself." Mora did not dispute Abad y Queipo's facts,
but implied that Abad did not give the whole story, since in reality so much had been borrowed on private estates that the clergy
was the virtual owner of a great proportion of rural holdings. As
Mora explained, many of the donations by individuals to establish
chaplaincies or to advance pious works were in the form of a portion of annual cash income from a family estate. The landowners
themselves then began to borrow freely on their property from the
surplus funds accumulating in the chaplaincy treasuries, an easy
thing to do because the church cared little about security for its
loans. Thus landed property was in a state of crisis by 1810, only
made worse by the turmoil of the revolutionary decade.[70]

The 1833 reformers were divided in their efforts to advance
legislation for the disentailment of church property. The matter
was first entrusted to a committee consisting of Mora, Couto, and
Espinosa de los Monteros. However, their deliberations were disrupted by a sudden proposal introduced into the chamber of

in 1827 (London, 1828), *1*, 333–34; Harry Bernstein, *Modern and Contemporary
Latin America* (New York, Lippincott, 1952), pp. 35–36. The *consolidación*, its
impact in Mexico, and the economics of landholding before and after independence
would be fruitful areas for study.

69. Mora, *Obras*, pp. 95, 309, 336.

70. Mora, *Revoluciones*, *1*, 504–05. The point at issue related to rural holdings,
for, according to Mora, 90 percent of urban real estate was held directly by the
clergy. The delinquent payment of interest on capital borrowed from the church,
especially during the revolution when land was not producing up to normal,
brought on a deluge of legal problems. Mora referred (p. 506) to a "famous dissertation" on the question by José María de Jáuregui, his former colleague in the
state congress: *Discurso en que se manifiesta, que deben bajarse los réditos a proporción del quebranto que hayan sufrido en la insurrección los bienes y giros de
los deudores* (Mexico, 1820). Jáuregui, as advocate before the audiencia, had written
the memorial on behalf of various landholders affected by a royal decree of 1819.

deputies by Lorenzo de Zavala on November 7. Zavala's plan called for the immediate occupation by the government of clerical real estate and its sale at public auction. The government would receive half the proceeds in cash and half in installments. The proposal alarmed Gómez Farías, who immediately directed the Board of Public Instruction, of which Mora and Espinosa were members, to forestall Zavala's proposal by offering one of their own. The result was a law submitted to the congress by Espinosa on February 17, 1834, but never passed. It was received by the chamber, said Mora, with "a very distinct coolness." Whether this was a result, as Mora suggested, of clerical influence, whether it reflected hostility by partisans of Zavala, or merely a reluctance of the majority of the deputies to nationalize church property, is unclear. Nevertheless, these measures became the model for the Ley Lerdo of 1856.[71]

Mora, as we have seen, used the ill-conceived royal decree of 1804 as justification for combating Zavala's scheme. Mora feared, as had Abad y Queipo, that the arbitrary expropriation and auction of mortmain property would bring ruin to the great number of people tied economically to the church. Since there is no money generally available to purchase the holdings, said Mora, the price would be forced down. "Better to give [the properties] to the first passers-by in the street" than to sell them for paper which would benefit only the speculators.[72] Instead, Mora intended that the

71. Manuel Payno, La Reforma social en España y México (Mexico, UNAM, 1958). Writing in 1861, Payno justified the reform laws of 1855–60 on the basis of historical precedents in Spanish regalism, the ideas of Jovellanos, and the measures of 1833. Payno also confirmed (or repeated) Mora's contention that Zavala had ties with speculators who hoped to buy up church property sold at auction. Zavala's proposal elicited Mora's famous characterization of his rival as "a man of little delicacy in all areas, but especially in matters of money" (Obras, p. 84).

72. Editor's note (probably by Mora) to Mirabeau, "Discurso sobre el derecho de la sociedad para ocupar los bienes del clero," in El Indicador, 3, 205 (Mar. 26, 1834). Mora claimed he only reprinted the Mirabeau discourse to "enlighten the subject" since "we agree with the author in almost nothing." It is clear, though, that despite the method pursued by the National Assembly in 1789, the French precedent was important for Mora. Mirabeau concluded by saying that his principal point in the speech was that "every nation is the sole and true owner of the property of its clergy." For Mora's plan, see "Bases presentadas . . . para el arreglo de la deuda interior de la federación mejicana" (Nov. 20, 1833), in Obras, pp. 331–38. It is followed (pp. 346–63) by the more moderate but comparable proposal presented by the Espinosa committee on Feb. 17, 1834.

properties should pass to the present tenants at a price, 5 percent of which (4 percent in some cases) would equal their present rent. Generous installments could then be arranged by the government for amortizing the principal. The government would also assume the mortgages held by the church on private property, and appropriate interest and amortization schedules could be arranged.

It is important to reiterate that disentailment would be tied to the regulation of the size and number of convents, to the reorganization of dioceses, and to the fixing of ecclesiastical salaries. Of several French and Spanish precedents for the liberal program to disentail church property, the one of most immediate significance was the legislation of the Spanish cortes of 1810–14 and 1820–22. In fact, it was the law of September 27, 1820, "suppression of entails of all types," lay and ecclesiastical, that was specifically cited in the 1833 proposals and that provided the point of departure for the new legislation.[73] The influence of Pedro Rodríguez de Campomanes and especially of Jovellanos on both the Spanish cortes and the Mexican reformers is also apparent. The inspiration for Mora's specific plan to turn church property over to the present tenants was most probably from Jovellanos, though the latter's "Informe de ley agraria" dealt largely with lay holdings and only moderately and briefly with the church.[74] Moreover, Mora referred to several state laws of the 1820s as foreshadowing the 1833 program. He and Jáuregui had been successful in winning acceptance for article 9 of the Mexico state constitution, forbidding

73. Art. 52, pt. vi of the Espinosa committee proposal (ibid., pp. 355–57) specifically repealed art. 14 of the Mexican law of Aug. 7, 1823. The latter article in turn had abrogated arts. 14 and 15 of the 1820 law, pertaining to ecclesiastical entails. Mora called this action of the 1823 congress "absurd." See *Obras*, p. 366. On the cortes precedent for the 1833 measures, see also James M. Breedlove in Benson, *Mexico and the Spanish Cortes*, pp. 132–33.

74. See Jovellanos, "Informe de la sociedad económica de Madrid al real y supremo consejo de Castilla en el expediente de ley agraria," *BAE*, *50*, 103a. Jovellanos urged the church to sell its properties or to alienate them to individuals in emphyteusis. He acknowledged (ibid., p. 137a) his debt to Campomanes' *Tratado de la regalía de amortización* (1765). Campomanes' treatise was reprinted in 1821 (Madrid) to show, according to the editor, that the cortes was fully within its rights to encroach upon church property, and that it was necessary for the people "to break the chains that have perpetually bound them to the ecclesiastical bodies." Manuel Payno emphasized the importance of Jovellanos for the 1856 Ley Lerdo. See *Reforma*, pp. 18–20.

henceforth any church property in mortmain. The speeches favoring the measure made good use of French and Spanish prototypes.[75]

Though the liberal assault upon corporate privilege focused on the church, the army was also a major target. Discussions by Mora, Zavala, and others of "the privileged classes" and of the "fueros" always grouped church and army together. However, even a cursory analysis will reveal that the two presented very distinct problems. The church as an institution was the chief corporate obstacle to the expansion of rationalized state authority in the eighteenth century. Clerical influence was constantly under attack by the new utilitarian philosophy, the premise of which was a secular rather than a religiously oriented society. The case of the army was different. The nobility as a military class had declined in New Spain in the sixteenth century, and for two centuries the colonial military establishment was minimal. After the Seven Years War, however, Charles III ordered a rapid expansion of the colonial militia to meet the threat, real or imagined, of British encroachment. While curtailing the church, the Crown actually extended privileges to the army, and by 1780 it became firmly established as a corporate body enjoying the full *fuero militar* of the peninsula. Royal and viceregal efforts to limit the disruptive effect on justice of a newly intruding privileged body were generally defeated by the supposed need of an ever-larger army for defense. By 1810 the army was an autonomous and irresponsible institution. With the removal of the Crown, it emerged as the most powerful arbiter in national politics.[76]

José María Luis Mora maintained that Charles III had expanded the army in New Spain partly as an effort to counterbalance the influence of the clergy.[77] Whether true or not, the suggestion is interesting, for it points up the problem the liberals faced in confronting the army after independence. They were categorical in their condemnation of it as an organization. "The

75. *Actas*, 7, 435–36 (June 6, 1826); 8, 457–75 (Sept. 9–11, 1826). See also Mora, *Obras*, p. 308.

76. See Lyle N. McAlister, *The "Fuero Militar" in New Spain, 1764–1800* (Gainesville, University of Florida Press, 1957).

77. Mora, *Revoluciones, 3*, 271–72.

greater part of the political disorders and social disorganization of
the Mexican Republic stem from the militia considered as a privileged class," wrote Mora. *El Fénix* complained of the excessive
luxury of traditional uniforms; *La Oposición* raised the matter of
equality, calling such a privileged group completely incongruous
in a republic.[78] Mora, who described the military judicial system
in some detail, referred to the seventeen *comandancias generales*
(which served as military courts in the first instance) as a "copious
source of disorders." The privileged soldier is insolent toward civil
justice, he said, and commits all manner of civil crimes with
impunity. Moreover, the barbarous impressment of common soldiers causes great terror in the countryside. As Zavala put it, a
privileged army is always "an aggressor against the rights of the
community." [79]

The liberals universally recognized the military evil; the problem was how to deal with it. Mora acknowledged that the 1824
legislators were forced to tolerate the army. Their mistake, he said,
was to guarantee its existence by a constitutional provision "which
tied the hands of the civil power against seizing opportunities
. . . to abolish the military fuero." [80] The constitution-makers
were following a natural course by merely copying article 250 of
the Constitution of 1812. The problem, though, went deeper than
that, as both Mora and Zavala admitted: it was simply that no government could succeed without the support of the regular army.

Mora had himself supported Santa Anna in 1832 and placed
hope in a military-civilian coalition to overthrow Bustamante and
to usher in a reform government. Mora had first sought the leadership of General Mier y Terán who he believed would have risen
above corporate interests. Whether Terán would have tolerated an
assault on the military fuero, any more than did Santa Anna, is
questionable. In any case, the military problem was one of great
frustration for Mora. "When it is a matter of tearing down," all
factions call for the army; "all in turn detest it when the hour

78. Ibid., *1*, 436–37; *El Fénix*, Feb. 12, 1834; *La Oposición*, Nov. 24, 1834. See also
Reformador, Dec. 9, 1833.

79. Mora, *Revoluciones*, *1*, 414–16; Zavala, *Ensayo*, *1*, 352, 392–93. For interesting
details on the kind of conflicts that arose in the courts between civilians and
militiamen, see McAlister, *"Fuero Militar,"* pp. 58, 84–85, and passim.

80. Mora, *Revoluciones*, *1*, 409.

arrives to raise the edifice or to consolidate what has been built."
The army "is now tolerated as an evil whose necessity is temporary." Yet, warned Mora, if governments refuse to consult their
real interests and continue to seek their support in bayonets, "the
evil will be eternal."[81]

The hope for curtailing military privilege lay in the development of a civic militia, to be composed of citizens in the states and
in the Federal District. The Constitution of 1824 authorized congress to draw up the regulations for such a "local state militia,"
which it did in the law of December 29, 1827.[82] This force, sometimes referred to as the "national local militia," sometimes as the
"civic militia," was distinct from the "permanent" or "active"
militia, the traditional privileged body. As a citizen force constantly on call, the former could become a source of support for
civilian governments. Though Mora favored the institution, he
admitted it had its defects. Since governors and other local officials
cannot make use of the permanent and active militia, he said, they
have built up ad hoc civic militia units for their own personal support. "Military institutions under diverse names and forms have
multiplied everywhere." These units, technically authorized by
the 1827 law, "are composed of the most unruly men" who attack
property and cause all manner of havoc. In 1830 *El Observador*
called for the abandonment of the civic militia in favor of better-
disciplined regular units. Mora's answer, also proposed by Zavala
in 1833, was to staff the local militia entirely with property holders
who would for their own protection assure order in the countryside.[83]

81. Ibid., 99–100. Zavala expressed similar sentiments (*Ensayo, 1,* 214–15).

82. See Dublán and Lozano, 2, 49–51. The Constitution of 1812 (arts. 362–65)
provided for a militia to be raised in each province (presumably without fuero),
in addition to the permanent national army (arts. 356–61). On Aug. 3, 1822, the
Mexican congress passed a *reglamento de la milicia cívica* (ibid., *1,* 619–26) which
apparently was based on the constitutional provision. This reglamento in turn was
superseded by art. 50, pt. xix of the Constitution of 1824 and by the subsequent
1827 law. These later laws merely adapted the 1812 institution to the federal form
of organization.

83. See *El Observador,* 2d ser., *1,* 65–70 (Mar. 17, 1830); Mora, *Revoluciones, 1,*
104–06; Zavala, *Memoria,* p. 24. Money was also a major problem in the raising of
local militias. The reconvened Mexico state constituent congress passed a measure
(introduced by Mora and Jáuregui) that because of the financial plight of the
state, the civic militia would be kept up only in those communities that could sup-

Presumably, Mora's criticism of Gómez Farías for failing to deal vigorously with Santa Anna was based on the existence of three battalions of local militia for the Federal District, provided for in a law of April 16, 1833.[84] The only really effective local militia, however, was organized by Governor Francisco García of Zacatecas. As a volunteer force, it became a model for the liberals. Mora wrote that "the privileged classes have never been able to pardon Sr. García for his scheme to seize power away from them," adding that the clerical-military reaction of May 1834 was directed primarily against the civic militia of Zacatecas, which made a vain effort to resist.[85] Despite liberal enthusiasm for a civic volunteer militia, the problem of the army was, in the last analysis, baffling to Mora and his colleagues. A privileged army had to remain, said Mora, as a necessary evil, to be tolerated until civil power could be further consolidated.

The inevitable "reaction of the fueros" against the Gómez Farías regime came in May and June 1834, led by President Santa Anna himself. Mora admitted, however, that opposition to the reform government arose partly from within the ranks of the "men of progress." He pointed to Manuel Gómez Pedraza, and especially to Juan Rodríguez Puebla who opposed the educational policy of the vice-president, abolishing special education for Indians. Mora also said that beginning in January 1834, Santa Anna began to receive complaints from "all classes and colors" against the reform measures.[86] This evidence suggests that the reaction had a broader base than liberal propaganda would allow.

The political housecleaning was swift and effective. Mora closed down *El Indicador* on May 7, 1834, complaining that Santa Anna had gone back on the reform program. He left the Board of Public Instruction on June 11, three days before Santa Anna was ac-

---

port it from their own funds. See *Actas, 10,* 49, 270 (Apr. 26, July 8, 1830). It was asserted that out of 80,000 enlisted in the state civic militia, only 10,000 were effectives.

84. Dublán and Lozano, *2,* 506–07; expanded and partly superseded by law of Mar. 21, 1834 (ibid., pp. 684–87).

85. Mora, *Obras,* p. 161; also *El Fénix,* Nov. 18, 1833; *Reformador,* Jan. 25, 1834.

86. Mora, *Obras,* pp. 152–53.

claimed as a hero by the Ayuntamiento of Mexico City. Mora and Gómez Farías went into seclusion, arranged their affairs, and prepared to flee the country. Deprived of pay that was due him, Gómez Farías made a hard journey to Zacatecas in September 1834, with a pregnant wife and three small children. Mora, a bachelor, was in less difficult straits. He managed to liquidate much of his property, except for three run-down houses which were to plague him for the rest of his life. Mora left Mexico City permanently for France at the end of November, with the sum of 5,000 pesos, his books, and his manuscripts. After a long trip, including brief stopovers in the United States, he arrived at Le Havre the following July. The departure of Mora and Gómez Farías closed a chapter in the chronicle of liberal politics, though as Manuel Payno wrote, Mora's *Obras sueltas* kept the reform program before the public during the subsequent decade.[87]

The reform laws, the many legislative proposals, and the political writings of the early 1830s reveal the development of a liberal ideology that contrasted a vision of secular progress based on individual liberty and juridical equality with the corporate abuses of the colonial regime. To what degree did this period produce an ideological opposition? Can we speak of a liberal-conservative cleavage in the 1830s as we can after 1847? Mora and his colleagues would have us do so, but other contemporary evidence is less conclusive. Opposition newspapers sprang up, notably *La Lima del vulcano* and *El Mosquito mexicano,* but they featured personal attacks upon members of the liberal regime. The "reaction" embraced a very mixed group, such as the previously mentioned Juan Rodríguez Puebla, Quintana Roo, and Manuel Crecencio Rejón, all formerly "men of progress." There was also the case of José María Gutiérrez de Estrada, a close friend of Mora, who had been cited in the *ley del caso* and who then returned briefly as minister of relations under Santa Anna in 1835. Gutiérrez was purported to have left the government because of the impending change to the centralist system. His 1840 mon-

---

87. Payno, *Reforma,* p. 47. On Gómez Farías, see Hutchinson, "Valentín Gómez Farías," pp. 335–38. For Mora's life at this point, see Florstedt, "Liberal Role," pp. 409–28.

archist pronouncement represented the beginnings of an ideological conservatism, but it was not apparent in 1835.[88]

It is questionable whether centralism was adopted (1836) in the name of "conservative" principles. Although Mora had spoken often of upholding the "federation" against the "ancient constitution of the country," he did not mean by this "federalism versus centralism." Bernardo Couto, Mora's 1833 collaborator, who then served as a senator on the constitutional committee in 1835, saw the matter clearly:

> today there is grumbling about the federation; actually there would be grumbling about any other type of government established in 1824. . . . The outbreaks and agitation in Mexico arise from a principle more general and effective than her constitution . . . they are part of the universal movement which today agitates a good portion of the earth. . . . It [is the] conflict between new principles and old habits, institutions, and interests.[89]

The major conservative spokesman by midcentury was Lucas Alamán. Though his conservatism was slow to develop, we do see by 1834 indications of his future position. In that year he wrote a tract against the reform government, justifying his actions and those of the Bustamante regime. He referred to the "self-designated party of the people," a group that grew out of the former yorkinos and distinguished itself from those called "aristocrats." For Alamán, the latter was a term "which in our revolution, as in the French, denoted men of religion, of honor, of property, of education, and of virtue, whom [the revolutionaries] tried to despoil of their goods and deprive of all influence in public affairs." [90] The reformers were "Jacobins," pursuing "liberty and equality" against "public order" and the "fundamental principles of all political association." The Burkean overtones in these utterances are unmistakable. But Alamán remained on the fringes

88. On Gutiérrez see Mora, *Obras*, p. 162; also Gutiérrez, *Documentos relativos al ingreso y a la salida de la primera secretaría de estado de la república mexicana* (Mexico, 1835), p. 14.

89. *Dictamen de la comisión especial de la cámara de senadores sobre cambio de la forma de gobierno y voto particular del señor Couto* (Mexico, 1835), p. 28.

90. Alamán, "Defensa del ex-ministro de relaciones," *Documentos*, 3, 41–46.

of public life between 1834 and 1846, and his political conservatism advanced little until 1844. In short, it is difficult to find a consistent ideological conflict during the troubled decade from the "reaction of the fueros" to the war with the United States.[91]

Nevertheless, the elements of the liberal position had been clearly presented by 1837. The espousal of a reform program after 1830 marked a major shift of emphasis in Mexican political liberalism, epitomized by the ideas of José María Luis Mora. Mora's new argument drew its inspiration from the side of continental political liberalism which sought juridical equality under a financially strong state. Though the reform program of 1833 was an attack upon the regime of corporate privilege inherited from the Colony, it can hardly be termed a "denial of the Spanish heritage." In fact, the models of most relevance to Mora were Spanish: Charles III and the Cortes of Cádiz. The Spanish reform tradition was always akin to the French, and influences from the one and the other were closely related in Mora's thought. Yet after 1830, specifically French thought and experience became less germane to the problems Mora faced than they were in the 1820s. Mora intended to complete his historical writings with an account of Mexico's "constitutional revolution covering the years from the reestablishment of the Spanish constitution in 1820 until the end of 1833." [92] Unfortunately, Mora found that the major characteristic of this "constitutional revolution" was the fragility of the formal constitution in the face of Mexican political reality.

There was, however, another aspect of Mexican liberal thought during these years. What kind of society was to replace the one inherited from the Colony? Let us now turn to that social conception and the philosophy that underlay it.

91. Church property continued to be threatened by centralist "conservative" governments after 1834. See Alamán, *Historia,* 5, 866; also Michael P. Costeloe, "The Administration, Collection and Distribution of Tithes in the Archbishopric of Mexico, 1800–1860," *The Americas,* 23 (1966), 27. Costeloe's pioneer work came to my attention after this chapter was written.

92. Mora, *Revoluciones, 1,* viii–ix. This is what presumably became the "Revista política de las diversas administraciones que la república mexicana ha tenido hasta 1837," published in his *Obras.*

5

Utilitarianism and the Liberal Society

Mexican political liberalism, in both its constitutionalist and its anticorporate phases, contained a set of assumptions about society. These assumptions were derived from utilitarianism, essentially a theory of morals and human nature, which permeated the philosophy of the Enlightenment in Europe, and which became systematically developed as a doctrine by Jeremy Bentham between 1780 and 1815. Though Bentham was deservedly the most famous of utilitarians, "there is scarcely a writer on moral and political theory who is free from every taint of utilitarianism." [1] The protean and omnipresent character of utilitarianism makes it a difficult matter to discuss in relation to Mexican liberalism; and yet to omit it would distort our understanding of political thought and policy, and leave inexplicable liberal actions in the socioeconomic sphere.

In broadest terms, utilitarianism was based on a secular view of human nature in which the individual forms his ideas from experience and, if left free, will act rationally in his own interest and in the interests of others. Historically, it was influenced by the secular and individualist currents of the Renaissance, by the drive toward separation of religious and temporal spheres during the Reformation, and particularly by the intense scientific spirit of the seventeenth century. The critical period in the development of this new morality was the years from 1680 to 1715, just as it was in the rise of liberal political thought. [2] The idea that morals and ethics depended on revealed religion and dogma came under increasing attack by those who sought a "natural" and "rational" explanation

---

1. John Plamenatz, *The English Utilitarians* (Oxford, Blackwell, 1958), p. 1.
2. See Paul Hazard, *The European Mind, 1680–1715* (New Haven, Yale University Press, 1953).

for human behavior. Again, it was John Locke who provided the point of departure for this aspect of modern liberal theory. His *Essay on Human Understanding* (1690) put forth a psychology of sense perception. Locke rejected the notion of innate ideas and demonstrated instead that understanding was the product of experience.

The new psychology developed both in England with Hume and Paley and on the continent, but from the point of view of liberalism it developed most significantly in France. As expressed by Helvétius in his *Essays on the Mind* (1758), human behavior was subject to two motivating forces, desire for pleasure and dislike of pain. Man was not "bad" as religious moralists had said, nor was he dominated by evil passions which must be restrained. He was merely seeking happiness by pursuing his interests—that is, by searching for pleasure and avoiding pain. The basic problem was to reconcile individual interests and social interests, which Helvétius believed could be accomplished by providing knowledge and good laws. A "reflective egoism" became the basis of morality, and the general good became the product of individual efforts to attain happiness. Also important for Helvétius was the idea, generalized in eighteenth-century thought, that man's character was determined by his environment, particularly his social environment. By acquiring knowledge of the environment, or of what he was, man had the power to change society and ultimately to perfect the human species.[3] This theory was the basis of both the universal search for useful knowledge which characterized the Enlightenment, and its vision of human progress, best presented by Condorcet in 1795.

Jeremy Bentham, after completing his education in France, began one of his earliest works with a tribute to the contemporary explosion of scientific knowledge. In the physical world "everything teems with discovery and with improvement." He added that "correspondent to discovery and improvement in the natural world, is reformation in the moral."[4] By the age of twenty Bentham's mission in life had become to establish a science of

3. Plamenatz, pp. 49–50; also Martin, *Rise*, p. 122.
4. Bentham, *A Fragment on Government* (1776), ed. by W. H. Harrison (Oxford, Blackwell, 1960), p. 1.

morals, based on the fundamental axiom, "it is the greatest happiness of the greatest number that is the measure of right and wrong." For Bentham as for Helvétius, the aims of legislation and morality were the same, namely "the art of directing the actions of men in such a way as to produce the greatest possible sum of good." [5] Bentham was concerned first with developing a "moral calculus," that is, discovering how accurately and to what extent "lots," or sums, of human happiness could be measured and compared. He believed that only when the legislator had accurate knowledge of pains and pleasures could the greatest happiness be assured. Bentham's secondary concern, which occupied most of his time and which accounted for his great influence, was the practical task of reform. The "greatest happiness principle," or utility, was to become for Bentham a universal tool to test the validity of existing institutions. Bentham spent his long life applying the principle of utility with great thoroughness to a multitude of contemporary problems.

Bentham, like Helvétius, had great faith in individuals as "rational agents." They should be given "the greatest possible latitude," he said, for "they are the best judges of their own interest." The law must intervene, however, when individuals fail to perceive the connection between their own interest and the interests of others. The role of law is to enlighten individuals concerning this connection, and to bring about an artificial identification of interests.[6] Bentham's passion was to simplify the laws, reducing the body of accumulated legislation to civil, penal, and constitutional codes which would conform to the principle of utility and better promote the identity of individual interests.

Besides the juridical application of utilitarian doctrine associated with Jeremy Bentham, there was its equally significant use in economic thought by the French physiocrats between 1756 and 1778 and by Adam Smith. The economists saw a natural order

5. Bentham, *Theory of Legislation*, ed. by C. K. Ogden (New York, Harcourt, 1931), p. 60. This is an English translation of the *Traités de législation civile et pénale*, pub. and ed. in 1802 by Etienne Dumont, Bentham's Swiss associate, from various MSS. written (many in French) in the mid-1780s. It was this work by which Bentham was best known abroad. First Spanish translation, 1821.

6. Ibid., pp. 63–64. See also Elie Halévy, *The Growth of Philosophic Radicalism* (London, Faber, 1928), pp. 18, 36.

existing in the economic relations among men, governed by self-evident and universal laws. Foremost among these were, one, the desire of individuals to better their condition, and two, their propensity to exchange. From these drives arose the division of labor that Adam Smith saw as the basis of productive wealth in society. Though the individual pursuit of self-interest was for both Adam Smith and for the physiocrats the motive force in society, the latter conceived of a system that could only operate under "the exact regimen of perfect liberty and perfect justice." The physiocrats believed that only land was productive of wealth and that this wealth could only be forthcoming if there existed a wise Legislator to "discover" [or to enforce] the laws of nature.

In effect, as Adam Smith pointed out, the physiocratic system, by emphasizing the wealth of agriculture at the expense of other activities, such as manufacturing, had a restraint of its own. Smith was more optimistic than the physiocrats and believed that "the natural effort which every man [not just the agriculturalist] makes to better his condition" would of itself lead a nation toward wealth and prosperity, rendering unnecessary the authority of the Legislator.[7] The physiocrats always assumed an enlightened despot in their system of "perfect liberty." Adam Smith, on the contrary, believed more in the "spontaneous harmony of egoisms," or the natural identity of interests. It is evident that one of the critical problems within utilitarianism was the role government should play in bringing about the harmony or identification of interests in society. It was a problem that had particular relevance to Mexican liberalism.

The utilitarian spirit permeated Spanish thought and policy under Charles III. Through the agency of the economic societies, those groups of the provincial elite which met to discuss and to suggest practical reforms, a veritable "crusade" was launched to

7. See Adam Smith's critique of the physiocratic or "agricultural" system in *The Wealth of Nations* (New York, Random House, 1937), particularly pp. 638–42. Also Charles Gide and Charles Rist, *A History of Economic Doctrines* (London, Harrap, 1948), Chap. 1. Adam Smith, of course, generally admired the physiocratic doctrine as "generous and liberal." It may be stretching a point to term the physiocrats "utilitarian," since their conception was highly rationalistic and Cartesian in spirit, and not empirically based, as was that of Adam Smith. However, the mainspring of their system, self-interest, was utilitarian.

crats in France. This assumption led to an ambivalence toward state action, which was less pronounced for Adam Smith in England.

Though utilitarianism was applied broadly to political problems, it was not a theory of politics. Men of quite different political persuasions were utilitarians, aristocrats and democrats, historic constitutionalists and advocates of enlightened despotism. Edmund Burke, for example, who was a follower of Adam Smith in economics, used the argument of utility to support his conservative defense of established political institutions. "Man," said Burke, "acts from adequate motives relative to his interest, not on metaphysical speculations." These motives involved prejudices, such as religion and aristocracy, which had proved their utility as the product of long social experience. Whereas the utilitarian morality led Bentham to condemn sentiment and accumulated custom, Burke used it to glorify tradition, specifically the English constitution.[13] In the hands of Bentham, the aim of utilitarian doctrine was to reform society by a system of laws based on a mathematically precise analysis of moral sentiments. Ideally, this aim was nonpolitical, but since politics could not be avoided, Bentham found himself increasingly embroiled in political problems.

His reform efforts were from the beginning directed principally against the complications of the English legal system, which had been sanctified against need for change by William Blackstone in his *Commentaries on the Laws of England* (1765). Bentham's concern for simplifying the British constitution made him politically a Tory with an affinity for continental enlightened despotism. In 1789 Bentham confronted the doctrine of the natural rights of man, as presented by the French revolutionaries. Despite the logical affinity between Bentham's reform efforts and those of the new French "simplifiers," and despite their common attack upon corporate privilege, Bentham reacted sharply to the idea that there were certain imprescriptible or natural rights which were above the law. A right could not exist as an abstraction, he said. It must be subject to utility and thus be a product of concrete human laws. He attacked as an "anarchical fallacy" the idea that

13. See Plamenatz, pp. 56–58; Halévy, pp. 158–61.

laws negating supposedly self-evident natural rights could be resisted. He argued that "every law is an evil, for every law is an infraction of liberty."[14] Government, therefore, can only choose between evils, acting in such a way that the sum of pleasures resulting from a law outweighs the sum of pains. Likewise Bentham opposed the "principle that all men ought to enjoy a perfect equality of rights." This would "render all legislation impossible," since "the laws are constantly establishing inequalities." Granting rights to some necessarily means imposing obligations on others.[15]

It was the philosophical principle of abstract rights that Bentham objected to, not the political application of the principle in France. While remaining indifferent to the political debate that raged in England over the French Revolution, he became increasingly sympathetic to political democracy by expansion of the franchise. He was drawn into this position after 1815 because of the opposition to his legal reform schemes from a succession of conservative governments. Thus he and his followers, the Philosophic Radicals, proceeded "to justify on grounds of utility the very rights which the French were claiming on grounds of nature."[16]

It is evident that Benthamite politics had little affinity for constitutional liberalism. Montesquieu, Constant, and their followers turned to the English constitution as the model for a free people. They accepted the very system Bentham had made it his chief mission to reform. He was skeptical of the separation of powers which was held as dogma by constitutionalists. Bentham, as Halévy has said, was "continental" in orientation; his passion for codification was a French and not a British idea. In his political sympathies he "passed from a monarchic authoritarianism to a democratic authoritarianism [after 1815] without pausing at the intermediate position, which is the position of Anglo-Saxon liberalism."[17] Yet, since the very nonpolitical nature of utilitarian doctrine broad-

14. Bentham, *Theory*, p. 48. In 1795 he published *Anarchical Fallacies, Being an Examination of the Declaration of Rights Issued During the French Revolution.*

15. Bentham, *Theory*, p. 99. L. T. Hobhouse presented an interesting discussion of this problem of rights vs. utility in *Liberalism* (London, Oxford University Press, 1911), pp. 54–72.

16. Martin, p. 7.

17. Halévy, pp. 86, 375–76.

ened its appeal, we find that Bentham had considerable influence among Mexican constitutionalists. The impact was subtle and diffuse, because their principal concern, guaranteeing individual rights against arbitrary power, owed little to utilitarianism. This was equally true with Constant, though he spoke admiringly of "our century which esteems everything according to utility," and though he was a follower of laissez-faire economics.[18]

On several occasions José María Luis Mora revealed that he had absorbed Benthamite principles. He asserted that "the glory of the legislator does not consist in being an inventor, but in guiding his subjects (*comitentes*) toward happiness." The only aim of society, Mora said, is the happiness of the individual members. He made no particular effort to deal with the conflict Bentham saw between rights and utility, and regarded the constitutional protection of inalienable rights as equal to guaranteeing security and the free pursuit of individual interests.[19] Like Constant, Bentham was frequently quoted during the constitutional debates of the twenties and was treated with great reverence by the liberals. Juan Wenceslao Barquera referred to "the wise Bentham, the greatest political and economic writer of our day." Among several authors suggested for study in a proposed state academy, Bentham was singled out by José María de Jáuregui. "In Mexico he has enchanted the intellectuals, who have read him with pleasure and have consumed all the copies [of his books] that have arrived." Jáuregui himself claimed to have had the "good fortune" of reading Bentham since the age of eight, though he admitted not understanding him "right off." [20]

The idea of legal codification had great appeal to Spaniards in both hemispheres, for whom the liberal age meant an opportunity to bring order and simplicity to accumulated legislation. The Mexico state congress showed concern for codification, particularly

18. Constant, "De l'Esprit de conquête," *Cours*, 2, 140, 143, 158. He was speaking of commerce and peaceful material prosperity as opposed to the destructive glory of Napoleon's wars.

19. See *Actas*, 7, 424 (June 5, 1826); 5, 262 (Aug. 20, 1825); Mora, *Obras*, pp. 473, 677.

20. Barquera, *Disertación económico-política sobre los medios de aumentar la población de los estados-unidos mexicanos en su ilustración y riqueza* (Mexico, 1825), p. 34; *Actas*, 1, 84-85 (Mar. 26, 1824); 2, 389-90 (Oct. 13, 1824).

the drawing up of a penal code; and Bentham was the leading authority on the subject. Bentham was regarded as a "demigod" in Spain, where he took a lively interest in the work of the cortes and especially in the projected penal code of 1821.[21] Following the example of the cortes, the state congress entertained several proposals to establish a codification committee. We must have a penal code, insisted Mora, for our judges are blocked at every turn "by the monstrous complication of the criminal laws." Unfortunately, the proposals came to naught during this period, either on the national or on the state level. A few years later, Mora espoused the idea that legislation was "a science of moral calculus," while quoting at length from the master. Above all, said Mora, punishments should be calculated to dissuade others from violating the laws, not to mortify the guilty man.[22] On one judicial matter, however—trial by jury—the Mexican constitutional liberals did not follow Bentham. They shared Constant's enthusiasm for this English institution; Bentham regarded it as a typical example of needless complication in rendering justice.

Though Bentham rejected on principle the notion of inalienable or natural rights, he did not oppose the effort to guarantee individual civil rights—freedom of the press, property, or individual security. Utility was the measure of these rights, and he believed that it was in the public interest to uphold them. Thus the Mexican liberals used Bentham occasionally to support their position of the 1820s. In a key essay on individual civil liberty, Mora warned against excessive governmental authority among peoples newly freed from tyranny, lest governments "enter into such activity that they themselves commit the crimes they ought to avoid." Citing Bentham, Mora added that government must maintain a fine line between (1), extending individual freedom to the

21. Halévy, p. 297. The entry of Bentham's ideas caused more controversy in Colombia than in Mexico. Francisco de Paula Santander, his great admirer, decreed in 1827 that the *Traités* be taught in the schools. The decree was annulled by Simón Bolívar the following year. See Armando Rojas, "La Batalla de Bentham en Colombia," *Revista de historia de América, 29* (1950), 37–66. A thoroughgoing study of Bentham in Spain and Spanish America, which attempts to explain his impact, should be made.

22. See *Actas, 1,* 465, 2d ser. (June 23, 1824); Mora, "Discurso sobre los delitos políticos" (1827), *Obras,* pp. 557–66; also p. 687, on the "barbarities" of Spanish laws.

point where it encroaches upon the security of others, and (2),
guarding against such individual aggression to the point where the
government itself becomes the aggressor.[23]

Mora became angered that some were advocating the explusion
of the Spaniards on Benthamite grounds of public utility. He
agreed with Bentham that "not only is utility the origin of all law,
but also the principle of all human actions"; yet this was no justification for breaking faith on solemn treaties, such as those guaranteeing Spaniards their rights as citizens. One could never justify
explusion by studying "the analytical tables of benefits and evils,
or of pains and pleasures, which are the base of his [Bentham's]
system." All of this merely proves, concluded Mora, that "the
reading and understanding of Bentham is not for half-trained or
mediocre minds." [24]

Bentham's argument against abstract natural rights, especially as
a basis for equality, also had impact on Mora and his group. Quoting copiously from *Sophismes anarchiques* and *Sophismes politiques*, *El Observador* asserted on several occasions that "all is
unequal in this world" and that all the legislator can do is to
diminish inequality. True "public opinion" is a matter of general
utility and not, as Rousseau said, a function of the general will.[25]
Bentham always maintained that his doctrine of the greatest good
for the greatest number had universal application, despite political or cultural differences. As such, it may have had special appeal
to the Mexican liberals of the 1820s, who were seeking to rise
above factional politics and to establish a constitutional system
that could command universal respect.

Utilitarian theory was used even more in the attack upon corporate privilege. Bentham's main concern was reform; "the whole

23. Ibid., p. 508.

24. Ibid., pp. 581–82; see also Francisco Molinos del Campo (*El Observador*, 1st
ser., *1*, 155) who quoted from Chap. 4 of Bentham's *Teoría de las penas legales*,
probably the 1825 translation (2 vols. Paris).

25. See, for example, Z., "Política. Discurso sobre la opinión pública y voluntad
general," *El Observador*, 1st ser., *1*, 255–84 (Aug. 1, 1827); "Igualdad," *El Observador*, 2d ser., *3*, 169–82 (Sept. 8, 1830). A French edition of Bentham's *Essay
on Political Tactics*, published in Geneva in 1816 by Dumont, included both the
Traité des sophismes politiques and the *Sophismes anarchiques: Examen critique
de diverses declarations des droits de l'homme et du citoyen* (see Halévy, p. 536).
This edition is presumably the one the writers in *El Observador* read.

force of his criticism is concentrated not on the principles of metaphysics but on established institutions." [26] If the object of legislation was to bring about the identity of interests, the greatest obstacle to that end was the spirit of corporation, which always conflicted with the general interest of society. One of the confusing points in assessing the influence of utilitarian philosophy is that antiquated institutions and corporate privilege could be and were attacked both in the name of utility and of the rights of man. In the hands of activists who were less concerned with philosophical distinctions and more concerned with politics than was Bentham, the two doctrines became merged into one. Thus the Abbé Sieyès in *What Is the Third Estate?* (1789) assaulted the privileged legal position of the two upper estates on grounds of "the rights appertaining to all" and also because the "alleged utility of a privileged order to public service is only a chimera." [27] This confusion was equally true among the Mexican reformers.

In 1825 Mora called for the abolition of the old audiencia, not because he opposed the judges as individuals, but because it was a body with particular interests of its own. He maintained that his system of district tribunals, with a single judge in the third instance, was cheaper, more efficient, and better calculated to serve the public.[28] José María de Jáuregui, the great Bentham enthusiast, savagely attacked the lawyers' guild (Colegio de Abogados) in the style of the master when it opposed opening the new supreme court to nonguild lawyers. He was supported by his colleague Nájera, who said that "little could be expected from a body which tried to make old prerogatives compatible with new ideas." [29] Mora's later assault upon the espíritu de cuerpo made good use of utilitarian arguments. For Mora, it was basically a matter of "class interests" being advanced against "social interests," of "corporate interests" against the "public welfare." *El Indicador* announced as its objective the suppression of the "clerical and military aristocracy" which was obstructing the "bases of public liberty," the "solid establishment of individual prosperity, and the advances of private fortune." Among the specific problems posed by the cor-

26. Halévy, p. 34.

27. Sieyès in Stewart, *Documentary Survey*, pp. 43, 45.

28. *Actas*, 5, 348–49 (Sept. 24, 1825).

29. *Actas*, 5, 255–57 (Aug. 19, 1825); 7, 140 (Apr. 10, 1826). Jáuregui's attack is curious since he was himself a member of the Colegio.

porate spirit—juridical, economic, and political—Mora emphasized its relation to the "administrative order." As long as corporations exist, "the laws cannot reconcile interests that are difficult
and often impossible to combine." [30]

In assessing the political applications of utilitarian theory, we
may note a tension within the doctrine itself that is of relevance to
our problem. The test of utility—the greatest good for the greatest
number—could be used to support individual rights. And yet
Bentham's strongest affinity was with statism, for example continental enlightened despotism.[31] We have already seen a similar
conflict within political liberalism—irrespective of utilitarian considerations—between a strong state to attack corporate privilege
and a limited state to guarantee individual liberty. In one sense
the tension within utilitarianism merely reinforced this conflict
within political liberalism. Yet a new dimension was added, since
ideally utility was a theory that sought the identity of interests
above political conflict.

The apparent goal of many of Bentham's reform efforts was to
bring about modern and rationalized central administration in
England. It has been argued that his most enduring achievement
was to have suggested a whole fabric of modern administration—municipal reform, improvement of prisons, a national system of education, a civil register of vital statistics, legislation for
public health, and so on.[32] He took special interest in a uniform
system of weights and measures, which his country never adopted.
In all this, as Halévy frequently emphasizes, Bentham's orientation was continental, particularly toward France where administrative centralization was most advanced.[33] This aspect of utilitarian theory helps us understand Mora's statist aspirations, a vital

30. *El Indicador, 1*, iii–iv (Oct. 9, 1833) ; Mora, *Obras*, p. 59.
31. The tension within Bentham's thought between rights and rationalized
administration was particularly well demonstrated in *Theory*, pp. 449–67 ("General
Precautions Against Abuses of Authority") .
32. C. K. Ogden, Introd., ibid., pp. ix–x.
33. Halévy, p. 375. On weights and measures see Bentham, *Theory*, p. 412. The
Englishman Plamenatz makes less of Bentham's continental orientation than does
the Frenchman Halévy, and instead emphasizes the great unacknowledged influence of Thomas Hobbes on utilitarian political conceptions. "The utilitarians,
like Hobbes, regard the state as a means of reconciling men's selfish interests" and
not as a means of protecting their rights (Plamenatz, pp. 10–16) . A tie to Hobbes
would merely reinforce the statist implications of utilitarianism.

and permanent ingredient of Mexican liberalism. Bentham re-
ferred constantly in his earlier writings to the "great Frederick
[II]," for him a model legislator. Mora found inspiration in the
Hispanic enlightened despot, Charles III.

It was within this utilitarian context that Mora made his famous
assault on *empleomanía*—the evil of office seeking—which Zavala
called "the epidemic malady of all peoples of Spanish descent."
Mora looked upon colonial government in Benthamite terms as a
closed corporation with public offices monopolized by the privileged few. At independence, offices had been thrown open to
merit; but since old habits lingered on, there was a great rush to
obtain a secure place in the public employment. Such a mentality
among citizens is entirely antithetical to "work, industry, and
wealth, [qualities] which make men truly and solidly virtuous."
Nothing is "less productive than unnecessary public employees." [34]
In an 1825 debate, Mora even more explicitly defended the
concept of a modern bureaucracy of loyal and removable employees, as opposed to the old idea that an officeholder had a *property* or a *right* in office.[35] An impersonal and effective public administration was an important element of the modern state Mora
envisioned.

Underlying the anticlerical program of 1833 was the drive for
secularization—the fashioning of a society in which religious
values and the church as an institution would be of little consequence in the action of individuals. Of primary importance in
achieving that objective was the effort to destroy the corporate
power of the church in favor of the secular state, which we examined in Chapter 4. But secularization involved more than elimination of corporate power; more subtle, yet more decisive, was the
introduction of essentially utilitarian values into a culture saturated with religion. Though the achievement of a secular mentality was part of the Mexican liberal program, it remains to be seen
in what terms the liberals conceived of it. Here we must reempha-
size the distinction between utilitarian doctrine and the more

34. Zavala, *Ensayo, 1,* 320; Mora, "Discurso sobre los perniciosos efectos de la
empleomanía," *Obras,* pp. 531–37; also *Revoluciones, 1,* 95. Acting upon his convictions, Mora left instructions that his properties not be rented to any military
man or public employee (Mora Correspondence, 1794–1844, Apr. 8, 1836).

35. *Actas, 5,* 75–77 (July 12, 1825).

broadly disseminated utilitarian spirit. Utilitarian morality as espoused by Bentham and Helvétius was radically secular. Both were atheists and sharply out of tune with their times. Their thoroughgoing utilitarian morality, freed from all religious connection, made little headway, even in France and England. Thus it had even less chance of victory in Spain or Mexico, where religious orthodoxy reigned supreme.

Within the Hispanic world, the utilitarian spirit was applied to the reform of the church itself. This was an important theme in the Spanish Enlightenment, just as it came to be in the popular upheaval of 1808–12.[36] While assuming the importance of the church as an institution and while adhering to the doctrine it taught, reformers hoped to make the church serve a more useful function in society.

Such an advocate of clerical reform was the famous José Joaquín Fernández de Lizardi of Mexican letters. Known primarily for *El Periquillo sarniento* (1817), a social satire in the genre of the picaresque novel, Lizardi was (after independence) a prolific pamphleteer who became entangled in bitter disputes over his reform suggestions. Though there was little system to his ideas, and though his impact on politics was small, "he did the work of a pioneer" in his wide-ranging social criticism. He was excommunicated for heresy in 1822 after defending the Freemasons. Though he managed to reconcile himself with the church, his enemies continued to attack him; one of them, José María de Aza, was even tried for libel, but was eventually acquitted. Lizardi struggled vainly to finance his writings. Sickness overtook him in 1826, and his final effort, a slim periodical called *Correo semanario de México,* was written between attacks of tuberculosis. Overwhelmed by adversity, Lizardi died in 1827 in dire poverty, leaving his family destitute. He asked that his epitaph state only: "Here lie the ashes of 'El Pensador Mexicano' who did what he could for his country." [37]

36. See Sarrailh, pp. 614, 648, and passim; Artola, *Orígenes, 1,* 362–66.

37. Quoted in Jefferson R. Spell, *The Life and Works of José Joaquín Fernández de Lizardi* (Philadelphia, University of Pennsylvania Press, 1931), p. 52. Spell is the foremost authority on Lizardi, about whom there is a considerable bibliography. See also Paul Radin, *The Opponents and Friends of Lizardi,* Occasional Papers, Mexican History Series, California State Library (San Francisco, 1939). Lizardi

The monasteries and the monastic life were a favorite utilitarian target. One of the episodes in Lizardi's engaging *Conversaciones del payo [peasant in the city] y el sacristán* involved a discussion in which the sacristán tried to persuade the payo that his daughter Rosita should not become a nun. The payo was proud that his daughter of sixteen, influenced by her confessor and by a saint's life she had read, intended to take the veil. The sacristán then spoke with Rosita and after much persuasion made his point. The girl lost interest in the idea and decided on marriage instead. Though Mora had high praise for the "great and useful services" of the "truly apostolic" sixteenth-century friars, he considered the present-day religious a burden on society. "One will be unlikely, as hard as he may try, to discover the utility of monasteries, especially for women." [38] It was in this spirit that Mora advanced his proposals to limit the regular clergy and their wealth.

The reformers also emphasized the discrepancies of wealth and function between the high and low clergy. The canons of the cathedral chapters came under particular attack. Lizardi called them "insatiable leeches"; Mora asserted that "in their present state, it is difficult to conceive of an institution more useless." Likewise, he criticized the bishops for neglecting their real duties and living in luxury in Mexico City on the lion's share of the tithe money.[39] On the other hand, Mora had great respect for parish priests, and his proposals to nationalize and redirect church income were aimed largely at making this worthy group more effective.

The unfortunate priest, especially in the isolated parish, does not have a minute to himself. Deprived of assistants and of the means to pay them, he can be called at any hour of the

reaffirmed his religious orthodoxy in *Testamento y despedida del pensador mexicano* (Mexico, 1827), *1*, 2.

38. Fernández de Lizardi, *Conversaciones*, *1*, Nos. 7–25; Mora, *Revoluciones*, *1*, 272; *Obras*, pp. 301–02. Cf. Mme. Calderon de la Barca's description of a ceremony in which a young girl takes the veil (*Life in Mexico*, pp. 258–63).

39. *Correo semanario*, Jan. 3, 1827; Mora, *Obras*, pp. 298–99; also *El Fénix*, July 15, 1833. Mme. Calderon described the situation of the Archbishop of Mexico in 1840 as "the most enviable in the world to those who would enjoy a life of luxury, indolence, tranquility, and universal adoration. He is a pope without half the trouble, or a tenth part of the responsibility" (*Life in Mexico*, p. 284).

day or night, in the hottest sun, severest cold, or heaviest rain, to the exercise of his ministry in a sometimes distant place.[40]

Justo Sierra suggested that the midcentury reformers looked to the lower clergy as allies.[41] In his projections for the new society, Mora may have seen them in the same way—the vanguard of a secularized and reformed church.

Inherent in the secularization efforts of the 1833 reformers was the desire to instill in Mexican society a utilitarian code of ethics. According to Mora, it was nearly impossible to establish the foundations of public morality in a people where social and religious duties were confused. In Europe, he pointed out, the problem had practically disappeared, thanks to "the progress of social science." In Mexico, however, the masses, under the influence of the clergy, still see no difference between a crime against society and a religious sin. Though the clergy do not make it a general principle that civil laws should be disobeyed, they reserve the right to "give their opinion from the pulpit or in the confessional" and thus indirectly encourage lawbreaking.[42]

Lorenzo de Zavala suddenly turned moralist in the concluding pages of his *Ensayo histórico* and launched a bitter tirade against Catholic casuistry. He argued that Catholicism was unique among religions in the force with which it penetrated men's hearts and affected their characters. He contrasted the "catechisms of religious instruction" with the Benthamite "table of virtues and vices that are universally known because they are natural to man." The casuist, continued Zavala, replaces the natural virtues of sobriety and continence with observance of Fridays, fasts, vows of chastity, and virginity. The result is that "the murderer, still covered with the blood just shed, eats no meat on Friday . . . [and] the prostitute puts the image of the Virgin beside her bed." Zavala maintained that his generation had been catapulted into a new "moral

40. Mora, *Obras*, p. 300; also a similar passage in *Revoluciones, 1,* 117–18. Mariano Otero's *Consideraciones* (1848) quoted almost an entire page (34) of this latter passage.

41. Sierra, *Juárez*, pp. 78–79.

42. Mora, "Estado de la moral pública," *Revoluciones, 1,* 517–22. A decree was issued on June 6, 1833, forbidding the clergy from preaching on political matters. See Dublán and Lozano, *Legislación, 2,* 531–32.

sphere," but that the transformation was far from complete. New "desires" and "interests" have appeared, but they must be followed by changes in "ideas, actions, and thoughts." [43] Zavala was more radically utilitarian than Mora, who never attacked Catholicism itself. Yet both called for a new secular mentality in which morality was removed from the tyranny of the church.

A major obstacle on the road to secularization was the existence of article 3 of the Constitution of 1824:

> The Roman Catholic Apostolic is and will be perpetually the religion of the Mexican nation. The nation will protect it by wise and just laws and prohibit the exercise of any other.

Toleration was generally recognized as basic to a liberal society, whether seen from the point of view of utility or of natural rights. And yet Mexican and Spanish liberals were reluctant to establish it in fact. López, the translator of Benjamin Constant, substituted for Constant's chapter on religious liberty a statement of his own, saying he was obligated by the constitution not to introduce new ideas. He then proceeded to argue on cultural and historical grounds the case for official intolerance. Likewise, the Mexican translator of Daunou (probably Zavala) added as his only comment that he "was far from regarding as useful or just in our circumstances civil tolerance of worship." [44]

In the national constituent congress, sentiment was strongly in favor of official intolerance, and it went unchallenged in the Mexico state congress, even by Mora. Nor was Mora troubled by logic when he supported government prohibition of books condemned by the church, provided such a policy did not contradict freedom of opinion. [45] In the state congress there was much concern over which religious ceremonies should precede the election of deputies in juntas—masses or litanies to the saints—and over what the religious preamble to the constitution should be. Mora rejected one suggestion that reference should be made to the Trinity. We are a congress, not a church council, said he; "cer-

---

43. Zavala, *Ensayo*, 2, 383–85, 390–91.
44. See Constant, *Curso*, 2, 107–11; Daunou, *Ensayo* (1823), p. 147.
45. *Actas*, 2, 320–23 (Sept. 20, 1824); on the discussions in the national congress see Reyes Heroles, *Liberalismo*, 1, 334–45.

tainly such a mystery is not the basis of society." It was sufficient, Mora believed, to "consider the Supreme Being as author of society," without reference to a specific religion "which perhaps in time will pass away." [46]

The contradicition between official intolerance and liberal social aims soon became apparent. Fernández de Lizardi was an early champion of toleration, for which he was much maligned. His sacristán recounted an incident in which an English Protestant was murdered by a fanatic for failing to kneel when the Host passed on the street, en route to a dying parishoner. What if Michelena (the Mexican minister in England) were to be killed for being a Catholic, he mused.[47] That killing a "heretic" foreigner could be looked upon as "good" was for Mora an excellent example of the confusion of religious sins and social crimes. By 1831 Zavala called for tolerance, and Vicente Rocafuerte's bold *Ensayo sobre tolerancia religiosa* was as welcomed by the liberals as it was condemned by the Bustamante administration.[48] In discussing the reforms needed in the Constitution of 1824, Mora stated explicitly that "the article [3] on religion must be suppressed." Making special reference to his schemes for foreign colonization, he asserted that "everywhere intolerance is contrary to public prosperity and to the progress of enlightenment." The newspapers *El Telégrafo* and *Reformador,* both official organs, also championed the cause of toleration.[49]

Despite this apparently overwhelming sentiment, official intolerance was not removed in 1833; in fact, the anticlerical legislation that was passed assumed official "protection" (and thus regulation) of the church. Even Mora's notion of "separation" was advanced without the apparent necessity of constitutional change. Mora must have sensed strong popular opposition to instituting

46. *Actas, 2,* 133 (July 27, 1824) ; 7, 469–70 (June 9, 1826) .

47. Fernández de Lizardi, *Conversaciones, 1,* Nos. 2–3.

48. Alamán wrote a sharp reply, *Un Regalo del año nuevo para el señor Rocafuerte* (Mexico, 1832) , which was preparatory to a brief imprisonment for Rocafuerte. The cosmopolitan Rocafuerte then served as an editor of *El Fénix* and in 1833 returned to his native Ecuador to assume the presidency. For Zavala's views, see *Ensayo, 1,* 372.

49. Mora, *Revoluciones, 1,* 319–20; *El Telégrafo,* Sept. 11, 1833; *Reformador,* Nov. 28, 1833.

toleration; for in 1837, he concluded that it "can and must be deferred indefinitely, since there are no Mexicans who profess faiths
other than the Roman Catholic, nor are there as in other countries
urgent reasons which make it necessary to guarantee [other
faiths]." [50] Perhaps the key to Mora's ambivalence was expressed
in 1830 when he wrote that for such a reform to be permanent "it
must be gradual and be characterized by *mental revolutions* which
extend to all of society." [51] Caught between his instinctive attachment to Hispanic values and his utilitarian and liberal aspirations,
he counseled moderation, implying that tolerance was a matter
that must be left to education.

In the utilitarian system of Helvétius and Bentham the educator
shared with the legislator a principal role. "It should be the object
of public instruction," wrote Bentham, "to make each individual
perceive how the general interest involves his own." Men should
be taught to shun the spirit of family, caste, party, sect, or profession, "which militates against the love of country." [52] For Mora,
writing in 1827, education could also help the individual find "the
rules which must govern his actions and which must impose
obligations at the same time that they guarantee rights." He needs
more than "natural inspiration" (*luz natural*) to "know that community well-being results in individual benefit." [53] Mora saw
education in Mexico as part of "the work of regeneration," the
formation of "a public spirit." In passing from a "harsh despotism" to a republican system where citizens need "all the moral
virtues," it is indispensable to have knowledge of social science.

Utilitarians also believed that since man was a product of his
environment, social as well as physical, he must learn its facts and
discover its laws. In so doing man could find the keys to human
and social progress. Thus Mora's *El Observador* filled its pages

50. Mora, *Obras*, p. 54. First written after Mora left Mexico, this statement
represented Mora's final thinking on the matter during the 1830s. The previous
passage (see n. 49 above), though published in 1836, was merely reprinted from
El Indicador, 2, 237–38 (Jan. 15, 1834). It may have been written as early as 1830.
    51. Mora, "Noticias estadístico-políticas de Méjico escritas en 1830," *El Indicador*,
2, 57 (Dec. 4, 1833), reprinted in *Revoluciones, 1*, 129. Italics mine.
    52. Bentham, *Theory*, pp. 431–32.
    53. See "Pensamientos sueltos sobre educación pública," *Obras*, p. 523, a fine ex-
pression of Mora's utilitarian views.

with random "scientific" articles—on preserving meat, on mummies, on cultivating cacao (by Alzate), on yellow fever, an appeal to conduct experiments on barometric pressure and air temperature, and even a piece by Count Rumford on eliminating beggars in Munich—all in an effort to propagate useful knowledge in the country.[54]

El Observador, of course, was attempting to revive what Mora called the "Mexican Enlightenment," the enlivened scientific spirit that won Humboldt's praise in 1804 but was dissipated by the ruinous war of independence. This spirit was an extension of Spanish educational rejuvenation in which Jovellanos played a role that "cannot be overexaggerated." [55] Jovellanos was the chief educational authority in Spain between 1780 and 1810 and wrote voluminously on the subject. His great project was the Asturian Institute at Gijón (given a royal charter in 1794) which was to emphasize study of the natural sciences. Jovellanos' educational philosophy, analogous to that of the utilitarians, was derived from the sensualist psychology of Locke and Condillac.[56]

As noted previously, four of Jovellanos' essays, written for the Asturian Institute, were reprinted in Mora's El Indicador, interspersed with notices of Mexico's own reforms. The editor (Mora) noted that Jovellanos was calling for study of nature and its marvels, both to know and adore the Creator, and also "to discover

54. Rumford (El Observador, 2d ser., 3, 331–39) illustrates particularly well the applied utilitarian spirit that so impressed Mora. Rumford (1753–1814) was a typical eighteenth-century cosmopolite (born Benjamin Thompson, of Woburn, Massachusetts), a scientist, inventor, and army officer who left for England during the Revolution. He later served eleven years as minister of war for Prince Maximilian of Bavaria, during which time he reorganized the army and created state industries for Munich's beggars. As a Count of the Holy Roman Empire, Rumford (he took the name Rumford from his wife's birthplace, Rumford, New Hampshire, which is now Concord) returned to England, made important discoveries regarding heat, and was cofounder of the Royal Institution (1800). The Institution was dedicated to "diffusing the knowledge and facilitating the general introduction of useful mechanical inventions and improvements."

55. Sarrailh, p. 219.

56. See Polt, pp. 43–51. Besides the essays mentioned below, Jovellanos drew up (1797) at royal behest a plan for reforming university studies, before he was exiled to Majorca. In exile he prepared his long "Memoria sobre la educación pública" (BAE, 46, 230–67), and later, in 1809 for the Junta Central, "Bases para la formación de un plan general de instrucción pública" (BAE, 46, 268–76). His influence upon the Cortes of Cádiz was great.

useful truths for the advancement of the arts and of commerce."
Moreover, Jovellanos urged that the noble ideas and sentiments of
literature be combined with the useful sciences to produce worthy
public citizens.[57] The inspiration of Jovellanos was undeniably
present in Mora's educational ideas.

In Mexico after 1821, primary education was what first captured
the interest of reformers. The focus of enthusiasm was the "mutual" system of instruction, founded in England and soon popular
on the continent. The system, known as the "Lancasterian" system
after one of its founders, was an outgrowth of the numerous
church societies that sprang up in eighteenth-century England for
"promoting Christian knowledge" among the masses. It was established simultaneously (but independently) about 1800 by Andrew Bell, an Anglican chaplain in a children's asylum in Madras,
India, and by Joseph Lancaster, a Quaker, in England. The
scheme was to use a few older pupils as "monitors" who would
pass on the master's questions to many younger pupils. It was an
unusually cheap method by which one supervisor, through an
elaborate system of mechanical drill, could oversee the instruction
of a large number. Both its economy and its aspect of mechaniza-
tion struck the mind of the day. Lancaster won the patronage of
George III, who remarked that he would like to see every British
subject be able to read the Bible. Lancaster maintained that "on
this plan, any boy who can read can teach . . . for a boy who can
read can teach although he knows nothing about it." [58]

Jeremy Bentham was introduced to the Lancasterian system
through his colleague James Mill, and he seized upon it as the
ideal vehicle for a general plan of "utilitarian education." The result was his "Chrestomathia" (chrestomathic, "conducive to useful learning") in which he demonstrated its benefits by means of
elaborate notes, appendixes, and tables. Bentham believed the
mutual system could be extended to all education. Classical learning was to be eliminated: "By the middle ranks of life, for the use
of which the proposed system of instruction is designed, the useful

57. See note to Jovellanos, "Otra [Oración] pronunciada en el mismo instituto
asturiano" (1798), in El Indicador, 3, 338 (Apr. 16, 1834); also Jovellanos, "Oración que pronunció . . . en el instituto sobre la necesidad de unir el estudio de la
literatura al de las ciencias," in ibid., pp. 308–09.

58. Quoted in John Roach, "Education and Public Opinion," New Cambridge
Modern History, 9 (Cambridge, Cambridge University Press, 1965), 206.

and not merely ornamental instruction is required." [59] In great vogue on the continent, the Lancasterian system was favored by the foremost French society for primary education and was adopted in Spain in 1821. It was introduced to Mexico by Manuel Codorniu, founder of the newspaper *El Sol,* who came in 1821 with the Viceroy O'Donojú.

The first Escuela del Sol opened in the Palace of the Inquisition on August 22, 1822, converting that infamous spot, as Rocafuerte later remarked, into "a temple of reason." The new plan was the work of the constitutional monarchist group of 1822, later the escoces party, which included José María Fagoaga, Lucas Alamán, José María Luis Mora, and other members of the provincial deputation of Mexico.[60] Alamán wrote a detailed description of the system which gave no hint of his later conservatism. Support gradually widened. Vicente Rocafuerte returned from his post of chargé d'affaires in England as an agent for the British and Foreign School Society, the international Lancasterian organization. Sánchez, the governor of Jalisco, introduced mutual education into his reform plan of 1826.[61] Enthusiasm for the system filled the newspapers, especially, of course, *El Sol,* which on June 27, 1826, said that the purpose of the schools was "to form a new race of men, whose individual desires will be identified with independence and liberty." Ultimately, the mutual system of instruction was adopted as the official method to be used in the new primary-school system established in the Federal District in 1833.[62]

Mora appears to have had little direct involvement with pro-

59. Bentham, "Chrestomathia" (1816) in *Works,* ed. by J. Bowring (Edinburgh, 1838–43) , *8,* 16–17. See also Halévy, *Growth,* pp. 286–89.

60. Other enthusiasts were Eulogio Villaurrutia and Agustín Buenrostro. See Irma Wilson, *Mexico: A Century of Educational Thought* (New York, Hispanic Inst., 1941) , pp. 132–38.

61. See Alamán, "Instrucción para el establecimiento de escuelas, según los principios de la enseñanza mútua, presentada a la excma. diputación provincial de México, por . . . diputado en las cortes de España por la provincia de Guanajuato," in *La Sabatina universal, 1,* 266–74, 279–99 (Sept. 28, Oct. 5, 12, 1822) . On Rocafuerte see W. E. Browning, "Joseph Lancaster, James Thomson, and the Lancasterian System of Mutual Instruction, With Special Reference to Hispanic America," *HAHR, 4* (1921) , 96–97. On Sánchez see Luis Pérez Verdía, "Prisciliano Sánchez," *Biografías* (Guadalajara, Ediciones I.T.G., 1952) , p. 94. As Roach says, the Lancasterian system was a blind alley and was ultimately abandoned everywhere, but it did awaken the public to the possibilities of mass education.

62. See Dublán and Lozano, *2,* 576–77 (Oct. 26, 1833) .

moting the Lancasterian system, but he did become acquainted
with James Thomson, who came to Mexico in 1827 as agent for
both the School Society and the British and Foreign Bible Society.
Mora became so intrigued with the challenge of circulating the
Bible widely in a country where official intolerance reigned that
he agreed to act as Mexican representative for the Society. He even
translated the Book of Luke into Nahuatl. Between 1829 and 1833
Mora carried on an extensive correspondence with Thomson and
other officials, mostly concerning shipments of Bibles which the
Bustamante government had tied up in customs. He also kept
Thomson informed on the progress of tolerance (or the lack of it)
in Mexico, a subject of mutual concern. Both Thomson and Mora
regarded the activities of the Society as a corollary to enlightening
the masses through primary education. Spreading Bibles did not
conflict with utilitarian educational goals, except in the case of a
few individuals like Bentham, who were radical secularists. In
England, primary education had been left by default to the
churches, and most Englishmen, like Mora, placed education
within the context of religion, however broadly defined.[63]

Mora's chief interest, however, was higher education. He maintained a close connection with his own Colegio de San Ildefonso
during the 1820s, where he resided and introduced a course in
political economy. On January 22, 1822, he was named by Iturbide to a committee to prepare a plan of studies for consideration
by the congress. Mora's special assignment was San Ildefonso, for
which he drew up a reform proposal (now lost) that won the
praise of Lucas Alamán in 1823.[64] Other plans were proposed, but
there was generally little stir in higher education during the
1820s, except in the provinces. Prisciliano Sánchez's institute in
Guadalajara, probably inspired by Jovellanos, was described by

63. See Mora, "Sociedad de la biblia" (1828), *Obras*, pp. 615–16. There are
numerous letters to Mora from Bible Society officials in Mora Correspondence,
1794–1844. They have been studied carefully by Florstedt, "Liberal Role," pp.
234–40, 316–20, and by Pedro Gringoire, "El 'Protestantismo' del Dr. Mora," *Historia mexicana, 3* (1953), 328–66. Gringoire concludes from these and from material
in the archives of the Bible Society that Mora did not convert to Protestantism, as
Génaro García suggested, but that he merely took an ecumenical view of Catholicism. On Thomson's activities, see Browning, "Joseph Lancaster."

64. The cordial note from Alamán to Mora (Mora Correspondence, 1794–1844)
is the only record we have of direct communication between the two men.

Mora as the "most fortunate and complete effort of its day."[65] Curiously enough, little attention was paid to higher education by the Mexico state constituent congress.

Mora later acknowledged the value of a reform plan presented by Lucas Alamán, as minister, in 1830. It would have divided instruction into four branches, an existing colegio to house each; new subjects were to be introduced and useless chairs of theology suppressed. Alamán's plan was brief and moderate for, as he himself said, the Bustamante administration believed that in all things it was better to reform than to create anew. Thus the old university was to continue along with the new establishments. Mora said sarcastically that Alamán in 1834 did not reject the liberal reform; in fact, "in defending it [Alamán] does not disguise his pretentions to having inspired it." Mora's tone leads one to suspect some truth in Alamán's claim. At least, it is another indication that there were points of affinity in the two men's ideas.[66]

The short-lived educational reforms were at the heart of what Mora often referred to as the "revolution of 1833." All evidence indicates that though he was never officially minister of education, Mora was the chief architect of the changes. He served on the educational committee appointed by Gómez Farías (September 20, 1833), which later became the General Board of Public Instruction (Dirección General de Instrucción), the new government agency to control education. The reforms were revolutionary in that the university and most of the former colegios of the Federal District were abolished and replaced by six state-controlled "establishments," each devoted to a branch of learning. Professors and administrators were to be government appointed. The new legislation, of course, was directed against the university as a corporate body but even more against the great influence the clergy exerted through education. It was in part for this reason that *El Indicador*

65. Mora, *Obras*, p. 113.
66. See ibid., pp. 114–15, 131. Alamán's plan can be found in his "Memoria" (1830), *Documentos, 1*, 222–25. There are obvious similarities between the plans of Alamán and Mora, sketchy as the former was. Alamán even spoke of a Dirección General de Estudios, though he apparently intended that each of the four branches have more autonomy than did Mora. Alamán reported in 1831 that a committee had been formed but that "not a step had been taken." The 1832 report on education was reduced to one page.

reprinted the educational essays of Jovellanos, mostly written just after his dismissal as minister of justice in 1797, when the church opposed his reform plan. "Jovellanos is the best witness to the great difficulty of moving forward in public education," wrote Mora.[67] Despite the conscious effort to be radical, for instance by eliminating the old terms "university" and "colegio" in favor of the neutral "establishment," the reform stayed well within Hispanic traditions.

Mora, Zavala, and the reformist newspapers reserved their sharpest anticlerical rhetoric for the old system of higher education. "The education of the colegios," wrote Mora, "is more monastic than civil." The life of the student is filled with "devotions more appropriate to the mystical than to the Christian life." Religious festivals, processions, and burials take two hundred days out of the student's year, prolonging education and "keeping him from industrious and positive occupations." The profusion of religious holidays was always particularly infuriating to the utilitarian mind. In the colegios, said Mora, subjects relevant to today's society—constitutional law, political economy, "profane" history, commerce, agriculture—are ignored.

Under clerical control education can never foster "a spirit of investigation and doubt" but only the "habit of dogmatism and dispute." The favorite teaching method, according to Mora, was to select an outdated author, expound his doctrines, and then to uphold them against all contrary evidence. The dogmatic method even spreads to the natural sciences, paralyzing them. Mora conceded that many good men (like himself, no doubt) had come out of the colegios, but that later they had to forget all they had learned. In general, the education of the colegios "does not lead to the forming of men who are to serve in the world; moreover, it falsifies and destroys at the root all convictions that go into making a positive man." [68] To create a *hombre positivo*—the utilitarian

67. Editor's note in *El Indicador*, 3, 344 (Apr. 16, 1834).

68. Mora, *Obras*, p. 117. For Zavala's views see *Ensayo*, 2, 228, 386–89. See also *Reformador*, Feb. 17, 1834. On Nov. 6, 1833, *Reformador* announced that "we have the good fortune of living in the nineteenth century, which is that of the positive." Leopoldo Zea points to Mora as the precursor of positivism in *El Positivismo en México* (Mexico, Studium, 1953), pp. 81–109; also *The Latin American Mind* (Norman, University of Oklahoma Press, 1963), p. 129.

advance public utility and national prosperity.[8] The scope of this concern for improvement was wide, from reviving decadent industries, such as silk and linen, to establishing centers for technical education and creating a state system of hospitals, orphanages, and improved public works. The activity of the societies was based on the desire to accumulate useful knowledge about the country and its problems. Utilitarianism as a doctrine made slow progress in Spain, however, because of the universal attachment to political and religious orthodoxy. Royal patronage for reform was taken for granted.[9] Jovellanos, in his 1788 eulogy on Charles III, emphasized above all that "useful sciences, economic principles, and the general spirit of enlightenment" had advanced only because the king had prepared the country to receive them.[10]

Jovellanos became the chief Spanish advocate of the new utilitarianism in the economic realm. His "Informe de ley agraria" spoke the language of individual interest and laissez-faire in every paragraph. Writing in the name of the Economic Society of Madrid, he petitioned that

> Your Highness [Charles IV] deign to promote the study of civil economy, the science that teaches how to combine public interest with individual interest and to establish the power and force of empires upon the fortunes of individuals.[11]

Though some guidance was necessary, Jovellanos believed that free competition would more likely produce a rational "balance" of interests than would direct legislation. He then proceeded to identify the various obstacles, physical, moral, and political, which, if removed, would allow the free play of individual interests, the basis of general prosperity. There is some debate as to whether Jovellanos was more decisively influenced by the physiocrats or by Adam Smith.[12] For our purposes it may be said that Jovellanos assumed the presence of a sovereign as did the physio-

---

8. See Sarrailh, *L'Espagne éclairée*, pp. 169, 223, and passim; also Robert J. Shafer, *The Economic Societies in the Spanish World, 1763–1821* (Syracuse, Syracuse University Press, 1958).

9. Sarrailh, p. 183; Herr, *Eighteenth-Century Revolution*, p. 154.

10. Jovellanos, "Elogio," *BAE, 46*, 311–12.

11. Jovellanos, "Informe," *BAE, 50*, 121–22.

12. Polt has recently argued the case for Adam Smith in *Jovellanos*, pp. 15–43.

model of the industrious, enlightened individual in pursuit of his own interests, whose chief loyalty would be as a virtuous citizen to the civil state—was Mora's educational goal.

The university was suppressed by decree on October 21, 1833, causing the *Reformador* to comment that "the last bulwark of gothic errors has disappeared forever." The six new establishments provided for a diversified and specialized instruction under central control, as opposed to the former system in which most of the colegios duplicated each other and formed so many "bastard universities." The law elaborated the subjects to be taught in each and where each was to be located.[69] However, not all the former institutions were suppressed. Mora acknowledged that the third establishment, physical sciences and mathematics, needed few changes from the old Colegio de Minería (where it was also housed). The Colegio was created in 1783 as part of Charles III's effort to reform the mining industry, and it had become the source of much of the scientific awakening in Mexico before 1810.[70]

Mora's own establishment, the second (humanities and ideological studies), was to teach everything which "contributes to the use of natural reason, or the development of the mental faculties of man, known in the philosophical world as Ideology"—that is, history, the statistics and geography of Mexico, political economy, and literature.[71] The establishment was eventually housed in the Hospital de Jesús, one of the properties of Monteleone nationalized in 1833 to endow education. Mora himself moved into a luxuriously furnished apartment in the building.[72] The other

69. Dublán and Lozano, 2, 570–74 (Oct. 26, 1833).

70. Mora, *Obras*, p. 125. See also Chap. 8 below.

71. "Ideology," the science of ideas, was a term used by Destutt de Tracy (1754–1834), the last eminent representative of the sensualistic school of philosophy of Locke and Condillac. He pushed their principles to their logical conclusion by asserting in his *Éléments d'idéologie* (1817–18) that all of the faculties of the conscious life were varieties of sensation. To think is to feel. Tracy was popular among the liberals, both as a constitutional liberal who wrote commentaries on Montesquieu, and as a philosopher. Mora reported in 1834 that the students of his establishment were reading the first ten lessons of Tracy. See *El Indicador, 3,* 383 (Apr. 23, 1833).

72. In fact, it was so luxurious that Mora was attacked for graft by *El Mosquito mexicano* (Florstedt, "Liberal Role," p. 421). The educational endowment was to consist of several convents, Monteleone's property, and that of the former colegios. See Dublán and Lozano, 2, 574–75 (Oct. 26, 1833).

establishments were, the first, preparatory studies; the fourth, medicine; the fifth, law; and the sixth, ecclesiastical sciences. The General Board of Public Instruction was also to control the San Carlos fine arts academy, the national museum, and a public library.

The reports submitted to the General Board of Public Instruction in April 1834 indicated that the rejuvenation in education was of modest proportions. Manuel Eduardo de Gorostiza, secretary of the board, reported that the proceeds from the various educational funds amounted to 223,830 pesos, though many of the expropriated properties were in ill repair. Three hundred and thirty-four students were enrolled in forty-seven courses. Troncoso in preparatory studies, Espinosa in law, and Mora in humanities all emphasized progress. Mora claimed forty-five students, Troncoso fifty-six, including two who were studying Otomí and one, "Mexican." The physical plant left much to be desired. The director of mathematics and physics complained that though the Colegio de Minería was "the most beautiful building in America," its laboratories and equipment were in shambles, fossils were piled in heaps on the ground, and window panes were broken. Mora said that saltpeter was eating away at the foundations of the Hospital de Jesús to a height of twelve feet.

Probably the most prosperous of the new enterprises were the two Lancasterian schools established in the Belem convent and the Hospital de Jesús. Gorostiza claimed there were 1,885 students in the primary school and 386 artisans and apprentices studying at night. The secretary, though indicating that there was a struggle against both the "old prejudices" and some "newly created interests," concluded that the achievement of six months had been remarkable. "Today . . . instruction is in perfect harmony with public institutions." [73]

The educational program was to be the cornerstone of the new

73. Gorostiza's report and Mora's were printed in *El Indicador, 4,* 28–35, and *3,* 380–85. The others are in MS. in Mora Documents, 1806–38. See also Wilson, pp. 162–68, and Florstedt, "Liberal Role." Gorostiza's reference to opposition confirms Mora's mention of disagreement on education (see above, p. 144) . Apparently, the chief dissenter was Juan Rodríguez Puebla, an early member of the board and briefly director of the first establishment. Mora said that the conflict came over Indian education. See Chap. 7 below.

liberal edifice. But the laws on education were soon abrogated by Santa Anna, the "Attila of Mexican civilization," and secularization had to await Gabino Barreda, a generation later. The liberal plan was radical in that it tore down the bulk of the colonial establishment, with the notable exception of Charles III's Colegio de Minería. Despite some probable Napoleonic inspiration, the reform as a whole, however, went no further than anything Jovellanos had advocated in 1798 or in 1809. "Theology" was changed to "ecclesiastical sciences." Mora said that "since religion rests on facts, its study is and must necessarily be historical and critical." [74] If no longer queen of the sciences, at least it still occupied a conspicuous place in the curriculum. The reformers feared lest their reforms be interpreted (as they were) as too radically secular. It was for that reason that Mora inserted in *El Indicador* the notes from Juan Agustín Ceán Bermúdez' *Memorias para la vida de Jove Llanos* (1814). Ceán had protested that his great friend was no atheist, but a deeply religious man.[75] Nor did the Mexican reformers intend that the religious life of their students be impaired by secular learning. In the establishment of law one of the regulations was that "all students will attend daily the Holy Sacrifice of the Mass which is celebrated in the establishment, and at night the Rosary, or any other devotion instituted by the director." [76] Mora's *hombre positivo* was to be no Benthamite secularist, but an individual rooted in Hispanic culture.

Next, we must confront directly a question often hinted at earlier. What *form* was the new society to take? What were its class relationships and its economic center of gravity to be? After 1830, the liberals began increasingly to employ the word "society." Mora attacked the regime of corporate privilege not only as the "ancient constitution of the country" in the juridical sense, but also as the manifestation of the colonial social order.

The key to the new society can be found in the liberal concep-

74. Mora, *Obras,* p. 125.

75. See *El Indicador, 3,* 342–44. Ceán was referring to the accusations made against Jovellanos at the time the latter was dismissed from the ministry of justice in 1797.

76. Report of Mar. 15, 1834, Mora Documents, 1806–38. The director was also to enforce the reception of Communion annually and at all the "principal festivals of Jesus Christ and the Holy Mother."

tion of property. Alexis de Tocqueville remarked in 1849 that the "French Revolution, which abolished all privileges and destroyed all exclusive rights, has allowed one to remain, that of property." [77] When he added, prophetically, that "property will form the great field of battle," he was distinguishing the future from the liberal age just passed, when there existed general agreement on the sanctity of individual property. In Mexico, the views of Mora epitomized this consensus; it predominated during his generation, despite the rare expressions of agrarian radicalism so fondly regarded by some twentieth-century Mexican interpreters.

John Locke made property a natural or inalienable right (see above, page 48) by saying that every man "has a 'property' in his own person" derived from the product of his labor. Property became an extension of the individual's right to life itself, thus assuring that it would form a part of the statement of rights of every constitutional declaration. The utilitarians, despite their different philosophic premises, also concluded that property was inviolable. Both Bentham and Edmund Burke derived their arguments on property from David Hume who argued that justice, an "artificial" as opposed to a "natural" virtue, meant above all respect for existing conventions about property.[78] Property is what holds society together.

Bentham argued that respect for property was closely tied to security, a measure of the greatest good and a principal object of civil law. "A long time has been necessary to carry property to the point where we now see it in civilized societies," he wrote. He was impressed, moreover, by "how easily the savage instinct of plunder gets the better of the laws," and he concluded in effect that property rights must be protected.[79] The utilitarians established a social basis for property, which eventually led to an argument for abridging individual property in the interests of society; but this was a later development. In a sense, both natural rights and utilitarian theory converged in the early nineteenth century to exalt

77. Tocqueville, *Recollections* (New York, Meridian, 1959), pp. 10–11.

78. See Plamenatz, pp. 34–36, 42. Justice was an "artificial" virtue for Hume because it "arises from the circumstances and necessity of mankind."

79. See Bentham, *Theory*, pp. 109–13, 145. When it came to property, Bentham even seemed to be using Burkean "prescription" in its defense.

individual property as untouchable. Benjamin Constant, for example, who generally made little use of utilitarian arguments, said property was none other than a social convention; and yet he upheld it as if it were a right that predated society.[80]

Although the connotation property had for liberals underwent change in England with the early onset of industrialization, on the continent property continued to be thought of as land. In the economic system of the physiocrats "property is the foundation stone of the 'natural order'. . . . It is a 'divine' institution—the word is there." [81] In an agricultural society, the physiocrats were impressed by the artificial maladjustment imposed by the multiplicity of legal, juridical, and economic privileges of the vestigial feudal regime. Thus liberty and the realization of the "natural order" meant merely the removal of these barriers, and the free pursuit of interests by the class of landed proprietors. The French Revolution perpetuated the assumptions of the physiocrats. When the Abbé Sieyès said that the third estate was the nation, he meant the French bourgeoisie, the class that became the beneficiary to the distribution of aristocratic and clerical property. Constitutional liberals—the early revolutionaries, Benjamin Constant, and Mora in Mexico—saw the landowning citizen as the bulwark of a free society.

In Spain, Gaspar Melchor de Jovellanos in his "Informe de ley agraria" envisioned a regeneration of agriculture by the removal of obstacles that impeded the individual cultivator from freely pursuing his interests. Implicit in his attack on entailment, on the privileges of the Mesta (sheepherders' guild), and on the restrictions to internal trade, was his vision of a society resting on free property holders. The ideas of Jovellanos were implemented by the Cortes of Cádiz, "desiring," as it said, "to protect the right of

80. See Constant, "Principes de politique," *Cours, 1,* 112–14; also Ruggiero, *History,* pp. 28–32, a discussion of eighteenth-century notions of property. Reyes Heroles emphasizes the fact that several deputies in the national constituent congress of 1823–24, notably Carlos María de Bustamante, espoused a social theory of property, which he construes as an early interest in agrarian reform. However, more significant than what can now be logically deduced from this theory (one quite generalized at the time) was what the contemporary liberals actually did conclude from it. See Reyes Heroles, *Liberalismo, 1,* 127–41.

81. Gide and Rist, p. 40.

property" and to encourage agriculture "by means of rightful freedom in its speculations." Property was declared subject to enclosure, rental contracts were to be binding for a specific period, and the grain trade was to be free.[82]

From our examination of Mora's political liberalism, it is evident that he shared these French and Spanish assumptions. In his first political essay he justified independence on the grounds that the country belonged to those who cultivated it. He spoke of a "sacred right" to property "legally acquired," which could not be usurped by the king and a small coterie.[83] Mora's constitutionalism, like that of Constant, was predicated on the idea that only the individual property holder could freely exercise his rights and still be responsible to society. Mora's proposals to place property qualifications on citizenship, advanced first on the state and then on the national level, were based on the belief that property holders could control anarchy and guarantee the constitution.

Mora's vision of a rural bourgeoisie was even more explicitly developed in his program to disentail church property. He feared that unless his scheme to transfer the expropriated property to its present tenants was carried through, the reform would only benefit the wealthy. Looking for a model, he hit upon France.

> What would have happened in France if the property of the church had been sold to the nobles? Would they have become the prop of the Revolution, as are the present property holders created by those events? Would the French be free today, or would they remain as a class of colonists on the land of a great lord?

The Mexican recipients of church land under Mora's plan would likewise tie their destiny to the "revolution" of 1833; the reforms "would create a multitude of small proprietors who by their expansive force would be the base of public order."[84]

82. Decree of June 8, 1813 (Dublán and Lozano, *1*, 410–12). See also Artola, *1*, 444, 483. On Jan. 12, 1814, Jovellanos was declared *Benemérito de la Patria* by the cortes. The citation emphasized the importance of the "Informe" for agrarian reform (Polt, p. 31a).

83. Mora, "Discurso sobre la independencia del imperio mexicano" (Nov. 21, 1821), *Obras*, pp. 465–67.

84. Ibid., pp. 377 and 389. In 1859, Melchor Ocampo looked again to the French experience with the same goal in mind. See Sierra, *Juárez*, p. 168.

A persistent problem for the liberals projecting the new society was how to increase and fortify this class of small rural property holders. Redistributing the lands of the church was one way; colonization by foreigners was another. Colonization was regarded as a social panacea by liberals throughout Latin America in the nineteenth century. In Mexico it was uniquely attractive as a means of counterbalancing the preponderantly Indian character of rural society, a matter we will explore in Chapter 7.

Colonization was much discussed in Mexico during the twenties and thirties, and a basic law facilitating the process was passed in 1824. There was, however, a deep-rooted suspicion of foreigners, a legacy of three centuries of isolation from the outside world, which, according to Mora, Zavala, and Ortiz (and, for example, Alberdi in Argentina), posed great obstacles to any consistent colonization program. One of the points Mora used to designate the "party of progress" was the equality of Mexicans and foreigners in civil rights. He spoke of the "judaic spirit of isolation" which characterized Hispanic countries. Lorenzo de Zavala, who as we shall see had special interests in colonization, assailed the law of March 12, 1828, which demanded passports of foreigners and put many restrictions on their owning of land. The law "is another of the sad consequences of our Spanish habits." [85] Tadeo Ortiz, who pioneered by proposing a scheme in 1823 for settling Tehuantepec with veterans, called the additional limitations on colonization imposed by an 1830 law "absurd, ineffective, and contradictory." [86] In the early 1830s Mora emphasized particularly the need for toleration as a means of encouraging colonization (see above, page 165). Official intolerance meant that only Catholics could be truly welcome as colonists.

85. See Mora, *Obras,* p. 149; Zavala, *Memoria* (1833), p. 8. The Aug. 18, 1824, law can be found in Dublán and Lozano, *1,* 712–13, the 1828 law in ibid., *2,* 64–65.

86. Tadeo Ortiz, *México considerado como nación independiente y libre* (Bordeaux, 1832), p. 441. See also his *Bases sobre las que se ha formado un plan de colonización en el ysmo de Hoazcoalco o Tehuantepec* (Mexico, 1823). Ortiz also wrote numerous articles in *El Sol* during 1824–25, promoting the development of that region. For other early interest see Reyes Heroles, *Liberalismo, 1,* 141–46. The 1830 law (Dublán and Lozano, *2,* 238–40) provided for review by the central government of state colonization projects. The 1824 law had left colonization up to the states. Principally, however, the 1830 law put limitations on foreign colonization in Texas (see Chap. 6 below).

The colonization laws of 1824 and 1828 explicitly put limits on the size of holdings, reflecting a general conviction among the liberals that it was *small* property that should become the economic base of the new society. This brings us to one of the critical questions of Mexican liberalism: How did the liberals intend to deal with latifundia? Mora made it clear what results he anticipated from his disentailment proposals. They should encourage

> not the large and uncultivated possessions, nor the proud landowners who squander in the great cities the fruit of what they extort from the colonist, but rather the small and productive holdings, occupied by the owner whose presence and whose vital efforts make them valuable and productive.

Mora even asserted that the present landowners, with few exceptions, "far from being useful are highly pernicious to society." Zavala wrote that land division was essential for equality in a new nation.[87] What then should be done? Mora admired a scheme of Governor Francisco García of Zacatecas for selling state-owned property to colonists in small portions, and even for purchasing ("if this is possible," added Mora) some large private properties for distribution. A later governor-to-be, Luis de la Rosa, wrote a stinging indictment of private latifundia and offered to distribute his own properties as an example to other hacendados.[88]

The key to the problem of latifundia is revealed in one of Mora's phrases which appeared in both the discussions just cited: "since it is not possible to take direct measures to diminish these immense possessions." Here we encounter a basic premise, namely that "the legislator cannot make direct laws that affect private property." Unlike corporate property, Mora maintained that the right to individual property predated society (see above, page

---

87. Mora, *Obras*, p. 378; Zavala, *Ensayo*, *1*, 18–20.

88. Mora, *Revoluciones*, *1*, 512; Rosa, *Observaciones sobre varios puntos concernientes a la administración pública del estado de Zacatecas* (Baltimore, 1851), pp. 5–6, 52–54. Zacatecas had a tradition of small properties, unlike most of the Indian areas of the center. In fact, with the population growth of the late eighteenth century, there was increased pressure for more small holdings, which culminated in García's reforms. See F. Chevalier, "Survivances seigneuriales et présages de la révolution agraire dans le nord du Mexique," *Revue historique*, 222 (1959), 1–18. Rosa's testimony would indicate, however, that García's reforms came to naught.

134) and thus was inviolable. The land problem could only be solved indirectly, by distributing the land of the church in order to strengthen the rural middle class.

Mora used the French Revolution as a model, but it was really inapplicable to the unique society of Mexico. France was a country of peasant proprietors, even before the Revolution; Mexico was a nation of Indians living in communal villages or on haciendas as landless peons. Moreover, the French revolutionaries attacked the nobility along with the church as a corporate estate, and transferred the property of both to the third estate—"the nation." But as we have seen, there was virtually no nobility in Mexico (except for Monteleone). There were only the latifundistas, who in liberal terminology were individual property owners and did not form a legal estate. Because there was no legal division between different types of lay landowners in Mexico, the size of the holding became a relative matter. Thus, the liberal attack on latifundia was also undermined for social reasons, since most of the legislators themselves were landowners.[89]

Mora emphasized the distinction between corporate and private property. The first could be legally limited, the second could not. In making this distinction, Mora shared the assumption of the physiocrats and of Jovellanos that the real problem in society was not accumulation of wealth, but rather the obstacles preventing the individual from freely pursuing his interests. Thus for Mora, as for Jovellanos, it was corporate accumulation that became the target of policy. Mora disliked latifundia and yearned for a society of small farmers; but liberal theory and the peculiarities of Mexican society stood in the way of its realization.

The immense influence of Jovellanos in nineteenth-century agrarian thinking throughout the Hispanic world has often been noted. But the fact that he was used by later critics of lay latifundia, such as Ponciano Arriaga and Andrés Molina Enríquez,

89. Zavala accused the escocés deputies of the Mexico state constituent congress of delaying the constitution in order to retain control of politics on the national level. As large landowners, he said, their peons voted for them in the elections (Ensayo, 1, 375). All of the deputies to the national constituent congress of 1856 were landowners; see Jan Bazant, "Tres Revoluciones mexicanas," Historia mexicana, 10 (1960), 231. The social basis of liberal politics in the nineteenth century is a subject badly in need of further study.

can mislead us as to his true intentions. Jovellanos, like Mora, was not primarily concerned with inequality of distribution but rather with entailment of property. He emphasized civil entailment (the *mayorazgo*) whereas Mora emphasized entailment by the church, which is one reason why Jovellanos was popular later. Jovellanos recognized the evil of accumulation that might result from the free play of individual interests, but it was a "necessary evil." Moreover, it had its natural limits: "The natural vicissitudes of fortune make wealth pass freely from one person to another; consequently, [wealth] cannot remain immense in quantity nor long in duration for any one individual." [90] Jovellanos went even further and asserted that "given equality of rights, inequality of conditions can have very salutary effects." The example and the attainability of wealth can awaken and incite individual interest, which, after all, is the chief aim of the legislator.

By 1834 in Mexico we see an apparent contradiction within liberalism between the political emphasis upon a strong state and the socioeconomic emphasis on private property, individualism, and the free accumulation of wealth. Constitutionalism gave way to government force in the growing confrontation with corporate privilege; yet laissez-faire remained a liberal credo. We may be aided in understanding this problem by recalling the perpetual conflict between the "spontaneous" and the "artificial" identification of interests that existed within utilitarianism. Did the identity of interests come about naturally and spontaneously, or was it necessary to impose an artificial identification? Jeremy Bentham, concerned primarily with juridical problems, came to stress artificial identification and the necessity of state action. The conclusion of the economic theories stemming from utilitarianism, however, was that the identity of interests came about spontaneously, in accordance with natural laws. Adam Smith, the physiocrats, and Jovellanos argued that way, as did Bentham in economic matters. Since all sought to eliminate the spirit of corporation, in effect they all advocated a strong state in the political sphere.[91]

The double way in which the utilitarians regarded the identification of interests is particularly relevant to Mexico. Political and legal privilege were consistently attacked, though ideas did

90. Jovellanos, "Informe," *BAE, 50,* 98b. Cf. Mora, *Obras,* pp. 306–07.
91. On this general question see Halévy, pp. 36, 264, 498; Martin, p. 303.

not become effective policy until midcentury. On the other hand, given Mexico's unique structure (the lack of a "feudal" nobility whose property could be assaulted on legal grounds), liberal theory proved inadequate for the task of limiting private latifundia in favor of a rural bourgeoisie. Thus we discover within early liberalism the dichotomy between a strong Bourbon-inspired political state and rampant laissez-faire—a dichotomy that exists to this day.

Before taking leave of the social design put forth by the 1833 liberals, we should examine briefly the ideas of Mariano Otero. Not only was Otero's *Ensayo* of 1842 a remarkably perceptive piece of social analysis, but it represented a significant departure in Mexican social thought. Unfortunately, because of Otero's early death in 1850 at the age of thirty-three, and because of his involvement in politics after 1842, he did not develop his ideas further. Nevertheless, they are worth considering in this study, both in their own right and because they bring into relief some important characteristics of liberalism.

The occasion for the essay was the soon-to-begin constituent congress of June 1842, to which Otero was a delegate. The congress was established by the Plan of Tacubaya, a revolutionary agreement by Generals Valencia, Paredes y Arrillaga, and Santa Anna. The "revolution" was sparked by the revolt of the Guadalajara garrison under Paredes on August 8, 1841, and his subsequent Plan of Jalisco. Otero, perhaps because of his youth (he was twenty-three at the time), was impressed with Paredes y Arrillaga and with his plan which he cited repeatedly in the essay. The plan noted grave ills and dislocations in Mexican society, and Otero judged the revolution to be of profound character. His intention was to analyze the revolution and its causes, because "it embraces the true social question that is stirring in Mexico." [92]

There are two closely connected themes in Otero's social thought. The first is the primacy of history, historical inevitability, and the progress of civilization. The second is the interrelated nature of all of society and the necessity of viewing it as a whole, not just in parts. Otero opened his discussion with a quotation

92. Otero, *Ensayo,* p. 6. The pamphlet *Consideraciones* (1848), discussed in Chap. 1 above, was most probably written by Otero. Though a penetrating view of Mexican society, it added little to his concepts as presented in 1842.

from Mme. de Staël to the effect that the French Revolution was
not an accidental occurrence, the work of specific men, but rather
the work of history, the culmination of past events. Later he cited
a passage from the French scientist Laplace emphasizing that in
the physical world "we must see the present state as the effect of
the previous state, and as the cause of what is to follow it." Otero
maintained that what was true in the physical world was "rigor-
ously applicable to the moral state of societies." It is the march of
history that is remarkable, the interconnection of great events,
both the "colossal parts" and the "small modifications." When one
contemplates the impressiveness of this vast monument, history,
"how great are events and how small are men!" Therefore, continued Otero, we should forget the actors and concentrate on the
drama, leave the passions of the day and look to history.

Otero argued that Mexican society in its present state was not
the work of chance, but rather the product of "fixed and inevitable causes." Despite political confusion, Mexican society is re-
sponding to "the general law of humanity," the law of progress
and perfectability. Our society is the natural result of what the
Spaniards left us, but "the form it has is merely transitional."
Daily it is being undermined and destroyed. Progress is inevitable,
and civilization which surrounds us "is conquering the universe
with astounding rapidity." We have yet to achieve civilization, but
it "is a science already acquired" by other nations, one that we can
learn. Otero saw real signs that progress had occurred in Mexico
since independence. We have only to compare ourselves with what
we were twenty years ago, he said. Mexico is no longer isolated
from the world; "the well-to-do and educated class of society has
increased considerably"; even the most unfortunate groups share
more "in the benefits of society"; monopolies and entailed property have diminished; and so on. Progress is Mexico's destiny, and
the fruitless and pitiful efforts we see to forestall it are "like the
straw placed on a railroad track to hold up the powerful engine
that passes on unawares." [93]

The second theme of Otero's essay is the wholeness of interrelated nature of society. Civilization can only triumph in Mexico,
he said, if there is a "general change" in society, if "the diverse ele-

93. Ibid., pp. 98–99.

ments that compose it . . . change in the form necessary for that new state." Civilization is a unity, "no more than the whole of the means acquired for the satisfaction of the physical and moral necessities of man." It is in the material relations of society that change must begin. Otero thus turned to analysis to discover the relationship between society's elements. The principal element, "the generating principle," is property. Otero maintained that a good historian could complete the annals of obscure nations by analyzing their property relations, in the manner of a Cuvier studying fossils or a Laplace studying ancient monuments.[94]

It is evident that Otero was departing from the premises of the earlier liberals. Both the emphasis on history and on the wholeness of society were new. Mora wrote history; but when he analyzed the *espíritu de cuerpo* or when he sought the precedents for independence in the colonial period, he was in the modern sense unhistorical. He emphasized "society," yet he saw only parts of it. Mora spoke of "social science," but he shared the conviction of the utilitarians that the free individual, enlightened by education and pursuing his own interests, was the basis of society and institutions. Man was shaped by his environment, but it was a static environment, governed by fixed laws. To study this environment was to discover its laws. Social analysis was to uncover the obstacles that blocked the realization of a "natural order."

Otero partook of a new spirit in European social thought, which developed in reaction to the antihistorical and individualist doctrines reaching fulfillment in the French Revolution. He quoted frequently from Mme. de Staël, who emphasized that the Revolution resulted from causes deep-rooted in the past. Most of all, it appears that Otero was touched by socialist thought, particularly French. There is only one such reference in the essay—to Victor Considerant, the chief proponent of the ideas of Charles Fourier—but many of Otero's premises are unmistakably from that source.[95] Like the utopian socialists, Otero believed that the

94. Ibid., p. 35.
95. Ibid., pp. 70–71. Otero noted a new commercial class, mostly foreign, which had emerged since independence and now virtually controlled governments when they needed money. He quoted from Considerant's *Destinée sociale* (1834–38) on the corrupting influence of the mercantile spirit and of excessive competitiveness, a principal theme of the Fourier school.

method of social science must be historical. Through analysis he was attempting to discover the development of institutions and their function at a particular stage. Moreover, for Otero as for the socialists the development of society was bigger than individuals; there was a law of change which man could not control. Civilization, the end product of change, could be discovered but not created.[96]

Otero sharply criticized the 1833 reform movement. The majority of Mexicans, he maintained, were of liberal opinion after independence. Otero himself sympathized with the objectives of the reformers and found some of the leaders admirable. But the movement fell to extremists who caused an unnecessary schism in the country. Spiteful persecution of the antiliberal interests merely caused them to react more forcefully. Lacking in 1833 was a view of "the entire social problem." Otero maintained that the "antiliberal" elements were being undermined by change itself. The church, for instance, was losing ground. Its income was diminishing with the influx of new ideas which exposed the injustice of forced exactions on the populace. The church formed no party and dominated no administration in the early years after 1821. It reacted when challenged in 1833; but, concluded Otero, with the general spread of enlightenment, clerical influence was bound to decline.[97]

Otero's sharp analysis (exemplified better by what I have cited elsewhere than here) was blunted by his meliorist philosophy. When he left analysis and began to predict, his essay loses interest.

96. See Plamenatz, pp. 155–58, who compares the doctrines of St. Simon with those of the utilitarians. See also Gide and Rist, pp. 243 ff; and, in general, Carl Becker, *The Heavenly City of the Eighteenth-Century Philosophers* (New Haven, Yale University Press, 1932) , pp. 95–96.

97. Otero, *Ensayo*, pp. 61–62. Otero's criticism of the 1833 reformers might be compared to Domingo F. Sarmiento's sympathetic critique of the doctrinaire liberalism of Rivadavia in Argentina. Sarmiento described 1830 as an intellectual turning point in Argentina (quite different from 1830 in Mexico) . "From that time we learned something of races, of tendencies, of national habits, of historical antecedents." Constant, Bentham, and Rousseau were replaced by Sismondi, St. Simon, Michelet, Guizot, and later Tocqueville. Thus, the "historical" and "socialist" doctrines had a far earlier and greater impact in Argentina than in Mexico. The reign of corporate privilege in the latter country inhibited the new ideas, except in a secondary figure like Otero, and lent continuing significance (through the Reforma) to the liberalism of Mora. See Sarmiento, *Life in the Argentine Republic in the Days of the Tyrants* (New York, 1868) , pp. 122–29.

Despite Otero's emphasis on the inevitability of social change, he concluded with the assertion that a good government was Mexico's first necessity. Otero presented an apology for the federalist system which he hoped would be reinstituted by the coming congress. He regarded the adoption of federalism in 1824 not as imitation of the United States, but rather the response to a "universal law." The federalist principle "is the system of nature." From families to nations, men organize, he said, in "diverse associations" to best serve their needs. Thus for a large republic, like the United States or Mexico, federal organization is the natural form.[98]

Otero's federalist apology in the context of his social thought suggests an affinity for the "associative socialism" of the Fourier school, which maintained that voluntary association according to a prearranged plan was the key to social problems. Otero can be seen as a liberal of constitutionalist sympathies reacting against the strong state of 1833, as well as against the centralism of 1836. He explicitly condemned salvation through a caudillo. Yet Otero also viewed federalism within a broader social framework as an associative principle which would ultimately protect the individual. Federalism was more than mere political rhetoric; it formed part of his system of thought. Since it was a real issue for him, it affected his political action and made him a *moderado,* reluctant to seek a strong state against corporate privilege. Thus Mariano Otero, though introducing the new element of society into Mexican thought, departed from the mainstream of liberalism—the tradition of 1833 and of 1857.[99]

There remain for our attention two matters of relevance to the liberal plan for a new society. The first concerns the role of the United States as a model to be followed. The second concerns the Indian, whose presence as the majority element of the population could hardly be ignored. Let us turn first to the United States.

98. See Otero, *Ensayo,* pp. 117–20.

99. And, it might be added, of later positivism with its Comtean statist emphasis. Reyes Heroles devotes an entire chapter (*Liberalismo,* 2, 88–136) to a discussion of Otero's *Ensayo* and refers to him frequently elsewhere. The appeal of Otero for contemporary Mexico lies in the modernity of his method of social analysis, in his emphasis on the primacy of property and the need for complete social renovation, and perhaps in his attachment to federalism. See also González Navarro, "Actualidad de Mariano Otero," *Historia mexicana,* 2 (1952), 286–93, a more perceptive assessment.

6

Liberalism and the North American Model

On November 28, 1847, Lucas Alamán wrote to the Duke of Terranova y Monteleone, the Sicilian heir to the feudal patrimony of
Hernán Cortés: "Who could have then imagined that three centuries after the death of the great conquistador, the city he up-
rooted would be occupied by the army of a nation which in 1547
had not even seen the light of day?" [1] Immersed in his study of
Cortés, New Spain, and three centuries of Spanish history, Alamán
might well resort to bitter irony on seeing his ancient Mexico
overwhelmed by the armies of the upstart nation to the north. It
remains to be seen if Alamán's political opponents, though
shocked by the war into a greater realization of Mexican problems, were able to share his response to the United States. We
must ask what influence the model of North American experience
had upon liberals of the pre-Reforma period. Did Mexican reformers see in the social and political institutions of the United
States the goal toward which they were heading? Could they find
in American thought and policy a means or a method of achieving
that goal?

I am prompted to pose these questions because of two seemingly
contradictory facts, apparent to any student of postindependence
Mexico. One is the way American society and institutions were
idealized in much of the Mexican political writing of the nineteenth century, especially in the pre-Reforma era. A first reading
of the principal sources for this book yields the conclusion that the
United States was not only the contemporary symbol of progress
for Mexican liberals, but that its institutions, its social and economic policies, and even its cultural values were openly adopted
in Mexican reformist thought. The other fact is the presence of a

1. Alamán, *Documentos, 4,* 457.

heritage of conflict between the United States and Mexico, drama-
tized by the Texas episode and the war of 1847 in the nineteenth
century, and by the acrimonious relations during the revolutionary years in the twentieth. There were obviously cultural differences involved in these clashes; differences that went deeper than
boundary disputes or diplomatic rivalries.[2] The paradox of un-
bounded admiration for the United States on the one hand, and a
heritage of conflict on the other, is a matter that merits attention.

A convenient point of departure for considering the problem is
the interpretation presented by Louis Hartz in *The Liberal
Tradition in America*. In brief, Hartz argues that North American
thought and politics have been conditioned or even determined by
the heritage of a "liberal society," essentially unchanged since the
seventeenth century. This society was the institutional embodi-
ment of John Locke's concept of a group of individuals in the state
of nature. "Because the basic feudal oppressions of Europe had not
taken root, the fundamental social norm of Locke ceased in large
part to look like a norm and began . . . to look like a sober description of fact." [3] We have seen how Locke, the seminal figure
in political liberalism, was interpreted differently in England and
France, in the first case to support established political institutions
which would limit sovereign authority, in the second to foster the
strengthening of the state against corporate or aristocratic privilege. In North America, Locke's individualism, his "fundamental
social norm," was never challenged.

Hartz attaches particular significance to Alexis de Tocqueville's
observation that the Americans "have arrived at a state of democracy without having to endure a democratic revolution . . . they
were born equal instead of becoming so." [4] Tocqueville saw as
most striking in the United States the existence of "equality of
condition." The movement toward equality was for him a "provi-

2. This sense of cultural contrast between the United States and Mexico per-
meates contemporary Mexican writing. A good example is the way Octavio Paz
in *The Labyrinth of Solitude* (New York, Grove Press, 1961) frequently and perhaps
unwittingly refers to North American characteristics to point up by contrast some
point he is making about Mexico.

3. Louis Hartz, *The Liberal Tradition in America* (New York, Harcourt, 1955),
p. 60.

4. Tocqueville, *Democracy*, 2, 108.

dential fact," the "most ancient and most permanent tendency that is to be found in history." [5] Having been "born equal," Americans did not have to uproot a feudal order through a liberal and democratic revolution. Without a feudal tradition, Hartz argues, the United States lacked both a liberal ideology and a liberal party. "Ironically, 'liberalism' is a stranger in the land of its greatest realization and fulfillment." [6] The objectives of liberals—representative political institutions, a cohesive yet individualist society, a developing secular morality—all had been established before independence, so that the revolution was limited essentially to breaking political ties with England.

In apparent contrast to Hartz, R. R. Palmer has recently contended that America did indeed experience a democratic revolution, similar in its objectives to other movements in the Atlantic world in the last decades of the eighteenth century. Palmer stresses America's contribution to democratic theory—the idea of the "people as a constituent power." It was a concept that was novel to the French and used by them later, in 1789. Although Palmer's perspective is different from that of Hartz, their interpretations of the United States do not actually conflict. Palmer admits to the "ambivalence" of the American Revolution. Though it was really a revolution—subverting legitimate government, ousting the Tories, confiscating property, and establishing new juridical concepts—it entailed no real break with the past. The American Revolution was revolutionary in its general principles, not in its confrontation with an old regime. "In constitutional theory, in the belief that a people must will its own government by a kind of act of special creation," the American and French revolutions were similar.[7] Palmer, therefore, emphasizes the common body of liberal and democratic principles in the Atlantic world, of which America was a part. Hartz accentuates the uniqueness of the American social order vis-à-vis Europe, and the effect of this uniqueness upon subsequent thought and politics. The common element in both works is the comparative context.

In his most recent book, Hartz has expanded his interpreta-

5. Ibid., _1_, 3–6.
6. Hartz, _Liberal Tradition_, p. 11.
7. Palmer, _The Age of the Democratic Revolution_, _1_, 267.

tion—perhaps too far—to encompass Latin America and other new European societies, Canada, Australia, New Zealand, and South Africa. The result is a theory of "fragment" cultures. Each of the new societies, he maintains, is governed by the particular culture and ideology that was dominant in Europe at the time and place of fragmentation, or extention overseas. Thus Hartz uses the terms "Locke" and "bourgeois" for North America, and the term "feudal" to epitomize Latin America. What is common to the fragment cultures in their new environment is that the dominant ideology emerges free from challenge. A European ideology is identified in terms of its enemies in the social struggle. When it is detached and becomes master of a region, great changes take place. It becomes a universal assumption.[8] Though it is difficult to accept the degree of cultural determinism Hartz implies in his theory of new societies in the Americas, one element is clearly pointed up: the United States and Latin America fell heir to radically different traditions.

Mutual understanding in the Americas has been plagued by an imperfect appreciation of social differences, or by what Arthur P. Whitaker has called the Western Hemisphere idea, "the proposition that the peoples of this Hemisphere stand in a special relationship to one another which sets them apart from the rest of the world."[9] This idea has always been a superficial one, because it is based essentially on a series of deceptive parallels in the historical experience of the two Americas. One parallel which cannot be denied, in fact the primary one, is that of two new societies in this hemisphere in contrast with the Old World. This, of course, is the point of departure for Hartz, except that he goes one step further to ask what the components of these new societies were. The spokesmen for the Western Hemisphere idea never went beyond geography and material factors. The idea flourished first in the eighteenth and early nineteenth centuries, then subsided until the twentieth when it enjoyed a resurgence during the Good Neighbor era and World War II.

8. Hartz, *Founding*, p. 5. Morse, in his contribution to the Hartz volume, refuses to term Latin America "feudal." See above, p. 44 n.

9. Whitaker, *The Western Hemisphere Idea: Its Rise and Decline* (Ithaca, Cornell University Press, 1954), p. 1.

The earlier version of this assumption about the unity of the Western Hemisphere was in full sway at the moment of Mexican independence in 1821. A Creole sense of pride in hemisphere and in country had been kindled forty years earlier by an intellectual reaction to the denigration of the New World by certain spokesmen of Enlightenment Europe, notably Buffon the scientist, Robertson the historian, and de Pauw, a self-styled *philosophe*. Both Americas replied with a common voice to the suggestion that, because of an essentially hostile and barren environment, species both human and animal were degenerate in the New World. This defense of America against the Old World drew together such diverse individuals as Thomas Jefferson and two recently exiled Jesuits, Juan Ignacio Molina from Chile and Francisco Clavijero from Mexico. It is revealing, however, that only on the level of flora and fauna could a Jefferson and a Clavijero produce parallel arguments in response to Europe. Clavijero's principal emphasis was on the antiquity of civilization in Mexico, a point Jefferson could obviously not advance.[10]

It was Alexander von Humboldt who perhaps contributed most to the Mexican Creole's sense of pride in the Western Hemisphere. On his visit to New Spain (1804) Humboldt found achievements in the arts and sciences impressive, particularly in Mexico City. He envisioned a great future for the country, an estimate that has endeared him to Mexicans ever since. Again, though this work by one of Europe's most respected savants served to help solidify the defense of the New World against the Old, it drew no particular parallels between the two Americas. Though Humboldt contributed to a surge of Mexican national optimism in the immediate postindependence years, an optimism that generally identified a common destiny for all America, his study was confined to Mexico.[11]

10. Clavijero, for all his elaborate appreciation of Aztec culture, held to an essentially Creole view of Mexican nationality, introducing a Mexican issue that was foreign to North America. See *History of Mexico,* trans. Charles Cullen (London, 1807), 2, 327–28. The definitive work on the controversy over America is Antonello Gerbi, *La Disputa del nuevo mundo* (Mexico, Fondo de Cultura Económica, 1960).

11. The continuing enthusiasm for Humboldt is reflected by two recent volumes, José Miranda, *Humboldt y México* (Mexico, UNAM, 1962) and Juan Ortega y Medina, *Humboldt desde México* (Mexico, UNAM, 1960). On national optimism

The inadequacies of the Western Hemisphere idea can point up the principal question of this chapter. If the historical experience of these two new societies has been sharply divergent, how aware of this fact were the Mexican liberals? How were they affected by this awareness or the lack of it? How would they have reacted, for instance, to the contention that the Americans in founding their nation "offered both the best and the worst example, the most successful and the least pertinent precedent, for . . . peoples who in other parts of the world might hope to realize the same principles." [12]

We first encounter the problem of North American influence in attempting to explain the adoption of the federal form of organization in the Constitution of 1824. In Chapter 3 we saw that apart from the republican federalist form and the necessary two chambers instead of one, the constitution was drawn up from Spanish sources. Benson's investigations have demonstrated that the Mexican states of 1824 had institutional roots in the Spanish provincial deputations. It can be argued that federalism was a "natural" development and not the "artificial" result of imitating the North American system. The assumptions of North American influence are deep-rooted, however, and they have led to widespread criticism of federalism as an alien import.[13] The fact that the system in the long run has been a dead letter has lent continuing support to the critics of federalism. Whatever significance federalism may be judged to have had "politically" (see above, page 84), as a juridical form it has little real meaning. The explanation is not that federalism was an "alien," or "abstract" —that is, North American—solution imposed upon Mexican reality. Rather, it is that the federal system, as part of a European-inspired constitutionalist effort to guarantee individual rights in the 1820s, was overwhelmed by centralist traditions and by the dictates of a strong reformist state.[14]

---

see Luis González y González, "El Optimismo nacionalista como factor de la independencia de México," *Estudios de historiografía americana* (Mexico, El Colegio de México, 1948), pp. 153–215.

12. Palmer, *1*, 232.

13. See Edmundo O'Gorman, introd. to *Fray Servando Teresa de Mier*, Antología del pensamiento político americano (Mexico, UNAM, 1945), p. xxiii.

14. Nettie Lee Benson, in demonstrating the institutional roots of federalism, leaves begging the larger question of its significance. She misleads the reader by

Assumptions concerning North American influence in 1824 can, however, be derived from contemporary evidence. Judging from the writings of the day, the American political model engendered great excitement. José María Luis Mora could write in 1822 that the Constitution of 1787 not only had won the praise of all, "but it has also brought glory and prosperity in a firm and stable manner to the freest people of the universe." [15] The pamphlets of Vicente Rocafuerte, who wrote enthusiastically from Philadelphia on the North American system, were circulating freely in Mexico between 1821 and 1824. Some were reprinted. Any newspaper or periodical of this period reveals how closely Mexicans associated their destiny under republican institutions with that of the United States. Washington and Jefferson became momentary heroes of the stature of Bolívar, Morelos, and Hidalgo. One of the early ceremonies of the national constitutional congress was the placing of Washington's portrait in the gallery of heroes. Reprints of speeches by the American founding fathers found their way frequently into the journals. *El Sol* (August 1, 1823) announced with high excitement a Mexican printing of the United States Constitution, "one of the perfect creations of the human spirit . . . it is the base on which rests the most simple, liberal, and happy government that we know in history."

The identification with the United States was irresistible, and it is clear that the delegates to the constitutional congress believed

---

citing (Preface, *Diputación provincial*) the conservative centralist historian Lucas Alamán as a support for her argument. Though Alamán saw the origin of the federal system in the provincial deputation, his overall view (in 1850) was that not only federalism but the entire liberal system derived from the Cortes of Cádiz was foreign to Mexican traditions and should be rejected. See Alamán, *Historia, 3*, 276 and passim. Yet presumably Benson's position is that, having institutional roots, federalism has been a viable tradition of real significance in Mexican history.

15. See Mora, *Obras*, pp. 472–73. The first journal Mora edited, the *Semanario político y literario* (1821–22), reprinted numerous North American documents, including the Declaration of Independence, the Articles of Confederation, two speeches by Washington, and the Constitution itself: see Benson, "Washington: Symbol of the United States in Mexico, 1800–1823," *The Library Chronicle of the University of Texas, 2* (1947), 177–78. It is significant to note that Mora's statement on the United States appeared in his article, "The Supreme Power Is Not Unlimited," and was merely a prelude to his Constantian critique of Rousseau (see above, p. 76).

that North American progress was the direct result of its political institutions. The young delegate from Yucatán, Manuel Crecencio Rejón, answered proudly in response to centralist criticism: "What we are offering for the deliberation of the congress [in the draft constitution] is taken from . . . [the United States document] with a few reforms to fit the circumstances of our people." [16]

Later observers have been misled by this federalist euphoria, this expression of the Western Hemisphere idea, which envisioned in republican institutions throughout America the highroad to progress. In effect, the overt acknowledgment of imitation by the Mexicans in 1824 reveals the superficial engagement of the American model in Mexican constitutional liberalism. The American form was adopted enthusiastically in large part because it was the *symbol* of liberal progress. In the Mexico state constitutional congress, José María de Jáuregui referred, as did others, to United States as "the model (*tipo*) of liberty." Yet in matters such as the organization of municipal governments, the judicial system, and the procedure for elections, the point of reference for the deputies was French and particularly Spanish liberal experience. There is little indication that North American constitutional writing, for example the *Federalist Papers,* circulated widely in Mexico.[17] States'-rights literature, coming on strong in the United States by 1824, seems to have had no effect on these Mexican champions of provincial autonomy. An apology for the federal system (1825) by José María Bocanegra evoked North American federalism. But the theorists Bocanegra cited were Destutt de Tracy and Benjamin Constant, not John Adams or James Madison.[18] This was more

16. "Esposición de motivos del plan de la constitución," May 18, 1823, in O'Gorman, *Fray Servando,* pp. 89–90; Rejón, *Discursos parlamentarios, 1822–1847,* ed. Carlos A. Echánove Trujillo (Mexico, Sec. de Educación Pública, 1943), p. 81 (speech of Apr. 1, 1824). Jesús Reyes Heroles emphasizes the impact of the North American federalist model in 1824 (*Liberalismo, 1,* 426–27).

17. Selections from the *Federalist Papers* did appear in the liberal periodical *El Atleta,* but not until 1829 (Reyes Heroles, *Liberalismo, 3,* 345). For Jáuregui's statement, see *Actas, 2,* 301 (Sept. 14, 1824) in a passage urging a greater tolerance of diverse political opinions. For similar expressions by José Francisco Guerra and by Mora, see *Actas, 1,* 273 (May 13, 1824) and *3,* 475 (Feb. 12, 1825), respectively.

18. Bocanegra, *Disertación apologética del sistema federal* (Mexico, 1825), pp. 12–16. Bocanegra had been a sponsor of the "constitutional plan" of May 1823.

than mere eclecticism; for instinctively it was the experience of continental Europe that spoke to Mexican reality.

The most respected figure of the national constituent congress, Father Mier, was a man whose constitutionalism was formed in the revolutionary upheaval of Europe. Born in Monterrey in 1764, he became an effective preacher in the Dominican Order. At the age of thirty, Mier delivered a notorious sermon in the Basílica of Guadalupe, questioning the accepted tradition of the Virgin's appearance. He was tried by the church and exiled to Spain. In and out of confinement, Mier escaped to France in 1801, where he made friends among ex-revolutionaries, including the French constitutionalist bishop, Henri Grégoire. On obtaining secularization from the Pope, he returned to Spain where he ultimately fought as an officer against Napoleon in 1808. Convinced of the justice of Mexican independence in 1811, he left for London, joined the liberal Spanish émigré group, and in 1813 published his *Historia de la revolución de la Nueva España*. Mier argued against republicanism in this work and justified his country's independence on the basis of an original "social compact" between the conquistadors and the Spanish throne, a theory which "after much drudgery and many sleepless nights, he had dug out of the thick forest of colonial legislation." [19]

Influenced by two visits to the United States, before and after Javier Mina's abortive strike (1817) for Mexican independence, Mier renounced constitutional monarchy and embraced republicanism. Writing from Philadelphia in 1821, he maintained that liberty could be achieved only through republican institutions, the source of North America's astounding progress.[20] He contrasted the Holy Alliance of Old World monarchs with republican freedom in the Western Hemisphere. Kings, even in England, had only obstructed the march of the human spirit. As a convinced republican, Mier opposed Emperor Iturbide and emerged a political leader in 1823. Still, Mier's attitude toward adopting the

19. O'Gorman, Introd., *Fray Servando*, p. xxiii. See also Mier's *Memorias* (2 vols. Mexico, Porrua, 1946) and *Escritos inéditos* (Mexico, El Colegio de México, 1944). There is a University of Texas Ph.D. dissertation by Bradford K. Hadley, "The Enigmatic Padre Mier," 1955.

20. Mier, *Memoria político-instructiva . . . a los gefes independientes del Anahuac* (Philadelphia, 1821) , p. 14.

North American federal model was ambivalent. He was struck by
the woeful lack of political experience in the Mexican provinces.
From his broad experience in two worlds, he realized how different North American society was from his own.

> They were a new people, homogeneous, industrious, hard
> working, enlightened, with all the social virtues, educated by
> a free nation. We are an old people, heterogeneous, without
> industry, enemies of work, wanting to live from public em-
> ployment like the Spaniards, as ignorant in the mass as our
> fathers, and impaired by the vices of three centuries of
> slavery.[21]

In short, though Mier did not deny the general argument of the
time—namely, that republican institutions bring social progress—he wanted more central control than was necessary in the
United States. When the vote on article 5 of the Acta Constitutiva
(making Mexico a representative, federal republic) was taken on
December 16, 1823, Mier approved. On article 6 (which made the
states sovereign, independent, and free) he voted "yes" to "free
and independent" and "no" to "sovereign." [22] Mier, though
denying he was a centralist, had backed away from the doctrinaire
federalism of the majority. Despite his enthusiasm for the United
States, he came to recognize that North American forms were of
limited application to Mexico.

Mier's "realism," as it has been called, was appropriated by the
conservatives after the war of 1847, and he was made the prophet
of evils that would come with a federal constitution.[23] The liberals were thus outmaneuvered and robbed of one of their heroes.
Mier can be said to have initiated the critical school of Mexican
constitutional historiography. Yet the long debate over federalism
has really missed the mark. By acknowledging North American
influence, the federalists of 1824 were not in any deep sense implanting an alien system. They were merely on a more superficial
level bolstering their optimistic vision of the progress of free societies under republican institutions in the New World.

21. Mier, *Discurso que el día 13 de diciembre del presente año de 1823 pronunció . . . sobre el artículo 5 del acta constitutiva* (Mexico, 1823), pp. 3–4.
22. O'Gorman, *Fray Servando*, p. 140.
23. *El Orden*, Feb. 20, 1853; Cuevas, *Porvenir de México*, pp. 173–75.

With the shifting orientation of political liberalism after 1830 came increased criticism of the Constitution of 1824. Lorenzo de Zavala, like Mora, repeatedly pointed to the contradictions in the document. Though the Mexican code was clearly based on the United States model, he said, it kept the fueros, granted Roman Catholicism exclusive status in the state, permitted monastic establishments for both sexes, and in general encouraged "the abuses that spring from these principles so destructive of the envisioned republic." This was no longer the Zavala of 1824, who, optimistically, had seen in republican and federal forms the automatic assurance of social harmony and progress. Referring constantly to the United States, he now saw the contrast in Mexico between constitutional principle and social reality. His country had taken on

> the formulas, the phrases, the words, the names, the titles, in short all the outward constitutional effects of the United States; but much was lacking in order that the substance, the essence of the system, that reality itself corresponds to the principles professed.[24]

Zavala, like Mora, had lost his faith in constitutionalism as the sure road to the liberal society in Mexico. It is difficult to know, he mused, what kind of government best suits a country that has neither "republican habits nor monarchical elements." [25] It was in this mood that Zavala turned his eyes north.

In general, the Mexican liberals of the pre-Reforma generation approached North American society uncritically. So frequent and so laudatory were the great majority of commentaries that they become almost unreal for the modern reader, conditioned to the heady climate of contemporary *antiyanquismo*. Only a few liberals made the effort to know the United States. Little American writing was translated or read. A scant half-dozen Mexican travelers to the United States in the pre-Reforma period left memoirs of their voyages.[26] There was a group of political exiles in New Orleans in

24. Zavala, *Ensayo, 1,* 178, 405.

25. Ibid., p. 173. See also Zavala, *Viage a los estados-unidos del norte de América* (Paris, 1834), p. 364.

26. See José de Onís, *The United States as Seen by Spanish American Writers, 1776–1890* (New York, Hispanic Inst., 1952) .

the 1840s, which included Melchor Ocampo, Valentín Gómez Farías, and Guillermo Prieto; but no systematic discussion emerged from this contact with what was a very special segment of American culture. Tocqueville's *Democracy in America* aroused some interest among Mexicans after 1840, but mostly for his discussion of juridical and constitutional matters.[27] What, then, was the intrigue of North American society?

To Mexican liberals the United States was a utilitarian dream world. They found there "the reality of atomistic social freedom." Tadeo Ortiz, one of the most enthusiastic of the Mexicans, referred to the United States as "the classic land of liberty and order and the refuge of all the social virtues."[28] The Mexicans, like Tocqueville, saw there the reign of enlightened self-interest; North Americans seemed able to combine their own advantage with that of their fellow citizens. American democracy, rooted in the free individual property holder, provided the model not only of liberty and equality, but of political stability as well. It was a model that was both simple and static. The Mexicans were seemingly oblivious to the changes in American society between 1789 and 1830, and to the public controversies of the age of Jackson.

Lorenzo de Zavala visited the United States just after the election of Andrew Jackson. Since he was traveling with the Mexican legation's secretary, José Antonio Mejía, he was well received by the president-elect. The encounter took place in Cincinnati, and Zavala was struck by the spontaneity and naturalness with which the people greeted Jackson. How different such a scene is, he remarked characteristically, from a Mexican fiesta. Our fiestas are based on ceremonies "formulated in the days of court ritual, where in the faces [of the people] is never seen a single sign of true interest, nor the sentiment of fellow-feeling." Jackson, in contrast

27. There were references to Tocqueville in José María Tornel y Mendívil, "Discurso pronunciado por . . . ministro de guerra y marina . . . en la sesión de 12 de oct. de 1842, del congreso constituyente, en apoyo del dictamen de la mayoría de la comisión de constitución del mismo," *El Siglo*, Nov. 30 and Dec. 1, 1842. He used Tocqueville to support his contention that federalism was natural only to North American conditions and that for a country like Mexico centralism was more appropriate. Mariano Otero was also familiar with Tocqueville (Reyes Heroles, *Liberalismo*, 3, 339, 353–54).

28. Ortiz, *México*, p. 64.

to a Mexican leader, was "lodged in a modestly furnished house, seated in an armchair and surrounded by twenty or thirty people who by their dress seemed workers or artisans. His had become the simplest court in the world." [29]

It was the democracy of small property holders, artisans, and self-respecting laborers that Zavala saw in the United States, not the "absurd leveling of all marks of superiority, nor even less, the anarchical confusion of all social elements and interests." [30] Having now less faith in the magic of constitutions, Zavala concluded that government in the United States was "an appendage of society." Mariano Otero noted in 1842 that what was remarkable in the United States was not the implanting of a federal form of organization, which had had a long prior history, but the "realization of an internal [democratic] government" within that form.[31]

The utilitarian mainspring of American society was illustrated by a universal spirit of enterprise. Whether the Mexican observer was a partisan of agriculture and free commerce like Zavala or an advocate of incipient industrialization like Estevan de Antuñano, the United States could be held up as a model. Antuñano extolled the American principle of "useful and honest work by means of instruction in arts and skills." [32]

Zavala marveled at the manufacturing town of Lowell, "a forest ten years ago," which for him was a symbol of human progress through industry. He described the factory system in detail, particularly its moral and social features. Factory work there did not have the deleterious effect on morals, particularly of women, that European or Mexican shops did. He likened the strict regulations for female factory workers in Lowell to those of Mexican convents, but added:

> These nuns of the nineteenth century spin cotton and produce all kinds of fabrics, rather than busying themselves making reliquaries, scapularies, and sudaria. In Lowell there are

29. Zavala, *Viage*, p. 68.

30. Zavala, *Ensayo*, 2, 239.

31. Otero, *Ensayo*, p. 119.

32. See Antuñano, *Ampliación, aclaración y corección a los principales puntos del manifiesto sobre el algodón* (Puebla, 1833), pp. 12, 81. Antuñano's ideas are discussed in detail in Chap. 8 below.

no amusements or diversions; rather it is a peaceful town, inhabited by people dressed cleanly, neatly, and with gentility.[33]

Like Tocqueville, Zavala noted in conversations a universal concern with "commercial affairs and ways of making money," in contrast to an interest in "abstract questions"; but he was always less critical of American materialism than was the French aristocrat.[34] Zavala's view was closer to that of Domingo F. Sarmiento, the greatest of Latin American travelers to the United States during this era.

In accordance with changing liberal preoccupations after 1830, church-state relations and even religious customs in the United States took on special significance. Vicente Rocafuerte's essay on religious toleration caused a furor when it appeared during the proclerical Bustamante regime. Rocafuerte pointed to the beneficial effects of toleration in the United States and even asserted that "Protestants are more active, more industrious, and wealthier than Catholics."[35] Zavala praised the diversity of religious sects and the government's benign attitude toward that diversity: "each respects the others; all consider themselves as members of a common society." While traveling through Tennessee, Zavala was much taken by the electrifying atmosphere of the frontier camp meeting. He judged it to be a positive influence in purifying morals, quite in contrast to the popular Indian pilgrimages to Chalma and to Guadalupe. He found the democratic practice of appointing ministers to be "compatible with the system of popular equality."[36] One of the few jarring impressions revealed in his account was the discrimination toward Negro slaves in the Protestant churches. Whereas the floor of the New Orleans Catholic cathedral "is filled with folk of all colors," in the Protestant churches "the congregation is made up of well-dressed ladies sitting in their adorned pews." The colored were either excluded or

33. Zavala, *Viage*, p. 294.

34. A similarly benign view of American materialism can be seen in [Rafael Reynal] and Carlos Gastelú, *Viage por los estados unidos del norte* (Cincinnati, 1834), p. 159.

35. Rocafuerte, *Ensayo sobre tolerancia religiosa* (Mexico, 1831), p. 26.

36. Zavala, *Ensayo*, 2, 235; *Viage*, p. 131.

fenced into a corner, "so that even in that moment [of worship]
they are obliged to feel their degraded condition." [37] This was for
Zavala the one blemish on an otherwise model society.

Always implicit and often explicit in these observations is the
contrast with what was seen at home. Nothing can be more useful
for my compatriots, wrote Zavala in the Preface to his *Viage,*
"than the knowledge of the customs, habits, and government of
the United States, the institutions of which have been slavishly
copied." He reiterated the theme as governor of the State of
Mexico in 1833, calling on his people to achieve "the level of civilization which has been reached by those admirable masters of republican institutions." [38] It was generally recognized by the liberals that these differences had historical roots. For example, the
old patriot, Andrés Quintana Roo, contrasted the two colonial
regimes in his Independence Day speech of 1845.[39] The realization of differences led to no cultural hostility, however. Urged on
by the vision of a cosmopolitan liberal society transcending national boundaries, patriotism figured very little in the pre-1847
view of the United States.

Lorenzo de Zavala, the most articulate of the liberal admirers of
the United States, is an interesting case. He was a militant reformer and a respected analyst of Mexico's ills, yet he died a
traitor in Texas. Zavala's Texas career is well known, but certain
aspects are worth reviewing. Besides being a facile writer, Zavala
was a political activist and a major participant in the political
imbroglio of the late twenties. He was also an *empresario* for
whom the line between national progress and personal gain was
blurred. By the terms of the colonization law of 1824, Zavala
secured a grant of land in Texas between Nagadoches, the Sabine
River, and the sea, on the condition that he introduce 500 foreign
and Mexican families as colonists. His efforts aroused government
opposition since he had close dealings with Joel Poinsett, Anthony
Butler, and other North Americans. The law had said that no land
go to Americans. Zavala's travels to the United States in 1830 in-

37. *Viage,* p. 26. Cf. Calderon, *Life in Mexico,* p. 369.

38. Zavala, *Memoria,* p. 11; see also *Ensayo,* 2, 146, 173; *El Fénix,* Dec. 14, 1831;
Reynal, *Viage,* p. 4.

39. Quíntana Roo, *Discurso,* pp. 5–6; also Rosa, *Discurso* (1846) , pp. 47–48.

cluded many land negotiations, in which he paid little attention to the terms of his contract.

Upon resigning his post of minister plenipotentiary to France (1835), Zavala returned directly to Texas where he became embroiled in the Texas revolution against the new Mexican centralist government. Though ill a good part of the time, Zavala participated in the political movement which drifted from federalism to independence. He was a signer of the Declaration of Independence of March 2, 1836. Zavala became vice-president of the Texan Republic, but resigned the following month out of disgust with the incompetent President David G. Burnett. Soon thereafter he contracted pneumonia when a canoe carrying his son and himself overturned in Buffalo Bayou, and on November 15, 1836, he died—a Texan patriot and a traitor to Mexico.[40]

If we can believe his writings, Lorenzo de Zavala regarded his Texan involvement as more than a shrewd business opportunity or an effort to promote the independence of the region. He stated eloquently the case for Texan colonization by North Americans. Texas offered Zavala, the Mexican liberal, a way out of an increasingly frustrating problem. He had argued that it was impossible for Mexico to progress toward a liberal society merely by taking on ideal constitutional forms. Society itself must be changed, and the vestiges of the past rooted out. The ideal society of the United States should be the model for reformers. Yet, in conclusion he introduced a jarring note: "The model was sublime, but inimitable." [41] Zavala had come to the realization that a liberal utopia like the United States was unattainable for the ancient Hispanic and Indian society of Mexico. His thought represents an extreme case of the dilemma of early Mexican liberalism in confrontation with the North American model. Zavala did advance a solution for his country, though it was one that ultimately separated him from the mainstream of the Mexican liberal tradition.

40. Zavala's Texas career has been examined in great detail by Estep in *Lorenzo de Zavala*. An example of the Zavala-as-traitor judgment can be found in Alfonso Toro, *Dos Constituyentes del año 1824. Biografías de Don Miguel Ramos Arizpe y Don Lorenzo de Zavala* (Mexico, Museo Nacional, 1925), p. 114. Impressive evidence that Zavala is now gaining acceptance in Mexico is the publication of Vol. 1 of his *Obras*, ed. by Manuel González Ramírez (Mexico, Porrua, 1966).

41. Zavala, *Viage*, p. 363.

Zavala saw in Texas the germ of a new Mexico. The early Anglo-Saxon settlers, he said, particularly those led by Stephen F. Austin, had made the land flourish. An expansion of such settlements (in concessions such as his own) would make Texas the richest, freest, most enlightened part of Mexico, an "example for the other states which continue in the rut of semifeudalism." [42] Later he was more explicit. There would be two distinct Mexicos, and under the impulse of liberal principles from the one, civil war in the other would be inevitable.

> The end nevertheless will be the triumph of liberty in these
> [older] states. And, upon the gothic rubbish of indefensible
> privileges, will arise a glorious and enlightened generation.
> . . . The American system will gain a complete though
> bloody victory.[43]

Thus Zavala concluded his final work. He sensed the expansive force of North American colonization, and intimated that it might overrun Mexico, but he distinguished this "conquest of industry and civilization" from "those [European] wars of conquest" that were directed by the ambitions of some conquistador.[44] Ironically, Zavala can be called a prophet of the war of 1847, far as it was from his cosmopolitan liberal dreams. His version of liberalism was overwhelmed by the realities of nationalism, power politics, and war.

Zavala was admittedly extreme, both in the volume and intensity of his laudatory writing on the United States, and in the ultimate solution he proposed for a regenerated Mexico. His case dramatizes the problem to which this chapter is devoted. Turning from Zavala to José María Luis Mora, one is struck by how little the North American model figured in Mora's thought. For example, the American Revolution was the subject of only passing comment in Mora's works. He referred to it briefly as the first break

---

42. Zavala, *Ensayo,* 2, 170–71.
43. Zavala, *Viage,* p. 368.
44. Zavala, *Ensayo, 1,* 300–02. Historians from Zavala's home state of Yucatán have looked charitably on his Texas involvements, perhaps because Yucatán's connection with central Mexico during this period was also very tenuous. See e.g. Carlos A. Echánove Trujillo, *La Vida pasional e inquieta de Don Crecencio Rejón* (Mexico, El Colegio de México, 1941), p. 196.

between the Old World and the New, thus pointing to the inevitable independence of the Spanish colonies. By contrast, as we have seen, the French Revolution loomed large for him. In ambivalent terms, Mora saw the latter as

> a torch appearing in the midst of darkness. Not only has it shown the true road that all peoples and all governments must follow in the difficult task of social organization, but at the same time it has pointed out the obstacles to be mounted and the risks to be run. . . . This [French] revolution from its beginnings till now is a school open to the instruction of all peoples.[45]

The American Revolution, rooted in a distinct structure of society and politics, appeared to have little such relevance for him.

Mora shared with his fellow liberals an admiration for the United States Constitution. Yet, his constitutionalist endeavors in the State of Mexico yield amazingly few references to North American experience—and they are mostly on points of detail. The Americans restricted foreigners from "confidential" government posts, a practice Mora thought should be also followed in Mexico. Important appointments by the governor should be approved by the council, as they were in the United States by the Senate. A two-thirds majority should be required for approving important matters, as was the case in the United States.[46] George Washington won great praise in several of Mora's *El Observador* essays of the late twenties. Washington was an ideal statesman, a "profound politician," a "hero of reason and philosophy." In these cases, however, Washington the man emerged isolated from the context of American society and institutions. He was a great man, whose moderation, judgment, and reason led a new nation around the pitfalls of political turmoil.[47] Mora admired the climate of tolerance and the amicable relations between church and state that prevailed in the United States. In advocating a system of civil

45. Mora, *Revoluciones, 3,* 275. On the American Revolution see ibid., p. 285.
46. See *Actas, 1,* 31 (Mar. 8, 1824); 408 (June 5, 1824); 471 (June 21, 1824).
47. See Mora, *Obras,* pp. 588, 593, 596. On one occasion Mora referred to Hamilton in defending the rights of citizens against military power. See Reyes Heroles, *Liberalismo, 3,* 344.

militia he pointed to the North American precedent.[48] It is significant, though, that reference to the United States virtually disappeared from his reformist writings of the early 1830s.

How can we explain Mora's seeming indifference to the North American model? Zavala's intensity of interest in the United States came partly, it is true, from his practical, entrepeneurial involvements with Americans such as Poinsett, Butler, and Austin. As a restless man of action he was drawn into colonization schemes; and though intellectually brilliant, Zavala was always less thoughtful than Mora. His impatience led him, perhaps, to seek a utopia, to conjure up the model liberal society in a way that was largely irrelevant to Mora. Yet there were others, Tadeo Ortiz and Mariano Otero, for instance, to whom the United States meant far more than it apparently did to Mora. There is a better explanation, suggested by the limitations of American democratic theory when used in France in 1789. This theory could become in America *both* a "mechanism for revolution" and a means of constitutional "stabilization." In France that was not possible because of resistance to democratic ideas and because "more than purely political forms were at stake in the French Revolution. . . . The *method* of the Free Americans, was not, after all altogether suited to circumstances in France." [49]

As a theorist Mora searched for a method of instituting reform in Mexico, for theory which was applicable to the situation of his country. These he could not find in the United States, a society that was liberal from its origins. "If America was from the beginning a kind of idyllic state of nature, how could it suddenly become a brilliant example of social emancipation?" [50] In concluding his survey of Mexico for Europeans, Mora remarked that those who did not know Mexico believed that, once independent, the country "would move ahead with the same ease and rapidity as the United States of America." In North America, however, "everything was done before separation from the mother country"; in Mexico, "everything remained to be done." In overcoming resis-

48. Mora, *Obras,* pp. 81, 316.
49. Palmer, *1,* 263. Italics mine.
50. Hartz, *Liberal Tradition,* p. 36.

tance to the new principles, Mexico had "to run all the risks of a constitutional revolution." [51]

Mora's constitutionalism, even his federalism, was advanced in the spirit of Benjamin Constant, seeking guarantees for individual liberty against an authoritarian and centralized government. His attack on the corporations was modeled on Bourbon regalism and the policies of the Cortes of Cádiz, both radically alien to North American experience. Mora's social thought was rooted in utilitarianism, and Bentham was his oracle. Mora attempted to establish secular and utilitarian values in Mexico. Why should he turn to the United States where "there was no Bentham, no Helvetius, among the superlatively middle-class thinkers. . . . Benjamin Franklins in fact, the Americans did not have to become Jeremy Benthams in theory. Unchallenged men of business, they did not have to equate morality with it." [52] It was precisely Mora's indifference toward the North American model as method or as theory that made him so significant a figure in Mexico.

We began with the ironic musings of Lucas Alamán upon experiencing in late 1847 the United States army of occupation in Mexico City. For the liberals, the war was ironic in another, unacknowledged way. The model nation had turned antagonist. The ideal liberal progressive society under republican institutions had become an old-style aggressor, a phenomenon that was assumed to have vanished in the free air of the New World. The war had a critical impact in sharpening the ideological cleavage between liberals and conservatives. Yet the postwar flowering of liberal political writing did not show the change of attitude toward the United States one might expect. There was little display of anti-yanquismo among the liberals; rather the war was generally discussed for what it revealed about Mexican social disorganization and political weakness.[53]

The war introduced a major point of confusion into the liberal argument. Liberals would never have indulged in the reflections of Alamán, because it was the very newness and modernity of American society that they had most admired. The United States represented the realization of the reforms envisioned by many liberals. This made it difficult to find a cultural base for nationalist resistance to an aggressive North America.

Another of the ironies of the 1847 episode was the resurgence of federalism at the very moment the war was beginning. The centralist form of organization had prevailed since 1836 and, despite an effort at change in 1842, it persisted. A quasi-liberal political movement, led by José Joaquín de Herrera in 1845, against the dreary round of Santanista governments, had called for federalism. The cry was resumed in August of 1846, after hostilities were under way. The Mexicans went on to readopt a system of loose territorial organization at the very time they were being threatened by a foreign power. The need for effective defense against invasion had been a classic argument for centralization and against federalism.[54] Apparently, Mexicans were oblivious to this reasoning. The 1845–46 arguments for federalism were the familiar ones. "Federalism is the symbol of the middle and lower classes, of patriotism and of liberty . . . [centralism] the symbol of wealth and privilege, of egoism and slavery." Manuel Crecencio Rejón asserted that the country was too vast and populous to centralize all government, that the interests of the localities demanded federal organization, and so on.[55] Curiously unresponsive to current events, the *Republicano* of August 23, 1846, claimed that now, since Mexico had had a generation of political experience, and a population, area, and revenue far larger than the United States at independence, it was more than ready to take on the federal sys-

54. E.g. Destutt de Tracy's debate with Thomas Jefferson in Gilbert Chinard, ed., *Jefferson et les idéologues* (Baltimore and Paris, Johns Hopkins University Press, 1925). Also adopted in 1847 was what came to be the uniquely Mexican juridical system of constitutional defense, the *juicio de amparo*. It was inspired by Tocqueville's description of judicial review in the United States. Departing from the American pattern, amparo in Mexico is an autonomous suit, initiated by an individual against violation of his rights under the constitution. See Richard D. Baker, "The Judicial Control of Constitutionality in Mexico: a Study of the *Juicio de Amparo*" (Ph.D. dissertation, University of North Carolina, 1962); Tena Ramírez, *Derecho*, Chaps. 26–27.

55. *La Voz del pueblo*, Mar. 12, 1845; Rejón, *Programa de la mayoría de los diputados del distrito federal* (Mexico, 1846). Rejón's arguments for federalism were combined with an appeal to fight the invaders to the death.

tem. Juridical federalism, debated so vigorously in 1824, had now become a political doctrine, an irradicable part of liberal ideology.

In the revitalized liberal argument that emerged between 1848 and 1853, the assessment of North American society continued to be uncritical. In fact, America's strengths were now more acutely recognized. The war had demonstrated the power of a democratic society. *El Siglo* remarked particularly upon the enterprising and hard-working population, made up primarily of North European immigrants. That this society, in which "individual interest is the mainspring directing its actions," yet where there also existed a "spirit of association," might overwhelm Mexico was apparent to many liberal observers. There was in the United States a movement to annex all Mexico, and this idea was not without its supporters in Mexico itself. It is surprising that *El Siglo* could treat the problem so calmly. One editorialist concluded that Mexico, if annexed, would flourish, but that "the enterprising spirit of the sons of the north, taking advantage of our idleness, would only make us workers in their industry, instruments of their prosperity." [56]

The problem for the liberals was that they could conjure up no alternative values to replace those that made North America so strong and irresistible. A remarkable example of this liberal confusion was Rejón, writing in early 1848 in violent opposition to accepting the boundaries indicated in the Treaty of Guadalupe Hidalgo. He asserted that *"the acceptance of the treaty means the political death of the republic,"* pointing to Mexico's appalling weakness, America's strength, and the "inevitability" of future conquests. The pamphlet revealed anger and indignation at the injustice of the war, but then it went on to evoke all the virtues of the mercantile spirit and of individualism, as opposed to Mexico's colonial habits. Colonization, patterned after the United States, was Rejón's principal solution for a stronger Mexico. *El Monitor* made a similar proposal.[57]

56. *El Siglo*, Oct. 29, 1848, and Aug. 11, 1849. Although many writings of the day referred to the existence of strong annexationist sentiment within Mexico, I found little open expression of it.

57. Rejón, *Observaciones del diputado saliente . . . contra los tratados de paz* (Querétaro, 1848) ; *El Monitor,* June 17, July 29, 1848. Rejón's pamphlet is dated

Another surprisingly bland view of the United States appeared in an account by Luis de la Rosa, the first postwar Mexican minister to that country. Though it is apparent that he was less temperamentally addicted to American life than was, for example, Zavala, Rosa's trip evoked little bitterness or hostility toward the recent aggressor nation. Rosa purported to write only "nonserious" impressions, emphasizing natural beauty rather than economy and politics. Yet he admitted that his attention was drawn away unwittingly from nature to become fixed "on society, on industry, on arts and commerce." He was plagued by the thought that while the traveler was contemplating nature "or admiring the beautiful vistas, the majority of the natives of the country are making dollars." [58]

Rosa showed a glimmer of Hispanic pride in contrasting an "inferior" though "very useful and well-constructed" bridge with the great bridge of Guadalajara, or with those by Tresguerras in the Bajío. "These are the works built in Mexico by a people whom some writers in the United States call 'the degenerate and degraded Spanish race in the New World.' " [59] Rosa found the stark Protestant churches or even the "sad and desolate" Catholic cathedral in New Orleans unable to evoke the sacred mysteries or deep sentiments of Christianity. Yet these passing thoughts scarcely affected his general admiration for "this country of activity, of movement and life." Moreover, North American examples figured prominently in his recommendations for the reform of his home state of Zacatecas, written in 1851 while he was still in the United States. Rosa was particularly impressed by the reign of small properties, by the universally accepted property tax, and by the absence of the crippling sales tax.[60]

The persisting liberal adherence to the North American model found a dissenter in London. José María Luis Mora, appointed

---

Apr. 17. An even stronger expression of indignation than Rejón's can be found in Valentín Gómez Farías' correspondence. See C. Alan Hutchinson, "Valentín Gómez Farías and the 'Secret Pact of New Orleans,' " *HAHR, 36* (1956) , pp. 476–77.

58. Rosa, *Impresiones de un viage de México a Washington en octubre y noviembre de 1848* (New York, 1849) , pp. 47, 54.

59. Ibid., pp. 48–49.

60. Rosa, *Observaciones*, pp. 9, 16–19, 24. See also Justo Sierra O'Reilly, *Diario de nuestro viaje a los Estados Unidos* (2 vols. Mexico, Robredo, Porrua, 1938–53) .

minister to England in 1846, reacted sharply to the threat of the United States. During and immediately after the war, Mora worked assiduously to bring Great Britain into the conflict. He first attempted to sell England a portion of territory that would create a buffer between the United States and Mexico. His analogy was the European balance of power system, which had successfully maintained "the individual existence of the weak nations against the aggression of the strong." [61] Later he tried to persuade Great Britain merely to "guarantee" the boundries of the treaty of 1848 against further American encroachment. Lord Palmerston was cool to both requests, and urged Mexicans to "put their hands to the wheel" and build a nation that would be "solid and enduring." [62]

One of Mora's principal concerns in London was the promotion of European emigration to Mexico. Colonization, an important part of the liberal program of 1833, was revived enthusiastically in the postwar years. Mora viewed emigration as urgent, not only in face of the Caste Wars (see below, Chapter 7) , but also as a means toward avoiding another Texas. Mora claimed in 1837 that the Gómez Farías regime had foreseen the alienation of Texas and had thus opposed indiscriminate non-Mexican colonization of the frontier areas.[63] By 1847 Mora was advocating that Mexico bend all efforts to attract Catholic immigrants, French, Belgian, and particularly Spanish, as opposed to Anglo-Saxon Protestants.

> In effect [he wrote], the Spanish people is the only one on earth that will not be congenial (*simpatizará*) with the American race. On the contrary it very much will be with the Mexican, which is its own. . . . The principal concern is that the supposed colonists keep their nationality intact.[64]

61. Mora to Relaciones (Nov. 30, 1847) , Chávez Orozco, *Gestión*, p. 39.

62. Mora to Relaciones (June 30, 1848) , ibid., p. 80.

63. Mora, *Obras*, p. 150. Mora was inconsistent on colonization at this juncture, however, for he cited as one of the principles of the "party of progress" the equality in civil rights of foreigners and Mexicans (cf. ibid., p. 4 with point No. 8 on p. 54) . Mora's shift away from toleration referred to above in Chap. 5 might also have been related to his concerns about Texas.

64. Mora to Relaciones (Apr. 4, 1849) , Chávez Orozco, *Gestión*, pp. 148–49. On French emigration see letter of July 28, 1848, in ibid., pp. 86–87.

Unfortunately, his several attempts to attract colonists in the years 1848–49 failed. Mora's admirer Mariano Otero was watching the colonization proposals before the Mexican congress and reported in September 1848 that Mora's admonition—"the necessity of taking precautions lest the frontier population have more affinity with the United States than with us"—was being overlooked completely.[65] Thus, just before his death, Mora urged his government to build a society that would differ culturally from that of the United States. Unlike most of his fellow liberals, Mora appeared to have abandoned the North American model.

Nothing more clearly points up the ambivalence of the prevailing liberal attitude toward the United States in the wake of the war than a sampling of conservative literature. The conservative argument was unequivocal. The United States was not only a threat to Mexican existence, but its culture and its values were not ones Mexico should emulate. The conservative position had crystallized slowly over thirty years, a process in which growing friction with the United States played a crucial role. This development can be reviewed briefly in the ideas of Lucas Alamán. As we know, Alamán was a centralist in 1824 but also minister of relations from 1823 to 1826. His early ministerial reports showed a bland and even admiring view of the United States. He urged colonization and distribution of vacant land, citing the example of the "almost magical transformation of this type of land in the new states of the Northern Union." [66]

By 1830, however, Alamán was emphasizing the difference of historical development in the two countries, how natural the adoption of federalism had been in the United States and, by contrast, how unnatural it had been in Mexico. As Bustamante's minister in the early 1830s, Alamán began to attack the virus of Enlightenment philosophy which had infected Mexico. Though still generally neutral toward the United States, he became particularly sensitive to North American colonization of Texas.[67] Like Mora in 1837, Alamán realized that unless care was taken in select-

65. Otero to Mora (Sept. 15, 1848), García, *Documentos, 6,* 114.

66. Alamán, "Memoria" (1823), *Documentos, 1,* 102. The theme was repeated two years later in "Memoria" (1825), ibid., pp. 122, 159.

67. See Alamán, "Exámen imparcial" (1834), ibid., *3,* 245–46 and passim.

ing Mexican and other Catholic settlers, "Texas is going to cease to belong to the United States of Mexico." [68] The lesson of Texas and the threat of the United States were a central part of Gutiérrez de Estrada's argument for constitutional monarchy in 1840. Like Zavala, Gutiérrez recognized the mighty torrent of North American democracy which might soon overwhelm Mexico. But unlike Zavala he sought energetic resistance in a strong government consonant with Mexican traditions. If this program is not followed, he warned, "perhaps twenty years will not pass without our seeing the Stars and Stripes wave over the National Palace." He admitted that, like others, he had once been "sincerely addicted to the dominant principles of our neighbors." However, experience had proved their inapplicability to Mexico.[69] Gutiérrez, like Alamán before the war, still admired (as well as feared) the United States, for they both saw its republican institutions as a natural product of colonial history.

With the appearance of *El Tiempo, El Universal,* Alamán's historical writings, and the postwar pamphlets of Gutiérrez de Estrada, the tone changed. A principal tenet of fully elaborated conservatism was a deep hostility toward the United States. Mexico was now seen to have superior Hispanic traditions and cultural values which must be defended. The war, Alamán asserted, was the most unjust in history. Ironically, it was the product of ambitions, "not of an absolute monarchy, but of a republic which claimed to be in the vanguard of nineteenth-century civilization." [70] This was a point the liberals never acknowledged, at least not openly, and it was at the heart of their confusion. Alamán was clear about the United States. Its literary culture was derivative and had no ties with a glorious Hispanic past; its religion was mixed with the commercial spirit and the affairs of this world; its individualism was the solvent of morality, order, and good customs.

> We are not a people of merchants and adventurers, scum and refuse (*hez y desecho*) of all countries, whose only mission is to usurp the property of the miserable Indians, and later to

68. Alamán, "Iniciativa de ley" (1830) in ibid., 2, 542. Mora's views on Texas might well have been inspired by Alamán.
69. Gutiérrez, *Carta,* pp. 54, 57–58.
70. Alamán, *Historia, 5,* 688.

rob the fertile lands opened to civilization by the Spanish race. . . . We are a nation formed three centuries ago, not an aggregation of peoples of differing customs.[71]

Mexico must now try, as Iturbide (supposedly) had tried in 1821, to construct in its very institutions a barrier between itself and the United States. In June and July 1853, *El Universal* argued that a Hispanic alliance must be formed to meet the expansive threat of the new northern barbarians (see above, page 31). With the exception of Mora, the nationalist response to the war came from the conservatives, not from the liberals. For Mexican nationalism in the long run had to entail the effort of differentiating Mexican culture, society, and values from those of the United States. Although conservative politics reached a dead end in the "traitorous" appeal to a foreign monarch, Alamán's resistance to North American culture had a lasting effect.

In conclusion, we have seen that in the main liberals of the pre-Reforma era were mesmerized by the ideal society to the north, and by the spectacular material progress of the United States under republican federal institutions. They talked openly of imitating the United States in reforming Mexico. The more penetrating thinkers, such as Zavala and Mora, came to distinguish between the goals of liberal reform and the methods for achieving those goals. For them the United States could serve as a model for goals but not for methods. The two societies and their respective histories were too different. Zavala's liberalism went bankrupt in Texas, whereas Mora's provided the roots of a continuing tradition. An important aspect of Mora's significance is the fact that he was less drawn to the United States than were many of his colleagues. Still, the nagging question of the North American model persisted to become a permanent feature of the liberal tradition in Mexico. Mora's problem was how to modernize a traditional Hispanic society without Americanizing it and thereby sacrificing its national identity. The problem is yet to be solved.[72]

71. *El Tiempo*, Feb. 4, 1846.
72. Daniel Cosío Villegas expressed deep concern on this question in his "Mexico and the United States" (1947) in *American Extremes* (Austin, University of Texas Press, 1964)

7

Liberalism and the Indian

We have become accustomed in the twentieth century to accord
the Indian a central role in Mexican culture. Mexico, we are told,
is an "Indian country." Even the casual traveler is impressed by
the strength of the indigenous presence in the murals by Rivera,
in the archeological sites at Teotihuacán, in the motifs of the
Ciudad Universitaria, and most recently in the splendid and
dramatic Museo de Antropología. These public symbols of Mexican culture challenge and perhaps even overpower the great Spanish baroque cathedrals, the neoclassic Chapúltepec Castle, and the
Victorian Fine Arts Palace. Our traveler need only wander out
from the center of the largest cities, or into the countryside, to
have his impression confirmed by the physical appearance of the
populace. *Indigenismo,* the effort to redeem the oppressed Indian
population and to demonstrate the indigenous roots of the Mexican nation, has formed a significant part of the revolutionary experience since 1910. The preoccupation with the Indian cannot be
separated from agrarian reform, from rural education, or from the
philosophical search for *lo mexicano.* Like so many of the concerns
bound up with the Revolution, however, twentieth-century indigenismo can cloud our analysis of the nineteenth century.

The place of the Indian in the thought of the pre-Reforma
period presents a problem to those Mexicans who seek the origins
of nationalism and liberalism. Francisco López Cámara argues that
concern for the native element was inherent in the Creole use of
"America" and "Americans" during the Revolution for Independence. Leaders such as Hidalgo, Cos, and Morelos conceived of a
"national community" of Indians and Creoles, united against
Spaniards and the colonial past. López Cámara concludes that a
"vindicating indigenismo becomes fused with the ideals of liberal-

ism, as one of its social elements." [1] We are left, then, with the implication that liberal precepts and indigenismo became joined together in postindependence thought—but unfortunately López Cámara's book ends at 1821. Luis Villoro's philosophical treatment of *Los Grandes Momentos del indigenismo en México* takes us from the ideas of Father Mier (1813–21) to those of Manuel Orozco y Berra (1880) without a word on the intervening period. Jesús Reyes Heroles devotes three volumes to *El Liberalismo mexicano* from 1808 to 1867 without ever touching directly upon the Indian problem.[2] All of this suggests the obvious, that the pre-Reforma liberals were not preoccupied with the Indian, that indigenismo was not a characteristic of the period.

It is further symptomatic of the problem that we have been able to discuss liberal political and social thought here for six chapters without confronting the Indian directly. The question of the Indian, however, must be singled out for special treatment; to do otherwise would be to fall prey to the assumptions of nineteenth-century Creole liberals themselves and to discard our critical perspective. The fact is that we must always be mindful of the indigenous element in the country's culture, lest in our search for affinities of structure between Mexico and Western Europe we conclude that the Mexican liberals were merely transplanted Frenchmen or Spaniards. The Mexican Indian was more than a depressed peasant or proletarian in the European sense. He was ethnically as well as socially different from the Creole elite.

In the sixteenth century the European medieval concept of estates became altered to fit the society of New Spain. Unlike the mixed-blood Castes, the indigenous population was regarded as a distinct juridical entity, and it constituted a "peculiarly American Estate." [3] Though the Indians shared with the Castes the onerous tribute, they were accorded a fuero—special courts and immunity from some taxes. Ethnically and juridically separate from the Creoles, they were also the living reminder of an indigenous civilization that predated the Spaniards. After 1821 this civilization theoretically constituted a heritage for the independent country.

1. López Cámara, *Génesis*, p. 271.
2. He treats matters concerning the Indian, particularly land, at length in a section entitled "Social Liberalism" in Vol. 3. His emphasis is upon identifying preagrarianist ideas.
3. McAlister, "Social Structure," p. 358.

The question of Mexico's national identity necessarily involved coming to terms with the Indian.

The problem is further confused, however, by the reality of post-Conquest society. Aztec institutions, as Charles Gibson has definitively shown, disintegrated under Spanish rule. "The [Aztec] empire collapsed first, and the civilization was fragmented in individual communities." Only the "local and less comprehensive" structures of Aztec life were permitted to survive.[4] Above the local and rural level, Mexico in 1821 was institutionally a Hispanic nation; and even in the countryside it was the Creole hacienda that dominated. Thus if the liberals dealt with the problems of political and social organization in a continental way, it was for understandable reasons. Yet, the physical presence of the Indian as the ethnic majority of the population continued to confront them, particularly when they turned to the problems of local organization. The *vecinos* of the ayuntamientos were simply not French and Spanish peasants. Moreover, when heretofore sedentary Indians broke into open rebellion against the government in 1847–49 (as in 1810), they could not be ignored.

The formal writing of the postindependence period reveals both an indifference to Mexico's indigenous heritage and a doctrinaire effort to remove the designation "Indian" from Mexican life. Whatever degree of indigenismo or *neoaztequismo* was present in the anti-Spanish pronouncements of the independence era passed from the scene in 1821. Both Alamán and Mora condemned those who had interpreted Hidalgo's revolt or Iturbide's empire as retribution for three centuries of Spanish domination. The legal proclamations of the years 1810–21, both those of the Spanish cortes and those of the insurgents, bequeathed to independent Mexico the doctrine of equality under the law. The tribute was suppressed. Racial, caste, and class distinctions were legally abolished, and all inhabitants were to enjoy equally the rights and responsibilities of citizens.[5] It was of great concern to the legislators of the State of Mexico, among others, that this concept be upheld.

4. Charles Gibson, *The Aztecs Under Spanish Rule. A History of the Indians of the Valley of Mexico, 1519–1810* (Stanford, Stanford University Press, 1964), pp. 403, 409.

5. See Moisés González Navarro, "Instituciones indígenas en México independiente," *Métodos y resultados de la política indigenista en México* (Mexico, Inst. Nacional Indigenista, 1954), p. 115a.

A few days after the congress convened, deputies José María Luis Mora and Alonso Fernández proposed that "*indio, in common acceptance as a term of opprobrium for a large portion of our citizens, be abolished from public usage.*" [6] On another occasion, Mora expressed disapproval of a suggestion by Carlos María de Bustamante that a monument to the liberator Morelos be placed in the Church of Loreto because it was known as an "Indian parish." We must insist, said Mora, that by law "Indians no longer exist." [7] Yet the term continued to appear in the debates of the 1820s, though usually modified as "those called Indians (*los llamados indios*) ."

Mora's doctrinaire views on the Indian can be seen clearly in his judgment of Juan Rodríguez Puebla, the fellow reformer of 1833–34. Mora, as architect of the education plan of 1833, objected strongly to Rodríguez Puebla's attempt to introduce a separate curriculum for Indians in the first establishment (preparatory studies) . Rodríguez Puebla, said Mora, wanted to keep intact the "ancient civil and religious privileges of the Indians" and, without explicitly saying so, to "establish a purely Indian system." The basis of the conflict is obscure and may well have involved a personal rivalry between the two men. It is certain, though, that Mora looked unfavorably upon the principal lifework of Rodríguez Puebla, which was to redevelop the Colegio de San Gregorio, a Jesuit school for Indians suppressed in 1767. Mora could not understand Rodríguez Puebla, whom he said even "claimed to belong to the [Indian] race"; for the latter had been a man of "progress," a partisan of "liberty." Why should he now work for the "exaltation of the Aztec race"? The encounter with Rodríguez Puebla led Mora to affirm characteristically that the Gómez Farías regime "did not recognize in government acts the distinction of Indians and non-Indians. Rather it substituted poor and rich, extending to all the benefits of society." [8] A doctrinaire liberal

6. *Actas, 1,* 52 (Mar. 13, 1824) .

7. *Actas, 3,* 9 (Nov. 3, 1824) .

8. See Mora, *Obras,* pp. 152–53. Rodríguez Puebla, a rare pre-Reforma *indigenista,* might prove an interesting figure for further study, if information could be found. Born in 1798, son of an *aguador* (water carrier) , he studied at San Gregorio and San Ildefonso on royal scholarship. After 1826, besides serving several terms in both houses of congress, he became the beloved director of San Gregorio, where he

regime had no place for a would-be nativist, and Rodríguez Puebla was forced to join the political opposition.

The corollary to this legalistic liberal attitude toward the Indian, dubbed by Manuel Gamio as "sociological myopia," was a general indifference toward Aztec Mexico. The pre-Conquest period was not a theme that attracted historians, and treatment of the Aztecs was always incidental to other concerns. We have seen Mora's view that Hernán Cortés was the founder of the Mexican nation, that nothing before him much mattered. Mora noted briefly that the Aztecs had no extensive agriculture. (How could they without tools as the Europeans knew them, and without yoke animals?) Therefore, he continued, the pre-Conquest population must have been small, for agriculture is the only means of supporting a large country. Large Indian population was a myth created by the missionaries and conquistadors to magnify their own deeds.[9] Mora's view of the Aztecs drew its inspiration from the European school of Robertson and de Pauw, rather than from Francisco Clavijero.

The Aztecs fared better with Alamán and Zavala, in each case for different reasons. The Hispanophobe Zavala maintained that pre-Cortesian Mexico was more populous than in his day and that "the Indians under their national governments were beginning to develop some ideas." For him, it was the Conquest that cut short "the spirit of invention," reducing the Indians to a state of slavery. Lucas Alamán refuted William H. Prescott's epithet of "barbarous," as applied to the Aztecs: "Only the religion which they professed merited such a name." [10] Yet Alamán limited his discussion of Aztec civilization to a very few pages, and one can conclude that he regarded its place in Mexico's heritage as insignificant.

Though Mora, Zavala, and Alamán were all amateur archeolo-

remained until his death in 1848. See Francisco Sosa, *Biografías de mexicanos distinguidos* (Mexico, 1884), pp. 907–10. On San Gregorio, see Gibson, p. 383; González Navarro, "Instituciones indígenas," p. 135a; Juan A. Mateos, *Historia parlamentaria de los congresos mexicanos* (Mexico, 1877–86), 2, 966. The latter contains a successful proposal by Rodríguez Puebla (Oct. 8, 1824) that the property formerly of the Hospital de Naturales be applied to the Colegio "for the purpose of educating youths *de los llamados indios.*" His speech (Oct. 11) supporting the proposal can be found in *Águila*, Oct. 19–20, 22–23, 1824. It was an eloquent refutation of the doctrinaire view on "equality."

9. Mora, *Revoluciones, 3,* viii.

10. Zavala, *Ensayo, 1,* 11–13; Alamán, footnote in Prescott, *Historia, 1,* 15.

gists, the developing interest in Mexico's ancient civilization during these years was mostly the work of foreigners. Only an occasional notice can be found in the newspapers of the day announcing a national expedition or find. L. Z. (undoubtedly Lorenzo de
Zavala) reported in *El Sol* (October 25, 1827) that ruins of a city
perhaps comparable to Tenochtitlán had been found north of
Huichapan in the State of Querétaro. The *Aguila* said that Father
Mier was heading a commission to dig up a statue of Teoyaomic,
an Aztec death god, and it invited him to write up the expedition.[11] *El Fénix* of October 14, 1833, commented on a book published in Paris by Waldeck on the ruins of Mitla and Palenque:
"It would be desirable for Mexican antiquaries to devote themselves to . . . a philosophical examination of these monuments."
L. F. B. Trioen, identifiable only as a Belgian doctor of laws and a
professor of medicine in Mexico, wrote in 1841 a thirty-five page
sympathetic account of ancient Mexico.[12] Francisco Zarco, probably influenced by Prescott, submitted to *El Siglo* on January 12,
1852, a romantic account of the great city of Texcoco and its decline. While living in France, José María Luis Mora agreed to
translate into Spanish an elaborate French work on Mexican
antiquities.[13] Apparently, Mora had studied Nahuatl for we have
seen that he translated the book of Luke into the Mexican language for the British and Foreign Bible Society. These items constitute thin evidence, however, and hardly indicate that the postindependence generation was much stirred by Mexico's ancient
origins.

The liberals were quite aware of the depressed condition of the
Indian population, a condition brought about by conquest and
persisting to their own time. True to their precepts of utilitarian
individualism and legal equality, they sought the cause of Indian

11. *Aguila*, Apr. 26, 1823.

12. Trioen, *Indagaciones, sobre las antigüedades mexicanas, pruebas de la civilización adelantada de los mexicanos en el xv siglo . . . y comparación de su civilización con la de sus descendientes en 1841* (Mexico, 1841). Trioen was almost unique
in referring to the present-day Indians as "the true Mexicans." He called for compassion toward the Indians and advocated a policy of education.

13. The 1,000-franc contract, dated Aug. 9, 1836, can be found in Mora Correspondence, 1794–1844, the 150 translated pages in Mora Documents, 1806–38. The
work was A. Lenoir, *Antiquités mexicaines* (Paris, 1833–34), an account of three
voyages in 1805–07 (particularly to Mitla and Palenque) by Dupaix.

degradation in the paternalism of the Spanish colonial system. Lorenzo de Zavala characteristically leveled his attack on the Laws of the Indies which kept the Indians segregated from Europeans, inhibited their learning of Spanish, and prevented them from entering the "rational world." Mora attacked the "privileged" status of the Indians in Spanish law, resulting in their inability to carry on the "social transactions of life." Worst of all, under the Spanish regime they could not acquire the sense of personal independence which came from the "sentiment of property." [14]

On the matter of the Indian, however, we are faced again with Mora's ambivalence toward the colonial regime. Though he had no liking for colonial paternalism, he concluded his discussion of Indian "privileges" by saying that the Laws of the Indies had been the subject of overly partisan conflicting interpretations. We must not forget, he added, that Spain's first consideration was to "maintain the submission of the colonies" and to guard against rebellion. Viewed in this light, most of the legislation was "judicious and prudent." [15] We are reminded of Mora's benign view toward Manuel Abad y Queipo's defense of clerical immunities in 1799 (see above, page 136). They could perhaps be justified as a means of strengthening control over the Indian population.

Mora was more consistent in his attack on the colonial missions, which he blamed for perpetuating the notion of communal property among the Indians. The missionaries, he asserted, kept the indigenous population "in a condition of stationary infancy." [16] Liberal spokesmen tended to look more favorably on the work of the missions in the late 1840s when the country was faced with rebellious Indians; still, it was the doctrinaire view that prevailed. The missions, except perhaps for the heroic efforts of the earliest sixteenth-century pioneers, were incompatible with the spirit of "personal independence," as were all the works of the "monastic regime." Thus the Gómez Farías government in 1834 secularized the remaining missions, first in Upper California and then in the entire country. In doing so the liberal regime was following precedents established by Charles III in expelling the Jesuits in 1767,

14. Zavala, *Ensayo*, *1*, 12–15; Mora, *Revoluciones*, *1*, 202 ff.
15. Ibid., 205–06.
16. Ibid., pp. 273–74; also p. 198.

by the Spanish cortes in 1813 (legislation reissued in Mexico in 1821), and by the efforts of the Guadalupe Victoria government in the mid-twenties.[17] The proclerical reaction of 1834 reinstated the missions, but they were suppressed finally in 1859.

Despite the legal view that the "Indian" no longer existed, there were occasional expressions of concern over his present-day condition. The logical liberal conclusion was that the Indian's plight had improved, now that he was legally a free citizen. An editorialist in 1846 announced that Indians are "admitted into all the professions . . . into all the educational establishments." Even if equality has not been fully realized, its proclamation "has greatly prepared the way by removing the principal obstacles." [18] Tadeo Ortiz had high hopes for the progress of the Indian population under its new legal condition.

Most liberals were not as sanguine as Ortiz, however, and while citing legal gains, admitted that the real condition of the present-day Indian was grim. The ever-critical Fernández de Lizardi, in his *Testament and Farewell* (1827), left the Indians in a state unchanged since the Conquest. Most lamentable is "the indifference with which the legislatures have regarded them, as can be seen by the few and uninteresting sessions in which [the Indians] have received attention since the first congress." [19] Zavala noted the shameful lack of concern for educating the Indian. Guillermo Prieto acknowledged that exploitation by landowners and moneylenders continued as before. *El Siglo* in 1853 went as far as to say that despite declarations of equality, "the Indians have taken on all the burdens of society, without enjoying any of the benefits." [20]

17. See C. Alan Hutchinson, "The Mexican Government and the Mission Indians of Upper California, 1821–1835," *The Americas*, 21 (1965), 335–62. Hutchinson demonstrates the complexities involved in secularizing the missions. See also González Navarro, "Instituciones indígenas," pp. 139–42. The very brief national secularization decree stated merely that the missions were to be converted into parishes within four months, according to limits set by the states (Dublán and Lozano, *Legislación*, 2, 689–90 (Apr. 16, 1834).

18. *Memorial histórico*, Feb. 16, 1846.

19. Fernández de Lizardi, *Testamento*, 1, 6; also *Conversaciones*, 2, No. 12. For a similar 1820 assertion by Lizardi, see Reyes Heroles, *Liberalismo*, 1, 50. For Ortiz' statement, see *México*, p. 334.

20. Zavala, *Ensayo*, 2, 387; G. Prieto, *Indicaciones sobre el origen, vicisitudes y estado que guardan actualmente las rentas generales de la federación mexicana*

In a general survey of Mexican society intended for Europeans, José María Luis Mora presented a similarly bleak picture of the indigenous population. He attested to the legal gains which had come with independence and said that pre-Conquest history had proved the Indians could govern themselves. Yet, "in their present state and until they have undergone considerable changes, [the Indians] can never reach the degree of enlightenment, civilization, and culture of Europeans nor maintain themselves as equals in a society formed by both." Mora depicted the Indian as resigned and melancholy, as one who covers his true feelings and "makes a mystery of his actions." Moreover, the Indian clings obstinately to his former customs, making it difficult for him to progress. Though explicitly denying a belief in superior races, Mora betrayed a deeper conviction that the Indian was inferior to the white and that there was little hope of bettering his status. In short, he said, these "backward and degraded (cortos y envilecidos) remains of the ancient Mexican population," while eliciting "compassion," cannot be considered the base of a progressive Mexican society.[21]

Mora explicitly stated that it was in the white race "that Mexican character is to be sought." [22] He believed that with a concerted program of European colonization, Mexico could, within a century, see the complete fusion of the Indians and "the total extinction of the Castes." Thus Mora, whose father publicly attested to his son's "refined lineage" and "clean blood" in 1812 (see above, page 72), could not conceive of nationality as residing in any group other than his own. Mora's sentiments were repeated later by Guillermo Prieto.[23] There was little dispute with this prevailing Creole conception of Mexican nationality during Mora's generation.

(Mexico, 1850), p. 386; El Siglo, July 8, 1853. See also Melchor Ocampo, "Representación" (1851), in La Religión, la iglesia, p. 28. Ocampo, as an enlightened hacendado, deplored the continuing evils of peonage. In general, however, peonage was not much discussed during this period.

21. Mora, Revoluciones, 1, 63–73.

22. Ibid., p. 75.

23. Prieto, p. 432. It was this Creole view that led Manuel Gamio to remark in 1916 that "nadie sabia donde quedaba la patria." See Forjando Patria (Mexico, Porrua, 1960), p. 68. Gamio emphasized how Benito Juárez separated himself from his race, once he had attained power (pp. 177–78).

The question of the Indian did not enter national politics except briefly with the coming of Vicente Guerrero to the presidency in 1829. Lorenzo de Zavala's account of the episode conveys a sense of social upheaval, which saw "a triumph of the popular party" and the ascendancy of an Indian president. Guerrero, said Zavala, made no effort to renounce his Indian origins; they were consistent with his democratic principles and his adherence to the policy of expelling Spaniards.[24] There apparently were some who welcomed Guerrero's assumption of power as signifying an Indian triumph. One pamphlet referred to him as "that immortal hero, favorite son of Nezahualcoyoltzin." The pamphleteer even foresaw "the reconquest of this land by its legitimate owners."[25] Zavala asserted that there was considerable opposition to Guerrero by "the new Mexican aristocracy" and by "señoras of a certain class" who were envious of the status suddenly attained by a darker-skinned family.[26] Though we must use Zavala with caution, his observations do suggest that the 1829 upheaval had a nativist strain. Perhaps the "unanimous" adoption of Bustamante's Plan of Jalapa, as described sympathetically by Mora, was in part a Creole reaction to the frightening prospect of the Indian in politics. Undoubtedly, Zavala himself became uneasy. His 1833 pronouncement on the futility of democracy (see above, page 123) revealed a man who would have had difficulty supporting Guerrero.

At the heart of the Indian question is land, a fact made unforgettable by the agrarian revolution initiated by Emiliano Zapata in 1910. Therefore, to better understand how the nineteenth-century liberals confronted the Indian, we must go beyond their general observations and plumb certain features of the formation of land policy in the postindependence years. We have seen that the cornerstone of the liberal edifice was the individual property-

24. Zavala, *Ensayo*, 2, 57–59, 133–34, 150. Zavala was a Guerrero partisan in 1829 and served briefly as his minister of finance.

25. E. A. D., *Los Indios quieren ser libres y lo serán con justicia* (Mexico, 1829). There followed a response by Otro Indio, *Todos los Indios son libres, y no hay que se los dispute* (Mexico, 1829), which took the doctrinaire liberal view.

26. Zavala, *Ensayo*, 2, 59. Cf. the description of "the hordes of savages called the Army of the South," entering Mexico City when Juan Álvarez assumed the presidency: Manuel Siliceo to Manuel Doblado (Nov. 17, 1855), García, *Documentos*, "Los Gobiernos de Álvarez y Comonfort según el archivo del general Doblado," *31* (Mexico, Bouret, 1910), 42.

owning citizen. Liberal adherence to the sanctity of private property also meant the necessary though reluctant acceptance of lay
latifundia. The implications of these postindependence assumptions for the Indian rural community are obvious and have been
often stated in a general way. The communal property of the villages was now threatened by liberal theory as well as by the traditional encroachment of the large landowner.

Precedents for the breakup of Indian communal property in
America were well established in peninsular Hispanic policy. The
government of Charles III, largely inspired by Pedro Rodríguez de
Campomanes and Pablo Olavide, initiated legislation intended to
promote agriculture in Spain by distributing common lands
among individual peasants. This common land included both
traditional pastures and wooded areas (*ejidos*) and also the *tierras
de propios,* town property rented out to individuals for cultiva-
tion. The rent from the *propios* was added to the *arbitrios,* local
direct taxes, to provide the basis of municipal finance. Charles III,
through the intendants, appointed syndics to intervene in town
finances and to promote the distribution of propios to poor peasants, either by low fixed rent or by public auction. These reforms
of the 1760s and 1770s, advocated again by Jovellanos in 1795,
were ineffectual, both because of efforts of local town officials to
appropriate common lands for themselves and because of the late
eighteenth-century expansion of private latifundia (*señoríos* and
mayorazgos) .[27]

The Ordinance of Intendants (1786) carried this Bourbon
policy to New Spain. The document mentioned briefly that communal property "shall be allotted by the intendants in pieces of
ground suitable for married Indians." [28] The matter was little
pursued prior to independence, however, except by Manuel Abad
y Queipo who advocated a series of reforms to alleviate the
onerous burdens borne by the Indians and Castes. Among them
was the distribution of communal lands among individuals of each

27. See Jovellanos, "Informe," *BAE, 50,* pp. 86–92; Herr, *Eighteenth-Century
Revolution,* pp. 90, 113–16, and passim. There was also much interest in developing colonies of foreigners.
28. Lillian E. Fisher, *The Intendant System in Spanish America* (Berkeley, University of California Press, 1929) , p. 139.

village.[29] The main law affecting postindependence thinking on
land policy was issued by the Cortes of Cádiz on January 4, 1813.
It decreed the reduction to private property of all unoccupied,
royal, and town lands (propios and arbitrios) "except for the
egidos which the towns need." The provincial deputations were to
carry out this distribution in Spain and America according to local
conditions.[30]

There were few formal measures on the national level between
1821 and 1856 pertaining to Indian communal property. The
delegates to the national constituent congress were generally hostile to village lands, but the Constitution of 1824 had no specific
provisions affecting the municipalities. These, as we have seen, in
a federal system were to be left to the states. National legislation
was limited to an 1824 measure providing for the distribution of
the property of the parcialidades of San Juan and Santiago, the
two traditional subdivisions within Mexico City. The matter was
not settled until 1868, largely because of the dispute as to whether
the property should be distributed to individuals or to towns.[31]
We must turn to the state level to see the specific problems of
formulating a policy for village lands. Let us consider one case, the
State of Mexico.

Concern for upgrading the degenerate municipalities of the
state was one of the distinguishing features of constitutional liberalism. José María Luis Mora advocated local "liberty" as a
counterweight to despotic power (Chapter 3 above). Yet we
found that "liberty" for Mora meant instituting some measure of
administrative decentralization at the lowest level. He did not in-

29. The other reforms recommended by Abad were the abolition of tribute for
Indians and Castes, the suppression of criminal laws prejudicial to the Castes,
free distribution of royal lands among Indians and Castes, the opening to the
people of uncultivated lands of large proprietors, the permission for all classes to
settle in or near Indian towns, and appropriate salaries for territorial judges (sub-
delegados). See Abad, "Representación" (1799), in Mora, Obras, p. 208.

30. See Dublán and Lozano, 1, 397–99.

31. See González Navarro, "Instituciones indígenas," pp. 123–25. The law can
be found in Dublán and Lozano, 1, 744 (Nov. 27, 1824). "San Juan" referred to
San Juan Tenochtitlán, "Santiago" to Santiago Tlatelolco (Gibson, p. 37). This
was a national issue because the Federal District was administered by the central
government. See also Alamán, "Memoria" (1830), Documentos, 1, 218–19; Chevalier,
"Conservateurs et libéraux," p. 463.

tend that the ayuntamientos develop as self-governing local units. The prefect system was established in an attempt both to curb the reign of local oligarchs and to encourage the municipalities to take on petty administrative duties themselves.

It was land that would form the material basis of the strengthened and reorganized towns; land consequently became the subject of much debate in the congress. These debates and the resulting legislation on municipal property followed two general and conflicting lines. One was the prevailing impulse to alienate village lands to individuals. The other was the more pragmatic effort to strengthen municipal finances so that the towns could pay their way and be responsible adminstrative units. Specifically, this second effort focused on the formulation of a measure to "designate and give propios and arbitrios to the towns of the state." Since one of the two chief functions of Indian town governments had been to collect the tribute, its abolition meant the possibility of reorganizing municipal finances in all towns on a uniform Hispanic basis.[32]

In one of the early discussions of municipal property, José María de Jáuregui called for a reading of the 1813 law "reducing common village lands to individual ownership." The law, he added, is "a hundred times" more beneficial here than in Spain. Indians will become proprietors and "true citizens under the tutelage of nobody," which is what they most desire.[33] One of the important functions of the prefect, instituted in the provisional Ley Orgánica (article 39, xvi) and preserved in the Constitution of 1827 (article 155, viii), was to distribute communal property "according to the laws on the subject" (presumably the 1813 decree of the cortes). The hostility to communal property, as we might expect, ran strong among the delegates. Yet actual cases involving distribution to individuals seldom came before the congress. One such rare case involved the prefect of Tula who wanted more specific legislation empowering him to divide lands, in view of the complications of existing laws. The committee decided that

32. "Late colonial Indian governments functioned principally to collect tribute and to dispense minor punishments" (Gibson, p. 191).

33. *Actas, 2,* 380 (Oct. 11, 1824).

article 39 of the Ley Orgánica was sufficient and instructed him to proceed in the distribution.[34]

More frequently the congress faced petitions from villages for grants of communal property. José Domingo Lazo de la Vega supported a petition from San Pedro Atzompán requesting a *fundo legal* (the basic communal grant provided for in colonial legislation) to be made up of lands taken from Ozumbilla. Mora reacted strongly to the request, saying that by the Constitution of 1812 not even the king himself had the power to "occupy the property of an individual or a corporation" and that the congress should explicitly annul the old laws regarding the fundo legal. Earlier he had maintained that such laws "are by their very nature annulled, because they conflict with the present system which disavows those privileges formerly extended to those called Indians. Today there are no caste distinctions nor does the law recognize any title other than that of citizen."[35] Lazo de la Vega retorted that it was not a question of Indians but of villages which should be granted necessary lands. The then president of the congress, egalitarian José Ignacio de Nájera, supported Mora's position, and the petition was rejected.

Mora was even more hostile toward a petition from the Ayuntamiento of Huehuetoca that the hacienda of Jalpa be forced to rent out lands to the village. We cannot attack property, said Mora, nor despoil proprietors of the very rights we are trying to guarantee. The petition should be returned to Huehuetoca "with the contempt a request of this type merits."[36]

Mora, Nájera, and Jáuregui showed particular disfavor toward

34. *Actas, 8,* 219–21 (Aug. 5, 1826); 419–22 (Sept. 4, 1826). The case involved villages dispersed during the revolutionary years in the mountains of the *partido* of Ixmiquilpan. The prefect complained of constant dispute among the villages (they were not really villages, he said), which frustrated his attempt to apply the new law.

35. *Actas, 4,* 56 (Mar. 16, 1825). Mora's later assertion was made on Apr. 29, 1826 (*Actas, 7,* 257–60). The case dragged on for two years. The provincial deputation had recognized this village of two hundred people (forty was sufficient), but the state audiencia reversed the decision. See *Actas, 7,* 52–53 (Mar. 10, 1826).

36. *Actas, 7,* 20 (Mar. 4, 1826). Apparently the petition related to lands traditionally occupied by the villages but now no longer available. In his formal writings Mora frequently condemned the fundo legal as a creation of the sixteenth-century clergy. See *Revoluciones, 1,* 198, 273–74.

lands that had been accumulated by the *cofradías,* or parishioners associations. The importance of these organizations increased greatly in the late colonial period, since they provided the one focus for communal solidarity when other community institutions were disintegrating.[37] To Mora, it was a "misunderstood piety" by which a "great part of the Indian lands have passed to the cofradías." The prefects should distribute cofradía lands to individual villagers, he said, so that their property rights might be protected against what was really clerical encroachment.[38] The report of the committee on community funds (see below) emphasized that the cofradías had absorbed an undue amount of land and called for a local investigation to distinguish legitimate from illegitimate cofradía holdings. In one case (Tenango del Valle), said the report, "it appears that the entire town has been already converted into parish lands and that the priest is the absolute owner of all." Moreover, the *mayordomo* of the cofradía puts inordinate funds into "useless expenses" on fiestas.[39] The committee, however, recommended no immediate intervention in cofradía lands. It appears that despite the militancy of Mora, Jáuregui, and Nájera, the matter was left unresolved.

The effort to strengthen the basis of municipal finance was an important concern of the congress. In the second month of session Benito José Guerra urged that a copy of the regulations drawn up by the provincial deputation on community funds be secured so a committee could move quickly. Action was imperative, he added, because of the miserable state of the municipalities.[40] The matter, as we have seen, was entrusted to the *gobernación* committee which sent out a request that each municipality indicate the sum of its community funds (propios and arbitrios). By September 1824 so many replies had come back that Guerra suggested they be extracted before being presented to the congress. One village, Tesoyuca, replied frankly that the measure on propios and arbitrios was useless "if it was not preceded by another which speaks

37. See Gibson, pp. 127–35.

38. *Actas,* 2, 12–13 (July 2, 1824); also 2, 441–43 (Oct. 26, 1824).

39. See *Dictamen de la comisión de gubernación sobre señalar y dar propios y arbitrios a los pueblos del estado de México* (Mexico, 1824), p. 10. Dated May 31, 1824.

40. *Actas, 1,* 119 (Apr. 6, 1824).

of giving the pueblos the lands they lack." The majority of the villages do not have propios, "some because [their propios] have been usurped by the hacendados, others because their ancestors have sold lands illegitimately." Tesoyuca itself had no fundo legal. It had been taken by hacendados who then defended themselves successfully against all village litigation.[41]

The evidence from Tesoyuca supports our general picture of rural changes in the late colonial period. The hacienda had become the supreme community. The *cabecera* concept had given way to terms such as "pueblo," "rancho," "hacienda," which reflected the real condition of rural areas. The guarantees for a minimal communal holding (fundo legal) became meaningless in the face of an expanding hacienda which was actually abetted by the law.[42] The alcalde of Tesoyuca complained that villagers, out of poverty, were forced to work as laborers on the haciendas for two and one-half *reales* a day. We are tyrannized by the hacendados, he added. They seize our cattle and "charge us fines at their whim, though we have done them no wrong." The petition called for lands that could be cultivated "for the individual interest of each one." This would stimulate prosperity in the village and aid in the establishment of schools. You must not think, said the alcalde, that "the pueblos because they are Indian have no desire to become enlightened." [43] The state congress was deluged with similar local petitions, asking not only for lands but also for the permission to collect tolls and special taxes to meet financial ob-

41. MS., dated Aug. 23, 1824. This document and an earlier (May 20) and more general petition are located in the Archivo de la Cámara de Diputados (Toluca), Carpeta 19, expediente 273, and Carp. 20, exp. 212, respectively. Extracts of the replies were read in the congress beginning Sept. 28, but unfortunately these extracts were not recorded in the *Actas*. Apparently they were never printed, though Mora suggested they should be. The two documents from Tesoyuca are the only ones of this category existing in the Cámara de Diputados archive. Perhaps others can be found in the Archivo General del Estado [de México], which unfortunately was closed to the public at the time of my visit.

42. Gibson, pp. 57, 408, and passim.

43. Tesoyuca's desire for individual holdings and for education should be compared with the concerns of other communities. Tesoyuca, a town of 413 families (1,260 individuals) located near Texcoco, was not isolated. Yet the petition spoke of larger nearby communities "which send their sons to the capital or to other towns to be taught."

ligations. The particular new obligation was the *alcabala* which in effect had been substituted for the colonial tribute.[44]

In framing legislation on municipal funds, the principal point debated was the basic right of the ayuntamiento to hold property. At first Mora's position was rigid. He recommended that the whole proposal be thrown out: "There are no rights in nature and in society except those of individuals." [45] Benito José Guerra said communities could hold property and cited Vattel to prove it. Guerra outlined in detail the categories of communal property, distinguishing between the fundo legal (the basic colonial grant [*casco*] to measure 600 *varas* square from the center of the village) ; miscellaneous *bienes comunes* from other sources (which included the propios) ; and "those called cofradía lands." Mora, in another context, dismissed such distinctions and said that all communal property should be lumped together. He gave in reluctantly to the view of the gobernación committee (as did José María de Jáuregui) and agreed on December 7, 1824, that "it was indispensable that the ayuntamientos have some [property]." [46]

The committee recommended adhering to the provincial deputation's proposal of February 12, 1822: present communal property should be distributed to individuals on a rental basis rather than as outright property. Such a measure, the committee maintained, would forestall further alienation of these lands, either through usurpation by nearby hacendados or through imprudent sale by villagers. The individual resident was too poor to develop lands held as private property. The committee's report included detailed provisions for renting out the various categories of community property. It is clear that the proposal was only a temporary measure designed to meet the pressing needs of the ayuntamientos.

44. See *Actas, 7,* 53 (Mar. 10, 1826). There were also references to increased population in the villages, which put pressure on existing land. A study should be made of economic and social changes affecting the municipalities after 1810.

45. *Actas, 2,* 353 (Oct. 1, 1824) ; also 2, 435 (Oct. 22) .

46. *Actas, 3,* 177–83. The previous discussion pertained to what came to be art. 39, sec. vi of the Ley Orgánica: the prefect shall supervise the administration of communal funds. For Guerra's presentation, see *Actas, 2,* 356–58 (Oct. 2, 1824) . On the fundo legal, a nineteenth-century and not a colonial term, see Gibson, p. 285.

Once the replies from the questionnaire to the villages have come in, the report said, "the laws which our present system demands can be considered and established." [47]

The committee's recommendation was allowed to stand. Articles 100 to 112 of the ayuntamiento law of February 9, 1825, defined the municipal funds. "The propios of the villages," stated article 101, "will consist of the landed property which they hold peacefully." [48] Nevertheless, the matter of communal property was left in legal confusion, since in the constitution the prefect was given power to distribute community property (see above, page 227), presumably in accordance with the 1813 law of the cortes. The absence of distribution cases in the debates indicates that the views of the gobernación committee prevailed in practice over the outright distribution principle, at least in the 1820s. Thus by force of necessity, the congress departed from doctrinaire liberal views and reaffirmed, however tenuously, the right of the Indian community to hold property. [49]

In formulating municipal policy, the deputies always adhered to the principle of paternalism. Despite the repudiation of colonial "privileges" enjoyed by the Indians, traditional notions of tutelage continued. We saw in Chapter 3 that Bourbon centralist assumptions ran deeper than the constitutionalist principle of municipal liberty. The prefect's powers were not unlike those of the intendant. For instance, the prefect was to supervise municipal funds in order to prevent money being squandered on wasteful

47. *Dictamen*, p. 11. The proposal was signed by Guerra, Lazo de la Vega, and José Figueroa. The first two, of all the deputies, showed the most consistent concern for the economic plight of the ayuntamientos. The committee's recommendation to preserve communal property won the praise of Andrés Molina Enríquez in 1909. He cited a key passage from the *Dictamen* in *Los Grandes Problemas nacionales*, Problemas agrícolas e industriales de México, 5 (Mexico, 1953), 38b. It might be noted that the *Dictamen* included a brief discussion of five distinct categories of Indian towns holding communal property, with citations on each from colonial legislation (pp. 7–9).

48. See *Decretos, 1*, 65–66.

49. Apparently, the provincial deputation and the gobernación committee were contradicting the intention of the Jan. 4, 1813 law. In sec. i it had instructed the deputations to substitute new funds for the yield from propios and arbitrios, since the latter were to be turned into individual property. The rental principle had been used earlier in Spain under Charles III as an alternative to outright alienation of communal lands.

fiestas or on works such as the bridge built at Xochitepec. Deputy
Pedro Valdovinos claimed that this bridge and a similar project at
Tlaltizapan, though built at great village expense, were unusable;
travelers still had to ford the river.[50] One of the prefect's duties
was to "take particular care that the inhabitants of his district, dispersed in the countryside, be reduced to village life, so that once
established in society, they can receive the corresponding religious
and civil education." The implementation of this policy, a revival
of the colonial *congregación*, seldom came before the deputies. On
one occasion, however, the congress debated vigorously the merits
of uniting four *rancherías* into one pueblo and granting it cofradía land for a fundo legal. The debate revealed an awareness by
the deputies that this policy followed a colonial precedent and that
it might thus in principle be opposed to "the present system of
government." Nevertheless, the opinion prevailed that "public
utility demands that these unfortunate citizens begin to enjoy the
benefits of the free system." [51]

Congressional policy toward Indian villages and their lands thus
emerged confused and unresolved. Communal property and Indian segregation were formally repudiated, and the 1813 principle
of reduction of communal property to private ownership found
strong support. Rural prosperity (apart from foreign colonization
schemes) was to be built upon individual property ownership. At
the same time, adherence to the doctrine of private property
merely abetted the hacienda, which was the dominant force in the
countryside. Recognizing the threat of the hacienda but unwilling
to attack it directly, the deputies departed from their anticommunal doctrines by accepting the proposal of the gobernación
committee. The concern for upgrading the municipalities (partly
so that they could pay taxes) led to a reassertion of late colonial
practices of close tutelage through the new prefect system. One
may conclude, then, that independence and liberal doctrines had

50. *Actas, 1,* 496 (June 20, 1824) , a discussion of art. 39, sec. xi of the Ley
Orgánica: prefects will propose to the governor improvements that need to be
made in their districts.

51. See *Actas, 9,* 479–82 (Jan. 29, 1827) . Mora was absent from the debate, but
he supported this function of the prefect (Ley Orgánica, art. 39, sec. xv) when it
was discussed. The article was omitted from the constitution in the abbreviated
enumeration of the prefect's duties.

little net effect in changing governmental policy toward the Indian villages, at least in the 1820s.[52]

Our discussion thus far has centered on liberal attitudes toward the sedentary indigenous population of the central and southern highlands of Mexico, the descendants of those peoples under Aztec hegemony in the sixteenth century. Except for 1810 and for occasional uprisings during the colonial period, these were peaceable peoples, different from the perpetually rebellious tribes of nomadic Indians which plagued the northern states of the country. Throughout the pre-Reforma period, several tribes, notably the Apache, Navajo, Ute, Comanche, and Kiowa, ranged widely over the vast region from Zacatecas to Coahuila to New Mexico and Arizona, destroying farms and ranches, attacking pack trains and mining camps, and taking human captives as well as material plunder and livestock. This Indian scourge became the dominant public issue for twenty years in such states as Chihuahua, Sonora, and Durango. There were some efforts made by the national government to aid state authorities, but generally the problem was ignored and left to the states themselves. The governors of Sonora and Chihuahua attempted vigorous military action and even hired North American scalp hunting adventurers to terrorize the savages. The raids subsided briefly during the occupation of Mexico by American troops, but broke out again in the fifties and sixties, until the dispersal of the Indian tribes in the United States after the Civil War.[53]

One finds only occasional reference to the *indios bárbaros* in Mexico City publications. Lorenzo de Zavala voiced concern over reports of uprisings by the Yaquis, Mayos, and Opatas in Sonora in 1825–26 and again in 1830. He maintained that a vigorous policy must be enforced. The "nation must compel the barbarous Indians to settle down in regular communities, or, like the North Americans, [force them] to leave the territory of the republic." [54] Mora ignored the problem, except on one occasion when he as-

52. Gibson's concluding remarks (*Aztecs*, p. 408) in large part characterize the policies of the Mexico state constituent congress.

53. See Ralph A. Smith, "Indians in American-Mexican Relations Before the War of 1846," *HAHR*, *43* (1963), 34–64. See also González Navarro, "Instituciones indígenas," pp. 158–64.

54. Zavala, *Ensayo*, *1*, 387; *2*, 335–36.

serted that colonization by European families would be the only feasible means of civilizing these peoples. Military colonies will only further arouse them, out of fear of extermination. Nor would missions be of any use. "The monastic system of the missions," has proved itself a failure over three hundred years.[55] The devastation of the North reached its peak in the early forties, and *El Siglo* conveyed through numerous articles in late 1842 the appeals of the frontier people for aid from the central government. On October 4, *El Siglo* depicted Mexico City as basking in luxury while "our brothers on the frontier are combating the *bárbaros*." The December 13 issue was devoted entirely to the problem.

El Siglo's brief concern for savage incursions included an obituary notice for Ignacio Zuñiga, a regional patriot from Sonora who had dedicated his life to the Indian question. His persistent objective was "to persuade [the Indians] by peaceful and political means to desire a social existence." Zuñiga founded a periodical in Mexico City in 1841 called *El Sonorense* and wrote several pamphlets popularizing his cause. He argued that the Apaches had stirred up the native tribes—Yaquis, Mayos, and Opatas—and had caused the great war of 1832. Military garrisons must be strengthened to meet this menace. If the Apache threat could be stopped, there was hope of peacefully incorporating the others. Zuñiga outlined a detailed program of provincial development, which included revitalizing the Franciscan missions, using Banco de Avío funds to reinstate the mining industry, and encouraging colonization.[56]

Zuñiga's enlightened attitude was exceptional on the hard-pressed frontier. More typical was the bald statement in 1851 from a clerical overseer on the gigantic Sánchez Navarro hacienda in Coahuila:

> If the legislature resolves to decree that 25 pesos be paid for every scalp, I swear I will grant each member of the legisla-

---

55. Mora, *Revoluciones, 1*, 160–61.

56. Zuñiga, *Rápida Ojeada . . . al estado de Sonora dirigida y dedicada al supremo de la nación* (Mexico, 1835). He died Mar. 27, 1843, at the age of forty-six. His obituary appeared in *El Siglo* on Apr. 4. On this question see also Robert C. Stevens, "Mexico's Forgotten Frontier: a History of Sonora, 1821–1846" (Ph.D. dissertation, University of California, Berkeley, 1963).

ture a plenary indulgence as soon as I am ordained, and it matters little that the legislators be excommunicated by those profound politicians in Mexico City who, preoccupied with their European theories, know nothing of the necessities which, unfortunately, must be adopted by our northern states.[57]

Thus, in the North it was frontier necessity, bearing little relation to political affiliation or ideas, which was probably the principal determinant of attitudes toward the Indian.

Mexico City's "profound politicians" could afford to be indifferent toward the raids of traditionally nomadic tribes on the remote northern frontier. The rebellions of sedentary Indians in Yucatán and the Huasteca, however, could not be ignored, for they raised the specter of social upheaval and race war. The uprising of the Mayas began in July 1847, at a time when the invading North American army was nearing Mexico City. It became a matter of grave concern for the entire country when rebels approached Mérida the following May, threatening to exterminate whites and mestizos or to push them into the sea. As in all peasant revolts, however, warfare followed the cycle of the crops. With the impending rainy season of 1849, Mayan soldiers returned to their fields, and Mérida was saved. The rebel forces divided between the leadership of Jacinto Pat and that of the fanatic Cecilio Chi. Chi was killed in late 1849, and by early 1850 the Yucatecan government had regained the upper hand.[58]

The war of Sierra Gorda in the Huasteca was less severe than that of Yucatán, but because of its proximity, was viewed with greater alarm in Mexico City. The center of the revolt was the town of Xichú, but it brought social turmoil to a large region touching the states of Guanajuato, San Luis Potosí, Querétaro, and Mexico. Beginning under the leadership of Eleuterio Quiróz in January 1848, it became entangled with a Santanista rebellion during 1849 and was not stopped until Quiróz was captured and

57. Quoted in Charles H. Harris, III, *The Sánchez Navarros: A Socio-economic Study of a Coahuilan Latifundio, 1846–1853* (Chicago, Loyola University Press, 1964), pp. 83–84.

58. For the events of the Caste Wars see Bancroft, *History*, 5, 537–39, 580–88; González Navarro, "Instituciones indígenas," pp. 154–56; Nelson Reed, *The Caste War of Yucatán* (Stanford, Stanford University Press, 1964).

shot in December 1849.[59] During 1848 and 1849, therefore, the problem of the Indian suddenly loomed large in Mexican thought.

The issues raised by the Caste Wars formed part of the larger national debate which took place in the wake of the 1847 defeat. Nevertheless, liberal and conservative responses to the Indian question were less divergent than it might seem from the polemics of the day. Liberal opinion, as seen principally in the newspapers *El Monitor* and *El Siglo*, showed confusion and inconsistency. *El Monitor* refused to recognize that the Sierra Gorda revolt was "the work of the indigenous class," as the Yucatán rebellion had been. Rather, it is "one of those riots lacking political objectives, aimed only at pillage and crime," and led by a group of brigands who have managed to stir up the Indian population. *El Monitor* admitted, however, that as "one of the sad legacies left to us by Spanish domination," the threat of a real Caste war was great. The editorialist concluded with a suggestive reference to 1810.[60] General Anastasio Bustamante, who ordered the execution of Quiróz, termed the rebels "communists." On April 20, 1850, *El Siglo* attacked a group in the State of Mexico who were opposing the moderate government of Mariano Riva Palacio. Calling themselves "liberal progressives," said *El Siglo*, they are borrowing communist ideas from Europe and are making their appeal to the Indians by promising lands, free priests, and Indian judges. Such irresponsibility can result only in a Caste war and in the "annihilation" of property.

The standard liberal explanation of the war was that the Indians were revolting against three centuries of abuse under the colonial system. *El Monitor* charged the Spaniards with "systematizing, by more or less hypocritical measures, the divorce of the races." Independence, said *El Siglo*, "has been unable up to now to tear from the [Indians'] hearts the bad seed, rooted there by three centuries of abjection and servility." The Indians became accustomed to viewing the whites only as the usurpers of their lands and their rights.[61] *El Monitor* admitted to continuing

59. See González Navarro, "Instituciones indígenas," pp. 151–52; Cotner, *Herrera*, pp. 237–39.

60. *El Monitor*, Apr. 22, 1849.

61. *El Monitor*, Apr. 1, 1853; *El Siglo*, Feb. 23, 1849. See also *El Monitor*, Apr. 22, 1849; *El Siglo*, Sept. 15, 1850.

abuses by the haciendas and particularly by the church but always identified the basic cause of the rebellions as rooted in colonial policy.[62] In 1853, *El Siglo* was drawn into a vigorous debate with the polemical conservative daily, *El Orden*. On August 13, *El Siglo* (probably Francisco Zarco, the editor) asserted that the recent rebellions were abetted by those who live under the "cruel yoke of the community," frustrated by the lack of private ownership. The "communal vice," maintained *El Siglo*, is outmoded and must be suppressed. Dubbed "socialist" by its antagonist for advocating the division of vacant and communal property, *El Siglo* jubilantly cited Thiers and Jovellanos as the inspiration for its views. The pressure on land must be removed, concluded the editorialist; the Laws of the Indies must give way to the stimulus of individual interest.

Two remedies were offered by liberal spokesmen. One was to await the eventual results of republican equality of opportunity; the other was to formulate a policy for "civilizing" the Indian. "If Indians are talented and become educated," argued *El Siglo*, "they attain the highest posts of the state." Through legal equality, the Indian is daily becoming more closely identified with the interests of the white race.[63] For the most part, however, the liberals believed some positive actions must be taken. On November 23, 1848, *El Monitor* cited the fear of a "universal rising of the indigenous class" and asserted that the alternatives were simply "to exterminate it or civilize it, mixing it with the others." *El Monitor* rejected the first method as barbarous.

Evidence that extermination or forced removal was advocated by some in central Mexico came in an article taken from a Veracruz newspaper and reprinted by *El Universal*. The article praised Anglo-Saxon Indian policy for at least assuring self-survival, "which is the primary law." Moreover, the spokesman from Veracruz maintained that conflict between the races was inevitable and that humane measures would only postpone the day of reckoning.[64] *El Siglo* and *El Monitor*, however, spoke in moderate and general terms of the need for education, for colonization by for-

62. *El Monitor*, July 1, 15, 1849.
63. *El Siglo*, Sept. 15, 1850; also Apr. 20, 1850.
64. From *El Arco Iris de Vera Cruz*, reprinted in *El Universal*, Dec. 11, 1848.

eigners, and even for reviving the missions. As *El Monitor* remarked, the numerical superiority of the Indians must be eliminated; otherwise Caste wars will continue to threaten us.[65]

The mildness of the public response to Indian revolt, as indicated by the chief liberal newspapers, can be contrasted with the
alarm revealed privately by several Mexican leaders in correspondence with José María Luis Mora. Bernardo Couto wrote
that the Caste Wars were of greater concern than the United States
invasion. Mariano Otero lamented the destruction of the army by
the 1847 war, since it weakened governmental efforts to "curb
these Indian uprisings." [66] A year earlier, Luis de la Rosa, then
minister of foreign relations, wrote to Mora of the "new and terrible element of discord" which he claimed had been fomented by
North American policy. He added that if the uprisings in Yucatán
and the Sierra de Xichú became more severe, the next congress
might decide to remove the political rights of Indians. "I would
very much like to know your opinions," wrote Rosa, "on the best
means to civilize the Indian race and to amalgamate it with the
white or Creole race of Mexico." Mora responded that once peace
with the United States was concluded, "the most urgent necessity
is to repress the colored classes." Rosa had mentioned in his letter
that a number of American officers offered their services to
Mexico, presumably to combat the Indians. Mora advised that
their offer be accepted "without hesitation," provided these Americans serve in the interior and not on the frontiers.[67]

It appears that Indian rebellion struck deeper fears in Mora
than even the continued threat of the United States. Moreover,
these views came from a man who was working vigorously to iso-

65. *El Monitor,* May 21, 1849. See also *El Monitor,* July 1, 15, 1849; *El Siglo,* July
5, 1848, June 20, 1851.

66. Couto to Mora (May 14, 1849), García, *Documentos, 6,* 145; Otero to Mora
(May 13, 1849), ibid., p. 140.

67. Rosa to Mora (Apr. 11, 1848), Correspondencia particular del ministro de
relaciones interiores y exteriores (Sec. Rel. Ext.). I am indebted to the late Luis
Chávez Orozco for providing me with a typescript copy of this MS. and Mora's
response (May 31, 1848) to it. The exchange is summarized by Chávez Orozco with
excerpts in Arturo Arnáiz y Freg, ed., *La Intervención francesa y el imperio de
Maximiliano* (Mexico, Inst. Francés de la América Latina, 1965), p. 39. The Mexican government was located at this time at Querétaro, very close to the heart of the
Sierra Gorda revolt.

late the United States diplomatically and to promote Hispanic and Catholic immigration as an anti-American bulwark. When faced with Indian upheaval, Mora reacted as a Creole, just as he had reacted to Hidalgo's revolt of 1810. Mora's anxiety was equally manifest in his official correspondence as minister to England. On June 26, 1848, he appealed without formal instructions to the British government for aid in repressing the Indians of Yucatán who are "pursuing with monstrous barbarity the plan for exterminating the white class." [68] Palmerston was unmoved by Mora's appeal and only agreed blandly that "nothing is more important to you than whitening your population" through colonization. Above all, Palmerston advised, you must offer security to immigrants, for colonization "is absolutely incompatible with the public disorders which up to now have formed the habitual state of Mexican society." [69]

Mora took seriously the request that he act as informal adviser to his government, and he reiterated officially the urgent necessity for "the fusion of all races and colors" by means of colonization in the "already populated part of the republic." Above all, white colonists must be favored by the government over the Indians in every way possible short of an open violation of justice. "Ever since independence, we have been enumerating, repeating, and exaggerating *ad nauseam* the supposed grievances of the colored races against the white. Sooner or later it all had to result in what we now see." The Indians are only capable of turning this propaganda into "irreconcilable hatred" and fruitless "bloody revolutions." The net result, concluded Mora vehemently, would be to "undermine [even] the most solidly established social edifice." [70]

Mora rigidly opposed British efforts to mediate in Yucatán on the basis of a truce that would recognize the Indians "collectively." We can deal with the Indians only as individuals, perhaps by consenting to grants of vacant land to cultivators. He said to

68. Mora to Palmerston, Chávez Orozco, *Gestión*, pp. 78–79.

69. Mora to Relaciones (June 30, 1848), ibid., pp. 81–82. As reported by Mora, Palmerston's attitude toward Mexico was supremely arrogant and condescending. See also ibid., p. 75 (May 31, 1848).

70. Mora to Relaciones (July 31, 1849), ibid., pp. 151–52. Similar sentiments on the urgency of colonization were expressed by Mora in the private letter to Rosa cited above.

Palmerston that "it would be better to lose that part of our territory than to cede it to tribes which have scarcely entered civilization." Mora was also well aware that the mediation proposal was a cloak for British designs to establish an Indian protectorate in Mexican territory, and he spent the final weeks of his life combating the British effort.[71]

The liberal appeal for colonization reached a peak of intensity in the years 1848–50. Colonies of foreign immigrants were seen to provide security on the frontier against further North American invasions, against attacks by savage tribes, and generally against Indian rebellion. A decree establishing a colonization bureau was issued in 1846, but a general law failed to emerge, largely because of the congressional dispute over provisions for religious toleration.[72] Several decrees were issued, however, establishing military colonies for the purpose of satisfying both military and colonizing objectives. First instituted (July 19, 1848) on the new frontier with the United States, they were extended to the Sierra Gorda region in late 1849, after the defeat of the rebels. Also, 478 rebel prisoners from Sierra Gorda were dispersed to colonies in several northern states. These measures represented a governmental response to crisis, rather than the formulation of a major policy; and "Mora's dream of a barrier of purely Mexican settlements" was never realized.[73]

Liberal confusion in confronting the Caste Wars may be contrasted with conservative clarity. As in other aspects of the post-1847 debate, the conservative argument showed vigor and consistency. Numerous articles appeared in the conservative press,

71. His communication of Apr. 30, 1850, reiterated opposition to a truce (ibid., p. 198). Mora also protested to Palmerston that there was a traffic in arms from British Belize to the rebels in Yucatán.

72. See above, p. 35. The Nov. 27, 1846, decree can be found in Dublán and Lozano, 5, 217–18. Carlos Sartorius, a longtime resident and promoter of immigration, who was of German extraction, attested to the convergence of pressures for colonization in the postwar years. See *Importancia de México para la emigración alemana* (Mexico, 1852), p. 34.

73. The phrase was Guillermo Prieto's (*Indicaciones*, p. 373). The decrees for military colonies are in Dublán and Lozano, 5, 422–26, 551–52, 632–37, 639. See also González Navarro, "Instituciones indígenas," pp. 152–53; and Cotner, *Herrera*, pp. 311–15, who notes that military colonization was closely related to Herrera's efforts to reform the army after the 1847 war.

particularly in *El Universal,* using the Caste Wars as an opportunity to discredit the republic and to contrast its failures with colonial peace and stability. In view of the present upheavals, the argument ran, it is remarkable to note that under colonial rule the Indians "lived in peace, obeyed without complaining, worked their lands quietly, and were not overburdened with taxes." [74] During three centuries, said *El Universal* earlier, the Spaniards instituted an effective system of "moral force," as opposed to the alternative of "physical force." Their rule thus depended upon the "development of the religious principle" and a "profound respect for authority." Crown and missionaries cooperated in establishing these principles, with the amazing result that there was no significant standing army in Mexico until the mid-eighteenth century. Soldiers were not needed when there existed "a true and positive love for the government." [75]

This beneficent system was completely overturned in 1810. With the proclamation of the "dogma" of equality, "the wise Laws of the Indies were erased with one stroke." Moreover, continued the writer, it was pure folly for the revolutionary leaders to evoke the memory of Montezuma, to denounce Cortés, and to depict colonial rule as three centuries of white tyranny over the Indians. "Misguided by the ardor with which they embraced the cause of independence, those caudillos denied their own race and condemned it to extermination." [76] *El Universal* maintained that under republican policies the Indians had gained nothing. Whereas they were previously "free to dedicate themselves to agriculture, to commerce, to arts and letters, enjoying privileges and immunities," now they are in reality slaves, the victims of new forms of exploitation.[77]

With the "relaxation of the religious principle," said *El Universal,* all respect for government as a protective force emanating from God has vanished. The Indians now see authority as oppressive. In the name of the new authority, they are impressed into the

74. *El Universal,* Mar. 16, 1849.

75. Ibid., Dec. 9, 1848, one of five remarkable articles (Dec. 8, 9, 11, 14, 15, 1848) entitled "Guerra de castas," probably written by Lucas Alamán.

76. Ibid., Dec. 9, 1848.

77. Ibid., Mar. 23, 1850.

army, their lands are taken away, and they are forced to bear new and burdensome taxes. Disillusioned by the new system, the Indians begin to reason from its principles: "Sovereignty resides in the greatest number; we are the greatest number; therefore, sovereignty resides in us." How, then, can we be surprised by the Indian revolts, considering the course we have taken since independence? [78]

The remedies proposed by the conservatives were as clear as their analysis of the causes. In the first place, a policy of extermination must be rejected. We cannot, as some liberals are doing, evoke Anglo-Saxon policy as a model and thus condemn the Indian race to destruction. Mexico must turn to its own traditions for inspiration, to the policy that produced the Colegio de Santa Cruz in Tlatelolco, the Colegio de San Gregorio, and hospitals in all Indian communities. *El Universal* proposed first that a militia composed of property holders (not unlike an earlier proposal by Mora) be formed for local protection. Principally, however, the government must rely on "moral force" to pacify the Indians. On December 14, 1848, the newspaper urged a series of measures designed as a frank return to colonial Indian policy: abolition of required military service; reestablishment of a single tax (like the tribute); revival of old "privileges," including the Indians' status as minors. The dogma of equality ("that most precious discovery of progressivist philosophy") is inapplicable to a heterogeneous society like ours.

These conservative proposals were climaxed by an appeal to reinstate the mission system. Evidence from early Europe and from sixteenth-century Mexico shows that "the religious sentiment has been the most powerful civilizing agent in modern societies." The Indians' profound respect for religion may well be termed "fanaticism" by the liberals. Yet,

> that fanaticism did harm to no one. It tempered the fierce passions of the savage, softening his customs and making him useful to society. Costing the government nothing, it was an insuperable barrier against the furious torrent that is now overflowing to lay waste to the republic.[79]

78. Ibid., Dec. 9, 1848.
79. Ibid., Dec. 15, 1848.

The conservatives' response to the problem of Indian rebellion was, as we have seen in Chapter 1, the most effective weapon in their post-1847 campaign of psychological warfare. Alamán's history of the Revolution for Independence asked the liberals to make the choice between Hidalgo's Indians and Iturbide's Creoles. Interpreting the Caste Wars, *El Universal* could likewise exploit a deepseated Creole fear of social revolution—shared equally by conservatives and liberals—for conservative political ends. The liberals were the more vulnerable because social revolution revealed their Creole concept of nationality. The conservatives could thus lay bare the basic inconsistency between this concept and the professed liberal attachment to the "dogma of equality," while they themselves remained consistent.

The Caste War articles in *El Universal* were probably the frankest and most systematic defense of colonial paternalism to emerge during these years. Throughout the articles ran a thinly veiled urging of monarchy as the only form of government that could successfully keep the Indians in peace. The conservatives professed an interest in upgrading the Indian's position, maintaining that he could become better "civilized," better educated, and that he could rise more easily in a "protective" system. "The inequality which we ask for is, we repeat, for the benefit of the Indians themselves." The emphasis of the conservatives was always clearly on the side of order rather than social change. In another revealing discussion of Mexico's two races, *El Universal* admitted that "all activity, we might say almost all intelligence, resides in the Spanish race, with the result that the naturally docile Indian race becomes a kind of auxiliary mass which is invaluable if properly directed." [80]

The conservatives argued that the Caste Wars were not, as the liberals said, a delayed Indian response to three centuries of Spanish oppression. They were rather, like Hidalgo's rebellion in 1810, the direct result of liberal attacks upon the colonial system. It is out of place here to consider in detail the causes of the Caste Wars or to try to identify the historical process they entailed. We might note, however, that recent findings suggest (for obviously different reasons) the validity of the nineteenth-century conservative thesis.

80. Ibid., June 17, 1852. See also Alamán, *Historia, 1,* 27.

Howard F. Cline has argued that the Yucatecan upheaval came as an Indian reaction to Creole-directed economic progress. An isolated region suddenly enjoyed great development when opened to the outside world in 1821. Indian patterns were threatened by the demand for labor and lands, particularly from the expanding sugar industry.[81] Nelson Reed points out, moreover, that the rising was not primarily among the traditional peons of western Yucatán, but more in areas where white authority had only been recently imposed. "What was dangerous was not long oppression but sudden acculturation, the forced march from one world to another." [82] François Chevalier has interpreted the Zapata revolt of 1910 as a similar kind of process, again located within a sugar area where agriculture was rapidly becoming modernized at the expense of Indian lands and village traditions.[83] There are indications that the Hidalgo revolt resulted from social dislocation brought on by the expanding economy and population of the Bajío region.[84] One can only speculate about the causes of the Sierra Gorda rebellion, for it has not been studied in any detail. The rebel Plan of Rio Verde (May 14, 1849) called for land distribution and more village autonomy, but it also included the standard list of liberal and anticlerical demands.[85]

This fragmentary evidence suggests a Mexican tradition of peasant rebellion in reaction to changes influenced by liberal ideas and policies.[86] It is thus misleading to view Indian revolts of the nine-

81. Cline, "Related Studies in Early Nineteenth-Century Yucatecan Social History," Microfilm Collection of MSS. on Mid. Am. Cultural Anthropology (University of Chicago, 1950); "The Sugar Episode in Yucatán, 1825–1850," *Inter-American Economic Affairs, 1* (1948), 79–100; "The 'Aurora Yucateca' and the Spirit of Enterprise in Yucatán, 1821–1847," *HAHR, 27* (1947), 30–60.

82. Reed, *Caste War*, p. 48.

83. Chevalier, "Un Facteur décisif de la révolution agraire au Mexique: le soulèvement de Zapata," *Annales Economies, Sociétés, Civilisations, 16* (1961), 66–82.

84. The native population of the Bajío was less traditionally oriented and more responsive to economic change than was that of Yucatán and Morelos. See Hamill, *Hidalgo Revolt*, pp. 48–52; also the note by J. P. Berthe in *Annales Economies, 20* (1965), 1257.

85. See González Navarro, "Instituciones indígenas," p. 151. Many contemporaries saw the United States invasion as the main cause of the Sierra Gorda revolt. It was undoubtedly a factor (Reyes Heroles, *Liberalismo, 3*, 568–69).

86. *El Universal* (Dec. 26, 1848) pointed to Indians from Metztitlán in the Huasteca, who in a letter to *El Siglo* (Dec. 24) expressed nostalgia for the old

teenth century as "social liberalism," as merely one aspect of a broad-gauged liberal movement. If they are to be studied as *pre-agrarista* manifestations—precursors of twentieth-century agrarian revolution—care must be taken to define their exact relationship to contemporary liberal thought and policy.

In discussing liberalism and the Indian we have frequently used the term "Creole." Its use indicates the ethnic gulf that existed in Mexican society and the reluctance of the pre-Reforma liberals to frame a design for social reform that included the Indian masses. The most consistent liberal policy aimed at erasing all legal distinctions in society, theoretically upgrading the Indian to the universal category of "citizen." Yet this theory amounted to ignoring the Indian base of society, to saying in effect that the Indian no longer existed. The legalistic concept also encouraged a general hostility to communal traditions and property in the name of equality before the law; it connoted anticorporatism and the promotion of utilitarian values. According to liberal precepts, the Indian as a poor individual would progress naturally if barriers were removed. Yet these theories were meaningless in a rural society dominated by the hacienda. The deputies of the Mexico state congress realized this fact; and, when actually confronted with the problem of strengthening municipal finances, they retreated from doctrinaire attitudes and made some concessions to traditional communal landholding. The resulting policy was confused at best, and communal tenure remained fragile.

Mexican constitutional liberalism of the 1820s was strictly Creole in orientation. Benjamin Constant in France could romanticize local traditions or point with pride to a village savant (see above, page 60). He could find in peasant traditions strength for his "new kind of federalism." Mora could see in the Mexican villages only the remnants of a depressed, ignorant, and even alien race. The Creole concept of nationality prevailed among the reformers of the 1830s, and they repudiated dissenters such as Vicente Guerrero and Juan Rodríguez Puebla. Not only was the Indian ignored, but hope for the future was placed in a new class of

---

regime. Chevalier says that the conservatives during the Reforma found support among some Indian caciques reacting against liberal anticommunal policies. See "Conservateurs et libéraux," pp. 462–63.

bourgeois property holders, fortified by European immigrants. Even a "radical," such as Zavala, questioned by 1833 the feasibility of a democracy that included the Indians. The Caste Wars brought confusion, for they tended to further undermine liberal faith in legalistic and doctrinaire attitudes toward the Indian. This liberal confusion was effectively exploited by political conservatives who shared the Creole concept of nationality, but who could advocate a paternalistic Indian policy which was consistent with that concept.

The question of the Indian per se was not a point of ideological conflict between liberals and conservatives. This fact is made clear by Mora's reaction to the Caste Wars. Even more revealing is a long anonymous article on "colonization" that appeared in *El Siglo* on September 11, 1848, and which was preserved as a clipping among Mora's papers. It is a curious blend of liberal and conservative arguments. European colonization must be urgently promoted; individual interest must be given free reign; individual property must be enhanced. Yet the writer opposed religious tolerance, and generally praised Spanish colonial civilization. The burden of the piece, however, was a vigorous attack on Indian "conservatism"—meaning the unprogressive quality of Indian communal institutions, Indian exclusiveness (as exemplified by the present rebellions), and Indian resistance to civilizing efforts.[87] We are left with the conclusion that in the face of Indian resurgence, Creole social conservatism was stronger than the political issues of ideological conflict. Liberal doctrines of individualism and equality did have an ultimate democratic effect on Mexican social policy, but it was not apparent in the age of José María Luis Mora.

87. Mora could possibly have written the article. Except, perhaps, for the praise of the church, there is no evidence that rules him out.

8

Liberalism and Economic Development

In viewing a recent Mexican government film entitled *Ideal de la revolución*, I was struck by its official image of "revolutionary" Mexico. Following a few wax-figure representations of the heroic episodes of 1910–20 and faded portraits of Zapata, Villa, Carranza, and Obregón, the film moved quickly and abruptly to a brilliant technicolor panorama of a modern, urban, and industrialized nation. I saw superhighways, skyscrapers, modern hospitals and urban schools, steel mills and petroleum refineries. Rural and provincial Mexico was shown by the completion of a rail link in Chihuahua, by the giant Papaloapan dam, and by modern port facilities at Salina Cruz on the Pacific. There were infrequent glimpses of Hispanic architecture and there were inevitably the Aztec motifs at the university. But I saw no Indian peasant farmers, no ejidos, no rural schools. The emphasis was unmistakably on the modern and cosmopolitan metropolis. The film began and ended with a patriotic parade at the Monument to the Revolution.

This short film dramatizes the preoccupation with modernization and economic development that has engulfed Mexico in the last two decades. The concept "revolution" has been broadened from its earlier focus on political liberty and rural social justice to include as well industrial transformation and urbanization. Contemporary Mexico is undergoing a revolution, but it is no longer the revolution of 1910 or of 1935. Yet the persisting official designation of Mexico as a revolutionary nation has produced a tendency to seek in the nineteenth century an "integrated" liberal heritage for revolution. Economic development must now be a liberal idea, along with anticlericalism, individual guarantees, and agrarian reform. The relationship between economic development and liberalism in the nineteenth century is by itself a confusing matter. In Mexico it is made doubly perplexing by today's official assumptions.

A first reading of the postindependence literature on economic development reveals a seemingly simple conflict between those who advocated laissez-faire and those who urged direct or indirect government intervention in the economy. Free trade versus protection; commerce versus national industry. The issues appear classic and universal. The difficulty comes in trying to place the arguments for economic development within the broader context of political debate. When we attempt to identify the disputants and to draw some correlation between their political and their economic views, we find points of confusion at every turn. Moreover, in discussing liberalism and economic development, new figures emerge, Estevan de Antuñano and Lucas Alamán. We have used Alamán's ideas to point up by contrast those of the reformers. We now turn to him directly, as the central figure in post-independence economic development. How can this be justified in a study of liberalism? Do we need entirely new categories as we shift from politics and society to economic development in nineteenth-century thought? These are the questions that confront us.

Broadly speaking, two approaches to economic development can be distinguished in the post-1821 generation—the doctrinaire and the pragmatic. The ideas of José Maria Luis Mora best represent the first approach, those of Lucas Alamán and Estevan de Antuñano, the second. The two concepts are not rigorous, nor are the distinctions between them always sharp. Both owe much to classic liberal economic theory as they do in varying degrees to eighteenth-century Spanish policy. Moreover, both approaches are governed by the basic economic fact of nineteenth-century Mexican society, that it was overwhelmingly rural and agricultural. Despite these qualifications, it is significant to identify the two concepts. They will aid in completing our definition of liberalism and in clarifying the history of economic development in Mexico.

The doctrinaire approach by definition entailed a strict adherence to liberal economic theory. Its advocates regarded the "economists"—Adam Smith, Jean Baptiste Say, Gaspar Melchor de Jovellanos, and later, Álvaro Flórez Estrada—with great reverence. As authorities on economic questions these men went unchallenged. The great appeal of liberal economics lay in its simplicity. It identified a "natural system of liberty": an economy based on division of labor and the saving of capital, which sprang from the spontaneous desire of a myriad of individuals to better their situation. Liberal economics was closely related to utilitarian theory. The doctrinaire as contrasted to the pragmatic approach to development in Mexico cannot be separated from the social assumptions of liberalism discussed in Chapter 5. It was the very unity of social and economic ideas in one beneficent system that recommended them to the Mexicans. Political economy was now a science, which, as Say put it, "unfolds the manner in which wealth is produced, distributed, and consumed." As a science it was "essentially independent of political organization." [1]

The separation of wealth from political organization increased the allure of liberal theory in Hispanic nations. To peoples who had groaned under the burden of trade restrictions and had experienced an entanglement of public policy with economic pursuits to a degree exceeding that of the rest of Europe, the vision of a "spontaneous economic constitution" was captivating. Jean Baptiste Say emphasized this divorce of politics and economics even more than did Adam Smith. The latter could not break entirely from the traditional view of political economy as a practical guide for statesmen.[2] It was for this reason, as well as the fact that he was a simplifier and a systematizer of Smith's ideas, that Say was more translated and apparently more read in Hispanic countries than was his master. According to Say, the economist must be a detached observer, an analyst, a scientist. He must demonstrate "that political economy, in the same manner as the exact sciences, is composed of a few fundamental principles, and of a great number of corollaries or conclusions drawn from these principles." [3]

In the eyes of the economists, the great obstacle to realization of

1. J. B. Say, *A Treatise on Political Economy* (Philadelphia, 1830), p. xix. First published in 1803.

2. Gide and Rist, *History*, p. 126. Say makes this point in the introd. (pp. 8–9) to the first Mexican edition (1814) of his treatise, a reprint of the Spanish 1804 edition.

3. Say, *Treatise*, p. xxviii.

a natural or spontaneous system was the presence of monopoly. Like Bentham in the political realm, Adam Smith exposed at every turn in his *Wealth of Nations* the injurious effects of special interests, of protectionist restrictions, and of the spirit of corporation. Book Four of his treatise, the one that most interested his contemporaries, was devoted primarily to identifying and attacking the privileges of mercantilism. "Monopoly of one kind or another," he wrote, "seems to be the sole engine of the mercantile system." [4] The book proceeded to expose the numerous devices (Hispanic countries loomed large in his discussion) used to advance a favorable balance of trade and thus to insure the inflow of gold and silver—tariffs on importation of foreign goods, bounties for the export of home products, drawbacks, restrictions on the export of currency.

In the "commercial or mercantile system of political economy" these restrictions and monopolies are imposed in the interest of merchants and manufacturers. If their interests are advanced by special privilege, it can be done only at the expense of the consumers at large; for "consumption is the sole end and purpose of all production." [5] This, according to Smith, was a self-evident maxim. In the natural system of political economy, production must be determined by market demand, not by artificial stimulants. Freedom of trade will only increase the demand for products and the subsequent division of labor. Since labor is the sole origin of wealth ("the exchangeable value of things"), the policies that extend special privileges can never be productive of wealth in society.[6] Gaspar Melchor de Jovellanos shared Smith's particular antipathy to the privileged merchants and manufacturers, and concluded that Spain's natural economy rested on agriculture.[7]

The traditional economy of the Iberian peninsula was already experiencing rejuvenation when the doctrines of Smith and Say made their appearance. The broadly disseminated utilitarian

4. Smith, *Wealth of Nations*, p. 595.

5. Ibid., p. 625.

6. Say, *Treatise*, p. xxxviii. Say said "industry" should be substituted for Smith's term "labor."

7. See above, p. 177, cf. Smith, *Wealth of Nations*, p. 461. Smith had a broader view of the economy than did Jovellanos, who here revealed his physiocratic leanings.

spirit encouraged the enlightened elite to criticize nonpolitical institutions. It is significant to note, however, that in the economic
realm there was no sharp distinction between renovation guided
by mercantilist assumptions and renovation guided by liberal
theory. Compomanes and Jovellanos can be associated as leaders of
the economic societies, as opponents of guild restrictions, as advocates of secular education. Yet Campomanes concerned himself
particularly with revitalizing manufacturing and thus always assumed a large role for the state in the economy. He argued that
the export of raw materials needed for home industry be prohibited, as well as the import of foreign manufactured goods. The
economic societies themselves did not depart entirely from mercantilist assumptions. Economic reform in late eighteenth-century
Spain emphasized *fomento*—special stimulus to national industries through extention of privileges—as well as the freeing of
trade and the attack upon traditional restrictions.[8]

The most outspoken of the early economic liberals in Spain was
Gaspar Melchor de Jovellanos. His "Informe de ley agraria" of
1795, however, caused considerable reaction and led to his period
of royal disfavor. The first Spanish edition (1794) of Adam
Smith's *Wealth of Nations* was put through a mercantilist sieve by
translator José Alonso Ortiz, and it emerged mutilated, abridged,
and full of qualifying footnotes. J. B. Say's *Traitè d'economie
politique* (1803), on the other hand, was translated in full within
a year of its appearance and promptly went through several editions. The Cortes of Cádiz, doctrinaire in so many of its liberal
decrees, had as its president in 1810 Ramón Lázaro de Dou, a reluctant Smithian. Dou called Smith the Newton of political economy at the same time that he espoused high tariffs for industry in
his native Catalonia.[9] It was Álvaro Flórez Estrada who became
the first systematic liberal theorist in Spain. Though his formal
treatise, *Curso de economía política,* did not appear until 1828,

8. See James C. La Force, Jr., *The Development of the Spanish Textile Industry,
1750–1800* (Berkeley, University of California Press, 1965) p. 156; Shafer, *Economic
Societies,* Chap. 1; Krebs Wilckens, *Campomanes,* pp. 182–83 and passim.

9. See Robert S. Smith, "The *Wealth of Nations* in Spain and Hispanic America,
1780–1830," *Journal of Political Economy,* 65 (1957), 104–25; Edith Helman,
"Some Consequences of the Publication of the *Informe de ley agraria* by Jovellanos," *Estudios hispánicos: Homenaje a Archer M. Huntington* (Wellesley, Wellesley College, 1952), pp. 253–73.

the elements of his economic liberalism were embedded in two
political pamphlets of 1811 and 1818. In short, liberalism had
made permanent inroads in Spain by 1821, though not without
considerable resistance.[10]

There were reasons why doctrinaire liberalism was even more
attractive to Mexicans than to Spaniards. The restrictions of the
mercantilist system bore most heavily on the colonies. The privileges of merchants and manufacturers which the system fostered
were enjoyed by Spaniards and not by native Mexicans. Commercial freedom came increasingly to be identified with the triumph
of enlightenment and political liberty. In his discussion of the
policies of Charles III, José María Luis Mora put most emphasis
on those reforms that removed restrictions on commerce. They
appear to have symbolized for him the general rejuvenation of the
peninsula. He noted the great increase of commerce following the
decrees that freed intercolonial trade (1774) and trade with Spain
(1778). After that, there could be no turning back.[11] The reforms only further awakened the Mexicans to the possibilities of
free trade with the non-Hispanic world. The logical result, both of
Spanish commercial reforms and of the impact of liberal doctrine,
was the decree of December 15, 1821, opening the ports of independent Mexico to the ships of all nations and to foreign goods at
a uniform tariff of 25 percent ad valorem.

The mood of the day was one of national optimism. The enthusiasm for free trade was part of the constitutional euphoria noted
in Chapter 3. "Commerce is the inseparable companion of liberty
and national wealth," wrote Vicente Rocafuerte in 1821. Another
pamphleteer asserted that through commerce Mexico would be
lifted from its former servitude and become in time "the foremost
world power because of its great size, its fertility, and its geo-
graphic situation." [12] This was an expression of what Cosío Villegas has termed "Mexico's legendary wealth," a myth dissemi-

10. The economic liberalism of Benjamin Constant was endorsed enthusiastically
in 1820 by Marcial Antonio López, his Spanish translator, who saw freedom of
industry as rounding out the list of constitutional guarantees for individual liberty.
See "Observaciones" in Constant, *Curso, 2,* 137–47.

11. Mora, *Revoluciones, 1,* 232; also *1,* 85, 217–20.

12. Rocafuerte, *Ideas necesarias a todo pueblo americano independiente que
quiera ser libre* (Philadelphia, 1821), p. 16; F. X. H., *Observaciones importantes
sobre el comercio libre* (Mexico, 1821), p. 1.

nated by foreigners from the conquistadors to Alexander von Humboldt. Alamán noted the role of Humboldt in giving Mexicans of the independence era an "extremely exaggerated notion of their country's wealth." To a nation thus convinced, Adam Smith's concept of an international division of labor had special appeal. "By distributing men in different climates and countries, nature wisely bestowed on them diverse products and varied industries." [13]

It soon became evident, however, that there were many who rejected the opportunity for independent Mexico to find its natural place in the international division of labor. In 1822, a pamphleteer from Guadalajara, expressing the sentiments of scores of provincial petitions, asserted that the 1821 law would put 2,000 people out of work in that center of artisan manufacture. A struggle over tariff policy was begun.[14]

The late colonial period saw resurgence and then decline of the traditional artisan industries, the most important of which were those devoted to crude woolens and coarse cotton cloth (manta). Royal policy restricted colonial textile manufacture in order to provide a market for goods produced in Spain. Despite restrictions, the artisan industries had continued because Spanish manufactures were high in price and because freight charges were based on volume, encouraging merchants to export high-cost, low-volume items. The renascence of peninsular industry in the late eighteenth century threatened these artisan industries, but Spain's war with England from 1796 to 1800 curtailed trade and gave de facto stimulus to the colonials. It was estimated that in 1803 one-half the population of Puebla was employed in cleaning and spinning cotton for 1,200 weavers of the city. The expansion of the artisan industries was underwritten by local Spanish capital. Puebla was the leading cotton center, as Querétaro was for woolens, but artisan industries were established throughout the provinces. They were soon disrupted, however, first by the decree of 1804, opening Veracruz to goods from the United States, then

13. Daniel Cosío Villegas, "Mexico's Legendary Wealth," in *American Extremes*, pp. 154–76; Alamán, *Historia*, *1*, 142; *El Sol*, Jan. 6, 1824.

14. See Robert A. Potash, *El Banco de Avío de México: el fomento de la industria, 1821–1846* (Mexico, Fondo de Cultura Económica, 1959), pp. 33 ff.

by the disastrous decade of warfare from 1810 to 1821, which put Spanish capital to flight. Independence threatened the obsolescent artisan industries with extinction by initiating a flood of cheap factory-produced English textiles.[15]

The artisans found their champions among the new group of provincial leaders who emerged with the overthrow of Agustín de Iturbide in early 1823. The provincial delegates to the two constituent congresses had a keen sense of regional autonomy, resulting both in the adoption of federalism in 1824 and in a sharp revision of the low tariff of 1821. The law of May 20, 1824, placed a large number of items on the prohibited list, including crude cotton and most varieties of common cotton cloth.[16] In the debates that preceded passage of this decree, prohibitions were defended by deputies who were relatively untouched by theoretical considerations, and by others for whom the interests of their constituents clashed with liberal doctrine.

Francisco García from Zacatecas was the most eloquent of this latter group. His *Exposición* of July 6, 1823, attempted to demonstrate that the "theory of the science" as expounded by J. B. Say could not be rigidly applied to Mexican local realities. What most concerned García was the displacement of capital and labor that would result from permanent free trade. "Is it so certain that industrious men, who become unemployed by the importation of foreign manufactures, will always find a new area in which to apply themselves?" García attacked the argument that a prohibition is a burden imposed on the consumer in favor of the producer. All consumers are also producers, he said, and it is fruitless to obtain cheaper goods "if at the same time we deprive ourselves of the means of acquiring them." Besides urging prohibitions to protect the artisans, García urged "the introduction of machines which simplify work"; moreover, he wanted the country opened to "industrious foreigners." Though these suggestions hinted at a

15. See La Force, pp. 17, 133, and passim; Jan Bazant, "Evolution of the Textile Industry of Puebla, 1544–1845," *Comparative Studies in Society and History*, 7 (1965), 66–67; Potash, *Banco*, Chap. 1.

16. See Dublán and Lozano, *Legislación*, *1*, 706–08. This coalescence of political federalism and defense of local industries might be compared to the process described by Miron Burgin in *Economic Aspects of Argentine Federalism* (Cambridge, Harvard University Press, 1946).

broad plan for development, it remained very much in embryo in his twelve-page pamphlet. Absent were any positive measures to form the capital necessary for modernizing and expanding industry.[17]

The most vigorous exponent of the doctrinaire view in the mid-twenties was Manuel Ortiz de la Torre, a native of Sonora and a professor at the Colegio de San Ildefonso. His two *Discursos* of 1823 and 1825 showed close familiarity with Smith and Say, and demonstrated the unity of utilitarian social theory and liberal economics. As a professor, he recommended the science of political economy "as one of the most noble, useful, and worthy to engage the study of every good citizen." [18] The wealth of the nation can only be stimulated by individual productive activities, freely pursued. Government should limit itself to guaranteeing "liberty and knowledge relative to production, and the greatest possible security in the possession of what is produced." Ortiz argued vigorously against prohibitions in 1823. Also urging free trade was the newspaper *El Sol*, whose pages between 1823 and 1827 were filled with articles on the subject. On July 29, 1825, an editorialist admitted that it was a noble desire to have industry, but added that "we lack laborers, we lack knowledge, and we see no evidence of sufficient capital being dedicated to the development of factories." [19]

17. See García, *Exposición sobre el dictamen en que la comisión ordinaria de hacienda consulta la prohibición de ciertas manufacturas y efectos extrangeros* (Mexico, 1823). The tariff debates are treated in detail in Reyes Heroles, *Liberalismo, 1,* 165–212. He views García as a precursor of the post-World War II rejection by underdeveloped nations of the international division of labor in favor of "their own theory of development" (*Liberalismo, 1,* 196). Reyes Heroles also calls García a "liberal protectionist," representing a basic combination in Mexican liberal thought—economic "heterodoxy" and orthodox adherence to political liberty (ibid., pp. 210–12). He singles out García, Prisciliano Sánchez from Guadalajara, and later the editors of *El Siglo* (see below, n. 85), apparently because they were political liberals (as opposed to conservatives) arguing for protection.

18. Ortiz de la Torre, *Discurso sobre los medios de fomentar la población, riqueza e ilustración de los estados-unidos mexicanos* (Mexico, 1825), as quoted in Robert S. Smith, "Manuel Ortiz de la Torre, economista olvidado," *Revista de historia de América, 48* (1959), 515. The arguments of Ortiz's *Discurso de un diputado sobre la introducción de efectos extrangeros* (Mexico, 1823) were similar. See also Reyes Heroles, *Liberalismo, 1,* 172–77.

19. It is worth noting that concern for good relations with England, at a time when the recognition of Mexican independence was pending, was an argument for

Between 1824 and 1827 the tide turned once again toward free trade. President Guadalupe Victoria was a confirmed economic liberal, who also recognized that the principal financial support for his government came from tariff revenue. The result was the law of November 16, 1827, which imposed ad valorem duties of 40 percent on all articles except some fifty-six which were prohibited. Common cotton cloth narrowly escaped prohibition.[20] The principle pursued was to keep duties high enough to produce sufficient revenue, but low enough to discourage contraband. The cause of the artisan industries reached its high point in 1829 when Vicente Guerrero assumed the presidency. Local industry was now championed by a popular leader of strong regional ties and humble background. We have noted the nativist strain in the Guerrero movement. The new congressional decree, prohibiting foreign goods that competed with artisan industries, was related to a measure excluding foreigners from retail merchandising, and to the second decree expelling Spaniards from the country. Guerrero, on assuming office in April, asserted that "the spurious *(bastarda)* application of liberal economic principles and the thoughtless freedom given to foreign commerce has aggravated our poverty." [21]

Guerrero's minister of finance, Lorenzo de Zavala, wrote later that he had heartily opposed the prohibition measure. He regarded it as "a narrow policy . . . conforming to the popular prejudice that it could be a way to diminish the export of specie." Zavala expressed the belief, common to doctrinaire liberals, that economic policy should be framed for the majority element, the consumer. Zavala was quick to detect colonial mercantilist assumptions. "Nothing is more difficult to dispel than a deeprooted prejudice." It is not at all surprising, then, that Zavala underwrote the publication of the second edition (1831) of Álvaro Flórez Estrada's *Curso de economía política*. The Spanish economist paid special tribute to his "worthy friend and former companion" at

---

free trade used by both Ortiz (Smith, "Manuel Ortiz," p. 510) and by *El Sol* (Jan. 6, 1824) .

20. Dublán and Lozano, *Legislación*, 2, 26–46; Potash, *Banco*, p. 47.

21. Potash, *Banco*, p. 54. The law of May 22, 1829, was a simple listing of some fifty prohibited items of artisan or handicraft manufacture (Dublán and Lozano, 2, 109–10) . On the move against foreign retail commerce see Reyes Heroles, *Liberalismo, 2,* 172–74.

the Cortes of 1820, who was "convinced of the utility which could result for both countries by generalizing the knowledge of political economy." [22] Besides attacking Guerrero's measure, Zavala also condemned the temporary removal of prohibitions for cotton goods the following year by the Bustamante regime. It was for him a disingenuous measure. The 1830 government had new economic goals in mind, as we will see, but they won little favor with Zavala.

The doctrinaire liberal approach to economic development crystallized between 1830 and 1834 as part of the anticorporate and secularizing movement for reform. Economic liberalism during the 1820s was directed primarily toward the specific issue of the tariff; after 1830 it permeated a more broadly conceived liberal ideology. The reform of 1833–34, however, was an abortive movement; its immediate effect on actual economic policy was small. Until 1847, doctrinaire liberalism was forced to give way to the opposing pragmatic conception of Lucas Alamán and Estevan de Antuñano.

Though economic theory was not José María Luis Mora's primary concern, he was always an enthusiastic follower of the "economists." The establishment of a chair of constitutional politics and political economy was his main proposal for reform of San Ildefonso in 1823. Apparently, the colegio was a center for the dissemination of the new economics, since both Mora and Manuel Ortiz de la Torre taught the subject there in the mid-twenties. Mora took little part in the tariff debate, for he was deeply engaged in the constitutional labors of the State of Mexico and in his law studies.[23] In fact, it was not until the reappearance of *El Observador* in 1830 that he came to apply the doctrines of economic liberalism to national problems. Enlightening the public in

22. See preface to Flórez Estrada, *Curso de economía política* (2 vols. Paris, 1831). Zavala's *Ensayo* (Vol. 1) was published the same year by the same publisher (Gaultier-Laguionie). Zavala went to Paris after he was ousted from the governorship of the State of Mexico by the Bustamante revolt. For Zavala's reaction to the Guerrero measure, see *Ensayo*, 2, 154–60, 304–05. A similar concern for the consumer was expressed in a speech by Manuel Crecencio Rejón on May 10, 1827 (*Discursos*, p. 249).

23. It is curious that the free trade–protectionist controversy caused little stir in the Mexico state congress from 1824 to 1827. Admittedly, it was a national, not a state issue, but one would suppose the matter to have figured prominently in the Zacatecas, Puebla, or Jalisco debates of the same period.

political economy formed part of the journal's mission to spread knowledge of the useful sciences.

The free operation of a natural economic system rested on eliminating the spirit of corporation and monopoly. Mora frequently referred to the "miserable (*mezquinas*) ideas of public economy which reigned in the peninsula" and which still formed a part of the Mexican mentality. The deputies of Puebla sacrificed the interests of the entire country to those of a single city, he noted, by obstructing the plan for a straighter road from Veracruz to Mexico City. Local road tolls are turned into public revenue, and the proceeds are not even put into road maintenance. Apparently he did not oppose tolls completely, however, for in the Mexico state congress he maintained that toll rights should be auctioned off to individuals for a small profit. "The government ought never to set itself up as an entrepreneur." [24]

Mora viewed prohibitions as so many "Spanish prejudices," as the effort to seek government aid in "monopolizing all branches of production among the natives, to the ruin of commerce and foreign enterprises." Another good example for Mora of this inherited Spanish penchant toward monopoly was Lucas Alamán's government investment bank, the "celebrated *banco de avío*" (1830) designed to "establish a forced industry." Such a plan committed the greatest of economic errors, that of trying to convince the people they were self-sufficient. Moreover, argued Mora, "Without freedom of industry, the creation of capital is very sluggish, the active faculties of man lack stimulus; and instead of being promoted, a nation's [prosperity] is considerably retarded." [25] Mora was consistently hostile to the idea of fomento. For him it was a Spanish mercantilist concept, involving government manipulation of the economy, and was thus injurious to true progress.

The chief example of monopoly for Mora was the church. Liberating the vast capital in mortmain and putting it into circulation was a principal objective of the anticlerical campaign of 1833. Yet two features of the attack on church property must be noted. The first was that fiscal objectives took precedence over economic

24. *Actas, 10*, 177 (June 1, 1830). On Mora's suggestion the congress abolished a proposed office of state director of roads; see also *Revoluciones, 1*, 55–56, and *El Indicador, 3*, 3–4 (Feb. 5, 1834).

25. *El Indicador, 1*, 48 (Oct. 16, 1833); Mora, *Obras*, p. 627. See also *El Fénix*, Feb. 17, 1834.

development per se. Second, the reform revealed a fundamental orientation toward land.

The proposals and projected legislation of the Gómez Farías regime (see above, Chapter 4) envisioned using church capital as a base for public credit. At the same time, disentailed church lands would pass as private property to the present tenants, upon purchase from the new owner—the government. Manuel Abad y Queipo had argued in 1805 that church property was mostly in specie and not in land, thus serving as working capital throughout the economy. Mora acknowledged the justice of Abad's argument for its day, but believed that by 1830 fiscal matters commanded top priority (see above, page 137). The politically weak and financially bankrupt state must be strengthened as an administrative unit. At the same time, since the new science of political economy dictated the separation of "wealth" and political process, the state should refrain from fomento. Disentailed church property should not be used directly for development purposes. It was not state power that Mora opposed but state manipulation of the economy.

The economic assumption underlying the reform of 1833–34 was that Mexico was by nature an agricultural and mining nation. Disentailed church property should fortify the class of (hopefully small) rural proprietors. Like Jovellanos in Spain, Mora believed that capital would accumulate naturally once the obstacles blocking the enterprise of the individual cultivator were removed. It is significant that the context of one of Mora's attacks on the Banco de Avío was a discussion of ways to increase small landed properties. "We Mexicans are not nor can we be for a long time manufacturers," announced El Observador in 1830. To turn such a vast nation, "with a soil ready to be cultivated for the abundant production of excellent commodities sought and needed by the entire world," toward manufacturing "is to try to disregard nature."[26]

Several articles appeared at this time on the mining industry, their theme being that until agriculture grew in importance, mining was the country's sole export. In a world of free international exchange, the untaxed export of specie was a necessity for

26. "Indicaciones," El Observador, 2d ser., 1, 43 (Mar. 10, 1830). For the attack upon the Banco de Avío, see Mora, Revoluciones, 1, 512. See also El Sol, May 28, 1830.

Mexico. *El Observador* quoted long passages from Flórez Estrada, Say, and Humboldt on the advantages both of instituting "absolute and general freedom of commerce" and of recognizing the primacy of mining in Mexico. Mining, agriculture, and commerce; the free pursuit of these activities would realize the cosmopolitan liberal ideal, as expressed by Flórez Estrada in 1818: "The interests of all nations are so united that the happiness of one never results in harm to any other." [27]

Mora's economic ideas, like those of Adam Smith, Jovellanos, Flórez Estrada, and the early J. B. Say, were preindustrial in orientation. The *Wealth of Nations* was "far from constituting a prophetic manifesto of the new [industrial] age." [28] Moreover, one of the distinctive features of Smith's school, as opposed to the ideas of Malthus and Ricardo, was its optimism. There remained a vision of the essential harmony of economic classes in a natural economy, divorced from politics and still rooted in the land. Mora shared these assumptions. With Mora, however, the strengthening of state power to combat the corporate wealth of the church loomed larger than specific measures to realize broad development through laissez-faire. Mora's obsession with clerical power strengthened an orientation toward land as wealth in a rural society. In Mora's conception the rural property holder, whether small or large, emerged as the central economic element.[29]

Next, let us consider the pragmatic approach to economic devel-

27. Álvaro Flórez Estrada, "Representación hecha a S. M. C. el señor Don Fernando VII en defensa de las cortes" (1818), written while in exile in England (*BAE, 113*, Madrid, Atlas, 1958, 210 n.). This was the work cited above in "Indicaciones," *El Observador*, 2d ser., *1*, 36. See also "Observaciones sobre la esportación de oro y plata," *El Observador*, 2d ser., *1*, 49–64 (Mar. 10, 1830); "Economía política. Minería," ibid., pp. 332–39 (May 5, 1830); "Disertación sobre el modo de promover en Méjico la industria mineral," *El Indicador, 3*, 3–23 (Feb. 5, 1834); *El Telégrafo*, Sept. 10, 1833. Valentín Gómez Farías expressed similar doctrinaire liberal views in 1841 (Hutchinson, "Valentín Gómez Farías," p. 504).

28. Gide and Rist, p. 83. J. B. Say, after writing his treatise in 1803, acquired a spinning mill and became an active industrialist. Later editions of his work show an increasing recognition of the role of the entrepreneur and of manufacturing in the economy. His basic assumptions remained unchanged, however. See Gide and Rist, pp. 118–33.

29. It might be argued that Mora, for this reason, inclined more toward the physiocrats than toward Smith and Say. There is no evidence of direct physiocratic influence on Mora, only indirect through Jovellanos: see above, p. 152. Mora's constitutionalism also revealed his attachment to land, as did that of Benjamin Constant. See above, p. 61.

opment after 1821. In identifying this conception, it is important to realize that the leading exponents were themselves entrepreneurs. Their own interests were closely tied to the theories and policies they came to advocate. These pragmatists were always more responsive to tradition and past experience than to liberal doctrine, though they by no means excluded the latter. The pragmatic approach can be seen first in the efforts to revitalize the mining industry during the 1820s. The leading figure in these efforts was Lucas Alamán.

The postindependence endeavor to rejuvenate the mines was an extention of Bourbon policies of the late colonial period. In the eyes of the Crown, mining was New Spain's most vital enterprise, the chief source of royal revenue, of commerce, and thus of colonial purchasing power for Spanish manufactures. A principal motive of the famous royal visit (visita) by José de Gálvez in the 1760s was to lay the groundwork for reviving the flagging industry. Quicksilver for amalgamation was in short supply. Capital for expansion was lacking. Labor disorders were rife. Many techniques were antiquated. After much investigation and several reports, came the creation in 1773 of a formal corporate guild of miners (Cuerpo de Minería), presided over by a tribunal and a crown-appointed director. Fausto de Elhuyar, a Spanish mineralogist, was called back from study in Germany in 1786 to take the post of director. Two years later he arrived in New Spain with a party of German mining experts. Elhuyar remained the chief figure in Mexican mining until independence.[30]

Charles III's mining policy followed the characteristic pattern of economic reform in the peninsula. Under the impetus of the new passion for useful knowledge, technology and expert advice were sought from abroad. Mining reform in New Spain was conducted in the spirit of the economic societies of the peninsula, concerned about all manner of practical improvements and particularly about technical education. The most significant innovation in New Spain was the establishment of the Colegio de Mi-

30. On the Mining Guild and Bourbon policies, see Walter Howe, *The Mining Guild of New Spain and its Tribunal General, 1770–1821* (Cambridge, Harvard University Press, 1949), and Clement G. Motten, *Mexican Silver and the Enlightenment* (Philadelphia, University of Pennsylvania Press, 1950).

nería, finally opened by its director Elhuyar in 1792. It was merely one of a number of specialized institutions founded in the Spanish Empire after 1750.[31]

There was a continual cry from the Mexican mineowners and increasingly from Elhuyar himself to remove burdensome taxes on the minting and export of silver. The principal royal concession in this regard (before 1810) was to relinquish one-half of the double seigniorage tax for the purpose of establishing a *banco de avíos*, or capital fund, to finance new ventures.[32] Direct investment in colonial mining was central to royal reform policy, as it also was, for instance, in the development of the peninsular textile industry. The chief instrument for economic revival was to be a new corporate body, modeled explicitly on the existing merchant guilds (*consulados*), "in order that in this way its individuals [miners] may achieve the permanence, encouragement, and aid which they lack." [33] In mining policy, as in peninsular economic reform, Enlightenment liberalism was combined with mercantilism, and utilitarian philosophy with the creation of new corporate bodies.[34]

In his first report as minister of relations in 1823, Lucas Alamán began the section on mining as follows:

It is an established principle among the economists that the most direct stimulus that can be given to agriculture and industry is to facilitate the consumption of its products and the sale of its artifacts. If we were to consider our mines from this point of view, we would find that nothing contributes as much as they to the prosperity of those [other] essential branches of public wealth.

Thus Alamán, under the influence of the new liberal economics, sought to continue the revival of mining begun by Charles III.

31. Cf. La Force, pp. 159–61. It must be noted, though, that the economic societies, both in Spain and America, disparaged the role of mining itself in the economy. See Shafer, *Economic Societies*, pp. 109, 128, and passim.

32. See royal decree of 1776 in Howe, pp. 50–51. On seigniorage, see ibid., p. 27.

33. Royal decree of 1773 in ibid., p. 38. José de Gálvez used the model of the consulado in his earlier report, ibid., p. 28.

34. La Force (p. 157) speaks of royal policy as "liberalized mercantilism." See also Herr, *Eighteenth-Century Revolution*, p. 56.

Alamán's promotion of the Mexican mining industry had roots in his personal background and interests. After serving in the Spanish cortes, he left for Paris and London in search of funds to rehabilitate the Cata mine of Guanajuato. Its "great bonanza" in the early eighteenth century had "made my grandparents rich." [35] When his family fled Guanajuato in 1810, the young Alamán naturally enough began his studies at the Colegio de Minería. In 1814 he departed for a six-year grand tour of Europe, highlighted by the study of mineralogy and mining technology at Paris and Freiburg. He became close to Francisco Fagoaga, descendant of another rich mining family which had been prominent in the Mining Tribunal. In the company of the Fagoagas, Alamán left Paris for Mexico in November 1822, eager to recoup his family fortune as well as to reinstate Mexico's leading industry after the disastrous years of revolution.[36]

Between 1822 and 1824, the revival of mining became a topic of prime economic concern in Mexico, second only to the question of the tariff. There were in Alamán's view two obstacles to be overcome. One was the taxes which burdened production and the export of ore. The other was the colonial laws restricting foreigners from acquiring interests in mining. Alamán could report by 1823 that the first barrier had been cleared. An 1821 decree of the Spanish cortes, instituting a single tax of 3 percent on gold and silver (in place of the former *quinto,* seigniorage, and other taxes) was confirmed by the Mexican provisional junta in November of the same year.[37]

The second obstacle was attacked by Alamán in a vigorous speech on September 5, 1823, supporting a proposal of the congressional mining commission. Alamán argued the need for allowing the free entry of foreign capital. Citing Adam Smith, he said that the Mexican mines should take advantage of the "natural

35. Alamán, "Memoria" (1823), *Documentos, 1,* 92; *Historia, 5,* Appendix (Doc. No. 25, p. 81).

36. On Alamán's early life, see Valadés, *Alamán,* Chaps. 1–4.

37. See Alamán, "Memoria" (1823), *Documentos, 1,* 93; decree of Nov. 11, 1821, in Dublán and Lozano, *1,* 563–64. On the cortes decree, which embraced proposals previously advocated by Elhuyar, see Howe, p. 432. Alamán took a leading role in the cortes discussions on alleviation of mining taxation. See Benson, *Mexico and the Spanish Cortes,* pp. 172–73, 183–84.

tendency" of foreigners to seek profitable areas of investment abroad. "They will direct their investment here without needing further encouragement." Mexican capital is lacking, he insisted. Either it has left the country or it is not invested out of fear of political instability. He refuted the contention that Mexico might become dominated by foreigners. Alamán argued optimistically that once attracted to its shores, foreigners would see its good government and its "delightful" climate and would "seek spontaneously the naturalization papers which in a certain sense we are now wanting to force them to take out."[38]

The result of Alamán's persuasion was the law of October 7, 1823, suspending colonial legislation that restricted mining contracts with foreigners. From an eclectic blend of personal economic interests, respect for past experience, and liberal economic theory, Alamán had urged successfully that the door be opened to private foreign capital. Still, he did not exclude government investment out of hand. As he explained in his 1823 "Memoria," the Mining Tribunal could have served as a banco de avío for mining; but under present circumstances that was not feasible—the tribunal had no funds and was even burdened with debt. Alamán did suggest that the government-supported metal exchanges (cajas de rescate) of the revolutionary years be restored as a further source of investment capital.[39] We have at least one piece of evidence, the testimony of Jared Sparks, editor of the North American Review, that Alamán was seen at the time as the enlightened and liberal statesman of Mexico's economic revival.[40]

38. Alamán, speech of Sept. 5, 1823, quoted in Valadés, Alamán, p. 167. For the full text see Águila, Sept. 6–7, 1823. See also Mateos, Historia, 2, 500–01.

39. Alamán, "Memoria" (1823), Documentos, 1, 94. The cajas were set up in the provinces after 1812 to allow miners to convert bullion to currency at a time when transport was restricted. They could thus have ready cash for their enterprises. See Howe, pp. 402–03. For the law of 1823, see Dublán and Lozano, 1, 681; also Potash, Banco, p. 35. The Mining Tribunal was abolished by decree on July 26, 1826. A junta of miners was created to make an accounting of the tribunal's assets in agreement with the government. The assets were to go primarily to supporting the Colegio de Minería, which was to continue unchanged. See Dublán and Lozano, 1, 795–96. Alamán complained in 1830 of irresponsible management by the junta ("Memoria," 1830, Documentos, 1, 207–08).

40. Sparks was a doctrinaire economic liberal who after describing the fallacies of Spanish colonial mercantilist restrictions, announced enthusiastically that "the prospects of Mexico never shone more brightly than at the present moment." His

Alamán's promotional efforts, first in Europe in 1822 and later in Mexico, led to the creation of the United Mexican Mining Association, underwritten by British capital in 1824. Alamán was its chief agent. The venture initiated a frenzied period of speculation, which saw the formation of numerous mining companies, the importation of much machinery, and even an ill-fated migration of Cornish miners.[41] The great mining revival, which Alamán foresaw as the basis of general economic development, achieved only limited success. The foreign venture was poorly planned and managed. Alamán himself came into conflict with British agents and in 1828 resigned from the company. He reported officially in 1830 that the mines "are already on a footing to subsist by themselves, production sufficing to cover costs." Though he still referred to mining as "our peculiar industry," his tone had changed, reflecting new economic concerns.[42]

Alamán's ideas of the 1820s, infused with economic liberalism, resembled those of the doctrinaires. Like them he spoke of the rehabilitation of mining and of its primacy in the country's economy. He welcomed foreign capital and argued against colonial restrictions, much as did Mora and Zavala. Mora's discussion of mining in 1830 indicated that he was sympathetic to Alamán's efforts of the previous decade.[43] The difference between Alamán and the doctrinaire liberals lay in the use Alamán made of economic theory. As an entrepreneur, continuing in the ways of his ancestors, Alamán adapted the new economic doctrines to his con-

---

article, a commentary on the report of the mining committee, emphasized the leading role of Alamán ("Gold and Silver in Mexico," *North American Review, 21,* 1825, 429–43).

41. This episode was described by H. G. Ward, British chargé d'affaires in Mexico from 1825 to 1827, who wrote trying to buoy up investor confidence in the mining industry after the speculative spiral had collapsed (*Mexico, 2,* 60–81 and passim). See also N. Ray Gilmore, "Henry George Ward, British Publicist for Mexican Mines," *Pacific Historical Review, 32* (1963), 35–47. Alamán announced the formation of the Compañía Unida de Minas in a letter to *El Sol,* May 12, 1824, and urged mineowners to join.

42. Alamán, "Memoria" (1830), *Documentos, 1,* 207; cf. "Memoria" (1825), ibid., p. 149. On Alamán's conflicts with the British agents, see Gilmore, p. 40; Valadés, *Alamán,* p. 226.

43. Mora, *Revoluciones, 1,* 26–40, contains a good review of the speculative ventures of the twenties, critical of the organization and methods of the foreign companies but not of Alamán. Mora concluded on an optimistic note (p. 38), referring to Alamán's "Memoria" (1830). See also Zavala, *Ensayo, 2,* 224–25.

crete and pragmatic plans for restoring Mexico's leading industry.[44] Funds were no longer available from the colonial banco de avíos of the Mining Tribunal, so he turned to private foreign investment, first for his personal interests, later for the industry in general. Through educational exposure to European advances, Alamán was receptive to improved technology. He wanted to modernize the industry, just as did Fausto de Elhuyar a generation earlier.

Alamán's positive and nondoctrinaire conception of development embraced more than mining. In 1823 he mentioned briefly that it was necessary to encourage manufacturing through protective (but not prohibitive) tariffs, while allowing the free entry of machines from abroad. The goal would be cheaper manufactures to compete with foreign goods. Francisco Arrillaga, the minister of finance, even made some specific proposals for mechanizing the textile industry.[45] In short, there were differences between Alamán and the economic liberals during the 1820s, but they remained subtle.

In 1830, the sharp divergence between the two approaches to economic development became manifest. Concurrent with the political reaction to Vicente Guerrero's popular regime was a reaction in economic thought to Guerrero's prohibitive legislation favoring the artisan industries. The doctrinaire liberal position was consolidated under the leadership of Mora and Zavala. The response of Lucas Alamán was of a quite different nature.

Between 1825 and 1830, Alamán remained outside government and turned his immense creative energy to private interests. He purchased property in Celaya, and had visions of developing that city of small workshops into a factory center for woolens. In doing so, he gradually liquidated his Guanajuato mines. He also pur

44. Alamán cited Smith but not Say. Perhaps the *Wealth of Nations* appealed to Alamán, because practical example loomed so large in it, as opposed to Say's more systematic treatise, and because Smith did not radically separate economics from statecraft. There may be some significance in Bernardo Couto's statement about Mora that he "professed the doctrines of the school of Smith, according to their explanation by Say" ("Mora," p. 888b).

45. See Potash, *Banco*, pp. 36–37; Alamán, "Memoria" (1823), p. 100. The concern for importing machines was of course not original with Alamán and Arrillaga, for the 1821 tariff law had decreed free entry to "all kinds of machines useful for agriculture, mining, and crafts (*artes*)." Francisco García also suggested the introduction of machines in 1823 (see above).

chased the rundown Hacienda de Trojes and attempted to turn it into a profitable enterprise with financial support from his father-in-law and from several chaplaincies. Valadés gives us an engaging portrait of the Alamán of these early entrepreneurial years, striking out with great energy in mining, agriculture, and textiles. In the elegant mansion of the Count of Santiago in Mexico City, he lived *"como un gran señor."* Entrepreneur, hacendado, and austere Hispanic nobleman; this was the man who in January 7, 1830, again became minister of relations.

A month after taking office Alamán reported to the congress that manufacturing "is reduced almost to nullity" because it had been promoted by the wrong methods. He went on to attack "the purely prohibitive system" and said that abundant population, capital, and adequate machinery were also prerequisites for industry. Alamán was announcing a plan for government promotion of modern industry in selected areas, to be implemented by a series of laws and orders over the next two years. Factory production was to be limited to cheap fabrics of cotton, wool, and linen, "necessary to clothe the most numerous class of our population." Mexico should continue to import luxury products from more industrialized nations. Alamán's plan for industry drew from both the free trade and the protectionist (for example, Francisco García's) arguments of the 1820s. Yet in announcing positive governmental efforts to modernize industry, it was a departure from both.

A law of October 16, 1830, provided for "the establishment of a Banco de Avío to promote national industry." Its capital was to be formed from one-fifth of the revenue received from import duties on crude cotton cloth. The 1829 prohibition on cotton cloth was to be lifted "for the time necessary, and no more," until an investment fund of one million pesos could be accumulated. The junta of the Banco, composed of the minister of relations and two others, was to import machinery and to distribute it at cost on easy terms to worthy enterprises. Special consideration would be given to those in wool, cotton, and silk. The Banco de Avío was intended as a government investment bank to develop industry on a modern basis.[46]

How can we account for Alamán's change from mining to

46. See Potash, *Banco,* Chap. 4, a thorough discussion of the inception and ramifications of the plan.

manufacturing, and from laissez-faire to direct government intervention? The explanation lies partly in the shift of Alamán's personal entrepreneurial interests between 1825 and 1830. It lies also in the little-studied history of capital in Mexico during the 1820s.[47] There was a sizable withdrawal of British funds, following the frenzied speculation of 1824–26 and the subsequent panic. Whatever Spanish merchant capital remained after independence was put to flight with the expulsion decrees of 1827 and 1829. The church traditionally invested in land. Alamán had turned to foreigners to finance the mines in the absence of private domestic funds and because the Mining Tribunal was bankrupt. Disillusioned by the absence of investment from other sources, Alamán now turned to the state. In doing so he may also have been trying to undermine the kind of regional and patriotic opposition that the artisans of Puebla had raised to a British-Mexican industrial company proposed by Juan Ignacio Godoy in 1829.[48] It would be difficult to attack Alamán's scheme on grounds of partiality, either to foreign interests or to the interests of a particular region.

The Banco de Avío was inspired by Bourbon economic institutions of the 1770s. Alamán's bank was none other than a recreation of the banco de avíos of the Mining Tribunal, now applied primarily to manufacturing. The method of funding the two investment institutions was similar. In each case a portion of government revenue derived from the particular industry in question was to be diverted into promotional purposes. Beyond the specific parallel with the mining fund of the 1770s, Alamán's conception of development in 1830 bears strong resemblance to the general policy of peninsular economic rejuvenation under Charles III.[49]

47. Stanley J. Stein's forthcoming study of the merchant class should enlighten this subject. See also the research of J. Fred Rippy, especially "Latin America and the British Investment 'Boom' of the 1820s," *Journal of Modern History, 19* (1947), 122–29.

48. Godoy was a large mineowner (Alamán, *Historia, 5,* Appendix, Doc. No. 25, p. 83) turned industrialist who sought the privilege of importing cotton thread (then prohibited), in exchange for introducing textile machinery into the Federal District and elsewhere. See Potash, *Banco,* pp. 57–61; Chávez Orozco, *Historia,* pp. 220–27; Miguel A. Quintana, *Estevan de Antuñano, fundador de la industria textil en Puebla* (Mexico, Sec. de Hacienda y Crédito Público, 1957), *2,* 53–61.

49. In promoting Spanish textiles, however, Charles III emphasized the production of fine cloth, even in defiance of market demands. In fact, the inattention to market forces was the single major defect of royal fomento, according to La Force.

Alamán's development scheme should not be seen as an outright repudiation of liberalism in favor of mercantilist conceptions. He had been responsive to laissez-faire during the 1820s and apparently turned to government financing only in the absence of private capital. Nor was he hostile to foreign entrepreneurs. Potash demonstrates that in the twelve years of the Banco's existence the great proportion of investment in modern manufacturing was of private origin, both from natives and from resident foreigners (particularly merchants). Two of the six spinning mills financed by the Banco were controlled by British and French interests. As in Spain, the introduction of foreign artisans and technicians was officially encouraged in the interests of modernization. The Banco de Avío was a means of initial stimulus, not a way of excluding all foreign interests. It may be significant that at least one contemporary observer, Tadeo Ortiz, found no conflict between the Banco de Avío and free trade. He said Mexico could become "the emporium of commerce from the Old World and the New." Later he showed equal enthusiasm for the newly founded Banco.[50]

Ortiz was, of course, an exception in his day. Resistance to the Banco de Avío was widespread and sustained. Artisan interests immediately attacked the plan, since it stemmed from a temporary removal of the 1829 prohibitions on textile imports. Puebla was the center of opposition, but it came from other parts of the country as well. The artisans were generally more concerned by the immediate threat that arose from removal of prohibitions than they were by the potential threat of displacement by machines.

The principal attack on the Banco, as we have seen, came from the doctrinaire liberals. Lorenzo de Zavala said that Alamán's tariff decree, "if not as antieconomic [as that of Guerrero] in its consequences, was at least as absurd, ridiculous, and petty." Under Alamán's plan, "the government [would be] establishing itself as the inspector general of these manufactures. . . . All the masters of this [economic] science raise their voice against such government activities." Zavala and Mora were equally hostile, both to

---

Alamán was more responsive to the market (following Adam Smith) and emphasized crude cotton cloth. It was also true that Mexico had no tradition of fine cloth manufacture.

50. See Ortiz, *México*, pp. 286, 305.

indirect support for obsolescent artisan industries through prohibitive tariffs, and to direct support for modern textile factories.
In his survey of Mexico in 1830, Mora stated flatly that the
"manufacturing industry has never been of consequence in Mexico"; the Alamán policy was merely a narrow effort to "nationalize foreign industry." [51] Industrial modernization, as proposed by
Alamán, was ideally a nonpolitical policy, independent of ideology. But this was a subtlety that went unnoticed by the doctrinaire reformers.

The Banco de Avío faced difficulties from the start. Despite his
leadership in founding the Banco, Alamán hoped that its governing junta would be an administrative entity not totally dependent
on the particular government in power. This, of course, was impossible in the period of extreme political instability between
1832 and 1835. Imported machinery for Banco-financed enterprises rusted on the docks at Veracruz. Customs duties earmarked
for the Banco were appropriated by rebellious generals. The
Gómez Farías regime on several occasions diverted Banco funds to
other purposes. Except under one minister, Francisco Lombardo
(December 1833), relations between the junta and the government were strained. Besides political obstacles, the Banco was
plagued with poor investment decisions. Most of the potential
enterprises were unrealistic. Lending was often determined by
personal favoritism. The junta took on too many projects. The result was that by 1835 all Banco-financed ventures had ended in
failure, with one notable exception—the cotton factory of Estevan
de Antuñano in Puebla.[52]

We know little about the life of Estevan de Antuñano, who, between 1833 and 1846, became Mexico's leading entrepreneur and
propagandist for national industry. Born in Veracruz in 1792,
Antuñano was educated in Spain and later in England, where he
was undoubtedly influenced by the dramatic expansion of industry. In 1821 he tried to establish a small spinning mill, using imported machines and child labor, which he called the "House of
Training for Children." His products failed to compete with

51. Zavala, *Ensayo,* 2, 304–05, 328; Mora, *Revoluciones, 1,* 41–42.
52. See Potash, *Banco,* pp. 87–129. Between Apr. 1833 and Mar. 1834 there were
ten ministers of finance and four of relations.

imported textiles. He also became a large landholder, managing throughout his lifetime properties inherited by his wife. On December 16, 1831, Antuñano and Company received a loan of 30,000 pesos from the Banco de Avío. Four years later, the appropriately named Constancia Mexicana, Mexico's first modern water-driven textile factory, began operation.[53]

We know Antuñano chiefly through his writings, over fifty pamphlets of varying lengths, many newspaper articles, and a voluminous correspondence, only a small portion of which has come to light.[54] This correspondence, including sixty-three letters to Lucas Alamán between March 1844 and October 1845, reveals a zealot in the cause of industry who bent every effort to disseminate his locally published pamphlets. Week after week he importuned Alamán with hundreds of copies of various writings, which the latter was to distribute in congress and elsewhere in the capital. Antuñano even asked Alamán, apparently without success, to reprint pamphlets at his own expense.[55]

Estevan de Antuñano regarded himself as the "founder of Mexican industry." He gave credit to Lucas Alamán, with whom he maintained close relations for over a decade, and he referred to the Banco de Avío as "the greatest idea to come forth since Mexico became a nation." But he had no doubts about his own role: "My

53. Actually, Mexico's first modern cotton mill was founded by Pedro Sáinz de Baranda in Yucatán (1833). It was one-tenth the size of Antuñano's factory and, because of Yucatán's isolation, never attained recognition. See H. F. Cline, " 'Aurora Yucateca,' " pp. 30–31. On Antuñano's early life, see Potash, *Banco,* pp. 107–09; Quintana, *Estevan de Antuñano, I,* 11–13; Bazant, "Evolution," p. 68.

54. There is a bibliography of Antuñano's published writings compiled by José Miguel Quintana, "Estevan de Antuñano," *Boletín bibliográfico de la secretaría de hacienda y crédito público,* June 15, 1955. Many of the pamphlets have been conveniently reprinted in M. A. Quintana, *Estevan de Antuñano.*

55. See Antuñano to Alamán, Mar. 19 and 27, Apr. 21, 1844; Mar. 8 and 22, Apr. 19, Aug. 1, 4, and 9, 1845, Antuñano Correspondence. I am indebted to José Miguel Quintana and to Jan Bazant for the opportunity of examining these letters (from a copybook of the era). Many of the letters, to Cayetano Rubio (a cotton dealer), to Isidoro Romero (an agent), and to numerous others, concern Antuñano's business dealings. Antuñano said on two occasions (Sept. 29, 1844, and Jan. 28, 1845) that he had had copies made of all correspondence sent and received since 1831, as well as "a great many very interesting documents which my children will be able to exhibit." He also referred to memoirs. The discovery of this wealth of material, probably still located in Puebla, poses a challenge to some future investigator of early entrepreneurship in Mexico.

enterprise called the Constancia Mexicana has become the model and stimulus for all other enterprises of modern industry." Antuñano often signed his later pamphlets "the first insurgent of Mexican industrial independence." The city of Puebla became the "Dolores of industrial independence"; January 7, 1835, became "comparable in obtaining industrial independence . . . with September 16, 1810, in gaining political independence." [56] He saw himself always as a lone combatant in the cause of industry, even though he was aided during the 1840s by Lucas Alamán, by *El Siglo,* and by other occasional spokesmen.

National greatness through industry was the predominant theme of Antuñano's pamphlets. "If Mexico is not great in manufacturing, it will be nothing," he wrote in 1846. Antuñano justified modern textile production as the rebirth of a traditional enterprise, established by the Aztecs and continued during colonial times. Puebla was a great center of textile production in the later colonial period, he said in 1834, but now it is ruined. It was entirely natural to open our ports to the ships of all nations in 1821, but the act "turned our artisans into beggars." With the artisan industries in ruins, Mexico must now revive textiles on a modern basis.[57]

Antuñano and his fellow spokesmen became increasingly preoccupied with the threat that Mexico might become an economic colony of the industrialized nations. In 1844 Antuñano attacked the primacy of mining. It was appropriate to the colonial period "because then the political economy of Mexico was guided by the mercantile convenience of the metropolis." Now, however, it is time for Mexico to break "the feudal charter" and "to fulfill its role as a civilized nation." In the 1840s Antuñano saw Mexican merchants and European nations conspiring to perpetuate free-trade doctrines, to stress Mexico's natural role in agriculture and

56. Antuñano, *Ampliación,* p. 24; *Economía política en México* (Puebla, Oct. 1845) ; *Economía política en México* (Puebla, Dec. 1845) ; also letters to Alamán, June 28, 1844, and May 27, 1845, Antuñano Correspondence.

57. Antuñano, *Economía política en México. Insurrección industrial* (reprint, n.p., n.d., of letter to *El Monitor,* Oct. 23, 1846) ; *Discurso analítico de algunos puntos de moral y economía política de México* (Puebla, 1834) , p. 35; *El Primer Asunto de la patria, el algodón. Manifiesto sobre el algodón manufacturado y en greña* (Puebla, 1833) , pp. 4–8; also *El Siglo,* Aug. 23, 1842.

mining, and to ruin industry. "Insurrection" was the cause of the day in 1845 and 1846, and Antuñano became its self-appointed leader.[58]

Development had become a patriotic matter. "For our republic the promotion of industry is not a mere calculation of profit, but a matter of honor and independence," asserted the newspaper *El Cosmopolita* on December 24, 1842. In one of his typically ingenuous efforts to dramatize industry, Antuñano sent a bolt of cloth from his factory to Santa Anna, so the general's daughters might wear dresses "in honor of Mexican industry." [59] Private investment in many of the companies underwritten by the Banco de Avío came as a result of pressure by state governors and *jefes políticos*. In some instances the ecclesiastical hierarchy participated in the companies and exhorted parishioners to invest, indicating that the church "saw the companies as semipublic institutions with patriotic or philanthropic ends, rather than as business concerns." [60]

The advocates of industry were much concerned by the lack of industrial values among the populace. In 1832, Alamán looked hopefully to the creation of a spirit of enterprise through the encouragement given to manufacturers by the Banco de Avío. Antuñano was less optimistic, but stated repeatedly that until the Mexican people were employed in productive industry, the country would remain economically impoverished and politically chaotic. His pamphlets were filled with maxims or catch phrases, *proposiciones* he called them, to demonstrate this simple thesis. "When the people become wealthy, they will grow in numbers,

58. Antuñano, *Economía política en México* (Puebla, Mar. 1844), pp. 3–4; *La Carta feudal de México o sea consejos de Mercator sobre la industria mexicana* (Puebla, 1846), p. 7; letter to Alamán, Apr. 6, 1844, Antuñano Correspondence; *Economía política* (1846); *Insurrección industrial. Economía política en México* (Puebla, 1846); "¡¡¡Mexicanos!!! El primer asunto de la patria—insurrección para la independencia industrial fabril de México," in *El Siglo,* Dec. 2, 1845. Antuñano reacted particularly to a work published by a British commercial agent, Robert C. Willie, called *México. Noticia sobre su hacienda pública bajo el gobierno español y después de la independencia* (Mexico, 1845), which argued against protection for industry.

59. Antuñano, *Economía política. Documentos (en doce cartas [to Santa Anna]) para la historia de la industria moderna de algodones en México* (Puebla, 1843), p. 13.

60. Potash, *Banco,* p. 98. The most important group of shareholders in the Industrial Company of Celaya were public employees.

they will become enlightened, and a public spirit will be created";
"As long as the majority of the people are not usefully and hon-
estly employed, Mexico cannot be governed by mild laws"; and so
on.[61]

Antuñano, as much as any reformer of 1833, sought the creation
of a utilitarian mentality in the people. Mexico has inherited the
vices of the Spanish colony, the scorn of work and the aspiration
after public employment. The only way these evils can be rooted
out is by useful employment in industry. What is needed is a national policy "promoting with determination these classes which
produce wealth, and diminishing within reasonable limits ex-
penditures on public administration of every kind." Like Mora
and Zavala, Antuñano attacked the profusion of religious holidays,
the bane of productive enterprise in the country. He advocated
labor by women in factories, another favorite utilitarian idea.[62]

It is apparent that Antuñano, and even the early Alamán, did
not oppose the utilitarian ideals which formed the basis of liberal
social philosophy. Antuñano maintained that "individual material
labor, directed by the mind, is the only solid pedestal upon which
a strong, rich, civilized society can be founded and made to
progress." [63] As we have seen, he pointed to the United States as a
model society. Antuñano wanted to instruct people in "political
economy," words that figured in the titles of most of his pamphlets. Unlike Mora, however, Antuñano was not a systematic
thinker. His ideas had little consistency. He could espouse economic individualism, utilitarian values, "political economy," and
at the same time maintain that national economic development
through industry could only be advanced by a frank policy of gov-

61. Alamán, "Memoria" (1832), *Documentos, 1,* 365; Antuñano, *Ampliación*
(1833), p. 37; *Memoria breve de la industria manufacturera en México* (Puebla,
1835), p. 4; *Economía política en México* (Puebla, June 1839), pp. 1–5; *Economía
política en México* (Puebla, July 1838), p. 3.

62. Antuñano, "Economía política en México. Insurrección industrial," *Republicano,* Aug. 15, 1846; *Ventajas políticas civiles fabriles y domésticas que por dar
ocupación también a las mujeres en las fábricas de maquinaria moderna que se
están levantando en México, deben recibirse* (Puebla, 1837). Jovellanos had advocated work by women as a way toward giving them equality with men (Sarrailh,
Espagne éclairée, pp. 516–17). On holidays see Antuñano, *Economía política* (June,
1839), p. 6. The government secured papal consent to the reduction of feast days
in 1836, but clerical protests deferred the edict until 1839 (Potash, *Banco,* p. 237).

63. Antuñano, *Economía política en México* (Puebla, Feb. 1839).

ernment fomento, including the extention of privileges to "the productive classes of society."

In abstracting certain general themes from Antuñano's writings, we must remember that he was in large part lobbying for specific government policies to aid his own enterprises. Of principal concern to Antuñano was tariff policy, and his pamphlets provide a means of following its complicated history during the thirties and forties. Alamán, in his "Memoria" of 1832, called in effect for a reinstitution of prohibitions, now that the textile industry had been established and there existed the means of replacing foreign imports. Prohibitions were not actually restored, however, until March 11, 1838. Both Antuñano and Alamán envisioned an integrated national system in textiles in which industry would utilize domestically grown cotton. Antuñano's early pamphlets argued strenuously for prohibitions on both crude cotton and manufactured cloth. He spoke of natural ties existing between Puebla and Veracruz (where most of the cotton was grown). The two regions cannot live separately. Antuñano called prohibition "the moral base of industry." [64]

During the next decade he fought any tendency toward tariff relaxation. He was aided by El Siglo and by the newly founded Dirección de Industria, which replaced the Banco de Avío. The general argument was that infant industries needed prohibitions to develop. Even in the very nations where liberal doctrines originated, industries "owe their progress to the prohibitive system." [65] Certainly, then, we are justified in demanding it. Santa Anna, as dictator in 1842, flirted briefly with lower tariffs in the

64. See Antuñano, *Pensamientos para la regeneración industrial de México* (Puebla, 1837), p. 13. For his advocacy of the prohibition of crude cotton see *El Primer Asunto* (1833), pp. 17–20; *Breve Memoria del estado que guarda la fábrica de hilados de algodón constancia mexicana* (Puebla, 1837), p. 9. See also Alamán, "Memoria" (1832), *Documentos, I,* 371. Crude cotton was prohibited Aug. 9, 1836. A new tariff law was passed on Mar. 11, 1837, with the prohibitions on cotton cloth to be put into effect after one year. The struggle to reinstate prohibitions was complicated by the fact that the Banco de Avío was also dependent on tariff revenue. See Potash, *Banco*, pp. 134–37, 189–99.

65. *El Siglo*, Aug. 25, 1843. The paper devoted much space during this year to industry. See also Mariano Gálvez, "Discurso leído en la sesión de industria el 27 de febrero de 1844" in *El Ateneo mexicano, I,* 33. Gálvez pointed particularly to France. Gálvez was the permanent secretary of the Board of Industry (see below).

interests of revenue, but cotton goods were still kept on the prohibited list. He finally yielded, and a rigid prohibitionist clause was written into the constitutional law of 1843 (the Bases Orgánicas): no articles harmful to national industry could be imported without the prior approval of two-thirds of the departmental assemblies.[66]

There was, however, a complication in the campaign to maintain the prohibitive system. After 1837 it became evident that domestic cotton was neither abundant enough nor cheap enough for the needs of the textile industry. The number of factories had grown; the demand for cotton had increased. With no outside competition possible, the temptation to speculate in the price of crude cotton was irresistible. Estevan de Antuñano began to advocate importation of cheap raw cotton from the United States. His new argument ran as follows: "Crude foreign cotton, providing useful occupation to Mexicans, will give them wealth and all its benefits. Foreign cotton manufactures will cause them poverty and all its fatal consequences." [67] There was scarcely one of his numerous pamphlets between 1840 and 1846 that did not include a reiteration of his new position on prohibitions. An intense conflict ensued between the cotton growers, "monopolists" Antuñano called them, and the manufacturers.[68]

The problem of obtaining cheap crude cotton became an obsession with Antuñano during 1844 and 1845. Daily he wrote to Alamán, the director of industry, and to other officials, calling for a loosening of restrictions. When his general arguments failed, he sought special concessions from government officials. In April 1844, Ignacio Trigüeros, the minister of finance, granted him permission to import three to four thousand quintals of crude cotton.[69] On April 21, Antuñano told Alamán he would use the privilege only if he felt unduly pressed by "the plot of national

66. See Potash, *Banco*, pp. 208–10. When Santa Anna agreed to continue prohibiting foreign textiles, *El Siglo* announced the "triumph of national industry" (Aug. 12, 1842).

67. Antuñano, *Economía política en México. Teoría fundamental de la industria de algodones en México* (Puebla, Aug. 1840), p. 5.

68. See the comment by *El Mosquito mexicano*, Apr. 4, 1843.

69. Letter, Antuñano to Trigüeros, Apr. 21, 1844 (Antuñano Correspondence), calling the latter a "true friend," and thanking him for the favor.

and foreign monopolists, [which is] sustained by the malice and ignorance of almost all the manufacturers and public officials of Puebla." Apparently, Antuñano did pursue the privilege, for his letters increasingly complained of persecution. By 1845 he was close to paranoia. He spoke of the "almost savage ignorance shown by the majority of the first men of Mexico toward the manufacturing industry and toward its founder and sustainer." Puebla's most respectable men seem to have adopted the "principle that everything against Antuñano is just." [70] In these straits, he looked to Alamán as a companion in the lone fight to sustain the cause of manufacturing.

Was Antuñano more than a lobbyist who developed elaborate arguments to promote his particular interests? He was obviously first of all a practical industrialist, a fact that limited his overall view of economic development in Mexico. Lucas Alamán was also an industrialist; but his enterprises were always secondary to public service, as closely tied as the two often were. Antuñano had no interest in public service, but his concerns did go beyond his cotton factory. He took particular pride in a paper mill, the Beneficencia Poblana, which he claimed had been rescued from failure and was now being run efficiently by his son-in-law, José María Loustalet.[71] In 1837, Antuñano began to advocate the establishment of machine-tool factories, after losing a "large and select collection of spinning machinery and a twenty-horsepower steam engine" in a shipwreck near Florida. He later called for promotion of the iron industry, which might in time become "the material base of Mexican industry." [72] On different occasions Antuñano

70. Letter to Alamán, Mar. 1, 1845, Antuñano Correspondence; also Apr. 19, July 15, Aug. 20, 1845. He referred often to his deafness, which made him embarrassed to receive people and undoubtedly added to his sense of isolation. Financial difficulties had overtaken him. He had to remortgage his factory in 1845 to keep creditors from the door.

71. Letter to Alamán, Apr. 26, 1845, Antuñano Correspondence. The mill won the support of El Monitor constitucional independiente, which devoted much space to the paper industry in Mar. 1845; see also Alamán, "Memoria sobre el estado de la agricultura e industria de la república" (1845), Documentos, 2, 290–91.

72. Antuñano, Pensamientos (1837), p. 12; Economía política (June 1839), p. 7; also Potash, Banco, p. 167. Antuñano reported his loss in a letter to Alamán on Mar. 22, 1837, Antuñano Correspondence.

also urged improvement of canals and roads, colonization of the coasts, and the propagation of foreign plants and animals.[73]

It was Lucas Alamán, however, who remained the statesman of economic development in Mexico. After the fall of the Bustamante regime, he returned to his own enterprises, which included the establishment of a spinning mill at Cocolapam near Orizaba in 1836. The Banco de Avío was strengthened by further capitalization in 1835 and lent money lavishly during the next two years. Alamán, incidentally, was one of the beneficiaries, receiving 60,000 pesos for his mill. The earlier problems of the Banco returned to plague it, and by 1840 its funds were exhausted. Moreover, there was increasing sentiment that it be replaced by an organization more directly controlled by the new industrialists themselves and less dependent on the government.[74] The result was the Junta General de la Industria Mexicana, a corporate entity modeled on the Mining Guild of the 1770s. Regional *juntas de industria* were to send representatives to Mexico City to meet every two years as the General Junta. Authority was lodged in a board *(dirección)*, the director of which was to be named by the President of the Republic, just as the director of the Mining Tribunal had been named by the Crown. Lucas Alamán served as director during its four years of existence.[75]

By 1844 Alamán had abandoned his earlier view that mining was "our proper activity"; he was now urging development on several fronts. He sought means to reconcile the interests of agriculture and manufacturing, including an attempt to expand cotton growing.[76] Alamán's plan for development, which was also

73. Antuñano, *Discurso analítico* (1834) ; *Economía política* (Mar. 1844) .

74. Potash, *Banco*, Chaps. 8–10; *El Siglo,* Oct. 16, 1841.

75. The junta fell apart with the reinstitution of federalism in 1846, when state governors gained control of the regional organizations. The Dirección was absorbed by the newly created Dirección de Colonización e Industria. In 1853 it became part of the Ministerio de Fomento, the direct predecessor of the modern ministries of Economía Nacional and Agricultura y Ganadería. See Potash, *Banco,* pp. 205–08.

76. By 1845, though, Alamán finally yielded to Antuñano's barrage of petitions in favor of the importation of crude cotton. See Alamán, "Memoria" (1845) , *Documentos, 2,* 270–79. For his earlier views see "Observaciones" (1841) , ibid., p. 512; "Memoria . . . agricultura e industria" (1844) , ibid., pp. 141–43. For his changed

advocated by Antuñano, was a reenactment of Bourbon peninsular fomento, adapted to the circumstances of a politically independent Mexico. The objective was to advance the cause of national regeneration through an independent, balanced, and modernized economy. Government stimulus in selected areas through
direct investment, special tax concessions, manipulation of the
tariff, importation of machinery, and foreign technology—these
Bourbon policies of a "liberalized mercantilism" were reborn in
post-1830 Mexico. The eclectic and pragmatic approach to development allowed special privilege, even monopoly, to coexist with
the search for a utilitarian spirit of enterprise. The plan was
riddled with doctrinal inconsistencies, as had been Bourbon policies in Spain, but such inconsistencies were its very essence.[77]

In identifying this Bourbon-inspired conception of development shared by Alamán and Antuñano, we must note again its tie
to land. Antuñano and Alamán were both large landholders. As
men of enterprise they were closer to the continental type of the
aristocratic entrepreneur, in contrast to the English industrialist
who typically formed part of a new social class, having few ties to
land, family traditions, or to older activities like mining.[78]

Antuñano wrote twice to Alamán of a cherished scheme for establishing a "Valley of Mexican Industry" along the pleasant
banks of the Atoyac River where he held nine haciendas. It would
be made up of twelve hydraulically powered factories and ten or

---

opinion on mining see "Memoria . . . agricultura e industria" (1843) , ibid., p. 24.
It is worth noting that the entrepreneur Alamán, in a letter of July 23, 1842, to
El Siglo, petitioned for the entry of foreign crude cotton to supply his factory at
Cocolapam.

77. Reyes Heroles suggests Bourbon inspiration in saying that Alamán attempted
in 1830 to fortify "the cadre of privileged classes with a new class which would
also spring from privilege" (*Liberalismo, 3,* 457) , or again when he attributes to
Alamán the idea of "colony with industry and the industrial branches following
colonial inspiration" (ibid., 2, xvi) . The confusion comes when he labels Alamán's
approach "conservative"—"integrally" tied to political conservatism—as opposed
to that of Antuñano. Reyes Heroles sees the latter as a "liberal" prophet of a
future industrial class to rise up against "traditional privileges" (ibid., 2, 346–47) .

78. See David Landes, "The Industrial Revolution," *Chapters in Western Civilization* (New York, Columbia University Press, 1962) , 2, 165. Landes explains why
industrialization on the continent lagged behind that of England. The social and
cultural factors he identifies on the continent are particularly relevant to understanding economic development in Mexico.

twelve villages of workers living as tenants on Antuñano's lands. Workers would alternately till their lands and work in the adjacent factories, and in so doing become "artisans of moral betterment." [79] Antuñano would presumably watch over the thriving community as a beneficent lord. Hacienda and factory would become merged in one harmonious system of production. His Constancia Mexicana was already located on one of these properties, Santo Domingo. Mme. Calderon de la Barca visited the factory in the company of the aristocratic entrepreneur himself in 1841, and was greatly impressed by its luxuriousness. "It is beautifully situated, and at a distance has more the air of a summer palace than of a cotton factory." [80] The owner of this enterprise could hardly be called the spokesman of a new industrial class.[81]

Though modern factory manufacturing had gained a foothold in Mexico by 1846, it faced serious challenge in the grave economic crisis occasioned by the war with the United States. The searching postwar debate embraced economic as well as sociopolitical questions. Particularly notable was the resurgence of economic liberalism, in retreat since 1834. The issues and the arguments, although similar to those of earlier decades, were now brought into bolder relief by the chaos of war. By 1845, the rigid prohibitive system of 1843 showed signs of strain. The war cracked it completely. A new tariff law was issued in 1845, lowering slightly the general list of duties while retaining prohibitions on crucial items

79. Antuñano to Alamán, May 12, 1844, Antuñano Correspondence; also June 18.

80. Calderon, *Life in Mexico*, p. 409. Led by Antuñano, the party visited several institutions in Puebla, including a foundling home, where Antuñano donated $200 "as a memorial of our visit."

81. There have been suggestions that both Alamán's and Antuñano's ideas show the influence of Henri Comte de St. Simon, the French prophet of an industrial society that would be bound together organically by the spirit of enterprise and directed by an artistic and scientific elite. See González Navarro, *Pensamiento*, p. 84; Quintana, *Estevan de Antuñano, 1*, 24–26. Though this matter warrants further investigation, I suspect that such influence was only felt after 1867. The technocratic strain in the thought of the pre-Reforma period owed more to Campomanes and Floridablanca than to St. Simon. Alamán edited a journal in 1841 entitled *Semanario de la industria megicana*, which included at least one European article ("Revolución industrial," *2*, 68–78, 94–96, 101–08), evoking the conflicts of the new industrial society. It was inserted without comment, however. Most of the articles were either drawn from earlier figures (Jovellanos, Campomanes, and even Colbert) or were the standard contemporary arguments for industry.

such as textiles and crude cotton. Early in 1846, President Paredes y Arrillaga finally released the ban on crude cotton, for which Antuñano had fought so long, but the war soon cut off the source of supply.

The North American occupation opened Mexico's ports of entry to foreign products of all kinds and deprived the Mexican government of its vital customs revenue. The boundary changes of 1848 compounded the difficulty of controlling contraband. Soon after the peace treaty, on May 3, 1848, the Mexican government was forced to lower duties to 60 percent of the 1845 level in order to recoup customs revenue and to allow new importations to compete with those that flooded the country during the war. In 1846, Alamán's Board of Industry was replaced by the more liberal Dirección de Colonización y Industria, which over the following years began to advocate suppressing prohibitions and to emphasize colonization as a solution to Mexico's economic problems.[82] Manuel Payno, as minister of finance in July 1850, continued to press for the tariff by initiating a liberal proposal in the congress.

The context of the postwar debate over tariff policy was similar to that of 1821. The established economic and fiscal system had been upset by war. Industries that had existed by protection now faced ruin by the de facto entry of foreign goods. Disruption of former restrictions aroused interest in establishing an ideal liberal system. There were, however, two new factors that conditioned postwar discussions. The first was that the intervening period had seen the assertion of a liberal reform ideology not present in 1821, which was bound to entangle political and economic issues. This matter we will examine shortly. The second was that the economic liberals now faced an established postindependence industrial tradition based on modern factories, and not merely obsolescent artisan industries. Artisan industries could be branded as the remnants of a discredited colonial mercantilism. Modern factories could not. The doctrinaire liberal position, as expressed earlier by

82. Law of May 3, 1848, in Dublán and Lozano, 5, 356; "Documentos que publica la dirección de colonización e industria, sobre el proyecto de levantar las prohibiciones del arancel de aduanas marítimas" (1848), Chávez Orozco, ed., *Los Industriales mexicanos y el comercio exterior de México, 1848–1852,* Colección de documentos para la historia del comercio exterior de México, 3 (Mexico, Banco Nacional de Comercio, 1959), 167–97; also Reyes Heroles, *Liberalismo, 3,* 494 ff.

Ortiz de la Torre, by Zavala, or by Mora, was bound to be modified in the postwar era.

A resurgence of the earlier economic liberalism was apparent in Mariano Otero's *Consideraciones* (1848), the pamphlet that struck so incisively at Mexico's political and social ills. Mining is the only industry that is flourishing today, said Otero. Thus mining should be encouraged, and not the textile industry, which "can subsist only in the shadow of prohibitions and privileges." It is contrary to all reason to keep out good foreign cloth in favor of the poor local product. Otero assailed the Banco de Avío, much as had Mora and Zavala.[83] Such an extreme expression was uncommon, however, in the postwar years. Both *El Siglo* and *El Monitor* wavered on the crucial question of the tariff, the former tending toward strong protection, the latter toward relaxation. But like the government itself during these years, their position was seldom doctrinaire. Newly established industries simply could not be eliminated.[84]

Defense of prohibitions was vociferous and widespread, partly because the government itself was opposed to them. On the national level the most forceful and complete defense appeared in two series of articles, one in the politically moderate-liberal *El Siglo,* the other in the conservative *El Universal*. The arguments presented by the two newspapers were remarkably similar. *El Universal* opened its series with a tribute to the "illuminating" articles published previously in *El Siglo* and to the important questions they had raised.[85]

83. Otero, *Consideraciones*, pp. 14–17.

84. In contrast to its 1850 stand, *El Siglo* (Nov. 2, 1848) had urged "the establishment of protective duties," adding that "the prohibitive system is renounced as harmful to the moral and physical progress of nations." Examples of *El Monitor's* liberal stand can be seen on July 17, 1851, and Feb. 7, 1852, a shift from 1848 and 1849. On Aug. 19, 1848, *El Monitor* had said it was impossible for the country to progress with free trade; "it is necessary that we adopt the prohibitive system, rationally understood and practiced."

85. *Alza de prohibiciones. Artículos publicados en el periódico titulado: el universal* (Mexico, 1851), p. 4. The three articles contained in this pamphlet are undated but presumably appeared early in 1851. Another similar series of four articles appeared in *El Universal*, Dec. 5, 13, 20, and 24, 1851. As noted above, Jesús Reyes Heroles emphasizes the 1850 arguments of *El Siglo* as exemplifying "liberal protectionism," i.e. political liberals arguing for high tariffs. He fails to mention *El Universal* (Reyes Heroles, *Liberalismo, 3,* 497–503, 529).

For both newspapers, industry was the road to national wealth and true independence. Must we remain "a nation of rustics and miners, having no other agreement with the world than to pay for its manufacturers and contribute to its greatness?" asked *El Siglo*. By so doing, said *El Universal*, "our country would only go backward on the road of civilization and true liberty." [86] Both spokesmen raised the specter of economic "vassalage" to the European powers and showed how Spain and France, and even on occasion England, had made use of prohibitive tariffs to advance their industries. *El Universal* even quoted a long passage from M'Culloch, the liberal economist and editor of David Ricardo's works, to demonstrate the role of the cotton industry in England's international power position. Arguing as had Antuñano a few years earlier, *El Siglo* asserted that "the [system] called free trade is nothing but colonial slavery and opprobrium on the Mexican name and character." [87]

Both advocates of prohibitions saw 1830 as the beginning of modern Mexican industry. Manufacturing, according to *El Siglo*, was from that time adapted to the advances of the century. The former industries were rejuvenated, "no longer in the old form, but mounted *a la europea*, that is, guided by science and stimulated by large capital investments." There followed in the article a long list of specific technological improvements which had been instituted. *El Universal* demonstrated the folly (as had Alamán in 1830) of merely protecting the artisan industries during the 1820s, while European production was being revolutionized.[88] Mexican industry also had to be modernized. *El Siglo* claimed fifty-five modern factories with a fixed capital of 16,500,000 pesos as of 1846. Both spokesmen pursued in detail the problem of the scarcity of crude cotton, concluding that importation from abroad must be temporarily continued.[89]

El Universal was joined in its defense of industry and of the

86. *Colección de artículos del siglo xix, sobre alzamiento de prohibiciones* (Mexico, 1851), p. 40 (Oct. 18, 1850); *El Universal*, Dec. 20, 1851; also *Colección*, pp. 38, 59–60 (Nov. 1, 1850), and passim.

87. *Alza de prohibiciones*, p. 15; *Colección*, p. 98 (Nov. 27, 1850).

88. *Colección*, pp. 19–21 (Oct. 6, 1850); p. 109 (art. undated); *Alza de prohibiciones*, p. 16.

89. *Colección*, pp. 138–39 (Jan. 16, 1851); *Alza de prohibiciones*, pp. 17–19.

prohibitive system by other politically conservative newspapers. Throughout March 1853, *El Orden* attacked *El Siglo* which, according to the former, had now changed its position. *El Omnibus* introduced another issue into the debate by comparing the defense of industry with that of political nationality: "If our race is threatened by conquest from the Saxon race, our industry is also [threatened] by another more alarming conquest." [90] Despite the remarkable temporary coalescence of *El Siglo* and *El Universal*, it was difficult for politics and economics to remain separated for long in the ideologically charged postwar era.

Opposition to the projected liberalization of tariff policy came both from defenders of modern factories and from spokesmen for the artisan industries. Small shops had by no means been replaced by water-driven factories. In 1843, less than half the thread used in Puebla was woven mechnically. [91] Artisans had opposed Alamán's temporary lowering of prohibitions in 1830. After the reimposition of prohibitions in 1838, however, there was little evidence of disharmony between artisans and new industrialists. Thus it is difficult to distinguish between the two in the flood of provincial petitions from 1846 to 1851 urging prohibitions on textiles. Though modern factories had become established, the life of the artisan industries behind prohibitive barriers was indefinitely prolonged. [92]

In conclusion, let us return to the problem posed at the begin-

90. *El Omnibus*, Dec. 17, 1851. *El Monitor* maintained a consistently liberal position from 1850 to 1853. See its debate with *El Universal*, May 1852.

91. Bazant, "Evolution," p. 68. Antuñano in 1833 said that a few textile factories would not harm existing weavers, since the country could support two to three hundred such factories (*Ampliación*, p. 69).

92. Several of these petitions, particularly from Puebla, appear in Chávez Orozco, *Los Industriales mexicanos*. See also *Representación de la junta de industria de Puebla . . . con motivo de las pretensiones para que se reformen las leyes que protejen la industria nacional* (Puebla, 1846), pp. 4–6; *Representación . . . al exmo. ayuntamiento de la capital de Puebla con motivo del alzamiento que se pretende de las leyes prohibitivos* (Puebla, 1851). Note should be taken of Guillermo Prieto's contention that both the establishment of modern industry and the importation of foreign products had led to the displacement of Indian village artisans, causing their further alienation from the whites. Prieto, however, urged removal of prohibitions along with a program of selective European colonization (*Indicaciones*, pp. 378, 397–99, 405, and passim); also Reyes Heroles, *Liberalismo, 3*, 504–08.

ning of this chapter—the relationship between economic development and political liberalism. I have tried to demonstrate that the terms "liberal" and "conservative" cannot profitably be used to designate concepts of development. The looser categories, "doctrinaire" and "pragmatic," are more appropriate. Lucas Alamán, the chief architect of economic development through modern industry, was also the ranking political conservative of the pre-Reforma era. His political conservatism, however, developed slowly and became a hardened ideology only after 1846. His earlier approach to both political and economic problems revealed some responsiveness to liberal theory.

Estevan de Antuñano, the other principal advocate of modern industry, was largely oblivious to politics. His comments on political and social issues were few, and before 1846 they tended to be conservative. In 1834, probably in reaction to the anticlericalism of the Gómez Farías regime, he expressed respect for the church and opposed curtailing its temporal powers. He defended tithes, but said they should be paid by the consumer rather than by the producer. He opposed small landholdings, except in "very civilized countries where the sciences and useful arts have augmented population, wealth, and good taste." In Mexico, however, subdividing land to stimulate agriculture would be profitless.[93] In 1839 Antuñano expressed preference for centralism as an antidote to anarchy, but also admitted that the centralist-federalist arguments of his day had not been profound. His general position seemed to be that the best government was one that fostered the creation of wealth through industry. He deplored the constant revolutions of his time and the general preoccupation with ephemeral political matters rather than with economic development.[94]

Antuñano's final publication revealed a conversion to political liberalism. In 1846, he announced a "political rudiment (*embrión*) of social regeneration, or a platonic plan to make Mexico content under the federal regime." His suggested reforms included closing the colegios of theology and jurisprudence for twenty

93. Quintana, *Estevan de Antuñano*, 2, 144–45; Antuñano, *Discurso analítico*, pp. 11–14.

94. Antuñano, *Economía política* (Feb. 1839), p. 7; "Economía política" (*Republicano*); letter to Alamán, Apr. 6, 1845, Antuñano Correspondence.

years, suppressing male religious communities, reducing the secular clergy by one-third, and instituting freedom of worship and colonization. Finally, he proposed disentailing mortmain property to underwrite a banco de avío in each state, for the purpose of promoting manufacturing and agriculture.[95]

Thus, Antuñano became a political liberal at the very time that Lucas Alamán's conservatism hardened into an ideology. Did these political positions, now crystallized, have any effect on economic ideas? Antuñano died in 1847, but his earlier economic arguments were expressed forcefully by the moderate-reformist *El Siglo* in 1850. Yet they were *also* presented by *El Universal*, perhaps even by Alamán himself. At first glance, then, the answer to the question appears negative.

This nineteenth-century tangle of political and economic views is part of the same one encountered in the all-embracing present-day concept of "revolution." What is confused are two kinds of change, two kinds of revolutionary transformation, rooted in distinct though intersecting historic models. The one revolution was political. Its model was France, but it embraced the entire Atlantic world. Identifying the principles of that revolution in the context of Mexico has been the main concern of this book. The other, the Industrial Revolution, coincided roughly in time with the political revolution. It entailed ideally, however, a process that bore little relation to politics—the change from an agrarian and rural society to one that was industrial and urban. Industrialization can coincide with political liberalization; it can be guided by liberal economic doctrine, as in England and the United States. Yet we have now learned from twentieth-century experience that economic development through industrialization can take place within a variety of political systems, guided by differing ideologies.

It is thus futile to force nineteenth-century approaches to the economic development of Mexico into the categories of political debate. Alamán and Antuñano, however imperfectly, introduced

95. Antuñano, *Economía política* (1846). His statement here is not to be taken necessarily as direct argument for the federal system. He was saying rather that, by accomplishing certain reforms, Mexico could be content under the federal system, then in process of being readopted.

into Mexico the idea and the reality of modern industry. They drew from the doctrines of economic liberalism, but they drew even more from Bourbon mercantilist policies of the eighteenth century. There was, of course, more consistency between political and economic views by those who advocated the doctrinaire approach to development. Mora, Zavala, and Manuel Ortiz de la Torre saw economic development as a spontaneous, or natural process, resting on the actions of the free individual. The effort to free the individual from corporate and monopolistic restrictions could be pursued in the economic as in the political sphere. In postindependence Mexico, however, this approach could be discredited as not leading to development at all, but rather to the perpetuation of a colonial economy, rural and agricultural at its base. Alamán and Antuñano by no means envisioned a modern urban, industrial society; but their ideas, rooted in eighteenth-century Spain, did initiate the "style" of economic development that has emerged in our time.[96]

There remains one final problem. Though *ideally* independent of political categories, in reality the debate over economic development was inevitably drawn into politics. The crucial element in this entanglement was the church. Several observers have pointed to the principal defect of Alamán's approach to development—that it attempted to ignore the entailed capital of the church. Alamán was even less anticlerical than were the architects of Spanish development, who at least had disentailed Jesuit property. This, of course, is one of the reasons why Jesús Reyes Heroles calls Lucas Alamán an "integral conservative," conservative in economics as well as in politics.[97] Alamán may have hoped that the church would invest voluntarily in industry, and indeed there is evidence that it did. Still, the vast temporal power of the church

96. Cf. Robert M. Will, "The Introduction of Classical Economics into Chile," *HAHR, 44* (1964), 1–21. Will stresses the durability of Bourbon conceptions of fomento "long after the teachings of the classical economists and the champions of economic liberalism were known in Chile" (p. 21).

97. Reyes Heroles, *Liberalismo, 3,* 425, 429, 457. He compares Alamán to Edmund Burke. See my critique of this view in "Alamán, Antuñano y la continuidad del liberalismo," *Historia mexicana, 11* (1961), 228–31. On Alamán and church capital, see also Chávez Orozco, *Historia,* pp. 357, 372–76. Chávez Orozco applies Marxist criteria and argues that it was necessary for Mexico, as for any nation, to eliminate feudal modes of production prior to industrialization.

was incompatible with the "spirit of enterprise" and with the modern industry that Alamán wanted to implant. It was the doctrinaire liberals, led by José María Luis Mora, who advanced a solution to this critical problem.

The inconsistencies of Alamán's position did not become apparent, however, until 1846, when the liberal-conservative debate burst forth. This may possibly explain Antuñano's final call for anticlerical reforms as a prerequisite to economic development. Except for the *El Universal* articles, which may or may not have been Alamán's, economic development figured little in the latter's postwar writings. His defense of the church, his attack upon liberal doctrines and the utilitarian spirit, his evocation of Hispanic values and traditions against the threat of the new society of the United States—all would logically close the door on economic modernization by any means. The debate over economic development thus became enmeshed in the ideological struggle which emerged after 1846, a struggle that was not resolved for two decades.

9

The Continuity of Liberalism

After leaving Mexico in 1834, José María Luis Mora spent his remaining years in exile. His life in Europe, mostly in Paris, was one of isolation, frustration, and in his eyes one of extreme poverty. He did find support in his long-time devoted servant, Juana Nava, who said Mora was like a father to her. In 1842 he apparently established a liaison with his housekeeper, an English-woman named Eliza Hoy, who claimed after his death that she bore him three children and that she deserved a share of his estate.[1] Mora kept in touch with Mexico through a considerable correspondence, and he had an occasional visit from a traveling countryman. For the most part, though, before 1846 he lived in obscurity.

Mora's publishing efforts ended in frustration. After the appearance of three volumes of *Mexico y sus revoluciones* in 1836 and of his *Obras sueltas* in 1837, his publisher Rosa turned over the manuscripts for the remaining five volumes of *Revoluciones* to an unknown "bookseller," Lecointe. We lose track of the negotiations thereafter, and of the manuscripts, which may today be collecting dust in some obscure corner of Paris. Mora did occasional legal chores for Mexicans in Paris; he began some translations. But by 1839 he was appealing to the Mexican minister in Madrid for work, any kind at any salary. "I am down to my last penny," he wrote.[2]

1. See Florstedt, "Liberal Role," pp. 544–48. There are two letters in the Mora Correspondence, 1845–56 (University of Texas), from Juana Nava, registering her deep feelings for him. Interestingly enough, she supported Eliza Hoy's claims to 3,000 pesos from Mora's estate.

2. Mora to Ignacio Valdivielso (Nov. 21, 1839), García, *Documentos, 6,* 21–22. There is an insurance policy in the Mora Documents, 1806–38, evaluating the possessions in his five-room apartment (13 Rue Blanche) at 44,000 francs. His was a genteel poverty, at worst.

Mora's correspondence during the dark years 1835–46 reveals at least three matters that continuously engaged his attention. He was a passionate bibliophile. This interest, already great in the 1820s, only increased when he found himself at the source of supply and without active involvements. If Mora was down to his last penny in 1839, it was partly because he put all his money into books. His papers contain hundreds of invoices from Paris book-sellers. He also bought regularly for his friends in Mexico, and they responded appreciatively.

Two of these friends, Bernardo Couto and Francisco Fagoaga, more than returned the favor by their patient and devoted atten-tion to Mora's three dilapidated properties—two large houses in Tacubaya and one on the Callejón de los Pajaritos in Mexico City proper. In 1834 Mora entrusted the rental and care of the proper-ties to Manuel Martínez del Campo and Fernando Batres. For several years they complained constantly of the problems of getting steady tenants (one of the houses was humid), of collect-ing rent, and particularly of the impossibility of securing a steady return for Mora after the repair bills were paid. Mora grew impatient at the lack of revenue. Batres resented Mora's implica-tion that he had managed poorly and dishonestly, and after 1840 withdrew. Ultimately, the thankless burden fell to Couto and Fagoaga. Throughout the early forties there was talk of selling the properties and furnishings, but both men were reluctant to pro-ceed because offers were low, and because, as Fagoaga put it, "you [Mora] will think them poorly sold." [3]

Couto and Fagoaga urged Mora to return and settle his affairs for himself. The problem of returning to Mexico obsessed Mora during the early 1840s. Another close friend, José María Gutié-rrez de Estrada, wrote, just prior to issuing his monarchist "letter," that only "with a complete variation in the political organization of the country," could Mora be assured of safety. [4] Fagoaga was

3. Fagoaga to Mora (Sept. 28, 1844), Mora Correspondence, 1794–1844. Fagoaga finally reported on Oct. 12, 1848, that he had sold all the furnishings except a Vermeil service. The properties, however, could not be then sold because the market was depressed. Many clerical holdings were being liquidated to pay bills of exchange the clergy had accepted during the war (García, *Documentos*, 6, 116). Mora's real estate was finally sold after his death, as was his library (see above, p. 77 n.).

4. Gutiérrez de Estrada to Mora (July 8, 1840), Mora Correspondence, 1794–1844.

more philosophical. In 1843 he said that Mora's situation in Mexico would be no different from that of the "rest of us."

> You would live . . . a martyr to the rage which it is impossible not to show continually on seeing the arbitrary manner in which everything is carried on. [Those in power] have no plan whatsoever of conduct other than getting what they can with miserable greed.[5]

Mora repeatedly questioned his friends on the advisablity of returning; repeatedly they concluded that there was little risk in his doing so. But Mora could never quite muster the resolve. On February 26, 1846, Fagoaga wrote welcoming Mora's apparent decision to come home the following August.[6] But the outbreak of the war or some other unknown obstacle intervened, and Mora never set sail. Instead, in December, he was rescued from oblivion by his appointment as minister to England by the newly established government of Valentín Gómez Farías.

Amid the bewildering events of 1847–49, liberal governments found themselves naturally turning to the man who had been the intellectual leader of the earlier reform movement. Mariano Otero and Luis de la Rosa, foreign ministers at this time, sought Mora's advice on policy questions. Both his diplomatic and extraofficial efforts were vigorous, as we have seen, but short-lived; for Mora's health was poor and could not withstand the rigors of London's climate. Mora had suffered from a tubercular condition for many years. By 1848 it became critical. During the summer of 1849 he went to France, seeking "a less misty sky and a less humid atmosphere," as well as relief in the spas of Vichy and Enghien. By December, however, he was writing Couto that "my illness is getting worse with the season. . . . Farewell, my dear Bernardo. I am exhausted." [7] His letters became briefer and more morbid. He again sought help in France, but this time he succumbed, in Paris on Bastille Day, 1850.

Mora's death was attended only by his faithful Juana; his burial was hastily arranged for by the Mexican consul. Benito Gómez

---

5. Fagoaga to Mora (July 22, 1843) , ibid.
6. Fagoaga to Mora, García, *Documentos, 6,* 54.
7. Mora to Couto (Dec. 1, 1849) , Mora Correspondence, 1845–56.

Farías, who was serving under Mora in London, hurried to Paris and obtained permission to have the body exhumed and reburied with appropriate solemnity in Montmartre Cemetery.[8] There it rested until June 1963, when his remains were brought to Mexico City, to be deposited permanently on June 24 in the Rotunda of Illustrious Men. The event was accorded modest commemorative importance.[9]

Mora had a small but important circle of friends. As we know, he was a leading figure in the Colegio de San Ildefonso during the early 1820s, and it seems that many of his closest associations were formed from his experience there. Bernardo Couto, Mora's most intimate friend, was first his student at San Ildefonso. Francisco Fagoaga, a few years his elder, was also a graduate. Luis Gonzaga Cuevas signed a letter to Mora in 1849, "your old friend and fellow collegian." [10] At least two of Mora's colleagues in the Mexico state congress, Domingo Lazo de la Vega and José Nicolás de Oláez, as well as the governor of the state, Melchor Múzquiz, attended San Ildefonso. José Julian Tornel and José María Bocanegra, both prominent in politics during the 1820s, were Mora's classmates.

His friendships with Francisco Fagoaga and with José María Gutiérrez de Estrada are of particular interest. Fagoaga came from one of the wealthiest and most distinguished Mexican families of the era. Fagoaga's father was the noble Marqués del Apartado, a leader along with his brother (Juan Bautista) and nephew (José María) in the mining revival of the preindependence era. The Fagoaga family had a wide reputation for its pious philanthropy.

8. Just prior to his death, Mora had named Benito Gómez Farías (son of Valentín) executor of his now-lost will. For the details of Mora's last days and the inglorious epilogue concerning the execution of his estate, see Florstedt, "Liberal Role," pp. 538 ff.

9. For the presidential decree, referring to Mora as a "precursor of the Reforma and of the Revolution," see El Nacional, June 20, 1963. Excerpts from the eulogy by Jesús Reyes Heroles, delivered in the chamber of deputies, can be found in Excelsior, June 25, 1963.

10. See García, Documentos, 6, 144. Early in 1840, Mora had been encouraged to return to Mexico by the fact that Cuevas was minister of relations. However, Luis G. Gordoa (another old friend from San Ildefonso) wrote on Oct. 26, informing Mora that Cuevas had just left the ministry and that he should postpone his plan (Mora Correspondence, 1794–1844). On Cuevas (1799–1867) see the introd. to his Porvenir de México, by Francisco Cuevas Cancino.

Francisco, in his later years, was given the responsibility of distributing his brother's fortune to numerous hospitals, convents, and orphanages. Fanny Calderon de la Barca was taken in by the three Fagoaga sisters in the 1840s, lived briefly in one of their haciendas, and accompanied them in many of their charitable works. Except for a brief period as foreign minister in 1832, Francisco, like his relatives, generally remained outside of politics; but one can assume his sentiments to have been conservative.[11]

One of Mora's closest friends was José María Gutiérrez de Estrada, the monarchist of 1840. Gutiérrez had married María Loreto Cortina, a sister of José Gómez de la Cortina (1799–1860), the inheritor of a noble title. Though born in Mexico, the count and his sister spent their early life in Europe where he served in the Spanish diplomatic corps until 1832. The Cortina family formed part of the Hispanophile aristocracy of Mexico City, which welcomed so warmly Spain's first ambassador to Mexico and his wife in 1840.[12] Between 1835 and 1847, Gutiérrez was Mora's most frequent correspondent. During much of that time Gutiérrez was also an expatriate, which undoubtedly drew the two men together. Though our evidence comes entirely from letters Gutiérrez wrote to Mora, it seems that Mora was undisturbed by his friend's monarchist pronouncement and increasingly conservative tendencies. Earlier, Mora had praised Gutiérrez' *Memoria* of 1835 (written upon leaving the post of minister of relations) as a "document which is destined to become immortal." Curiously enough, the *Memoria* contained much that was con-

11. The readily available biographical material on the Fagoaga family is contradictory, because the family had several branches and thus lent itself to geneological confusion. See "Biografía de D. Francisco Fagoaga [1788–1851]" in Alamán, *Documentos, 3,* 337–45; Sosa, *Biografías,* pp. 357–59; García, *Documentos,* "Noticias bio-bibliográficas de algunos alumnos distinguidos del colegio de San Pedro, San Pablo y San Ildefonso de México," *19* (Mexico, Bouret, 1908), 209–11; Calderon, *Life in Mexico,* pp. 415–17, 503–04, 531, and passim; Howe, *Mining Guild,* passim. A study of such a prominent and respected, yet generally nonpolitical, family as the Fagoagas would reveal much about the era 1810–54.

12. The Calderons were on intimate terms with the Cortina family ("we dine [with them] nearly every Sunday"), including Gutiérrez de Estrada. See *Life in Mexico,* p. 275 and passim. In his later life, Count Cortina was an exceptionally prolific literary scholar who held several public offices (Sosa, *Biografías,* pp. 274–85). See also Manuel Romero de Terreros, "Prologo," *Conde de la Cortina, Poliantea* (Mexico, UNAM, 1944).

servative in tone. In 1842, Gutiérrez even wrote Mora that the two men were in complete agreement on the ills of the country.[13]

What conclusions can we draw from this scattered evidence on Mora's associations? It is apparent that social ties among Mexico's elite could transcend "liberal" and "conservative" lines. Mora was close to Valentín Gómez Farías, a middle-class doctor from outlying Zacatecas, who was the leading liberal politico of the era. But several of Mora's good friends were conservative aristocrats. Luis G. Cuevas wrote the pro-Iturbide *Porvenir de México* in 1851 and later served the conservative cause from 1858 to 1861. He married into one of the great families, the Vivancos. The Fagoagas and the Cortinas were two of the principal families of the metropolis.[14] Mora remained on the edge of this society, but his liberal principles did not cause personal ties to be broken, at least before 1847.

This study commenced with a description of the ideological conflict that became solidified between 1847 and 1853, in the cruel aftermath of foreign invasion. Conservatives and liberals, probing the causes and implications of national disaster, presented irreconcilable programs which by 1853 pointed to inevitable civil conflict. In subsequent chapters, however, we noted numerous areas of coalescence between "liberals" and "conservatives." José María Luis Mora and Lucas Alamán, for example, are often taken to represent the contrasting ideological positions of the pre-Reforma era, yet there were many points of similarity in their ideas.

On the one hand, we have seen Alamán's early attraction to liberal precepts. He advocated the Lancasterian system of education in the early 1820s. As a delegate to the liberal Spanish cortes he argued for a loosening of mercantilist restrictions on the mining industry. Adam Smith loomed large in his early economic

13. Gutiérrez de Estrada to Mora (Apr. 18, 1842), Mora Correspondence, 1794–1844. Gutiérrez' *Memoria de la secretaría de estado y del despacho de relaciones interiores y exteriores* (Mexico, 1835) attacked the "civil and religious tyranny" of 1833 (p. 13), praised the "solidification of institutions" in Chile (p. 2), and called for more study of colonial history (pp. 44–45). It also emphasized the necessity of individual guarantees. See also Mora, *Obras*, p. 162.

14. As indicated above, Mme. Calderon's account portrayed this postindependence society vividly. She was much impressed by the overt nostalgia for colonial times among those she knew. See *Life in Mexico*, p. 475.

ideas. During the twenties he admired the United States and showed no antipathy toward the utilitarian underpinning of its society. Alamán served the incipient republic as its chief minister for several years. In 1823 he congratulated Mora on the latter's proposed reform for the curriculum of San Ildefonso. Alamán's own educational reforms of 1830 may well have influenced Mora in 1833.

On the other hand, Mora showed affinity for a number of Alamán's conservative principles. Both were part of the constitutional monarchist party of José María Fagoaga in the early 1820s. Mora had centralist sympathies, despite his later adherence to doctrinaire federalism. He was ambivalent toward the heritage of Spain; he defended the memory of Cortés and the conquistador's role as founder of the Mexican nation. Alamán even quoted Mora's favorable estimate of Cortés in his *Disertaciones.* Alamán's newspaper, *El Tiempo,* also cited Mora in 1846, this time using Mora's faintly aristocratic constitutional liberalism as support for the newspaper's own notion that the country should be governed by an aristocracy of merit.[15] Like Alamán, Mora showed hostility toward the United States after 1847. He argued that colonization should be limited to Spaniards and Catholics in order to fortify Mexico's "nationality" against subversive North American influences. Most of all, we have seen Mora's reaction to the threat of Indian upheaval, both in his interpretation of the Hidalgo revolt of 1810 and in his extreme alarm over the Caste Wars of 1847–49. When faced with social revolt by Mexico's ethnic majority, Mora put forth a Creole concept of nationality similar to that of Lucas Alamán.

Despite these numerous areas of affinity and coalescence, we cannot escape the reality of ideological conflict. Upon what, then, did this conflict rest? In the first place, it did not really crystallize until 1846 with the appearance of a self-conscious, militant conservatism. Secondly, the clash embraced issues that were primarily political. The most obvious of these was the form of government itself—republic or monarchy. It may have been monarchism that

15. See Alamán, *Disertaciones,* 2, 61–62; *El Tiempo,* Jan. 26, 1846, which quoted from Mora's 1830 essay calling for citizenship to be legally limited to property holders (in *Obras,* pp. 631 ff.).

ultimately separated Mora and Gutiérrez de Estrada. Though we
have evidence that Mora was an early supporter of monarchy, after
1846 he became committed to defending the republic and sent
home reports on the activities of Mexican monarchists in Europe.
Correspondence between Mora and Gutiérrez de Estrada broke
off after 1847.[16] In 1853, Gutiérrez wrote to Alamán as a kindred
spirit, expressing his complete disillusionment with any ready
solution for Mexico's problems. Nevertheless, Gutiérrez de Estrada persisted for a decade until he found a willing candidate for
the Mexican throne.[17]

More profound than the clash over governmental forms, however, was the question of the church. In the case of Mora, anticlericalism was the one aspect of his thought that always stood out
in sharp contrast to that of Lucas Alamán. It was the proclerical
tendencies of the Bustamante regime after 1830 that drove Mora
into the reformist opposition. The periods that yield the most
evidence of coalescence between liberals and conservatives, 1821–
30 and 1834–46, were ones in which the church issue was muted.
The same can be said for the remainder of the nineteenth
century.

Anticlericalism was a deep and personal matter with Mora.
Couto wrote in 1856 that it had carried him to great extremes.

> Many years before his [Mora's] death, he had divorced him-
> self from the functions of the priesthood. This . . . explains
> the greater part of the events of his life which ran its course in
> affliction and bitterness of heart. Few men have experienced
> less peace and contentment of soul.[18]

Mora left explicit instructions that one-fourth of his estate be
given to charitable enterprises, provided they under no circum-

16. The last letter was Gutiérrez to Mora (Apr. 29, 1847), García, *Documentos,*
6, 90–94. They shared a hostility toward the United States, and both men sought
European aid to save Mexico from annexation. Cf. Gutiérrez, *México* (1848), pp.
17, 36, and above, p. 213.

17. See letter, Gutiérrez to Alamán (Jan. 20, 1853), Alamán, *Documentos, 4,*
92–95. Gutiérrez de Estrada later wrote *México y el archiduque Fernando Maxi-*
miliano de Austria (Mexico, 1863), describing his long efforts in behalf of monarchy.

18. Couto, "Mora," p. 888b.

stances be "ecclesiastical entails" or be "administered or supervised by ecclesiastical persons." [19] Though Mora's public concerns
were drawn to other matters after 1846, his correspondence reveals
a continuing militancy on the church. In 1848 Mora wrote privately to Luis de la Rosa that the church "is one of the corporations most interested in realizing such [monarchist] projects, and
this is a new and potent reason for stripping it of all civil power
and influence." [20] Up until his death, Mora continued to inspire a
revived anticlerical liberalism which was translated into policy a
decade later.

The clash of political ideas in the pre-Reforma period was
carried on within Mexico's social elite. Creole Mexico, whether
liberal or conservative, stiffened at the prospect of "democracy"
—active participation in politics by a Vicente Guerrero, by the
Maya Indians of Yucatán, or by the followers of Eleuterio Quiróz
in the Huasteca. Mora's friendships and associations demonstrate
that there were social assumptions that ran deeper than the liberal-
conservative conflict. Social and personal bonds among Mexico's
elite were strained after 1847, and partially cracked during the
Reforma, but the subsequent decades show that Creole social conservatism had great resilience throughout the nineteenth century.
In the long run, theoretical liberalism undermined traditional
social attitudes in Mexico, but there is little evidence that this had
happened by 1853. Despite the occasional (and peripheral) flashes
of social radicalism, liberalism during the age of Mora remained
an elite concept.[21]

We can discern the structure of Mexican political liberalism in
the years 1821 to 1834, principally in the thought of José María
Luis Mora. Central to this structure was a tension between aug-

19. Instructions to Fernando Batres (Apr. 8, 1836), Mora Correspondence, 1794–
1844.

20. Mora to Rosa (May 31, 1848), Correspondencia particular del ministro de
relaciones (Sec. Rel. Ext.).

21. Kalman Silvert has made the distinction in modern situations between
ideological conflict and the more critical form of *value* conflict in society. "Ideological conflict will always accompany value clash, but value clash will not always
accompany ideological dispute." Perhaps this distinction is relevant to mid-
nineteenth-century Mexico. See "Some Psychocultural Factors in the Politics of
Conflict and Conciliation: Setting up the Problem," Paper delivered at American
Political Science Association (1965), p. 11.

menting guarantees for individual liberty and strengthening state authority to combat corporate privilege. It was a tension that existed within liberalism throughout the Atlantic world and that can be most clearly seen in the dialectic of two typical forms, the French and the English. Historically, the French Revolution best revealed the contention within political liberalism, and thus became the point of departure for this study. France provides the classic example of a libertarian and egalitarian ideology directed against an old regime. The early phases of the French Revolution introduced the basic constitutional problem of relevance to Mexico—how to build a regime of constitutional limitation on authority in a situation where historic political institutions were weak. The problem in Hispanic countries was similar but more acute than in France. Not only were historic institutions weaker in Hispanic countries than in France, but the tradition of authority was stronger and the corporations more entrenched. The Revolution obliterated clerical and noble privilege in France. In Hispanic nations, at least clerical privilege remained intact.

Nevertheless, it was the postrevolutionary Frenchman, Benjamin Constant, who most clearly inspired Mexican constitutional liberalism in the first decade after independence. Mora and his colleagues identified their situation with his and tried to erect constitutional barriers to protect the individual. In the specific work of organization, the Mexican constitution-makers relied upon the more immediate Spanish Constitution of 1812, akin as it was to previous French models. But Constant provided the theoretical impulse for constitutionalism, just as he did for the reconvened Spanish cortes in 1820. Mora took seriously Constant's concern for "a new kind of federalism," based upon some measure of municipal administrative autonomy—difficult though this was to implement in Mexico. The delegates to the Mexico state congress struggled to establish independent judicial institutions (especially the jury system). They sought individual liberty and constitutional stability in the institution of private property. Moreover, Mora led a courageous and unpopular fight to apply constitutionalist precepts to a burning sociopolitical issue—the expulsion of the Spaniards.

The weakness of constitutional liberalism in the Mexican situation became apparent after 1830. The reality of entrenched corporate privilege—epitomized by the clerical and military fueros and by the vast property holdings of the church—could no longer be overlooked, as it had been in the 1820s. The state, obliterated by the removal of the Spanish Crown at independence, must recover its sovereignty if equality under the law, and ultimately individualism, was to have meaning. Thus José María Luis Mora turned his back on constitutionalism. Benjamin Constant and postrevolutionary France suddenly became less relevant to him, and he sought guidance instead in the Spanish reform tradition of Charles III and the Cortes of Cádiz.

In this phase of political liberalism it was Gaspar Melchor de Jovellanos who spoke most directly to the Mexican situation. As a liberal aristocrat, Jovellanos had sought a revival of Spain's historic constitution at the same time that he had supported the anticlerical reforms of Bourbon enlightened despotism. His dilemma became more acute when he found himself in 1809 at the head of a de facto revolutionary junta which rested implicity upon a doctrine of popular sovereignty. Mora saw this dilemma as his own in the Mexico of 1833. The "constitution," as he saw it, had to give way to a fiscally strong administrative state which could secularize society, institute legal equality, and yet avoid the democratic extremes of the French Jacobins or of the Cádiz radicals. Thus, it was the Spanish Bourbon tradition that provided the most relevant model for anticorporate reform in Mexico.

The social philosophy of Mexican liberalism was derived from utilitarianism. The concept of Helvétius, Bentham, and Jovellanos that society was ideally a multitude of individuals freely pursuing their own interests, had great appeal in Mexico. The test of "utility" could be applied universally to entrenched privilege and outworn institutions: Did an institution or corporate entity as it functioned enhance the greatest good for the greatest number? Though the utilitarian ideal could be and was used to reinforce the drive for individual rights during the 1820s, it figured most prominently in the reformist thought of the 1830s.

Mexican society, in Mora's view, must be based on the secular *hombre positivo*, the individual citizen of the nation, freed from corporate restrictions and loyalties in order to pursue rationally

his own interests. The result would be inevitable social harmony
and progress. At the heart of the utilitarian ideal was educational
reform. Education must be secularized and must emphasize the
useful rather than the theological. Utilitarian theory, as it was applied in the late eighteenth and early nineteenth centuries, also
strengthened the liberal attachment to private property. The
social objective of the 1833 reformers was an ever stronger class of
responsible property holders. This objective theoretically included
the Indian, but in practice it perpetuated traditional attitudes
toward the depressed majority of the population. Colonization by
Europeans was the liberal panacea for augmenting the rural
middle class and "fusing" the Indians with other groups.

Critical to the liberal social design for Mexico was the reluctant
acceptance of large lay properties. These could not be attacked as
the holdings of a legal estate as they were in France, and thus they
were tolerated as "private property" along with the preferred
small holdings. This attitude toward lay latifundia is one key to
understanding nineteenth-century liberalism as an elite concept.
In the economic realm Mora and his colleagues followed doctrinaire views. Under a regime of laissez-faire, the basic economic
unit of the new Mexico was to be the rural property holder.
Mexico was to continue primarily as an agricultural and mining
nation, following the international division of labor that characterized the "natural" system of the liberal economists. Mora had
little use for a national manufacturing industry, "forced" by
government intervention. His view of economic development was
essentially individualist, rural, and agrarian in its orientation.
Capital would accumulate naturally when corporate ecclesiastical
property passed into the hands of a rural bourgeoisie.

Except for the attack upon the church, the socioeconomic
theories of the reformers made important concessions to rural,
agrarian, and traditional patterns. There were also limits to the
degree of secularization intended by the liberals. This was the case
everywhere in the early nineteenth century, except in the mind of
an extremist like Jeremy Bentham. These limits, however, were
particularly apparent in Mexico. José María Luis Mora ultimately
balked on the question of toleration for non-Catholics, as did the
later constitution-makers of 1856. He was reluctant to advocate a

radical separation of church and state and settled instead for state control or "protection" of the church. His nationalized system of higher education provided for "ecclesiastical sciences" as one of its six divisions of study. He greatly admired Bishop Abad y Queipo and even condoned, in the context of 1799, the latter's defense of ecclesiastical immunities. Mora made frequent reference to the policies of "Catholic" countries, revealing his assumption that in such cultures there were inherent obstacles to achieving a "secular mentality." Thus, liberalism in Mexico cannot be considered as an integral philosophy of modernization.

Within this context, then, the distinguishing feature of Mexican liberalism was the predominance of a strong state in the political realm accompanied by an economic regime of unfettered individualism. There was a conflict within European utilitarian theory which supported this dichotomy, but it also grew from the particular situation of Mexico. Bentham had seen the necessity of a Legislator who would reconcile individual interests above political conflict, and he had favored enlightened despotism in his early years. Mora similarly admired Charles III and sought a fiscally strong state buttressed by a modern bureaucracy. Yet, like Bentham, he saw no need for the state to guide the economy. It should be left to autonomous interests. This dichotomy within liberalism has had a decisive effect on subsequent thought and policy in Mexico.

The United States as a model republic loomed large in the minds of pre-Reforma liberals. Its political institutions, particularly federalism, appeared to be the realization of constitutionalist ideals. To Mexican utilitarians like Lorenzo de Zavala, Estevan de Antuñano, or José María Luis Mora, North American society was a utopia where the spirit of enterprise prevailed and where individuals were able to combine their own advantage with that of their fellow citizens. Although the United States revealed the goal of liberal aspirations, whether constitutionalist, reformist, or utilitarian, it offered no method or theory for achieving this goal. Method and theory could only be sought in continental Europe, where social and institutional traditions were more analogous to those of Mexico. Mora saw more clearly than did some of his contemporaries the basic irrelevance of the United States as a model for liberal reform, a point which enhances his significance.

The United States invasion of Mexico in 1847 confused the liberals, for theoretically their liberalism provided no cultural or social values, other than those of the aggressor, upon which they could base a nationalist reaction. Mora called for Catholic immigrants in order to preserve Mexico's nationality, but it was a proposal that logically undercut his liberalism. Maintaining Mexican cultural identity in the face of a dazzling liberal society to the North has become a permanent problem in the modernization of Mexico.

It is in these structural elements that we can discover the continuity of Mexican liberalism since independence. We begin with the assumption that Mexican liberalism was a historic entity that formed part of a larger body of thought and policy in the Atlantic world. It arose from the interaction of outside ideological influences and native institutional peculiarities. Liberalism in Mexico cannot, then, be profitably regarded as a protean and all-embracing concept, adaptable to every turn of contemporary ideology. As a historic concept, early nineteenth-century liberalism had a central orientation that was epitomized in the thought of José María Luis Mora. A figure like Mariano Otero—however much his keen social analysis, his critical view of property relations, and his adherence to federalism might have present-day appeal—was essentially peripheral to this central orientation. The political contention of the 1820s and the 1830s between constitutional limitations on authority and the dictates of a strong reformist state can be seen reenacted during the Reforma and particularly in the years 1867–76. Constitutionalism was temporarily smothered by the organicist positivism of the Díaz period. It reemerged in the drive for federalism, municipal autonomy, and general limitations on authority, which characterized the ideas of Madero, Carranza, and the delegates to the 1917 convention. Yet the antistatist impulse of the years 1910 to 1920, as in prior periods of reform, was again forced to yield. The recovery of constitutionalism, however newly defined for our day, persists as a problem for contemporary Mexico.

Pursuing further the question of continuity, we can find in the age of Mora a model that will help us understand the present drift of socioeconomic policy in a Mexico emerging from revolution. Of most relevance to liberal political reform in the 1830s was the experience of Bourbon Spain. In turning from politics to economic development, it was again the inspiration of late eighteenth-century Spain that prevailed. The doctrinaire liberal approach to development was forced to give way to the more pragmatic conception of Lucas Alamán, rooted in Spanish efforts to modernize the mining and textile industries through government intervention.

Alamán and Antuñano did not reject economic liberalism, any more than did the architects of modernization under Charles III and Charles IV. Corporate economic monopoly was blended with liberal precepts in the interests of an independent national economy. Cannot Mexico's industrialization since 1940 be best seen in these terms? Vibrant economic individualism of utilitarian inspiration continues in concert with mercantilistic privilege, under the increasingly technocratic guidance of the state. The emergence after 1917 of new corporate entities, the peasant ejido and the labor union (in anomalous combination with revived liberal anticlericalism), has also followed the orientation of late eighteenth-century policy. Did not the anticlerical Bourbons create two corporations in New Spain, the army and the mining guild?

Mexico's twentieth-century effort to modernize a traditional Hispanic society can be more accurately interpreted as the continuity of Bourbon patterns, infused with liberalism, than as a recovery of the traditional Hapsburg patrimonial state.[22] To argue the latter is to regard Western liberalism as exotic to Hispanic American culture and to regard the period 1760 to 1920 as an alien interlude in Mexican history. It is undeniable that liberalism in Mexico has been conditioned by a traditional Hispanic ethos, and that as a system of values its strength has been

22. The latter has been argued by Morse, "Heritage," pp. 169–72. This view is also implicit in Frank Tannenbaum's interpretation of the Constitution of 1917, in *Mexico: The Struggle for Peace and Bread* (New York, Knopf, 1950). Ultimately, to test the relevance of the Bourbon as opposed to the Hapsburg model for twentieth-century Mexico, it will be necessary to distinguish carefully between the two in their own historical context, a major task ahead for historians.

diluted. Yet seen as a part of the continuity of Bourbon policies, the legacy of liberalism has been significant. A central assumption of this study is that one cannot properly separate "Hispanic" and "Western." Hispanic America, like Spain, is a part (albeit a peculiar one) of the Atlantic world of the West and can only be considered in that context. So, liberalism, a principal current of Western thought, has left its enduring mark on Mexico, just as it has on Spain itself.

Bibliography

This book rests primarily on published materials, some of them readily available, others quite obscure. My main concern has been to study the assumptions underlying thought and policy during the postindependence generation in Mexico. Liberalism was a political idea, and since the age was one of fervent political expression through books, pamphlets, journals, newspapers, and legislative debates, my first task has been to analyze these materials. I have also examined the legislation of the first half of the nineteenth century on a variety of questions related to liberalism. Laws are a good guide to the mentality of an age.

Since José María Luis Mora was the central liberal theorist of the years 1821–53 and is the focus of this study, his published works were my most important source. He was also editor of three weekly journals, *Semanario político y literario de Méjico* (1821–22), *El Observador de la república mexicana* (1827–28, 1830), and *El Indicador de la federación mejicana* (1833–34). Though he did not write all the articles published in these journals, there is little they contain that departs from his views. Mora's formal contributions were reprinted in his *Obras sueltas* (1837). But a close reading of the non-Mora articles in the journals, of the European material that was reprinted, and of the frequent comments by editor Mora, has aided me in understanding Mora's assumptions.

Almost as significant as Mora's formal writings are the debates of the first constitutional congress of the State of Mexico, recorded in the ten volumes of *Actas* (1824–31). They have seldom been used by historians. Not only do they provide further evidence on the general ideas of Mora and his fellow legislators, but they open up the investigation of many questions of special concern to the incipient Mexican state and nation. I found a few revealing manuscripts pertaining to congressional policy toward village lands in the Archivo de la Cámara de Diputados of Mexico State in Toluca.

Mora's official correspondence as minister to England has been edited by Luis Chávez Orozco (1931). Mora's voluminous personal papers (in three groupings) are housed in the García Collection at the University of Texas. Although more valuable to the biographer than to the intellectual historian, these papers have yielded a number of important items. A selection from the letters written to Mora was edited by Génaro García in 1906, but there are many still in manuscript which I have found of value. Unfortunately, the Mora papers include little written by him, nor was I able to track down such Mora manuscripts elsewhere.

I have studied the published writings of Lucas Alamán, Lorenzo de Zavala, Mariano Otero, Estevan de Antuñano, Melchor Ocampo (before 1853), Servando Teresa de Mier, José Joaquín Fernández de Lizardi, José María Gutiérrez de Estrada, and those of many lesser spokesmen of the era. I also utilized a collection of manuscript letters from Estevan de Antuñano to Lucas Alamán (1844–45). Some pamphlets and most newspaper editorials were anonymous. Unfortunately, no one has made a close study of early nineteenth-century newspapers, so there is still much guesswork involved in identifying editorial spokesmen. I have used with benefit the principal Mexico City newspapers, *Águila mexicana* and *El Sol* in the 1820s, *El Fénix de la libertad* and *El Telégrafo* in the early 1830s, *El Cosmopolita* and *El Mosquito mexicano* in the late 1830s and early 1840s, and *El Siglo XIX, El Monitor republicano, El Tiempo,* and *El Universal* in the 1840s and early 1850s. Numerous others were of occasional value.

Apart from the more easily obtainable material, I have found scarce newspapers and pamphlets in a dozen or so repositories, both in this country and in Mexico. In Mexico, the most useful were the Lafragua Collection of the Biblioteca Nacional, the Basave Collection of the Biblioteca de México, the Cuevas Collection of the Colegio Máximo de la Provincia Mexicana de la Compañía de Jesús, the private collection of Antuñano pamphlets held by José Miguel Quintana, the Hemeroteca Nacional (newspapers), and the Hemeroteca of the Secretaría de Hacienda y Crédito Público. In the United States, I have relied principally on the Bancroft Library of the University of California, Berkeley, the University of Texas, the Sutro Collection of the California State Library, San Francisco, the New York Public Library, and Yale University. I also found rare items in Widener Library and the Law Library of Harvard University, in the Library of Congress, and in the Lehigh University Library.

The following bibliographical guides have been particularly useful:

Castañeda, Carlos E., and Jack A. Dabbs, *Guide to the Latin American Manuscripts in the University of Texas Library*, Cambridge, Harvard University Press, 1939.

Colín, Mario, *Bibliografía general del estado de México*, 2 vols. Mexico, Jus, 1963.

Dictionary Catalogue of the History of the Americas, New York Public Library, 28 vols. Boston, G. K. Hall, 1961.

Gans, A. I., ed., *Supplement to the Catalogue of Mexican Pamphlets in the Sutro Collection*, 3 vols. San Francisco, California State Library, 1941.

Ker, Anita M., *Mexican Government Publications*, Washington, Library of Congress, 1940.

Luquiens, Frederick B., *Spanish American Literature in the Yale University Library*, New Haven, Yale University Press, 1939.

Millares Carlo, Agustín, *Repertorio bibliográfico de los archivos mexicanos y de los europeos y norteamericanos de interés para la historia de México*, Mexico, Universidad Nacional Autónoma Mexicana, 1959.

Palau y Dulcet, Antonio, *Manual del librero hispano-americano*, 7 vols. Barcelona, Librería Anticuaria, 1923–27.

Quintana, José Miguel, "Estevan de Antuñano," *Boletín bibliográfico de la secretaría de hacienda y crédito público*, June 15, 1955.

Radin, Paul, ed., *An Annotated Bibliography of the Poems and Pamphlets of J. J. Fernández de Lizardi*, Occasional Papers, Mexican History Series, 2, San Francisco, California State Library, 1940.

———, *Catalogue of Mexican Pamphlets in the Sutro Collection*, 10 parts, San Francisco, California State Library, 1939.

Sabin, Joseph, *Bibliotheca Americana. A Dictionary of Books Relating to America*, 29 vols. New York, Bibliographical Society of America, 1868–1936.

Spain and Spanish America in the Libraries of the University of California, 2 vols. Berkeley, University of California Press, 1928–30.

Union List of Latin American Newspapers in Libraries in the United States, comp. Arthur E. Gropp, Washington, Pan American Union, 1953.

Vance, John T., and Helen L. Clagett, *A Guide to the Law and Legal Literature of Mexico*, Washington, Library of Congress, 1945.

The alphabetical list of sources that follows is limited to items cited in the footnotes and in the text. *Hispanic American Historical Review* has been abbreviated to *HAHR*, Universidad Nacional Autónoma Mexicana to UNAM.

Abad y Queipo, Manuel, "Escrito presentado a Don Manuel Sisto Espinosa" (1809), in Mora, *Obras sueltas*, pp. 231–40.

———, "Representación a nombre de los labradores y comerciantes de Valladolid de Michoacán" (1805), in Mora, *Obras sueltas*, pp. 214–30.

———, "Representación a la primera rejencia" (1810), in Mora, *Obras sueltas*, pp. 258–64.

———, "Representación sobre la inmunidad personal del clero" (1799), in Mora, *Obras sueltas*, pp. 174–214.

Actas del congreso constituyente del estado libre de México, 10 vols. Mexico and Toluca, 1824–31.

Águila mexicana, Mexico, Apr. 15, 1823–28 (?).

Alamán, Lucas, *Disertaciones sobre la historia de la república megicana, desde la época de la conquista que los españoles hicieron . . . hasta la independencia*, 3 vols. Mexico, 1844–49.

———, *Documentos diversos*, 4 vols. Mexico, Jus, 1945–47.

———, *Historia de Méjico desde los primeros movimientos que prepararon su independencia en el año de 1808, hasta la época presente*, 5 vols. Mexico, 1849–52.

———, "Instrucción para el establecimiento de escuelas, según los principios de la enseñanza mútua, presentada a la excma. diputación provincial de México, por . . . diputado en las cortes de España por la provincia de Guanajuato," *La Sabatina universal, 1*, 266–74, 279–99 (Sept. 28, Oct. 5, 12, 1822).

[———], *Un Regalo de año nuevo para el señor Rocafuerte*, Mexico, 1832.

Algunos Mexicanos, *Manifiesto a la nación*, n. p., n. d. (1851?).

Alza de prohibiciones. Artículos publicados en el periódico titulado: el universal, Mexico, 1851.

Antuñano Correspondence, Quintana Collection, 1844–45.

Antuñano, Estevan de, *Ampliación, aclaración y corrección a los principales puntos del manifiesto sobre el algodón*, Puebla, 1833.

———, *Breve Memoria del estado que guarda la fábrica de hilados de algodón constancia mexicana*, Puebla, 1837.

———, *La Carta feudal de México o sea consejos de Mercator sobre la industria mexicana*, Puebla, 1846.

———, *Discurso analítico de algunos puntos de moral y economía política de México*, Puebla, 1834.

———, *Economía política. Documentos (en doce cartas) para la historia de la industria moderna de algodones en México*, Puebla, 1843.

———, *Economía política en México*, Puebla, July 1838.

————, *Economía política en México,* Puebla, Feb. 1839.

————, *Economía política en México.* Puebla, June 1839.

————, *Economía política en México. Teoría fundamental de la industria de algodones en México,* Puebla, Aug. 1840.

————, *Economía política en México,* Puebla, Mar. 1844.

————, *Economía política en México,* Puebla, Oct. 1845.

————, *Economía política en México,* Puebla, Dec. 1845.

————, "Economía política en México. Insurrección industrial," *Republicano,* Aug. 15, 1846.

————, *Economía política en México. Insurrección industrial,* reprint (n.p., n.d.) of letter to *El Monitor republicano,* Oct. 23, 1846.

————, *Insurrección industrial. Economía política en México,* Puebla, 1846.

————, *Memoria breve de la industria manufacturera en México,* Puebla, 1835.

————, "¡¡¡Mexicanos!!! El primer asunto de la patria—insurrección para la independencia industrial fabril de México," *El Siglo XIX,* Dec. 2, 1845.

————, *Pensamientos para la regeneración industrial de México,* Puebla, 1837.

————, *El Primer Asunto de la patria, el algodón. Manifiesto sobre el algodón manufacturado y en greña,* Puebla, 1833.

————, *Ventajas políticas civiles fabriles y domésticas que por dar ocupación también a las mujeres en las fábricas de maquinaria moderna que se están levantando en México, deben recibirse,* Puebla, 1837.

Archivo de la Cámara de Diputados, Toluca, Carpetas 19–20, expedientes 212, 273.

Arnáiz y Freg, Arturo, ed., *La Intervención francesa y el imperio de Maximiliano,* Mexico, Inst. Francés de la América Latina, 1965.

————, "Prologo," *José María Luis Mora, ensayos, ideas y retratos,* Mexico, UNAM, 1941.

————, "Prologo," *Lucas Alamán, semblanzas e ideario,* Mexico, UNAM, 1939.

Artola, Miguel, *Los Orígenes de la España contemporanea,* 2 vols. Madrid, Inst. de Estudios Políticos, 1959.

El Atleta, Mexico, Dec. 21, 1829–May 9, 1830.

Baker, Richard D., "The Judicial Control of Constitutionality in Mexico: a Study of the *Juicio de Amparo,*" Ph.D. dissertation, University of North Carolina, 1962.

Bancroft, Hubert H., *History of Mexico,* 6 vols. San Francisco, 1883–88.

Barquera, Juan Wenceslao, *Disertación económico-política sobre los medios de aumentar la población de los estados-unidos mexicanos en su ilustración y riqueza*, Mexico, 1825.

Bazant, Jan, "Evolution of the Textile Industry of Puebla, 1544–1845," *Comparative Studies in Society and History*, 7 (1965), 56–69.

———, "Tres Revoluciones mexicanas," *Historia mexicana, 10* (1960), 220–42.

Becker, Carl, *The Heavenly City of the Eighteenth-Century Philosophers*, New Haven, Yale University Press, 1932.

Belaunde, Victor A., *Bolívar and the Political Thought of the Spanish American Revolution*, Baltimore, Johns Hopkins University Press, 1938.

Belgrano, Mario C., "Benjamin Constant y el constitucionalismo argentino," *Boletín del instituto de historia argentina "Doctor Emilio Ravignani," 6*, 2d ser. (1961), 1–57.

Benson, Nettie Lee, *La Diputación provincial y el federalismo mexicano*, Mexico, El Colegio de México, 1955.

———, ed., *Mexico and the Spanish Cortes, 1810–1822*, Austin, University of Texas Press, 1966.

———, "The Plan of Casa Mata," *HAHR, 25* (1945), 45–56.

———, "Servando Teresa de Mier, Federalist," *HAHR, 28* (1948), 514–25.

———, "Washington: Symbol of the United States in Mexico, 1800–1823," *The Library Chronicle of the University of Texas, 2* (1947), 175–82.

Bentham, Jeremy, *A Fragment on Government and An Introduction to the Principles of Morals and Legislation*, ed. W. H. Harrison, Oxford, Blackwell, 1960.

———, *Teoría de las penas legales*, 2 vols. Paris, 1825.

———, *Theory of Legislation*, ed. C. K. Ogden, New York, Harcourt, 1931. Translation of *Traités de législation civile et pénale*, ed. Etienne Dumont, 3 vols. Paris, 1802.

———, *Works*, ed. J. Bowring, 11 vols. Edinburg, 1838–43.

Berlin, Isaiah, *Two Concepts of Liberty*, Oxford, Oxford University Press, 1958.

Bernstein, Harry, *Modern and Contemporary Latin America*, New York, Lippincott, 1952.

Berthe, J. P., "Note," *Annales Economies, Sociétés, Civilisations, 20* (1965), 1256–58.

Bloch, Marc, *Feudal Society*, Chicago, University of Chicago Press, 1961.

Bocanegra, José María, *Disertación apologética del sistema federal,* Mexico, 1825.

Browning, W. E., "Joseph Lancaster, James Thomson, and the Lancasterian System of Mutual Instruction, With Special Reference to Hispanic America," *HAHR, 4* (1921), 49–98.

Burgin, Miron, *Economic Aspects of Argentine Federalism,* Cambridge, Harvard University Press, 1946.

Burke, Edmund, *Reflections on the Revolution in France,* London, Dent, 1910.

Bustamante, Carlos María de, *Cuadro histórico de la revolución de la américa mexicana,* 6 vols. Mexico, 1823–32.

Calderon de la Barca, Frances E., *Life in Mexico: The Letters of Fanny Calderon de la Barca,* eds. Howard T. and Marion H. Fisher, Garden City, Doubleday, 1966.

Callcott, Wilfred H., *Church and State in Mexico, 1822–1857,* Durham, Duke University Press, 1926.

Campomanes, Pedro Rodríguez de, *Tratado de la regalía de amortización,* Madrid, 1821.

Ceán Bermúdez, Juan Agustín, *Memorias para la vida del excmo. señor D. Gaspar Melchor de Jove Llanos,* Madrid, 1814.

Chávez Orozco, Luis, ed., *La Gestión diplomática del Doctor Mora,* Archivo histórico diplomático mexicano, 35, Mexico, Sec. Rel. Ext., 1931.

———, *Historia de México, 1808–1836,* Mexico, Patria, 1947.

———, ed., *Los Industriales mexicanos y el comercio exterior de México 1848–1852,* Colección de documentos para la historia del comercío exterior de México, 3, Mexico, Banco Nacional de Comercio, 1959.

Chevalier, François, "Conservateurs et libéraux au Mexique. Essai de sociologie et géographie politiques de l'indépendance a l'intervention française," *Cahiers d'histoire mondiale, 8* (1964), 457–74.

———, "Un Facteur décisif de la révolution agraire au Mexique: le soulèvement de Zapata," *Annales Economies, Sociétés, Civilisations, 16* (1961), 66–82.

———, *La Formation des grandes domaines au Mexique,* Paris, Inst. d'Ethnologie, 1952.

———, "Survivances seigneuriales et présages de la révolution agraire dans le nord du Mexique," *Revue historique, 222* (1959), 1–18.

Chinard, Gilbert, ed., *Jefferson et les idéologues,* Baltimore and Paris, Johns Hopkins University Press, 1925.

Clavijero, Francisco, *History of Mexico,* trans. Charles Cullen, 2 vols. London, 1807.

Cline, Howard F., "The 'Aurora Yucateca' and the Spirit of Enterprise in Yucatán, 1821–1847," *HAHR*, 27 (1947), 30–60.

———, "Related Studies in Early Nineteenth-Century Yucatecan Social History," Microfilm Collection of MSS. on Mid. Am. Cultural Anthropology, University of Chicago, 1950.

———, "The Sugar Episode in Yucatán, 1825–1850," *Inter-American Economic Affairs, 1* (1948), 79–100.

Colección de artículos del siglo xix, sobre alzamiento de prohibiciones, Mexico, 1851.

Constant de Rebeque, Benjamin, *Cours de politique constitutionnelle ou collection des ouvrages publiés sur le gouvernement représentatif,* 2d ed. Edouard Laboulaye, 2 vols. Paris, 1872.

———, *Curso de política constitucional,* trans. and ed. Marcial Antonio López, 3 vols. Madrid, 1820.

———, *De la Religion considerée dans sa source, ses formes et ses développments,* 5 vols. Paris, 1824–31.

El Constituyente de 1856 y el pensamiento liberal mexicano, Mexico, Porrua, 1960.

Correo semanario de México, Mexico, Nov. 22, 1826–May 2, 1827.

Correspondencia particular del ministro de relaciones interiores y exteriores, Archivo de la Sec. Rel. Ext., typescripts Chávez Orozco.

Cosío Villegas, Daniel, *American Extremes,* Austin, University of Texas Press, 1964.

———, *La Constitución de 1857 y sus críticos,* Mexico, Hermes, 1957.

———, ed., *Historia moderna de México,* 7 vols. Mexico, Hermes, 1955–65.

El Cosmopolita, Mexico, Feb. 18, 1837–July 8, 1843.

Costeloe, Michael P. "The Administration, Collection and Distribution of Tithes in the Archbishopric of Mexico, 1800–1860," *The Americas, 23* (1966), 3–27.

Cotner, Thomas E., *The Military and Political Career of José Joaquín de Herrera, 1792–1854,* Austin, University of Texas Press, 1949.

[Couto, José Bernardo], Norberto Pérez Cuyado, pseud., *Disertación sobre la naturaleza y límites de la autoridad eclesiástica,* Mexico, 1825.

———, "Dr. D. José María Luis Mora," *Apéndice al diccionario universal de historia y de geografía,* ed. Manuel Orozco y Berra, 2 (Mexico, 1856), 887–89.

Cuevas, Luis G., *Porvenir de México,* ed. Francisco Cuevas Cancino, Mexico, Jus, 1954.

Cumplido, Ignacio, *Manifestación al público del impresor . . . con motivo de su prisión,* Mexico, 1840.

Daunou, Pierre Claude François, *Ensayo sobre las garantías individuales que reclama el estado actual de la sociedad,* Mexico, 1823.

Dealey, James Q., "The Spanish Source of the Mexican Constitution of 1824," *Texas State Historical Quarterly, 3* (1900), 161–69.

Decretos del congreso constituyente del estado de México, 1, Tlalpam, 1830.

De la Maza, Francisco, "Los Restos de Hernán Cortés," *Cuadernos americanos, 32* (1947), 153–74.

Díaz Mirón, Manuel, *Discurso que pronunció el 16 de septiembre de 1845, aniversario del grito de Dolores,* Veracruz, 1845.

Dictamen de la comisión de gubernación sobre señalar y dar propios y arbitrios a los pueblos del estado de México, Mexico, 1824.

Dictamen de la comisión especial de la cámara de senadores sobre cambio de la forma de gobierno y voto particular del señor Couto, Mexico, 1835.

Disertación que manifiesta la propiedad que los eclesiásticos tienen en sus bienes, Mexico, 1834.

Don Simplicio. Periódico burlesco, crítico y filosófico por unos simples, Mexico, Dec. (?) 1845–Apr. 24, 1847.

Dublán, Manuel, and José María Lozano, eds., *Legislación mexicana,* 34 vols. Mexico, 1876–1904.

E. A. D., *Los Indios quieren ser libres y lo serán con justicia,* Mexico, 1829.

Echánove Trujillo, Carlos A., *La Vida pasional e inquieta de Don Crecencio Rejón,* Mexico, El Colegio de México, 1941.

Estep, Raymond, *Lorenzo de Zavala, profeta del liberalismo mexicano,* Mexico, Porrua, 1952.

Excelsior, Mexico, June 25, 1963.

El Fénix de la libertad, Mexico, Dec. 7, 1831–June 4, 1834.

Fernández de Lizardi, José Joaquín, *Baratas del pensador para los cuchareros y la nación,* Mexico, 1824.

——, *Conversaciones del payo y el sacristán,* 2 vols. Mexico, 1824–25.

——, *Testamento y despedida del pensador mexicano, 1,* Mexico, 1827.

Figgis, John N., *Political Thought from Gerson to Grotius: 1414–1625,* New York, Harper, 1960.

Fisher, Lillian E., *Champion of Reform: Manuel Abad y Queipo,* New York, Library Publishers, 1955.

——, *The Intendant System in Spanish America,* Berkeley, University of California Press, 1929.

Flaccus, Elmer W., "Guadalupe Victoria: Mexican Patriot and First

President, 1786–1843," Ph.D. dissertation, University of Texas, 1951.

Flórez Estrada, Álvaro, *Curso de economía política,* 2d ed. 2 vols. Paris, 1831.

——, "Representación hecha a S. M. C. el señor Don Fernando VII en defensa de las cortes," *Biblioteca de autores españoles, 113,* Madrid, Atlas, 1958.

Florstedt, Robert F., "The Liberal Role of José María Luis Mora in the Early History of Independent Mexico," Ph.D. dissertation, University of Texas, 1950.

——, "Mora contra Bustamante," *Historia mexicana, 12* (1962), 26–52.

——, "Mora y la génesis del liberalismo burgues," *Historia mexicana, 11* (1961), 207–23.

Fuller, John D. P., *The Movement for the Acquisition of All Mexico, 1846–1848,* Baltimore, Johns Hopkins University Press, 1936.

F. X. H., *Observaciones importantes sobre el comercio libre,* Mexico, 1821.

Gálvez, Mariano, "Discurso leído en la sesión de industria el 27 de febrero de 1844," *El Ateneo mexicano, 1,* 33–40.

Gamio, Manuel, *Forjando patria,* Mexico, Porrua, 1960.

Ganshof, F. L., *Feudalism,* London, Longmans, 1952.

García, Francisco, *Exposición sobre el dictamen en que la comisión ordinaria de hacienda consulta la prohibición de ciertas manufacturas y efectos extrangeros,* Mexico, 1823.

García, Génaro, ed., *Documentos inéditos o muy raros para la historia de México,* "Papeles inéditos y obras selectas del Doctor Mora," 6, Mexico, Bouret, 1906.

——, ed., *Documentos,* "Noticias bio-bibliográficas de algunos alumnos distinguidos del colegio de San Pedro, San Pablo y San Ildefonso de México," *19,* Mexico, Bouret, 1908.

——, ed., *Documentos,* "Los Gobiernos de Álvarez y Comonfort según el archivo del general Doblado," *31,* Mexico, Bouret, 1910.

Gerbi, Antonello, *La Disputa del nuevo mundo,* Mexico, Fondo de Cultura Económica, 1960.

Gibson, Charles, *The Aztecs Under Spanish Rule. A History of the Indians of the Valley of Mexico, 1519–1810,* Stanford, Stanford University Press, 1964.

Gide, Charles, and Charles Rist, *A History of Economic Doctrines,* London, Harrap, 1948.

Gilmore, N. Ray, "Henry George Ward, British Publicist for Mexican Mines," *Pacific Historical Review, 32* (1963), 35–47.

Godechot, Jacques, *Les Institutions de la France sous la révolution et l'empire*, Paris, Presses Universitaires, 1951.

Góngora, Mario, *El Estado en el derecho indiano, época de fundación, 1492–1570*, Santiago de Chile, Editorial Universitaria, 1951.

González Navarro, Moisés, "Actualidad de Mariano Otero," *Historia mexicana*, 2 (1952), 286–93.

———, "Instituciones indígenas en México independiente," *Métodos y resultados de la política indigenista en México*, Mexico, Inst. Nacional Indigenista, 1954.

———, *El Pensamiento político de Lucas Alamán*, Mexico, El Colegio de México, 1952.

González y González, Luis, "El Optimismo nacionalista como factor de la independencia de México," *Estudios de historiografía americana* (Mexico, El Colegio de México, 1948), pp. 153–215.

Griffin, Charles C., "The Enlightenment and Latin American Independence," in A. P. Whitaker, ed., *Latin America and the Enlightenment* (Ithaca, Cornell University Press, 1961), pp. 119–43.

Gringoire, Pedro, "El 'Protestantismo' del Dr. Mora," *Historia mexicana*, 3 (1953), 328–66.

Gurria Lacroix, Jorge, *Las Ideas monárquicas de don Lucas Alamán*, Mexico, Inst. de Historia, 1951.

Gutiérrez de Estrada, José María, *Carta dirigida al escmo. sr. presidente de la república sobre la necesidad de buscar en una convención el posible remedio de los males que aquejan a la república*, Mexico, 1840.

———, *Documentos relativos al ingreso y a la salida de la primera secretaría de estado de la república mexicana*, Mexico, 1835.

———, *Memoria de la secretaría de estado y del despacho de relaciones interiores y exteriores*, Mexico, 1835.

———, *México en 1840 y en 1847*, Mexico, 1848.

———, *México y el archiduque Fernando Maximiliano de Austria*, Mexico, 1863.

———, *Le Mexique et l'Europe ou exposé de la situation actuelle du Mexique et des dangers qui peuvent en resulter pour l'Europe si elle ne prend des mesures efficaces pour y remédier*, Paris, 1847.

Hadley, Bradford K., "The Enigmatic Padre Mier," Ph.D. dissertation, University of Texas, 1955.

Hale, Charles A., "Alamán, Antuñano y la continuidad del liberalismo," *Historia mexicana*, 11 (1961), 224–45.

———, "José María Luis Mora and the Structure of Mexican Liberalism," *HAHR*, 45 (1965), 196–227.

Halévy, Elie, *The Growth of Philosophic Radicalism,* London, Faber, 1928.

Hamill, Hugh M., Jr., "Early Psychological Warfare in the Hidalgo Revolt," *HAHR, 41* (1961), 206–35.

——, *The Hidalgo Revolt: Prelude to Mexican Independence,* Gainesville, University of Florida Press, 1966.

Hardy, R. W. H., *Travels in the Interior of Mexico in 1825, 1826, 1827, and 1828,* London, 1829.

Harris, Charles H., III, *The Sánchez Navarros: A Socio-economic Study of a Coahuilan Latifundio, 1846–1853,* Chicago, Loyola University Press, 1964.

Hartz, Louis, "Comment" (in the symposium on his *The Liberal Tradition in America*), *Comparative Studies in Society and History, 5* (1962–63), 279–84.

——, *The Founding of New Societies,* New York, Harcourt, 1964.

——, *The Liberal Tradition in America,* New York, Harcourt, 1955.

Hazard, Paul, *The European Mind, 1680–1715,* New Haven, Yale University Press, 1953.

Helman, Edith, "Some Consequences of the Publication of the *Informe de ley agraria* by Jovellanos," *Estudios hispánicos: Homenaje a Archer M. Huntington* (Wellesley, Wellesley College, 1952), pp. 253–73.

Herr, Richard, *The Eighteenth-Century Revolution in Spain,* Princeton, Princeton University Press, 1958.

Hobhouse, L. T., *Liberalism,* London, Oxford University Press, 1911.

Howe, Walter, *The Mining Guild of New Spain and its Tribunal General, 1770–1821,* Cambridge, Harvard University Press, 1949.

Hutchinson, C. Alan, "The Mexican Government and the Mission Indians of Upper California, 1821–1835," *The Americas, 21* (1965), 335–62.

——, "Valentín Gómez Farías: a Biographical Study," Ph.D. dissertation, University of Texas, 1948.

——, "Valentín Gómez Farías and the 'Secret Pact of New Orleans,'" *HAHR, 36* (1956), 471–89.

Iguíniz, Juan B., *Disquisiciones bibliográficas,* Mexico, El Colegio de México, 1943.

El Indicador de la federación mejicana, 4 vols. Mexico, Oct. 9, 1833– May 7, 1834.

Jáuregui, José María de, *Discurso en que se manifiesta, que deben bajarse los réditos a proporción del quebranto que hayan sufrido en la insurrección los bienes y giros de los deudores,* Mexico, 1820.

————, "Voto particular del . . . vocal de la soberana junta e individuo de la comisión eclesiástica, sobre patronato," *La Sabatina universal, 1,* 261–66 (Sept. 28, 1822).

Jovellanos, Gaspar Melchor de, *Obras* (2 vols.), *Biblioteca de autores españoles, 46, 50,* Madrid, Atlas, 1951–52.

Krebs Wilckens, Ricardo, *El Pensamiento histórico, político y económico del conde de Campomanes,* Santiago de Chile, Editorial Universitaria, 1960.

La Force, James C., Jr., *The Development of the Spanish Textile Industry, 1750–1800,* Berkeley, University of California Press, 1965.

Landes, David, "The Industrial Revolution," *Chapters in Western Civilization, 2* (New York, Columbia University Press, 1962), pp. 140–93.

Lenoir, A., *Antiquités mexicaines,* 2 vols. Paris, 1833–34.

La Lima del vulcano, Mexico, Oct. 19, 1833–Aug. 30, 1836.

Locke, John, *Two Treatises of Civil Government,* London, Dent, 1924.

López Cámara, Francisco, *La Génesis de la conciencia liberal en México,* Mexico, El Colegio de México, 1954.

Lynch, John, *Spanish Colonial Administration, 1782–1810: the Intendant System in the Viceroyalty of the Rio de la Plata,* London, University of London Press, 1958.

McAlister, Lyle N., *The "Fuero Militar" in New Spain, 1764–1800,* Gainesville, University of Florida Press, 1957.

————, "Social Structure and Social Change in New Spain," *HAHR, 43* (1963), 349–70.

Machorro Narváez, Paulino, *Don Francisco Severo Maldonado,* Mexico, Polis, 1938.

Macune, Charles W., Jr., "A Test of Federalism: Relations Between the Province and State of Mexico and the Mexican Nation, 1823–1824," *Paisano, 4* (1965), 39–57.

Maldonado, Francisco Severo, *Contrato de asociación para la república de los estados unidos de Anahuac,* Guadalajara, 1823.

————, ed., *El Fanal del imperio mexicano,* 2 vols. Mexico, 1822.

————, *Nuevo Pacto social propuesto a la nación española, para su discusión en las próximas cortes de 1822 y 1823,* Guadalajara, 1821.

Martin, Kingsley, *The Rise of French Liberal Thought,* New York, New York University Press, 1954.

Mateos, Juan A., *Historia parlamentaria de los congresos mexicanos,* 10 vols. Mexico, 1877–86.

Mecham, J. Lloyd, *Church and State in Latin America,* Chapel Hill, University of North Carolina Press, 1934.

———, "The Origins of Federalism in Mexico," *HAHR, 18* (1938), 164–82.

Mellon, Stanley, *The Political Uses of History; a Study of Historians in the French Restoration,* Stanford, Stanford University Press, 1958.

Memorial histórico, Mexico, Jan. 1–Feb. 28, 1846.

Michels, Roberto, "Conservatism," *Encyclopedia of the Social Sciences, 4* (New York, Macmillan, 1931), 230–32.

Mier Noriega y Guerra, Servando Teresa de, *Diez Cartas, hasta hoy inéditos,* Monterrey, Impresos Modernos, 1940.

———, *Discurso que el día 13 de diciembre del presente año de 1823 pronunció . . . sobre el artículo 5 del acta constitutiva,* Mexico, 1823.

———, *Discurso . . . sobre la encílica del Papa Leon XII,* Mexico, 1825.

———, *Escritos inéditos,* Mexico, El Colegio de México, 1944.

———, *Historia de la revolución de la Nueva España,* 2 vols. London, 1813.

———, *Memoria político-instructiva . . . a los gefes independientes del Anahuac,* Philadelphia, 1821.

———, *Memorias,* 2 vols. Mexico, Porrua, 1946.

Miranda, José, *Humboldt y México,* Mexico, UNAM, 1962.

———, "El Liberalismo mexicano y el liberalismo europeo," *Historia mexicana, 8* (1959), 512–23.

Molina Enríquez, Andrés, *Los Grandes Problemas nacionales,* Problemas agrícolas e industriales de México, 5, Mexico, 1953.

El Monitor constitucional, Mexico, Dec. 21, 1844–Feb. 13, 1846.

El Monitor constitucional independiente, Mexico, Mar. 4–June 22, 1845.

El Monitor republicano, Mexico, Feb. 14, 1846–Apr. 30, 1853.

Mora Correspondence, 1794–1844, University of Texas.

Mora Correspondence, 1845–56, University of Texas.

Mora Documents, 1806–38, University of Texas.

[Mora, José María Luis], *Catecismo político de la federación mexicana,* Mexico, 1831.

[———], *Disertación sobre la naturaleza y aplicación de las rentas y bienes eclesiásticas, y sobre la autoridad a que se hallan sujetos en cuanto a su creación, aumento, subsistencia o supresión,* Mexico, 1833.

———, *A los Habitantes del estado de México su congreso constituyente,* Texcoco, 1827.

———, *Méjico y sus revoluciones,* 3 vols. Paris, 1836.

———, *Memoria que para informar sobre el orígen y estado actual de las obras emprendidas para el desagüe de las lagunas del valle de México,* Mexico, 1823.

———, *Obras sueltas,* 2d ed. Mexico, Porrua, 1963.

Morse, Richard M., "The Heritage of Latin America," in Louis Hartz, *The Founding of New Societies* (New York, Harcourt, 1964), pp. 123–77.

El Mosquito mexicano, Mexico, Mar. 14, 1834–Dec. 3, 1844 (?).

Motten, Clement G., *Mexican Silver and the Enlightenment,* Philadelphia, University of Pennsylvania Press, 1950.

El Nacional, Mexico, June 20, 1963.

Noriega, Raul, "El Liberalismo mexicano," *Novedades,* July 25, 1965.

El Observador de la república mexicana, 6 vols. Mexico, June 6, 1827– Jan. 2, 1828; Mar. 3–Oct. 27, 1830.

Ocampo, Melchor, *Obras completas,* 3 vols. Mexico, Vázquez, 1900–01.

———, *La Religión, la iglesia y el clero,* Mexico, Empresas Editoriales, 1948.

O'Gorman, Edmundo, ed., *Fray Servando Teresa de Mier,* Antología del pensamiento político americano, Mexico, UNAM, 1945.

———, "Precedentes y sentido de la revolución de Ayutla," *Plan de Ayutla* (Mexico, UNAM, 1954), pp. 169–204.

El Omnibus, Mexico, Oct. 18, 1851–Nov. 5, 1856.

Onis, José de, *The United States as Seen by Spanish American Writers, 1776–1890,* New York, Hispanic Inst., 1952.

La Oposición, Mexico, July 2, 1834–June 25, 1835.

El Orden, Mexico, Aug. 1, 1852–1855 (?).

Ortega y Medina, Juan, *Humboldt desde México,* Mexico, UNAM, 1960.

Ortiz, Tadeo, *Bases sobre las que se ha formado un plan de colonización en el ysmo de Hoazcoalco o Tehuantepec,* Mexico, 1823.

———, *México considerado como nación independiente y libre,* Bordeaux, 1832.

Ortiz de la Torre, Manuel, *Discurso de un diputado sobre la introducción de efectos extrangeros,* Mexico, 1823.

———, *Discurso sobre los medios de fomentar la población, riqueza e ilustración de los estados-unidos mexicanos,* Mexico, 1825.

[Otero, Mariano], *Consideraciones sobre la situación política y social de la república mexicana en el año 1847,* Mexico, 1848.

———, "Discurso que en la solemnidad del 16 de septiembre de 1841 pronunció en la ciudad de Guadalajara," *El Siglo XIX,* Oct. 22–23, 1841.

———, *Ensayo sobre el verdadero estado de la cuestión social y política que se agita en la república mexicana,* Mexico, 1842.

———, *Ministerio de relaciones interiores y esteriores,* Mexico, 1848.

———, "Oración cívica," *El Siglo XIX,* Sept. 23, 1843.

Otro Indio, *Todos los Indios son libres, y no hay que se los dispute,* Mexico, 1829.

Palmer, Robert R., *The Age of the Democratic Revolution: A Political History of Europe and America, 1760–1800,* 2 vols. Princeton, Princeton University Press, 1959–64.

Parry, J. H., *The Audiencia of New Galicia in the Sixteenth Century,* Cambrige, Cambridge University Press, 1948.

El Partido conservador en México, Mexico, 1855.

Payno, Manuel, *La Reforma social en España y México,* Mexico, UNAM, 1958.

Paz, Octavio, *The Labyrinth of Solitude,* New York, Grove Press, 1961.

Pérez Verdía, Luis, *Biografías,* Guadalajara, Ediciones I.T.G. 1952.

Plamenatz, John, *The English Utilitarians,* Oxford, Blackwell, 1958.

Plan de Ayutla, Mexico, UNAM, 1954.

Polt, John H. R., *Jovellanos and His English Sources,* Transactions of the American Philosophical Society, new ser. 54, pt. 7, Philadelphia, 1964.

Potash, Robert A., *El Banco de Avío de México: el fomento de la industria, 1821–1846,* Mexico, Fondo de Cultura Económica, 1959.

———, "Historiography of Mexico Since 1821," *HAHR, 40* (1960), 383–424.

Prescott, William H., *Historia de la conquista de Méjico,* 2 vols. Mexico, 1844.

Prieto, Guillermo, *Indicaciones sobre el orígen, vicisitudes y estado que guardan actualmente las rentas generales de la federación mexicana,* Mexico, 1850.

Quintana, Miguel A., *Estevan de Antuñano, fundador de la industria textil en Puebla,* 2 vols. Mexico, Sec. de Hacienda y Crédito Público, 1957.

Quintana Roo, Andrés, *Discurso pronunciado . . . en el glorioso aniversario del 16 de septiembre de 1845,* Mexico, 1845.

Rabasa, Emilio, *La Constitución y la dictadura,* Mexico, Porrua, 1956.

Radin, Paul, ed., *The Opponents and Friends of Lizardi,* Occasional Papers, Mexican History Series, San Francisco, California State Library, 1939.

Ramos Arizpe, Miguel, *Report that . . . Presents to the August Con-*

gress, trans. Nettie Lee Benson, Austin, University of Texas Press, 1950.

Real de Curban, Gaspard, *Derecho eclesiástico escrito en francés por M. de Real y traducido al castellano por J. M. M.*, 2 vols. Mexico, 1826.

———, *La Science du gouvernement*, 8 vols. Aix-la-Chapelle, 1751–64.

Reed, Nelson, *The Caste War of Yucatán*, Stanford, Stanford University Press, 1964.

Reformador, Toluca, Apr. 1, 1833–June 28, 1834 (?).

Rejón, Manuel Crecencio, *Discursos parlamentarios, 1822–1847*, ed. Carlos A. Echánove Trujillo, Mexico, Sec. de Educación Pública, 1943.

———, *Observaciones del diputado saliente . . . contra los tratados de paz*, Querétaro, 1848.

———, *Programa de la mayoría de los diputados del distrito federal*, Mexico, 1846.

Representación . . . al exmo. ayuntamiento de la capital de Puebla con motivo del alzamiento que se pretende de las leyes prohibitivas, Puebla, 1851.

Representación de la junta de industria de Puebla . . . con motivo de las pretensiones para que se reformen las leyes que protejen la industria nacional, Puebla, 1846.

Republicano, Mexico, Mar. 1, 1846–July 11, 1847.

Reyes Heroles, Jesús, "Continuidad del liberalismo mexicano," *Plan de Ayutla* (Mexico, UNAM, 1954), pp. 343–74.

———, *El Liberalismo mexicano*, 3 vols. Mexico, UNAM, 1957–61.

[Reynal, Rafael] and Carlos Gastelú, *Viage por los estados unidos del norte*, Cincinnati, 1834.

Rico González, Victor, *Hacía un Concepto de la conquista de México*, Mexico, Inst. de Historia, 1953.

Rippy, J. Fred, "Latin America and the British Investment 'Boom' of the 1820s," *Journal of Modern History, 19* (1947), 122–29.

Riva Palacio, Vicente, ed., *México á través de los siglos*, 5 vols. Mexico, 1888–89.

Roach, John, "Education and Public Opinion," *New Cambridge Modern History, 9* (Cambridge, Cambridge University Press, 1965), 179–208.

Rocafuerte, Vicente, *Ensayo sobre tolerancia religiosa*, Mexico, 1831.

———, *Ideas necesarias a todo pueblo americano independiente que quiera ser libre*, Philadelphia, 1821.

Rojas, Armando, "La Batalla de Bentham en Colombia," *Revista de historia de América, 29* (1950), 37–66.

Romero de Terreros, Manuel, "Prologo," *Conde de la Cortina, Poliantea,* Mexico, UNAM, 1944.

Rosa, Luis de la, *Discurso pronunciado en la alameda de esta capital,* Mexico, 1846.

———, *Impresiones de un viage de México a Washington en octubre y noviembre de 1848,* New York, 1849.

———, *Observaciones sobre varios puntos concernientes a la administración pública del estado de Zacatecas,* Baltimore, 1851.

Rousseau, Jean Jacques, *The Social Contract,* New York, Dutton, 1950.

Ruggiero, Guido de, *The History of European Liberalism,* Boston, Beacon, 1959.

La Sabatina universal, Mexico, June 15–Nov. 16, 1822.

Sabine, George H., *A History of Political Theory,* New York, Holt, 1937.

Sánchez Agesta, Luis, *El Pensamiento político del despotismo ilustrado,* Madrid, Inst. de Estudios Políticos, 1953.

Sarfatti, Margali, *Spanish Bureaucratic-Patrimonialism in America,* Berkeley, University of California, Inst. of International Studies, 1966.

Sarmiento, Domingo F., *Life in the Argentine Republic in the Days of the Tyrants,* New York, 1868.

Sarrailh, Jean, *L'Espagne éclairée de la seconde moitié du xviii⁰ siècle,* Paris, Impr. Nationale, 1954.

Sartorius, Carlos, *Importancia de México para la emigración alemana,* Mexico, 1852.

Say, Jean Baptiste, *Tratado de economía política,* 3 vols. Mexico, 1814.

———, *A Treatise on Political Economy,* Philadelphia, 1830.

Semanario de la industria megicana, Mexico, 1841–42.

Semanario político y literario de Méjico, Mexico, July 12, 1820–Mar. 27, 1822.

Shafer, Robert J., *The Economic Societies in the Spanish World, 1763–1821,* Syracuse, Syracuse University Press, 1958.

Sierra, Justo, *Evolución política del pueblo mexicano,* Mexico, Fondo de Cultura Económica, 1950.

———, *Juárez, su obra y su tiempo,* Mexico, UNAM, 1956.

Sierra O'Reilly, Justo, *Diario de nuestro viaje a los Estados Unidos,* 2 vols. Mexico, Robredo, Porrua, 1938–53.

El Siglo XIX, Mexico, Oct. 8, 1841–Dec. 31, 1845; June 1, 1848–July 30, 1858.

Silvert, Kalman, "Some Psychocultural Factors in the Politics of Conflict and Conciliation: Setting up the Problem," Paper delivered at American Political Science Association, 1965.

Smith, Adam, *The Wealth of Nations,* New York, Random House, 1937.

Smith, Ralph A., "Indians in American-Mexican Relations Before the War of 1846," *HAHR, 43* (1963), 34–64.

Smith, Robert S., "Manuel Ortiz de la Torre, economista olvidado," *Revista de historia de América, 48* (1959), 505–16.

——, "The *Wealth of Nations* in Spain and Hispanic America, 1780–1830," *Journal of Political Economy, 65* (1957), 104–25.

El Sol, Dec. 5, 1821–Dec. 29, 1832.

Sosa, Francisco, *Biografías de mexicanos distinguidos,* Mexico, 1884.

Sparks, Jared, "Gold and Silver in Mexico," *North American Review, 21* (1825), 429–43.

Spell, Jefferson R., *The Life and Works of José Joaquín Fernández de Lizardi,* Philadelphia, University of Pennsylvania Press, 1931.

——, *Rousseau in the Spanish World Before 1833,* Austin, University of Texas Press, 1938.

Spitzer, Alan B., "The Bureaucrat as Proconsul: the Restauration Prefect and the *Police Générale,*" *Comparative Studies in Society and History,* 7 (1965), 371–92.

Stevens, Robert C., "Mexico's Forgotten Frontier: a History of Sonora, 1821–1846," Ph.D. dissertation, University of California, Berkeley, 1963.

Stewart, John H., ed., *A Documentary Survey of the French Revolution,* New York, Macmillan, 1951.

Tannenbaum, Frank, *Mexico: The Struggle for Peace and Bread,* New York, Knopf, 1950.

El Telégrafo, Mexico, Jan. 11, 1833–Dec. 31, 1834.

Tena Ramírez, Felipe, *Derecho constitucional mexicano,* Mexico, Porrua, 1963.

——, ed., *Leyes fundamentales de México,* Mexico, Porrua, 1964.

El Tiempo, Mexico, Jan. 24–June 7, 1846.

Tocqueville, Alexis de, *Democracy in America,* 2 vols. New York, Knopf, 1954.

——, *Old Regime and the French Revolution,* Garden City, Doubleday, 1955.

——, *Recollections,* New York, Meridian, 1959.

Tornel y Mendívil, José María, *Breve Reseña histórica,* Mexico, 1852.

————, "Discurso pronunciado por . . . ministro de guerra y marina . . . en la sesión de 12 de oct. de 1842, del congreso constituyente, en apoyo del dictamen de la mayoría de la comisión de constitución del mismo," *El Siglo XIX*, Nov. 30–Dec. 1, 1842.

Toro, Alfonso, *Dos Constituyentes del año 1824. Biografías de Don Miguel Ramos Arizpe y Don Lorenzo de Zavala*, Mexico, Museo Nacional, 1925.

Trioen, L. F. B., *Indagaciones, sobre las antigüedades mexicanas, pruebas de la civilización adelantada de los mexicanos en el xv siglo . . . y comparación de su civilización con la de sus descendientes en 1841*, Mexico, 1841.

El Universal, Mexico, Nov. 16, 1848–Aug. 13, 1855.

Valadés, José C., *Alamán, estadista e historiador*, Mexico, Robredo, 1938.

————, "José María Gutiérrez de Estrada (1800–1867)," *Enciclopedia yucatanense* (Ed. Oficial de Yucatán, Mexico, 1944–47), 7, 141–204.

Villoro, Luis, *Los Grandes Momentos del indigenismo en México*, Mexico, El Colegio de México, 1950.

————, *La Revolución de independencia*, Mexico, UNAM, 1953.

La Voz del pueblo, Mexico, Jan. 25–Dec. 31, 1845.

Ward, Henry G., *Mexico in 1827*, 2 vols. London, 1828.

Whitaker, Arthur P., ed., *Latin America and the Enlightenment*, Ithaca, Cornell University Press, 1961.

————, *The Western Hemisphere Idea: Its Rise and Decline*, Ithaca, Cornell University Press, 1954.

Will, Robert M., "The Introduction of Classical Economics into Chile," *HAHR, 44* (1964), 1–21.

Willie, Robert C., *México. Noticia sobre su hacienda pública bajo el gobierno español y después de la independencia*, Mexico, 1845.

Wilson, Irma, *Mexico: A Century of Educational Thought*, New York, Hispanic Inst., 1941.

Zavala, Lorenzo de, *Ensayo histórico de las revoluciones de Mégico, desde 1808 hasta 1830*, 2 vols. Paris and New York, 1831–32.

————, *Juicio imparcial sobre los acontecimientos de México en 1828 y 1829*, Mexico, 1830.

————, *Memoria de la gestión de gobierno del estado de México durante el año de 1833*, Toluca, 1833.

————, *Obras, 1*, ed. Manuel González Ramírez, Mexico, Porrua, 1966.

————, *Proyecto de reforma del congreso*, Mexico, 1822.

————, *Viage a los estados-unidos del norte de América*, Paris, 1834.

Zea, Leopoldo, *The Latin American Mind*, Norman, University of Oklahoma Press, 1963.

———, *El Positivismo en México*, Mexico, Studium, 1953.

Zuñiga, Ignacio, *Rápida Ojeada . . . al estado de Sonora dirigida y dedicada al supremo de la nación*, Mexico, 1835.

Index

Abad y Queipo, Manuel (Bishop of Michoacán), 24; defends ecclesiastical *fuero*, 118 n.; influence on Mora, 135-39 passim, 260; views on Indians, 136, 221; advocates social reforms, 225-26. See also *consolidación* decree; *fueros*; property, ecclesiastical

Acta Constitutiva, Mier's vote on article *5*, 197. *See also* Constitution of *1824;* federalism

Acta de Reformas (*1847*), 34. *See also* Otero; federalism

agrarianism: and property, 177 n.; and Indian upheavals, 246. *See also* Indians; latifundia; property

agriculture: Mora's assumptions concerning, 260-61; Alamán supports cotton raising, 276, 279; Antuñano turns against domestic crude cotton, 277. *See also* industry; property

Alamán, Lucas, 8, 12, 109; interprets liberalism, 1-2; career and early life, 16-17, 20; uses history as a political weapon, 17-19, 213-14, 244; defends property of Monteleone, 18, 99, 120; ideas, compared with Mora's, 22-27 passim, 295-96; death (*1853*), 32; on Creole aristocracy, 45; on Freemasonry, 98; his developing conservatism (*1830s*), 146-47; advocates educational re-

forms, 169 ff.; hostility toward U.S., 188, 207, 212-14; on federalist origins, 193-94 n.; on Aztecs, 219-20; and economic development, 249; entrepreneurial career, 262, 263-89 passim; leads mining revival (*1820s*), 263-67; influenced by liberal economics, 263-67 passim; founds Banco de Avío, 268-69; correspondence with Antuñano, 272; ideas, compared with Antuñano's, 278-80, 286-89; as Director of Industry (*1842–46*), 279-80; and Gutiérrez de Estrada, 297. *See also* conservatism; monarchism

Alberdi, Juan Bautista, 179

alcabala, 113, 210, 213

alcalde de paz, 88

Alfonso X (Castile), 122

Álvarez, Juan: attacked by Bustamante, 109; Creole view of his presidency, 224 n.

Alzate, José Antonio, 167

American Revolution. *See* Revolution for Independence (U.S.)

Anahuac. *See* Aztecs

Antuñano, Estevan de, 8; admires U.S. spirit of enterprise, 200, 275; and economic development, 249; early life, 271-72; as propagandist for modern industry, 272-89 passim; economic ideas assessed, 275-76, 278-79; turns against domestic crude

view of, 26-27; regime overthrown, 81; opposed by Mier, 196. *See also* Plan of Iguala

Ixmiquilpan, 228 n.

Jackson, Andrew, receives Zavala, 199

Jacobins, 54, 146

Jalisco, 32, 92 n., 95, 169

Jalpa (hacienda), 228

Jáuregui, José María de, 102; favors control of municipalities, 89; on judiciary, 94-95; favors assumption of Patronato (*1822*), 127 n.; on church property, 138 n., 140, 229; on militia, 143 n.; on Bentham, 155; attacks Colegio de Abogados, 158; cites U.S. as model of liberty, 195; on municipal property, 227, 231. *See also* Constituent Congress (State of Mexico)

jefe político. See jefe superior

jefe superior: in Constitution of *1812*, 79-80; Mora's view of, 90

Jefferson, Thomas, 192, 194, 208 n.

Jesuits, 192, 218; praised by Alamán, 19; expulsion of, 62, 121, 221

John of Salisbury, 47

Jovellanos, Gaspar Melchor de: ambivalence on Bourbons, 62-63, 64, 66, 136, 152; constitutionalist principles, 64-69, 118; and Constant, compared, 68-69, 118; attacks *mayorazgo*, 119; influence on Mora, 121-25 passim, 172, 175, 181-82; interprets Spanish history, 122; on church property, 140; utilitarian theory, 152; role in Spanish educational reform, 167; advocates individual property rights, 177; cited by *El Siglo,* 238; economic theory, 250, 251-52, 261; advocates factory work by women, 275 n. *See also* Bourbon policy; constitutionalism; sovereignty

Juárez, Benito, 2, 3, 14, 223 n.

judiciary: Constant's views on, 59; organization of, in State of Mexico, 92-95. *See also fueros;* jury system

juicio de amparo, 34 n., 208 n.

Junta Central of Seville, Jovellanos' role in, 64-68, 122

Junta General de la Industria Mexicana, Bourbon inspiration for, 279. *See also* Alamán; Dirección de Industria

jury system: advocated by Constant, 59; adopted in State of Mexico, 95, 156. *See also* judiciary

Kiowa, 234

Laboulaye, Edouard, 59

laissez-faire. *See* free trade; mercantilism; property; Smith; utilitarianism

Lamennais, Félicité Robert de, 15 n.

Lancaster, Joseph, founds Lancasterian system of mutual instruction, 168

Lancasterian system: described, 168; in Mexico, 169-70; success in *1833,* 174

Laplace, Pierre Simon, Marquis de, cited by Otero, 184

latifundia: in New Spain, 41-43, 217; liberal acceptance of, 89 n., 134-35, 180-83, 301; attacked by Abad y Queipo, 137 n.; supremacy over municipalities, 225, 230; and industrial development, 268, 281; upheld by Antuñano, 286. *See also* feudalism; *mayorazgo;* property

Lausanne, 58

Laws of the Indies, 221, 242

Lazo de la Vega, José Domingo, 97; supports communal holdings, 228, 232 n.; attends San Ildefonso, 293

Lecointe, and Mora, 290

ley del caso, 28, 111

ley de curatos, 130